AMERICAN FARM COLLECTIBLES

Identification and Price Guide

Russell E. Lewis

©2004 Russell E. Lewis

Published by

krause publications
An F+W Publications Company

700 East State Street • Iola, WI 54990-0001
715-445-2214 • 888-457-2873
www.krause.com

Our toll-free number to place an order or obtain
a free catalog is (800) 258-0929.

Library of Congress Catalog Number: 2004091766

ISBN: 0-87349-823-2

30785983 9/04

Edited by Dennis Thornton

Designed by Kay Sanders

Photos by Russell E. Lewis

Printed in the United States of America

Table of Contents

Dedication

This book is dedicated to my wife Wendy, my sons Justin and Rob, my brothers Gord and Ron, and to my parents Gerald and Marian Lewis. Farming is about tradition and, without these folks, I would have none. Without my parents, I never would have had the opportunities afforded to me for farming and for education. Without my brothers, models for success would be fewer. Without my wife, I could not do what I do now. Without my sons, what hope is there for the future?

As a child, my father was known to family and friends as "Bob-the-White-Horse." He played for hours on end that he was the Percheron draft horse named Bob on my grandfather's farm. He hooked himself up to a crate with binder-twine harness and completed a variety of farm duties daily. This pattern of play set the stage for a life of dedication to farming and being in a position to pass down a tradition to his family. I dedicate this book to his memory and to all of the hard-working farming men and women like him who have made American farming the most productive in the world.

A Century on the Farm

This book covers items of a collectible nature related to farming in North America from shortly after the Civil War until approximately 1965. Many of our current farming collectibles were invented prior to 1900 and examples are still readily found for sale, with some of the items still in use on farms. These dates correspond to the beginning impact of the industrial revolution on farming in America and the manufacture of many items that have become collectibles and antiques. They are of interest to many collectors, not just farmers and those raised on the farm.

The time period selected also represents the evolution from a truly agrarian society to an urban society. Now, many people find farm collectibles of interest partly due to the "romantic" ideal of an agrarian society. As a farmer, I know that not all aspects of farming are as ideal as we like to think. However, I also know that this is an area of great interest to the general public. I hope this book is found helpful in identifying and pricing farm-related antiques and collectibles.

Not much has been written in this field, nothing in the past seven years. Only a handful of earlier works, now out of print, deal with this field. And the field is so large that many books could be written, covering each chapter in this book. But this is a beginning, a guidepost. Or should I say a "corner post?"

This is not a book just about tractors! Does that mean tractors are not a part of the book? Tractors are, of course, included, but many fine guides exist on full-size tractors. I have included items related to tractors and implements in the fields of advertising and toys. There is also a brief chapter on collectible tractors from the classic era of tractor development, from the 1930s through the 1960s.

Lefty Laughlin's 1948 Oliver 66 Row Crop qualifies as an antique, but still gets frequent use on his farm in Michigan.

Why should you listen to me? I have been farming since shortly after birth. I was the Gold Star State Dairy Farmer for the FFA in Michigan in 1965, one of 22 youths selected for their knowledge and ability in farming out of a pool of 22,000 at the time, and the only youth selected for dairy farming. I still farm. I raise Percheron draft horses and North Country Cheviot, Oxford, and Scottish Blackface sheep with my wife Wendy. We have raised and milked Jerseys, Ayrshires, Brown Swiss, Holsteins, Milking Shorthorns, and even one Guernsey.

I have also spent many a Saturday over the past 30 years attending the ever present "farm auction" to look for treasures needed for farming or collecting. I amassed so many items over the years that I have had three fairly large farm auctions myself in the past few years. One held the record for "buyer's numbers" for some time at nearly 500 buyers. Also, as an anthropologist, I spent years working with and writing about the Old Order Amish. I lived within their communities in Indiana and Michigan while studying their agricultural techniques and the energy efficiency of horse agriculture. This familiarity with the older equipment used by the Amish simply added to my interest in farm antiques and collectibles.

My wife and I collect some items related to farming, especially tin dairy equipment signs such as DeLaval and Surge. And our house seems to be full of items related to farming and agriculture, including figures of chickens and sheep. I personally saw the transition from horse agriculture to tractor agriculture in our community as a child. I recall the last time that the Lewis family ever used horses to thresh grain and the threshing dinner afterward. As a growing boy, one of my neighbors, Neff Fisk, used to allow me to drive his team of horses, either on the way to my one-room country school or on the return home. He continued using horses his entire life.

All of these things have contributed to my interest in farming collectibles and farm antiques. Many of the items of collectible interest have been well covered in books about tractors or implements. But many of the smaller items have not been specifically covered in a book about farm collectibles. I hope that this book will become the basic text of farm collectibles and give the reader easy access to all types of farm collectibles in one source. This book is a mere beginning and I hope it has a long and wonderful life of revisions, additions, and expansions.

The book is in the format familiar to the collector: photos, descriptions of items, history and dates of items, and values. There is also a general introduction on dating and values. In addition, I have included suggested farm museums and living villages to help the current collector learn more and view items of interest.

The book is broken into the following chapters:

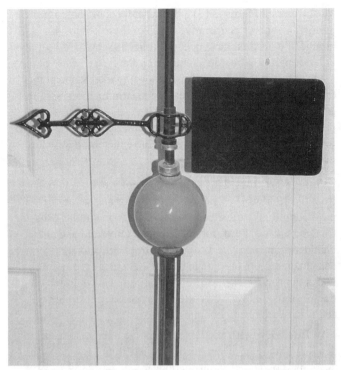

This beautiful cast iron weather vane and glass globe is a classic farm collectible and is valued at more than $100. *Art Smith Collection*

Sometimes the cast iron seat for a weathered antique hay rake or other implement could be worth more than the implement itself.

Introductory Comments. This section includes tips on collecting, valuation, using the Internet as a collecting and research tool, building a collection, and more. There is also a section on dating items that should be used in conjunction with the data provided in the book and the final chapter showing at least 65 years of advertising of farm items.

Farming in Print. This section includes the collecting of print items related to farming such as manuals, pamphlets, magazines, advertisements, and calendars. Many of the manuals for tractors and farm equipment have become highly collectible and highly priced. This section also introduces books of a collectible nature related to farming.

Farming in Advertising. This section includes non-print advertising items, such as "give-away" items from farm equipment dealers, seed companies, dairy companies, commodity companies (tobacco, cotton), and the all-important role of tin signs on the farm and in collecting. Items include everything from tape measures to key chains.

Small Scale Farming. This section includes the development of farm toys and related collectibles designed for children. Of course, there are books already out on toys and farm toys. This chapter will introduce the reader to the importance of farm toys and related child items.

Farming Implements. This section includes an introduction to non-tractor implements and their collectibility. Over the past 35-40 years, collectors have purchased cream separators to become garden flower pots, scalding kettles for the same purpose, windmills as decorations, one-row cultivators to sit in the yard, scythes to hang on the garage wall, hog scrapers because they looked interesting even though most did not

know what they were, and wool carders. Also included is a discussion of old implement seats and their values.

Farm Tools. This section concentrates on smaller tools of the farming trade, such as wrenches, hammers, shovels, rakes, and hoes. Again, there are books dealing with some of these items on the market. But there is nothing specifically about farming tools and some of the special wrenches and items needed to repair farm implements, such as the items needed to repair chains and sickle bars. Advertising and tools will also be covered regarding such items as Fordson and John Deere tools as well.

Horse Hardware. This section includes the growing popularity of collecting what we term horse hardware, items related to horse harness. This includes old collars, hames, ivory rings, bells, buckles, decorative brass, tugs, and even complete sets of harness. It also includes antique tongues for farm equipment made by a particular company, such as Deere or International Harvester. It also includes implements to care for horses such as picks, combs, halters, brushes, and tack boxes. Finally, it includes other barn and stable collectibles for other farm animals.

Farm Kitchen/Household. This section includes the items related to preparation and preservation of food. They were not unique to farms but of special importance to them, given the farms' isolation from "store bought" food in many cases. This will be an overview of important items and some items overlooked in the past. It will include canning items, pie safes, Hoosiers, early refrigerators, and small utensils. I have also included other items related to farm households that fit best in this category, such as household shutters, doors, windows,

Farm antiques, such as this hand wash-wringer, often find other uses. This serves as a planter in a farm garden, though the flowers have seen better days.

bells, lightning rods, and other decorative or functional items found on the farmstead.

Gardens. This section includes the one field still lasting into today's economy in large scale, the garden companies and their seeds. Each winter morning, one sits in anticipation of the seed catalog coming in the afternoon mail, bringing with it hopes of spring and abundance in the garden. There are many items of interest in this field: advertising specifically related to seeds and gardening, early gardening tools, seed packages, catalogs, and the comeback of "heritage or antique seed varieties" in recent years. Seed display units from old hardware stores are in demand, as are calendars and "give-away" items from seed companies. Not a lot of data is available for this category, but what is clear is that interest is growing for items of a vintage nature related to gardening. I am sure that this section will expand as revisions are made to this book in the future.

Farm Recreation. This section illustrates some of the special advertising that went into selling hunting, fishing, and other recreational items specifically to the farming community. Hunting, especially, was often a necessity to the farmer to provide needed food. It was commonly seen as an extension of food production. With this in mind, many companies marketed items to farmers in a different fashion. This will be examined as to its collectible value. Examples include the marketing of crow decoys and owl decoys to deter the crows as pests from your farm and the marketing of predator calls to eliminate those "bad" animals from your farm. Many fine books are already available that cover hunting and fishing collectibles (I have authored five books in this field). But I wanted to include a brief chapter on the subject to make certain that all new collectors are aware of the growing value of fishing lures, shotgun shell boxes, duck decoys, game calls, old wooden skis, old croquet sets, and other recreation items.

Farm Organizations. This section includes collectible items from organizations such as The Grange, 4-H, and FFA.

Most American farmers have been members of some form of organization or cooperative. Each of these groups has produced items that have become collectible by their scarcity or by design (toy tractors endorsed by the FFA). Many of the items in this category have an unknown market value at this time. But as our demand increases for farm memorabilia, it is anticipated that we shall see an increase in the trading of pins, awards, and certificates in much the same way as similar fraternal society and military items have increased in value over recent years.

Vintage Tractors. This section concentrates on tractors from the 1930 to 1965 period, with photos and values of the most commonly collected vintage tractors, including Allis-Chalmers, Case, Ford, John Deere, and Oliver. I have also included some valuation comments from collectors, restorers, dealers, and users of vintage tractors. There are many fine books in print on tractors; however, I have concentrated on tractors most likely to be collected by those of us in our 50s and 60s, i.e. the baby boomers.

An Interview with the Expert. This section includes a detailed pricing of recent auction values from "on-site farm auctions" conducted by an auctioneer who has 23 years of experience conducting farm and country auctions. Art Smith has been auctioning since 1981 and has specialized in farm items during his entire career. He has numerous antique dealers who follow his sales due to the quality of items he sells. And he has extensive knowledge of the values on farm collectibles, which he generously shares with the readers in this section. In addition, brief comments from other experts in the field appear in this section to give the collector additional information regarding values and their ideas regarding farm collectibles.

History of Farm Advertising. A review of many of the items that are now collectible is completed in this chapter by reprinting a number of advertisements from farm publications dating from 1903 until about 1965. Of special interest are all of the detailed ads from the 1903-05 period that show most of the items found in this book. One gets both an idea of how old many of the collectible items are and the fact that many farm items did not change greatly once invented in the late 1800s or early 1900s. For instance, fence-stretching tools, feeding equipment, and implements remained nearly the same until the advent of the tractor in the 1920s. Also, a review of the *Montgomery Ward Farm Catalog* of 1964 demonstrates that many of the early 1900s items are still in use and demand. This should also assist the collector in dating items to prevent them from buying "antique items" that are really only a few years old. I took photos of corn knives and hay hooks still for sale at the local New Holland dealership in 2003 to demonstrate this point. Many of the items passed off online as "antique" are really only 30 years old and may not be all that rare. Of course, some of the more recent items are still highly collectible. But the buyer should be aware of how long many of the farm items of a collectible nature were actually manufactured. It is very difficult to tell a hoof pick from 2003 from one from 1965. This chapter is offered as a great way to familiarize oneself with changes through the ages of American agriculture.

Chapter One:

Introduction and Dating Items

Prior to breaking down the specific sales data on farm collectibles and antiques, it is necessary to give a few precautionary words on collecting these items. Here are some dating hints for the uninitiated, as well. As an attorney, I am familiar with the term "Caveat Emptor," which simply means that the buyer should be aware. Also, we have the term "Carpe Diem," which means to seize the day. Sometimes when one is attempting to seize the day (the item), one forgets to be aware! This brief introduction is to remind all of you to be aware when attempting to build that collection with that all-important item.

First, remember that not all souls are pure in the antique and collectible business. Most are or try to be good, but many are very willing to skin you alive and sell you back your own skin. I have witnessed more than one person willing to dupe buyers in the area of sporting collectibles. Now I have observed many in the farm collectibles business equally willing to stretch the truth. However, with a little knowledge, most of the "sucker tricks" can be avoided. Here are a few things to be aware of in the farming collectibles field. Most observations are based upon a review of more than 1,000 recent online auction listings and the wording used in them. In addition, some of the comments are based upon observations made at auctions and at flea markets.

Many online auctions do whatever possible to claim an item to be "antique," i.e. 100 years old or more, to get into that special legal category. Some of the antique category tricks I have noticed include the following:

1. "The gentleman I purchased this from was 85 and he claimed his dad played with this item, making it over 100 years old." (Variations include, aunt, uncle, grandmother, grandfather, or neighbor.) When one encounters such a general description, it usually is "made-up" by the seller and not based upon fact or reality. If I am selling something from a person with a claimed age, I support it with facts, not generalizations.

2. "This item came from a farm sale in _____ and all of the items are very old." Again, this is mere puffery, as lawyers call it, and has no facts to support the age of the item.

3. "This is from an Amish farm." This is a fairly common attempt to mislead potential buyers. It seems to indicate that all Amish farm items are old. Of course, some could be, with the culture dating back to 1691 (I wrote my thesis on the Amish and have published extensively about their culture). However, most of the farm items sold online as "old Amish items" can be purchased in Wana Hardware (a large hardware owned by a Mennonite family in Shipshewana, Ind., serving the local

Old Order Amish community) or some such place today. Two recent examples stick out in my mind. The first was a canning bath lift tray made of steel. It was being sold as "from an old farm estate," but the same lift can be purchased in our local hardware store, if not at Wal-Mart. The second was a common Cyclone seeder that was supposedly old for two reasons: it was Amish and it had a patent date of 1925. Neither claim makes an item old.

4. The Cyclone seeder example leads to another common area of fraud, patent dates. Patent dates simply indicate when something was patented, when someone applied for a patent, or, in some cases, when an item had a patent pending. It is as though one finds an 1865 coin in an archaeology dig. One knows the site is at least as recent as 1865 but one does not yet know the age. An 1865 coin indicates the possibility of some age to the site, but the coin could have been dropped in either 1985 or 1865. An item with a patent date of 1898 does not mean it is from 1898. In the fishing lure arena, Skinner fluted spinners have very early patent dates and Skinner continued to use them through the 1950s on its lures. Old patent dates help prove the date of the patent, not the age of the item. Please see the next section for more on using patents as a tool.

5. Artificial weathering is another area of caution in any collecting field. Dishonest dealers have often purposely left duck decoys out in a field during winter to "age" them. The same things can be done with farm and farming collectibles with wooden parts or metal parts that will "age" when exposed to bad weather. I am sad to report that a friend of mine was taken in at a flea market by a dealer who had weathered a "primitive" apothecary. It was a very nice looking unit (made about one year before purchased) that was clearly "aged" in the field. My friend assumed the dealer was telling the truth and failed to check the item carefully for construction techniques that would have shown its true age.

6. "I am not really sure what it is, but I was told it was used for _____ on old farms and it is at least _____ years old." This is a nice way to add fluff to a listing that likely has a common item or one not even related to historical agriculture.

The above are not all of the tricks the unscrupulous have up their sleeves, but the ones discussed cover most of the obvious tricks used for online auction listings and in some other settings. A little common sense and a careful reading of the description and examination of the photos (or lack of photo details) usually will protect the buyer. But, remember Caveat Emptor.

How does one tell the age of an item? Well, solid research is the only solution. There are certain things that one can learn with a little exposure to farming and farm collectibles but some details will take significant research. There are some general

Horse-drawn implements, such as these spreaders, may be antiques, but they're still sought-after in the Amish community for regular use. The I-H sold for $800 and the New Idea for $1,750.

time periods that will become obvious with a little exposure to the field. We are all still learning other ways to date items with more accuracy. For instance, with the exception of some very large steam tractors, tractor-related items do not gain significance until the early 1900s. Horses and horse-drawn equipment were still the mainstay in the 1800s and up through the 1940s in some regions of America. Many of us recall the last team of horses in the neighborhood still being used in the 1950s or even the 1960s in my case (non-Amish, that is). Our family used horses in the mid-1950s for the last time.

Diesel power was not significant as an agricultural influence until the 1930s. It was not common until the post-war era of the early 1950s. Small farms did not purchase their first diesel tractor until the 1960s, or the 1950s at the earliest. This helps date oil industry-related items, such as cans. Milking machines became commonplace only in the 1950s, with earlier ones existing but being far more rare. Milk was shipped in cans commonly through the early 1960s, with bulk tanks replacing cans in the 1960s in most areas. The cream cans of the pre-Depression era gave way to larger milk cans in the 1930s-1960s. Some areas only shipped cream, without milk cans being used at all.

The introduction of certain materials, such as Tenite 1 and Tenite 2 (plastics developed during World War II and just before), are clear indicators of a post-war item in most cases. Early Tenite 1 was unstable and can be a sign of an item's age (1935-1941 in many cases). The addition of better plastic components was common in the 1940s as plastic, and then nylon, were seen as "miracle materials." Many manufacturers figured ways to incorporate these lighter materials into many items. Of course, some items were completely replaced by plastic items in the 1940s and 1950s.

Toys show a good evolution of materials, from wood to early rubber to cast iron to other forms of steel and tin and improved rubber. Then came vinyl and nylon and, finally plastic, replacing earlier materials. A cast iron Arcade toy farm tractor is older and we know it simply by the materials used to cast the toy. Misleading articles mentioned earlier were a tin lithograph barn made by Marx Toys and a set of Auburn vinyl animals being touted as "over 100 years old." Neither of these materials existed 100 years ago and both items dated from the early 1950s.

The most valuable way to date an item is to handle as many items as possible. Go to shows, visit reputable dealers, go to auctions, read club literature, visit Internet sites, talk to people. The following list is not comprehensive but is certainly a good overview of how to date items that are collectible:

1. **Catalogs and magazines** are invaluable aids to dating items. However, the catalogs themselves are too expensive for the average collector to acquire just for dating purposes. Magazines, on the other hand, are very affordable and can assist one in determining the first year of production of an item, production run, and trends in manufacturing. I have identified many items by scanning through old magazines and seeing the "only" advertisement ever run by a small company. It is common to still find magazines from the 1950s for only a few dollars each in mint condition. Earlier magazines increase in value greatly for each decade covered. Catalogs of manufacturers are also fairly inexpensive for the 1950s but go up fast. Earlier catalogs fetch $50 on up for the 1930s-40s and much more for earlier ones. They have not yet reached the prices seen for sporting collectibles catalogs, but they will not stay this inexpensive for too long, as interest grows in farm collectibles and antiques.

2. **Club literature** of the various tractor, toy tractor, toy, hardware, and kitchen collector clubs is another wonderful source of data. In addition, old issues of newsletters and of club magazines can assist one in identifying "unknown" items.

3. **Packaging** is a big clue in dating if you are lucky enough to find an item in its box or on its card. The first thing to look at is the address, to determine if a Zip Code is present. Zippy the cartoon character introduced the Zip Code for the U.S. Postal Service in 1963 and the Zip Code started appearing immediately on some packaging. However, the lack of a Zip Code may also simply mean that the company used up "in stock" packaging first or simply failed to comply with new postal regulations. The lack of a Zip Code is not a guarantee that an item is pre-1963, but it is one possible indicator. Also, I have noted that many companies used the Zip Code on a coupon or mailing label but not on the front of a package or catalog for the first few years of the 1960s. So beware. Lack of a Zip Code was often only a sign that a company was slow to react to new postal regulations and/or the layout department was using old copy for catalogs and advertisements.

4. **Package colors** and materials also evolved and are an obvious indication of approximate time of manufacture. Items packed in wooden crates are normally older than items found in cardboard boxes and the crates marked with a stencil painted label are older than others. Labels such as fruit crate labels ended for the most part by the 1950s and would indicate an approximate age of the item. Also look at the box construction itself with many of the cardboard boxes being dated by the maker even when the contents were not dated. Also, some catalogs and magazines showed the packaging and this would assist dating a found item if the package is still present. Regardless of the packaging, items can usually be dated to a range of years at the very least by the package type and/or color. Of course, addresses on the packaging may also help date a company if one knows the various locations of the company.

5. **Handle** many items for which you already know the dates. You can learn to compare by examination of similarities and differences. This is one of the advantages to the many collectible and antique shows that one can attend. You are able to walk around, pick up items, ask questions, make comparisons, learn, and not spend a cent. I know I have spent many days as an instructor, teaching others what I have learned. Most people who do the shows also enjoy helping one learn about the items they have for sale. So go, ask, learn, and maybe even buy an item or two! I no longer go to shows in anticipation of selling, as I believe the Internet is a far superior tool for that. However, I still enjoy seeing thousands of collectible items in one spot. It is a great social activity, too.

6. **Company names and packaging** can help date an item. Note the full company name, which often changed through the years, and the complete address of the company.

7. **Benchmarks** include literature or advertising introducing an item as "NEW." But, beware as some companies used the designation "NEW" for more than one year to sell their products. A review of the Heddon catalogs from 1970-1984 when researching for my fishing lure books demonstrated this over and over again. These can be catalogs, magazine advertisements, company brochures, call box inserts, separate wholesaler fliers or advertisements, or company histories. I think that the wisest investment the new collector can make is that once a direction for the collection has been decided upon, purchase the company catalog for the particular year of the beginning of the collection, if it's available. Then, attempt to follow the changes in following years through catalogs and advertising in trade magazines and popular literature. Research and collecting must both have a beginning. Once you have this foundation, the rest of your collection is built on the strength of knowledge of your product. Of course as collectors, we often only do the research once we accidentally discover some irresistible item that must become ours!

8. **Oral history** involves seeking out "informants" when attempting to learn the history of an area or subject. This is no different in farm and farming collectible history. I have included an interview with an experienced farm auctioneer as an example in this book. How many of us have listened to stories told by our fathers, mothers, grandparents, aunts, and uncles who are no longer here to jot their memories down? It is most important to the future of farming history and farm collectibles that we document all we are able to about the history of items. We can seek out individuals with knowledge and write down what they have to say while the information is still available. I have learned much of my information through discussions with farmers, family members, collectors, jobbers, and retailers in the trade. I can only hope that others are also documenting all they are able to, while it is fresh in the minds of those involved.

9. **Patents, trademarks,** trade names, and copyrights can be vital. One final way to date an item is to complete a patent search for the item on the U.S. Patent and Trademark Office Web site, www.uspto.gov, by entering the appropriate data. The site is quite easy to use and will result in finding great details on an individual piece. Sometimes the only information about an item is the patent number printed on it. This will result in a complete history by entering the number in the search process. There are limitations on certain searches unless you know the patent number. Keep in mind that the patent year only indicates when the item was actually granted a patent. Sometimes this is years after an item was "used in commerce." It is also possible to conduct trademark, trade name, and copyright searches for items. However, this is a bit more complicated than entering the patent number. Trademark and trade name searches are conducted through the U.S. Patent and Trademark Office, and copyright searches would be completed through the Library of Congress, the organization in charge of protecting copyrighted material in the United States. You can go from the www.uspto.gov site to the copyright site but the address for copyrights is http://lcweb.loc.gov/copyright/ and it tells one how to go about searches. Also, keep in mind that if you are printing items for publication, some of the materials on the U.S. government sites are protected by copyright and you will need permission to reprint certain items for publication.

Finding Items

It is tougher and tougher to find items "on the street," so to speak. However, it can still happen. I use every available technique to find items for my collections. Every once in a while, I get lucky and find a good item for a low price. But it all takes work and diligence to be successful. The ones finding items with the most regularity are not just "lucky," they are also industrious. I know one picker who is always finding great things. But he is out of bed early, at estate sales to get number 1, and works at least four days a week finding items. Also, he is willing to pay for an item. Many people think that good items are out there at ridiculously low prices just waiting to be discovered. Trust me, this is the exception and not the norm. The norm is that an estate dealer prices items fairly, with enough profit margin left for the dealer to also make a dollar or two. Thus, items at estate sales are not "cheap" but are fairly priced in most instances.

I have a real issue with those who do not want to pay a fair price for an item. Sure, we all like bargains if found. But please do not always try to beat down prices when someone has an item for sale.

In the same fashion, if one is asked the actual value of an item, I believe it is our ethical duty as collectors and dealers to tell the truth as best we know it. In other words, if I go to a garage sale and see a tin sign hanging on the wall, that is not in the sale but they are willing to sell, I should also be prepared to tell them the value of it when asked. This is not to say that we have to tell people the value of an item that is already priced. This I do not think is necessary.

But if one is relying upon our knowledge and experience, and we are after something of theirs that is not already priced, we have a duty to be honest about the value in that situation. Of course, I am not suggesting it is only fair to pay full retail for an item. Only that the seller has a right to know the full retail if asking. Each of us will make our own decisions on how much to pay, but we should be duty-bound to be fair and ethical in all of our dealings. I know that in my own experiences, this has resulted in positive repeat dealings with people. I have had access to collections that was denied others.

Using the Internet in Collecting

I have been involved in higher education for nearly 34 years as a professor and administrator. I only wish I would have had a microprocessor and the Internet when conducting research for my earlier professional writings! My students can find answers to many questions in less time today than it took me to drive or walk to the library. What does this mean for collecting? A lot.

The Internet became a viable tool for selling and buying collectibles and antiques beginning in 1995 with the birth of many online auction houses. Only a few remain today and most of the market is consumed and controlled by only one: eBay. (I have no ownership interest in eBay and it does not pay me for mentioning or trading on the site.) I spent a little time looking at eBay listings for farm collectibles for sale. These items were found under a number of related categories. I marveled that an entire farming collectible collection could be purchased without leaving the seat of my chair at my computer desk, including an 1800s Studebaker wagon.

This was no surprise to me, of course, as I make a substantial number of sales per year on eBay and use it as a tool on

Identification marks on this butter churn indicate it was made by the Union Mfg. Co., Toledo, Ohio. Those marks prove invaluable to determining the age of the item. This churn is valued at more than $300. *VanAlstine Collection*

Where to look

How does one find items? Well, a list could be quite long but I will attempt to summarize in the following list:

Dealers

Antique shops and malls, and flea markets

Farm and household auctions

Postings at feed, supply, and grocery stores

Advertising in local papers

Advertising in regional magazines

Advertising in retirement homes

Telling each and every friend of your interests

Buying advertising space on a billboard

Visiting shows dedicated to farming collectibles

Visiting areas rich in agricultural history

Visiting Internet sites where one can buy/sell/learn about farming collectibles and antiques

Visiting living agricultural museums and historical museums

Going to auctions dedicated to farming collectibles

Joining every organization related to farming collectibles

Joining a local organization dedicated to collecting

Giving lectures on the topic to community service groups

Giving lectures on the topic to local school groups

Developing a network of collector to collector exchanges

Lots of footwork, phone calling, emailing, and other contacts

Training and using a quality picker or pickers to assist you

a weekly, if not daily, basis. However, for many, this is a bewildering area still not trusted or understood. Even if you do not buy one farming collectible or antique over the Internet, it is still a great tool to learn about farms, farm history, farming antiques, and collectibles. More and more dealers, auction houses, and publishers are making online sites available for all of us to visit and expand our knowledge. Many collectors are sharing their collections and knowledge online by adding technically accurate listings of items for online with references given to major research works to verify the item for sale. I purchased a number of books and advertising items shown later in this book online. All of the listings had detailed factual data related to manufacture and time period of the items, supported by references in some instances.

One can buy and sell on the Internet with confidence if only a few simple rules are followed. The first and most important rule is to deal only with those dealers with a positive reputation. This is the same for online dealers or those with storefronts. Just as one usually selects a mechanic or an attorney based upon reputation, one should also select a dealer the same way. With online dealers, a mechanism known as "feedback" can easily be checked to determine how others have fared in their dealings with the dealer. If all others are happy with the service, the timeliness of delivery, the quality of the items, the proper description of the items sold, then it is likely you are dealing with a reputable individual or company. If the individual or company still lacks feedback, positive or negative, I would not spend a large amount of money in my purchases from them. But if someone has sold a number of related farm collectibles or antiques in the past year and all their feedback is positive, it is likely you are safe in your dealings with that person/company.

There are additional ways to guarantee your satisfaction with more expensive items. Make sure you know the seller's return policies. Also, for a $3,000 item, will the seller accept funds being escrowed to a third party until the transaction is completed? If not, that is not a guarantee of problems but it does give one more option for very valuable items. Also, most auction services and electronic payment services (such

as PayPal) are now offering guarantees that may be purchased at the time of electronic payment. For a $12 item, this is not necessary in most instances; however, it would be one more assurance for a $3,000 item.

Finally, the best guarantee is in past dealings with the seller personally. That way, one knows first hand if he/she is satisfied with the past performance of a seller and with the product(s) supplied. I buy and sell thousands of dollars worth of sporting collectibles per year on the Internet and have only had one really unpleasant experience. A phony photograph of "an old tackle box and contents" hoodwinked me. But with more than eight years of indirect and direct sales experience online, that is not a bad record.

So, my advice to all with access to a computer and the Internet is to get on the "Net" and learn to use it as a tool. Also, it is a great way to find items that trips to the local antique store would take years to find. Any item on the Internet is available to anyone for the looking and buying. It allows us to fill in our collections far more easily and more rapidly than any other technique, albeit at a more costly price in many cases. Yet, at the same time, bargains can be found when a seller lists an item with which he/she is not familiar or during times of a soft economy. I can attest that I have found some real buys on the Internet for both reasons. The most important advice is to learn by experience and have fun along the way.

The Internet is also an invaluable research tool and should be used to learn more about one's collecting interests. One great site to visit and then visit the actual living sites is www.alhfam.org, the site for the Association for Living History, Farm and Agricultural Museums. ALHFAM is the clearinghouse and society for information about many items related to early farm life in America. This site will lead you to many links and great information. Currently there are 125 member institutions listed in its information base and one can discover locations, hours, and special collections by a visit to the site. There are more than 80 international Web site links. Whether it is the great and extensive Greenfield Village, or one of the smaller but wonderful sites such as Conner Prairie

John Deere hit and miss engines from the 1910s or early 1920s are among farm antiques that have appreciated greatly in value over the past few years. They're worth $2,000 or more.

in Indiana, one can learn much about historical agriculture through the site itself and then visits to the museums. Most land grant universities, such as Michigan State, Cornell, Penn State and others, also have museums and major research collections on farming.

Value Trends

Gone are the days of a $5 DeLaval or Surge tin sign being found at the local antique shop, for the most part. Bargains can still be found in unique situations but overall most dealers now know the value of good farming collectibles, if they can identify them. Thus, even novice dealers easily identify advertising items due to the additional printed information on the item. However, one could find a tool or implement not identified because the items are not marked or the markings are coded and the dealer does not know the meaning. Also, estate sales can have some bargains. I went to a neighborhood estate sale and picked up two Ford wrenches for $1.50 because the dealer used masking tape to place the price on the wrenches and covered up the trademark. I noticed the "D" and bought them. I also picked up a very old Crescent brand 12" wrench for only $3.50 in excellent shape. The dealers were not specialists in tools so they priced these items cheaply compared to glassware and kitchen items. But if a dealer has resources available on prices, the prices will not be so low.

Values in antiques and collectibles are driven primarily by age, rarity, condition, and the desire created by a particular brand or maker. Obviously, the older the item, the greater the rarity. But not always. Also, the older the item, the less important is condition compared to a newer item. In other words, a farming magazine from 1919 is old, not necessarily real rare, but would be more acceptable with some wear and tear than would a common 1954 *Hoard's Dairyman*.

In the past 30 years, we have seen a revolution in pricing for fine collectibles and antiques, and it is now coming to farm and farming collectibles. Some recent changes include: cast

iron seats selling for $5 a decade ago now bring over $100; hit and miss engines bring hundreds, or even thousands, of dollars; good advertising signs reach into three figures commonly; certain antique tractor prices are on an upward spiral; toy tractors can reach astronomical figures if needed to fill a gap in a collection; and the list continues. The main thing keeping down some prices is the weight and bulk of some desired items makes it hard to move them, limiting their demand and prices. This may change as these items become more difficult to find and other items keep increasing in price.

For specific values, see the sections on different types of farming collectibles in the book itself. However, in general, items have been going up on a 10 percent to 15 percent per year basis the last few years, according to my own observations and those of others. Of course, this cannot be guaranteed to continue but will likely continue upward at some scale. Our economy is far weaker today than it was at the time of record breaking sales for many items registered in the years of 2001 and 2002, so I would expect at least a temporary softening of pricing on even the better items. However, they simply do not make some collectible items, so the market will likely continue to grow in the future for these better and rarer pieces.

I would suggest keeping up with the sales data from auction houses, going to local auction houses and farm auctions, visiting antique stores, and reading as much as you can find on farm antiques and collectibles. Also, prudent following of online auctions is an excellent test of what people are actually willing to pay for a particular item. As to deciding the best place for an investment, again, only you can decide. However, with that caveat, I think it important to note that better items retain and increase in value more rapidly than mediocre items. This is true in all antique and collectible areas. In other words, if you can afford to buy a rarer version of an Ertl die-cast John Deere, you will more likely see a quicker increase in value on your investment than a model found in greater numbers. But it is your choice to make, not mine nor anyone else's.

Chapter Two:
Farming in Print

This section covers the collecting of book and non-book print items related to farming such as manuals, pamphlets, magazines, advertisements, and calendars. Many of the manuals for tractors and farm equipment have become both highly collectible and highly priced within recent years. Farm books (books dedicated to farming and not advertising for farm items) are only briefly covered due to the enormity of the subject. However, I have listed a few books of collectible nature as examples of what is available to the collector.

One reason for the increased value of some of these items is that they have been the only source of data on the antique items themselves. Another reason is that they are often very colorful and full of nice illustrations. Finally, they take up little space and add significantly to the general knowledge base of one's collection.

Manuals and advertising items have always shown up at farm auctions, usually in a boxed lot of other paper items. However, the past 10 years or so, most auctioneers have noted with special interest the operating manuals for the more popular John Deere tractors (A and B) and I-H tractors (BN, Cub, C, H, M, and Super M) and Allis-Chalmers (B, C, WD, any of the D series). I recall selling one Deere manual online in 1998 for nearly $50 that I picked up at a feed mill auction for a few dollars. A recent farm auction saw manuals sell for $20-$260 each, depending on the age and the product. The least expensive advertising literature sold for $5 and ranged upward to $40 each at the same June auction.

The point is that this area of collectible has "come of age." Many folks are after these items now and recognize their values. However, it is an area where bargains can still be found at farm auctions and in antique stores. Online auctions will normally command a higher price, as bidders from around the world are normally viewing the same item and will not hesitate to bid up a nice item. When I still had an antique booth, I had a paper item priced at $2 that brought $28 when I put it in an online auction. It was there for the taking for a long time (nearly two years) but when it was offered to a broader audience, it jumped in price accordingly. Not all items do the same but, as a general rule, online auctions will at least net the highest possible viewing of an item.

What does one look for in selecting paper items to collect? Actually, this depends if one is considering investment potential or personal interest. Let us cover investment potential first. The most important attribute of paper items is "condition, condition, condition," as we antique dealers like to say. But with paper items, it is doubly true. A soiled paper item is of little value. A mildewed item, a torn item, a musty item, none of these are wanted in a collection. Not that a super rare piece will not be purchased. It is just that its value is no more than 10 percent of the value of a piece in fine shape, maybe only 1 percent. I have turned down paper items for free because they were so musty or dirty that I was afraid of ultimate damage to other items. Also, beware that paper items with must and mildew can also cause severe allergic reactions. I learned that by experience with one "find" I made of old sporting magazines that ultimately had to be thrown out due to the mildew causing a reaction.

So, whether for value or reference, only select clean items in fine shape. A tear or bent corner is not going to make an item worthless. These flaws are far easier to deal with than the areas of mildew and dirt. Some dirt will clean off with wallpaper cleaner and other cleaning items on the market, but this should be done only if an item is needed for research or to fill in a gap in one's collection.

Our first category is condition. What else affects value? I would say that with paper items the most important attribute is "brand recognition," followed by general attractiveness of the layout of the item. A John Deere item is almost always going to garner more attention than even an older item by a small manufacturer such as Rumely tractors and threshing machines. The Rumely item is likely more rare. But that is not as important as the fact that far more of us grew up with John Deere A and B tractors. We easily recognize them and want to collect items related to them. So one will find paper items related to John Deere, Farmall, Case, Allis-Chalmers, and Oliver to be the most popular tractor-related items, and Surge and DeLaval the most popular milking machine related items.

As a former college president of an art and design school, I can attest to the importance of the layout of a graphic item as being important for its "attention getting" ability. This is true today, it was true in the past, and it is very true for collectible paper items. The area of layout includes the color of the brochure or item, the quality of illustrations used, and the general design of the item and its use of illustrations. It is like the folk story of a blind person attempting to describe an elephant when one cannot see it. One recognizes it is an elephant but it is hard to describe. The same is true of good layout designs. They are easy to spot and hard to describe.

Look for nice strong colors, deep yellows and reds, a pleasing orange, an easily recognized green and yellow combination. Then add nice line drawings and the use of good illustrations or photography. Finally, make sure the print is pleasing and easy to read. If an item has all of these qualities and brand recognition, and is in pristine condition, it will command a premium price.

One final item of value is demand caused by other factors, including generation demand, crossover collector demand, and general attraction demand.

Generation demand is demand caused by one generation with a greater interest in an item, a brand, or an era. I have documented this type of demand in my fishing collectible books. It means that "baby boomers" are far more interested in the tractors of the 1950s (and 1930s and 1940s) than we are of the first tractors on the scene. This is because we recognize them, remember them, drove them, walked behind them, rode on them with our fathers or mothers or brothers or sisters. We saw them daily.

Crossover collector demand includes competition from collectors of related fields, such as tools. A John Deere or Fordson wrench is as much of interest to the tool collector as it is to the tractor collector. It is also of general interest to all farm collectors. This tends to drive up the price of an item. The classic example is a Winchester product. These items are sought by folks in many areas of collecting due to the name alone.

General attraction demand is best illustrated by something I first noticed in fishing lure collectibles, called the "cute factor." If an item is attractive, it is pretty, it is cute, it is colorful, its value will increase accordingly because collectors from other fields will also be after it. In fishing lures, there is a lure known as a Heddon Punkinseed that is very "cute." It looks like a little bluegill or sunfish. These lures have gone far beyond their "normal value" as they now attract a large cadre of followers that just like their appearance, even if they are not that interested in lure collecting. I am sure many areas of farm household collectibles would fall into this category as well, such as roosters, lambs, and calves.

One cannot discount the intrinsic value of an item either. If a person has a WD-45 Diesel tractor, he or she is far more likely to spend money on its manual than some general A-C collector would. Even if one simply had once owned the same WD-45 Diesel (as I did), one would then spend more on the same manual. If we need something for our own research or to make ourselves feel good about a memory, we tend to buy it, regardless of price. I have developed a mathematical formula as follows: **item + quality of memory = price**. In other words, the greater the quality of a memory related to a particular item, the greater will be its price. Only the buyer can determine this intrinsic value. It often will not be recovered in reselling an item unless one finds another buyer with similar feelings.

Paper collectibles

Where does one find these items? Paper collectors are fortunate because there are many dealers specializing in paper items. Some of these folks sell online and many offer "lists" or catalogs for their specialty goods. It is my opinion that the online auction is the easiest source for finding a specific item to fill in a collection. However, one also finds these items at every farm auction in America, sometimes only a piece or two, sometimes an entire box full of items. I attended a farm implement and tractor dealership dispersal auction at which one could have purchased a veritable warehouse of paper

What are paper collectibles?

So, what is collectible in terms of paper items? Well, just about anything that meets the qualifications set forth above. A list is provided as a guide:

Tractor manuals and advertising items
Implement manuals and advertising items
Milking machine manuals and advertising items
Brochures and advertising items for tools and hand-held implements
Advertising for breeds of farm animals
Manuals and advertising items for farm household items
Advertising for marketing farm products and goods
Catalogs for any of the above items
Early (pre-1950) farm magazines
Any other paper item related to farming

items related to farming: manuals, advertising items, give-away items, catalogs, and early magazines. However, even at this auction, the items went fairly high, as their value had already been realized. Many bidders were interested in buying large lots for resale online and elsewhere.

As with all items, the best way to find them is to ask. Ask your friends, relatives, co-workers, garage sale sellers, local auctioneers, farm dealerships, former milking machine route salesmen, the local veterinarian, cow and horse jockeys (no, not the riders, the traders). Ask anyone you can think of about these items. I have found items in the most unusual places by never being too shy to ask.

To give a range of values is both necessary and very difficult for this category, as it encompasses such a broad area. Most paper items start at about $2 retail and can easily go up to $100 for nice manuals of popular tractors and implements. Rare catalogs from dates earlier than 1940 can bring upwards of $200. I have purchased 1940s DeLaval manuals for $50 and sold them for $35-$75 the past few years. One, in an online auction, only brought $10.50 but was in rougher shape. Simple 8- to 12-page advertising brochures will often bring $5-$20 depending on the brand, item, and condition of paper. Most tractor manuals are easily worth $10 and more likely $25 as a minimum price if in pristine condition.

Crate label ends for the cedar fruit and vegetable shipping crates, and similar tobacco paper labels, usually begin at about $4 each. Some can bring up to nearly $200 if rare and/or if exceptionally interesting graphics are present. A superb site on the Internet dedicated to paper label collecting is www.paperstuff.com. This site has hundreds of labels for sale and gives a nice little history of these labels used primarily between 1920 and 1950 in America. As the site indicates, color lithograph labels have been used to identify products and their sources since as early as the 1880s. They had reached their demise by the mid-1950s due to the use of cardboard boxes. Many labels were found in storage throughout America and these are now for sale to collectors. Make sure you are not buying a reproduction, as its value is limited. The average price for a crate end label is less than $10. Tobacco labels, pins, and cigar box labels are similar in use, history, and value. The little metal tobacco pins were used to mark tobacco by the farm sending it to market. These are nice little advertising pins to collect.

The interesting thing about the crate end labels is that one can develop a collection within a collection by concentrating only on labels depicting farms and farming, or fishing, or wildlife, or just oranges, or just strawberries. Of course, some of the crossover labels, such as fishing and wildlife, tend to bring more due to competition among collecting fields. But there is likely not a more colorful area of farming-related collectibles covering 70 of our arbitrary 100 year history of farming collectibles.

As a general rule, most paper items are not worth a significant amount if post-1950. However certain manuals and catalogs would still command quite a bit up until about 1970. As one goes back in time, there is nearly a doubling effect every 10 years. In other words, if a 1940 brochure for a New Idea Spreader is worth $20, then it is likely worth twice that if from 1930. But one must factor in the generation demand for any particular item as well. I should think the most valuable farm paper in the near future will be from about 1930 until 1955, due to the interest of all of the "baby boomer" generation of farm kids and farm collectors. I know I would much rather see an advertising piece for something I recognize and may have once used than an obscure tractor or threshing machine that I only heard of or saw in an antique farm magazine.

This is a difficult area to give a price for particular items unless they have recently sold, due to market fluctuation and demand differences. This is illustrated by a recent request made to a major paper dealer online when I asked him to send me $200 worth of paper items to scan for this book. He replied that he would rather not, as he could not properly price it. He told me he would rather just sell it on an online auction and then he would know the value. He was very polite and understanding. He just did not want to sell an item for $15 that he later would see selling for $25. This is not uncommon among dealers, of course, however it does demonstrate the sensitive area of pricing and estimating prices for these types of items. But my purpose is to give some guidance.

Antique and collectible farming books seem to be even more volatile in terms of pricing than the paper advertising items. There are numerous value guides available regarding antique and collectible books. The serious collector should consult one or more of these books for more information on book valuation. However, I have found that books do not seem to have any easily determined formula in determining value in the field of farm and agricultural collectibles. I have recently purchased books from the middle to late 1800s for less than $20 that contained superb graphics, lithography, and even cut-out inserts showing the internal organs and bone

structures of farm animals. To me, these all seem like bargains. I hypothesize that there simply is not enough demand by collectors for farming books to be driving the prices to the hundreds of dollars one would see for similar books in hunting, fishing, wildlife, etc.

One general area of interesting books is the *USDA Yearbook of Agriculture* series published for a number of years by our U.S. Department of Agriculture. The research arm of the Department of Agriculture began in 1865. Many of the early *Yearbooks of Agriculture* have important information about early agricultural inventions and techniques of interest to the collector today. These books pick a topic and leading writers cover it in depth. The books were available from the USDA and/or the Government Printing Office. I once owned one with President Jerry Ford's signature. He had used it as a text at the University of Michigan. Oh why did I sell that one? These books usually bring from $5-$30, depending on condition. A 1906 version is shown.

The USDA also put out thousands of brochures and pamphlets on farming over the years. Some of these have minor collector interest, as well. Most of the brochures would only bring a few dollars at best. The reason the brochures are not of as much interest is that they are mainly black and white and are not very compelling in the design category. However, earlier ones would command some interest due to line drawings and/or photos of early farm equipment or tools.

Books such as *Silent Spring* by Rachael Carson had a major impact on agriculture, as it led to the banning of DDT and many related chemicals. In addition to it being a classic, it is a farm collectible. There were also many books written about soil conservation after the Depression that are collectible, such as the great works by Aldo Leopold and others. A search of any major Internet search engine on agricultural books by topic will generate hundreds, if not thousands, of "hits." I would suggest using www.ask.com or www.google.com to begin your online searches.

Some of the how-to books have a following, especially for some of the lost arts such as raising draft horses or the farm orchard. If the book is a first edition, it is almost always more valuable. I have included, as an example, a book from the Lippincott Series on farming from the early 1900s on raising sheep. Now that I own it, I want to complete the series on other farm enterprises due to the quality of that book. A very old book may or may not be more valuable, depending on how many were printed and circulated. A book with great illustrations is usually more valuable. The addition of the dust jacket usually increases the value. Finally, the signature of someone famous (President Ford), makes the book more valuable.

I have included a few examples of what I would consider collectible farm books due to their contents or their rarity. Any serious collector of rare books is directed to specialty dealers and references on rare books for more detailed information.

I researched more than 1,000 online auctions in reviewing pricing for this book. Most listings in this chapter, and in other chapters, without photographs represent some of those online auctions. Many of the items from the online auctions are also detailed with photographs in other sales data and/or in Chapter 14 on advertising.

Between the descriptions given and similar items listed elsewhere in the book, the reader should be able to clearly identify each item described. Also, each online item price was verified by actual auction sale results and/or interviews with experts in the field of farm collectibles and antiques.

Values of Print Items

Paper cover booklet, 5 1/2" x 8", 18 pages, A Brief History of Pneumatic Tires for Farm Vehicles, Goodyear Tire Press, 1938. This was a booklet publishing the results of a 1938 essay contest open to FFA members and showed in photographs many pieces of farm implements from the period. The booklet was in good condition, as the term is used by paper dealers, but collectors would have downgraded the "chew" on edge and normal wear. The item was clearly bought not to collect as much as for reference. It would be an excellent addition to farm implement references of the period. $22

Paper cover catalog, 6" x 9", 80 pages, 1932-33 Hertzler & Zook Catalog, publisher unknown, 1933. This Belleville, Pa., manufacturing company made a variety of items for sawing that attached to Fordson tractors, trucks, or hit and miss engines. In addition, 53 pages of the catalog are dedicated to early farm equipment such as anvils, wheelbarrows, concrete mixers, blacksmith tools, drill presses, pulleys, belting, kettles, fencing and supplies, and the Twin City tractor. It had a stain so would not be pristine for paper collectors. But what a great source of data on the 1930s! $23

Seven farm implement and tractor magazines and equipment newsletters from the 1960s-70s. These were all trade magazines for dealers and in good shape, but quite recent. $8

Paper cover catalog, 6 3/4" x 8 3/4", 64 pages, color covers, 1906 IRON AGE Farm Implements, publisher unknown. According to the sales pitch, this company was started in 1836 and later purchased by Oliver. This is the complete implement line for garden and horse-drawn farm items. They are shown in the 64 pages, illustrated and priced. Implements include: Advance Fertilizer Drill, Eureka Corn Knife, Bateman Hoe, various potato diggers, harrows, cultivators, wheeled plows, wheeled hoes for gardens, and seeders. $26

Advertising card, postcard size, no date, M & J Rumely Separators. A nice advertising piece shows a girl holding a flower and explains the qualities of the New Rumely Separator. Rumely made early tractors and threshing machines as well, and the card shows one of each of them. Address is La Porte, Ind., home to Rumely for years. $15.50

Advertising card, postcard size, no date, mailed in 1914, Lininger Implement Co., Omaha, Neb., published by American Trade Promoting Corp., also of Omaha. This card advertised farm implements, binding twine, wagons, buggies, gas engines, and automobiles. $12.25

Seven matchbooks (matches removed) for implement dealers from Belvidere, Ill., included John Deere, I-H, Ford, New Idea, and Oliver. Graphics on covers showed some fairly old ones (Oliver with a single walking plow on cover) and newer I-H books. $9

Hard cover book, 543 pages, 6" x 8 1/2", 1913 Implement Blue Book, published by Midland Publishing Co., Midland Building, St. Louis. This would be great to own. What a reference for advertising of the era, farm machinery and implements, vehicles, information about makers, and prices. .... $50+

Hardcover book, 432 pages, Twelfth Annual Report of the Indiana State Board of Agriculture for 1870. This contains numerous illustrations of major and minor manufacturers of farm implements, tools, and machinery from throughout the Midwest. Also, local agricultural reports by county and state fair results. $67

Paper cover catalog, 10 1/2" x 24" (folds to 7 3/4" x 10 1/2"), color photos, John Deere Hay Making Implements, 1934. This catalog shows four new items in the John Deere line for 1934: No. 4 Mower, Power Mower, Side Delivery Rake, and tractor-mounted Side Delivery Rake. This shows the strength of brand in bidding on items. Many of the items listed above have far more useful information but this item was being purchased for its "collector quality" and not for the data contained within its pages. "Nothing Runs Like a Deere" could be modified in farm collectible circles to "Nothing Runs Prices up at an Auction Like a Deere." $37.50

Five New Holland Farm Implement **catalogs** and a 1914 calendar. The catalogs included 1968 combine heads, 1967 combines, 1968 auto bale stackers, 1969 Equipment Buyers Guide, New Holland's own "Our First 100 years 1895-1995 history magazine," and the 1914 calendar. $10

WHERE ELSE CAN YOU FIND SO MUCH *Real Value* FOR YOUR WAGON DOLLAR?

(2)

FEATURES:

1. Quality Construction . . . In choosing your new farm wagon, it is important to consider that the modern wagons described in this folder are the product of a factory which has specialized in the manufacture of quality hauling equipment for nearly 90 years. What does this mean to you? It means that whichever "Big 3" Wagon you choose you are getting a wagon that is built to last, a rugged low-down wagon that will handle "pay loads" with safety, a wagon built entirely of new, high-grade material by skilled workmen.

2. Light Weight . . . Yes, a wagon *can* be built to last longer and still be *lighter* than other wagons. John Deere Rubber-Tired Farm Wagons are built with emphasis on quality materials, light-weight, simplicity, and precision, rather than sheer bulk.

3. Light Running . . . Owners report that John Deere Rubber-Tired Farm Wagons are extremely light running. Here again, long experience in wagon construction is your assurance that you are getting a wagon with just the right combination of strength and light-running qualities. You are sure to appreciate the new smoothness of pneumatic-tired wheels running on precision-built Timken tapered-roller bearings.

4. Non-Whipping . . . John Deere Rubber-Tired Farm Wagons are *trailers*—not whippers—even when running at rapid speeds under load. Rigid construction throughout, plus provisions for taking up any looseness that may occur after long hauling service, enable you to keep these wagons running like new.

5. Adjustable Tubular-Steel Reach The John Deere reach is extendable from 83 inches to 131 inches, making it easily adaptable to boxes and beds of various lengths. A means of taking up play in the reach is provided so that any looseness which would encourage whipping is prevented.

6. Demountable Wheels . . . Each of the "Big 3" Wagons is regularly equipped with strong, steel, automotive-type wheels, demountable at the hub.

7. Automatic Brakes . . . Some state laws require 4-wheel brakes if the wagon is to be used on the highway. Others require 2-wheel brakes. Both types of brakes are available with automatic control on the No. 953 Wagon.

(3)

"TOPS" AT HAVING TIME

Note extended reach

WITH A *Fast, Smooth-Running* JOHN DEERE YOU'RE IN COMMAND OF EVERY HAULING JOB ON YOUR FARM OR ON THE HIGHWAY

WITH A "PAY-LOAD" OF CORN

➤ HAULING COBS FROM THE SHELLER

A dependable wagon is one of the best assets your farm can have because practically every farming job begins and ends with some kind of hauling.

With a modern, light-draft hauling unit that operates safely and smoothly in your fields or on the highway . . . behind your tractor, truck, or motor car you speed up all of your hauling jobs. You'll find the sturdily-built John Deere wagons fill the bill completely. They're easy to handle . . . economical to own . . . dependable on every job.

Your John Deere dealer will be glad to give you the complete story on these wagons, to help you choose the one that best fits your needs. There is the No. 953 for all standard hauling jobs, the No. 963 if you want an extra heavy-duty wagon, and the No. 943 which meets all-around needs but is limited to the handling of smaller loads at slower speeds.

There is almost no end to the uses you will find for one of these smooth-running, sturdy hauling units. At all seasons a John Deere Rubber-Tired Wagon can be put to profitable use in field work, for fast trips to and from town, for marketing grain, cotton, fruit and livestock, hauling milk, wood, and a score of similar jobs.

These are the wagons that are playing such a big part in the conversion of farm hauling from a slow, tedious job to a speedy, low-cost operation. Plan now to own at least one of these modern hauling units. There is a variety of poles and hitches for tractor, truck, team, or motor car—the right one for your requirements.

WITH THE HAY CHOPPER

BEHIND THE CORN PICKER

ON THE WAY TO THE COTTON GIN

(5)

JOHN DEERE

RUBBER-TIRED

FARM WAGONS

NOS. 943...
953...963

THE BIG 3

IN MODERN FARM
HAULING EQUIPMENT

Paper cover catalog, John Deere Wagons for 1950, a nice color brochure on John Deere wagons. I somehow won this but lost out on the 1940 New Idea Manure Spreader brochure. All the Deere bidders must have been out in the hay fields that day. This shows the diminishing value of items once they hit that 1950 demarcation point. $7.50

An 1887 engraving of a farm scene in Iceland.............................$2

A Funks Seed Corn farm record book from 1940. This was for Rob-See-Co, a trade name for J.C. Robinson Seed Co. of Waterloo, Neb. I think this is inexpensive for this nice item and the condition was excellent. $2.50

A black and white photograph of an old farmhouse, dating from the late 1800s. $10

A farm diary written by a teen-ager describing his jobs around his family farm, dating from 1917-21. This would be a classic piece of research data for early farm life and the price seems low for this type of information. $16

A 19th century Alabama farm diary with line drawings. The diary was the product of L. Clarke Allison and dates from an earlier time period. But I would guess it is the value of the drawings that drove up the price of this farm diary. The seller estimated the value at $700-$900. ....$138.50

Mid- to late-1800s magazines with advertisements for farms. Most of these were volumes of *The Cultivator and Country Gentleman* published in Albany, N.Y. The issues contained about 20 pages, measured 9 1/2" by 12 1/2" and were clean, coming from a bound volume. These were offered for $12 and most sold for $12-$18. The advertisements were interesting, describing particular "farms" for sale, giving the details of crops, buildings, fencing, and the farm name. ....$12-$18 each

A *Farm Journal* issue from June 1946. It sold for $2, but the cover was quite ragged and this hurt the value. One in fine condition would have brought about $10 (see the magazines shown in Chapter 8 and those pictured later in this chapter).. $2-$10

A John Deere Tire Pump Operators Manual, five pages long. With no special graphics, it appeared to be from the 1950s or 1960s and was Operator's Manual OM-C6-654. ....$15

A beautiful engraving from 1887 showing a wagon being driven to the ranch..$1

A *New York Evening Post* advertisement for Swartwout Farm in Westchester County, N.Y., found in a formerly bound volume of the newspaper. The price was for the entire newspaper but it was the farm advertisement that was listed online to attract bidders. It did attract five active bidders and many more lookers.....................................$26

A 1919 Louden Farm Equipment Catalog made available on CD-ROM. A new item, not a collectible but a valuable research tool, this is a reprint of the 1919-20 general catalog of Louden Machinery Co., a company known for its barn equipment and hay unloading tools. Items included early hay carriers, door hangers, dairy barn equipment, litter, feed, merchandise and milk can carriers, hardware specialties, and more. The Louden cupola for barns had a weathervane with a cow on it. $25

Another advertisement from *The Cultivator and Country Gentleman.* This was the complete 20-page magazine, clean, from a bound volume being purchased. $20

A nice grain mill postcard from the Chaffee-Miller Milling Co. of Casselman, N.D. $5

A set of advertisements from 1954 for Ford, New Idea, Allis, I-H, and more. These were simply tear sheets from 1954 magazines. **$4**

A 1911 Pennsylvania Railroad book explaining the many wonderful uses of dynamite on the farm. As a lawyer, I found the book of interest telling all the folks how to use something that one would be held strictly liable for if harming someone or someone's property. The little 9", 112-page book explained how to increase production, blow up stumps and rocks, use dynamite to dig a well, and many other wonderful uses for this item. The book sold for $15.75 and undoubtedly would have done even better if the railroad collectors would have found it in the farm listings. **$15.75**

A DeLaval almanac from 1946. This was a surprise, bringing only $10.50. These often bring $25-$50. August often brings lower prices for online auctions and I think this is an example. **$10.50**

An 1878 engraving showing oxen pulling a plow. Like earlier engravings mentioned, this is an inexpensive but beautiful piece of Americana. **$2**

An advertisement for Delco Remy. The advertisement is on a page from a farm magazine showing a beagle, some farmers hunting, and their "Farmall" type tractor sure to start with its Delco Remy parts in the background. **$3.50**

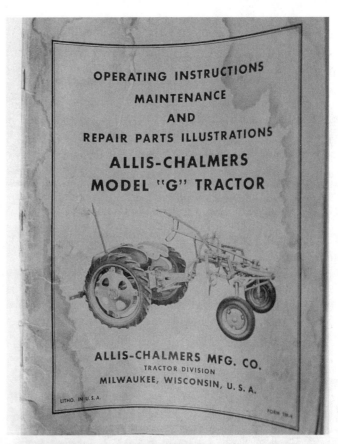

The *Lippincott's Sheep Manual* is a wonderful example of farm books that are collectible. There is an entire Lippincott's livestock series and it would make a nice set for any farm library, all published in the early 1900s. The sheep volume is from 1918 and contains many valuable color and black and white prints, in addition to valuable data on raising sheep. This volume is in excellent condition. *Lewis Collection*..**$23.50**

This Allis-Chalmers Model "G" Tractor manual should bring $25+ and the little manual for the mower for B and C tractors should start at $10 and go up from there. Even the Wheel Horse manual is worth at least $25 as well. *Paulsen Collection* ....**$25 each**

These magazines from the late 1930s and early 1940s should sell for $10-$20, minimum, each in clean condition. *Paulsen Collection*

....**$10-$20 each**

The Oliver 70 tractor advertisement is from the 1937 *Country Home* and the Farmall 12 advertisement is from the 1938 *Country Home* magazine. Even cut out and framed, these advertisements would have collector appeal to a tractor collector or farm enthusiast. See the real tractor in Chapter 12.

A Firestone Tractor Tire advertisement shows many vintage tractors. These advertisements were from the *Country Home* 1937 or 1938 magazines, as are the tractor advertisements.

A nice plate of a Jersey cow was once found inside a book called the *Biggle Cow Book*. This plate was removed and sold in an antique store. We paid a few dollars for it years ago. This is not especially valuable but is a nice addition to one's special area of interest and in a form capable of being displayed. *Lewis Collection* .... **$5-$10**

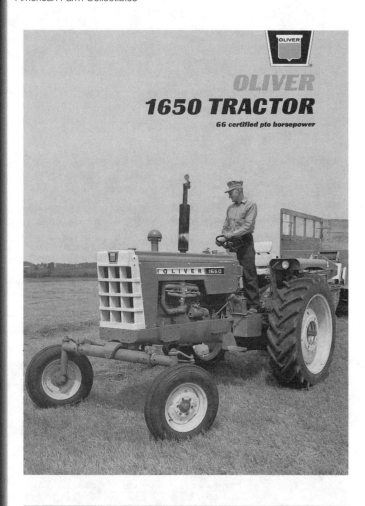

These Oliver catalogs from the mid-1960s are at the end of our era but are nice clean examples of collectible literature. They show many of the tractors available in the mid-1960s. They should sell for at least $15-$20 in this nice condition, maybe more if needed by a bidder that day. ....$15-$20 each

MORE OLIVER TRACTORS IN THE STYLE YOU PREFER

1850 —perfect choice for big acreages

This powerful new performer packs plenty of muscle—92 observed pto horsepower—to take 6 and 7-plow loads with outstanding economy. Engine choices include gasoline or LPG, plus the rugged and economical new Dyna-Diesel. The 1850 is available as a row-crop with dual or adjustable front ends; and as a Wheatland, Ricefield and 4-wheel drive model.

1950 for the most demanding power requirements

Now you can own Oliver's most powerful tractor in true row-crop styling—with either a tricycle front end or adjustable axle. With 105 observed pto horsepower, the 1950 has power to compare with today's biggest tractors, yet it's as maneuverable and easy to handle as a tractor half its size. It's powered by the world's finest tractor engine—the GM 2-cycle diesel. Also available in Wheatland, Ricefield and 4-wheel drive versions.

OLIVER CORPORATION • CHICAGO, ILLINOIS 60606

OLIVER
FOR MEN WHO GROW

This Minneapolis-Moline tractor catalog, also from the mid-1960s, is worth between $15-$20 and is in excellent condition......... $15-$20

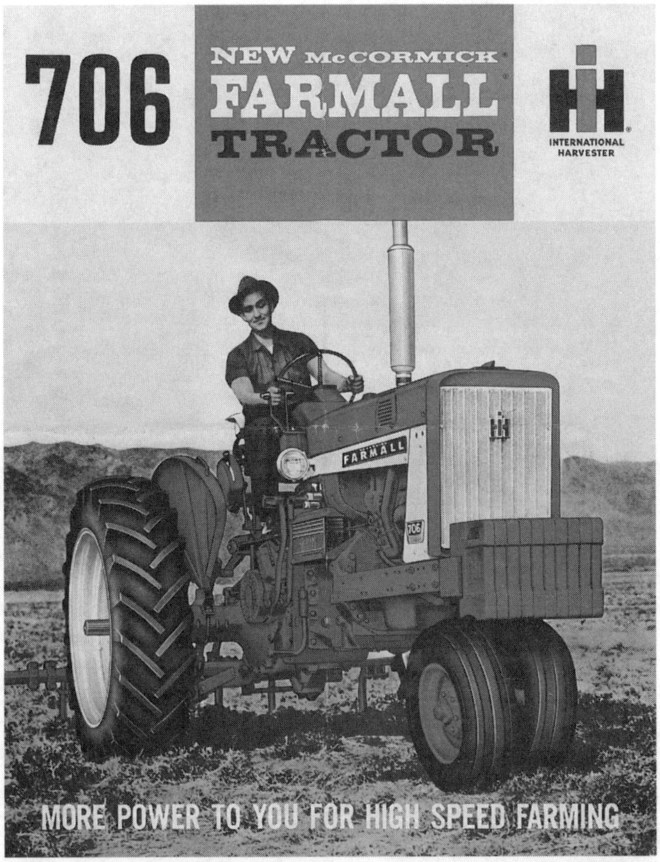
706
NEW McCORMICK
FARMALL
TRACTOR
INTERNATIONAL HARVESTER
FARMALL
MORE POWER TO YOU FOR HIGH SPEED FARMING

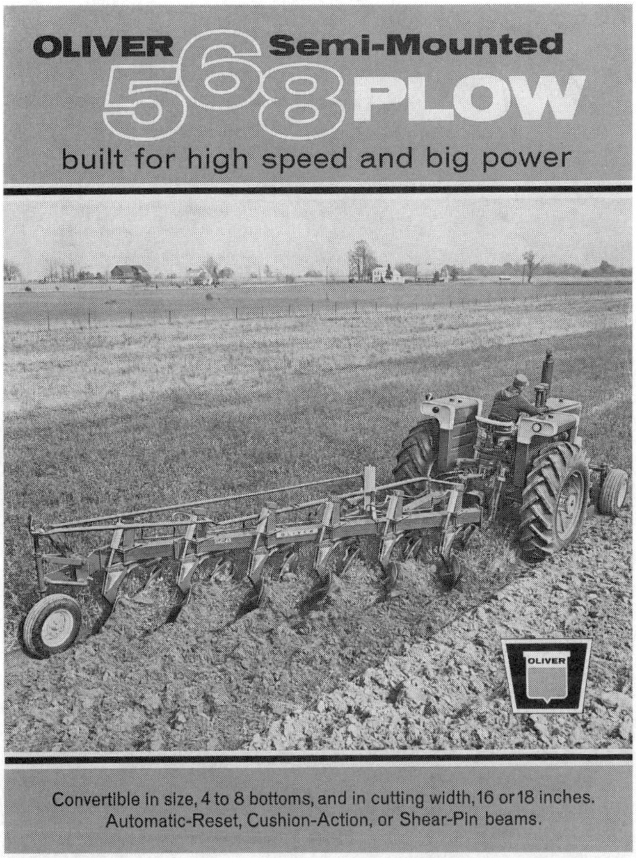
OLIVER Semi-Mounted
568 PLOW
built for high speed and big power
OLIVER
Convertible in size, 4 to 8 bottoms, and in cutting width, 16 or 18 inches.
Automatic-Reset, Cushion-Action, or Shear-Pin beams.

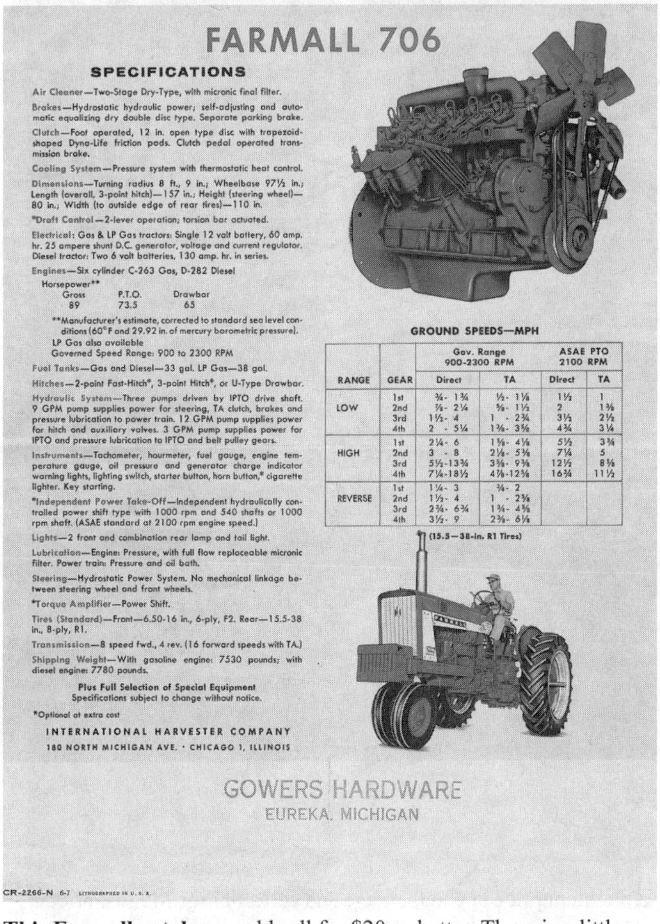

FARMALL 706

SPECIFICATIONS

Air Cleaner—Two-Stage Dry-Type, with micronic final filter.

Brakes—Hydrostatic hydraulic power; self-adjusting and automatic equalizing dry double disc type. Separate parking brake.

Clutch—Foot operated, 12 in. open type disc with trapezoid-shaped Dyna-Life friction pads. Clutch pedal operated transmission brake.

Cooling System—Pressure system with thermostatic heat control.

Dimensions—Turning radius 8 ft., 9 in.; Wheelbase 97½ in.; Length (overall, 3-point hitch)—157 in.; Height (steering wheel)—80 in.; Width (to outside edge of rear tires)—110 in.

*Draft Control—2-lever operation; torsion bar actuated.

Electrical: Gas & LP Gas tractors: Single 12 volt battery, 60 amp. hr. 25 ampere shunt D.C. generator, voltage and current regulator. Diesel tractor: Two 6 volt batteries, 130 amp. hr. in series.

Engines—Six cylinder C-263 Gas, D-282 Diesel

Horsepower**

Gross	P.T.O.	Drawbar
89	73.5	65

**Manufacturer's estimate, corrected to standard sea level conditions (60°F and 29.92 in. of mercury barometric pressure).

LP Gas also available

Governed Speed Range: 900 to 2300 RPM

Fuel Tanks—Gas and Diesel—33 gal. LP Gas—38 gal.

Hitches—2-point Fast-Hitch*, 3-point Hitch*, or U-Type Drawbar.

Hydraulic System—Three pumps driven by IPTO drive shaft. 9 GPM pump supplies power for steering, TA clutch, brakes and pressure lubrication to power train. 12 GPM pump supplies power for hitch and auxiliary valves. 3 GPM pump supplies power for IPTO and pressure lubrication to IPTO and belt pulley gears.

Instruments—Tachometer, hourmeter, fuel gauge, engine temperature gauge, oil pressure and generator charge indicator warning lights, lighting switch, starter button, horn button,* cigarette lighter. Key starting.

*Independent Power Take-Off—Independent hydraulically controlled power shift type with 1000 rpm and 540 shafts or 1000 rpm shaft. (ASAE standard at 2100 rpm engine speed.)

Lights—2 front and combination rear lamp and tail light.

Lubrication—Engine: Pressure, with full flow replaceable micronic filter. Power train: Pressure and oil bath.

Steering—Hydrostatic Power System. No mechanical linkage between steering wheel and front wheels.

*Torque Amplifier—Power Shift.

Tires (Standard)—Front—6.50-16 in., 6-ply, F2. Rear—15.5-38 in., 8-ply, R1.

Transmission—8 speed fwd., 4 rev. (16 forward speeds with TA.)

Shipping Weight—With gasoline engine: 7530 pounds; with diesel engine: 7780 pounds.

Plus Full Selection of Special Equipment
Specifications subject to change without notice.

*Optional at extra cost

INTERNATIONAL HARVESTER COMPANY
180 NORTH MICHIGAN AVE. · CHICAGO 1, ILLINOIS

GROUND SPEEDS—MPH

RANGE	GEAR	Gov. Range 900-2300 RPM		ASAE PTO 2100 RPM	
		Direct	TA	Direct	TA
LOW	1st	¾- 1¾	½- 1⅛	1½	1
	2nd	⅞- 2¼	⅝- 1½	2	1⅜
	3rd	1½- 4	1 - 2¾	3½	2½
	4th	2 - 5¼	1⅜- 3⅝	4¾	3¼
HIGH	1st	2¼- 6	1⅝- 4⅛	5½	3¾
	2nd	3 - 8	2⅛- 5⅜	7¼	5
	3rd	5½-13¾	3⅝- 9⅜	12½	8⅝
	4th	7¼-18½	4⅞-12⅝	16¾	11½
REVERSE	1st	1¼- 3	¾- 2		
	2nd	1½- 4	1 - 2⅝		
	3rd	2¾- 6¾	1¾- 4⅝		
	4th	3½- 9	2⅜- 6⅛		

(15.5—38-in. R1 Tires)

GOWERS HARDWARE
EUREKA, MICHIGAN

CR-2266-N 6-7 LITHOGRAPHED IN U.S.A.

This Farmall catalog would sell for $20 or better. There is a little more demand for Farmall products. **$20**

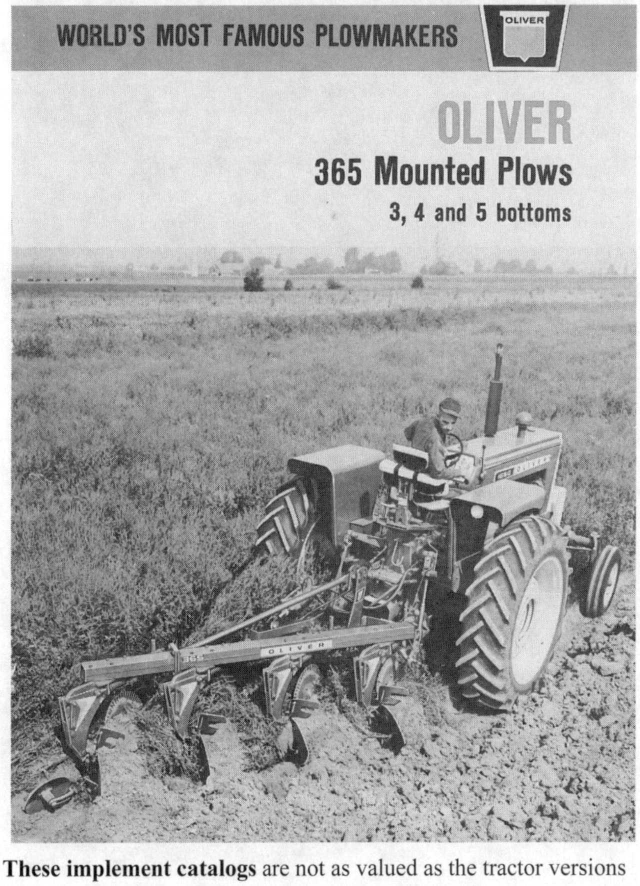
WORLD'S MOST FAMOUS PLOWMAKERS
OLIVER
OLIVER
365 Mounted Plows
3, 4 and 5 bottoms
OLIVER

These implement catalogs are not as valued as the tractor versions but still are in demand. These mid-1960s catalogs in pristine condition should bring $5-$15 each. These, and all of the manuals shown, are from the *Paulsen Collection.* .... **$5-$15**

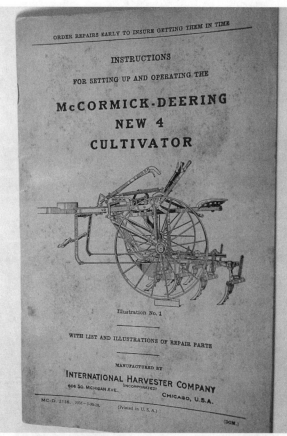

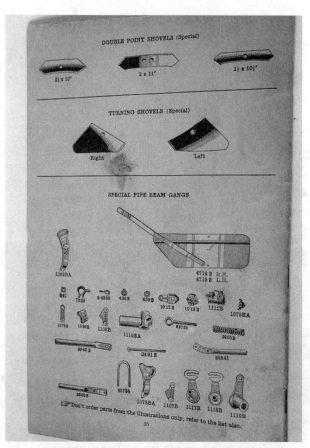

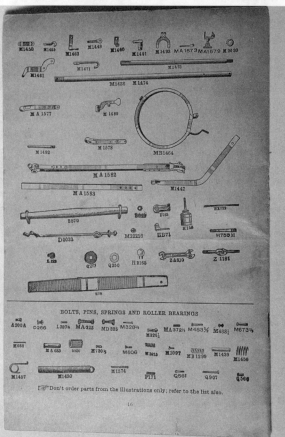

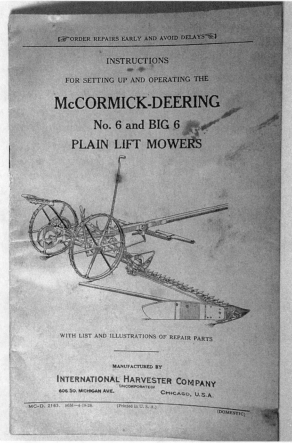

These manuals for McCormick-Deering implements from 1928 would bring a premium price due to their age and collectibility. Manual prices are detailed above and in the Art Smith interview later in the book. These should start at $50 easily enough. Here are the covers and some of the details from the manuals. Note the seat style typical of an International. Also note the use of eveners. ....$50+

McCORMICK-DEERING CORN PLANTERS AND DRILLS

Planter Precision that means Accurate Planting

VARIABLE-DROP PLANTERS

CHECKROW   DRILL

the checkrow planter into a hill-drop   The clutch dog has a bearing 2 inches wide.

Illust. 4. The McCormick-Deering No. 102 Checkrow Planter at work.

McCormick-Deering "100 Series" Corn Planters and Drills

Illust. 1. The McCormick-Deering No. 102 Checkrow Corn Planter. The full equipment includes reel and 80 rods of wire.

planter is No. 104. The drill is equipped with 30-inch wheels, and is No.106. All three are equipped with the variable-drop feature.

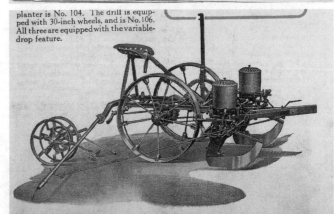

Illust. 2. No. 102 Two-row Corn Planter with open tire wheels. Planter is furnished with checkrow equipment which includes side reel, eighty rods of check wire and two steel stakes. The reel can be used on either side of the planter.

MOWERS AND KNIFE GRINDERS. McCormick-Deering Mowers, 1-horse 3½-foot vertical lift; 2-horse regular and vertical lift, 4½ and 5-foot cuts. Heavy-duty types, 4½ and 5-foot, regular and vertical lift, 6 and 7-foot regular lift only. Pneumatic-tired highway mowers. Trailing mower for tractor. Special Farmall and tractor mowers. McCormick-Deering Knife Grinders for mower knives. Tool and saw gumming wheels extra. McCormick-Deering Shredder Knife-Head Grinder.

RAKES (All Types) TEDDERS, McCormick-Deering Self-Dump Rakes, 8, 9, 10, and 12-foot; cornstalk rake, 11-foot. McCormick-Deering Sweep Rakes, three styles. McCormick-Deering Side Rakes and Tedders, 7¼ and 8-foot sizes. McCormick-Deering Tedders, 6 and 8-fork.

HAY LOADERS AND STACKERS. McCormick-Deering Windrow Loader, 6-foot. Double Cylinder Loader, Cylinder-Rake Loader, 6-foot. All unhitch from top of load. McCormick-Deering Stackers, two types, overshot and special high lift.

HAY PRESSES. McCormick-Deering one and two-horse type and power presses. Three sizes, 14x18, 16x18, and

CORN BINDERS AND PICKERS. McCormick-Deering Corn Binders, 1-row vertical and horizontal, 2-row power-drive. McCormick-Deering Corn Pickers, 1 and 2-row Farmall and pull type.

ENSILAGE CUTTERS. McCormick-Deering, four sizes with capacity of 3 to 25 tons cut ensilage per hour. Force feed, large throat and boiler plate steel flywheel. Six to 25 horsepower required. McCormick-Deering Running Ensilage Harvester and McCormick-Deering Ensilage Blower.

HUSKERS AND SHREDDERS. McCormick-Deering Steel Husker and Shredder. Large capacity, all-steel construction, combined snapping and husking rolls, all moving parts protected by shields, large and convenient feed tables.

CORN SHELLERS AND FEED MILLS. McCormick-Deering Shellers. Spring type, hand or power, mounted or down, 4 sizes. Cylinder Shellers, 2 sizes. McCormick-Deering Feed Grinders, 3 types in various capacities. McCormick-Deering Hammer and Roughage Mills.

FARM WAGONS AND TRUCKS. Weber Wagons; Keystone and Monarch

This catalog shows the complete McCormick-Deering line during the horse era. The cover portrays a farmer planting corn with a two-row corn planter. My thanks to Jerry Paulsen for sharing this and the other two McCormick-Deering manuals shown. This manual is in rough shape but the contents are valuable for research. I think it is still worth $50 even in this shape due to its age and contents. $50

for Disk Harrows, Offset Disk Harrows, Spring-Tooth Harrows, Peg-Tooth Harrows, One-Horse Cultivators with 5, 7, and 9 shovels, also 7, 9, and 14 teeth. Ridge Busters, for horses or tractors. Rotary Hoes, Soil Pulverizers, Field Cultivators, Rod Weeders, Land Packers, and Plow Packers.

KEROSENE ENGINES. McCormick-Deering, operate on kerosene as well as gasoline. Sizes 1½ to 2½ and 3 to 5 horsepower. Equipped with high-tension, rotary-type Wico magneto. variable-speed throttle governor, replaceable bearings, automatic splash lubrication, and enclosed crankcase. McCormick - Deering 4 and 6-Cylinder Industrial Power Units.

TRACTORS. McCormick-Deering, Models W-12, O-12, 10-20, W-30, WA-40, WD-40 (Diesel). Also Industrial Tractors with rubber tires, including Diesel types. Power Take-Off for tractor binder, ensilage harvester, corn picker, rice binder, etc. Tractor Hitches for all drawbar machines.

FARMALL TRACTORS. McCormick-Deering, 2- and 3-plow sizes, operate on kerosene or gasoline. Also F-12, the new Farmall for smaller farms. Fast, economical power for seed-bed work, planting and cultivating row crops, haying, harvest and belt work. Special

and electric driven types. Capacities, 350, 500, 750, 900, 1200, and 1500 pounds of milk per hour. McCormick-Deering Cream Separator Oil, a specially prepared light-bodied lubricant for cream separators.

MILKERS AND MILK COOLERS. McCormick-Deering Milkers, single and double units, single and double cylinder vacuum pumps, engine and motor drive. No-oil, no-spring pulsator assures satisfactory performance in hot and cold weather. McCormick-Deering Milk Coolers, 2 to 10-can sizes.

CANE MILLS, McCormick-Deering. Powerful three-roll mills that "get the juice." Upright, horsepower mills in four sizes, capacities from 35 to 90 gallons of juice per hour. Belt power mills, three-roll, horizontal, capacities 175 to 250 gallons per hour. Juice pumps.

GRAIN DRILLS AND LIME SOWERS, McCormick-Deering Grain Drills; sizes 5 to 57-furrow openers; 4, 6, 7, and 8-inch spacing. Press drills and press wheel attachments. Also fertilizer drills, beet drills, alfalfa drills, one-horse, endgate and broadcast seeders. McCormick-Deering Lime Sowers, Endgate Lime Spreaders, Fertilizer Distributors and Crop Dusters.

McCORMICK-DEERING LINE

GRAIN BINDERS, REAPERS, TWINE. McCormick-Deering Binders, 6, 7, and 8-foot cut. Special binders for rice. McCormick - Deering Tractor Binder, 10-foot cut. McCormick-Deering Reapers in 5 and 5½-foot cut.

HARVESTER-THRESHERS, WINDROW-HARVESTERS, HEADERS, PUSH BINDERS. McCormick-Deering Harvester-Threshers. Three sizes, 8, 12, and 16-foot cutting widths. Harvest and thresh small grains, peas, soybeans, sorghums, grass seeds, and other crops in one operation. McCormick-Deering Windrow-Harvesters, 8, 12, and 16-foot. McCormick-Deering Headers, 12 and 14-foot. Push Binders, 10, 12, and 14-foot.

MOWERS AND KNIFE GRINDERS. McCormick-Deering Mowers, 1-horse 3½-foot vertical lift; 2-horse regular and vertical lift, 4½ and 5-foot cuts. Heavy-duty types, 4½ and 5-foot, regular and vertical lift, 6 and 7-foot regular lift only. Pneumatic-tired highway mowers. Trailing mower for tractor. Special Farmall and tractor mowers. McCormick - Deering Knife Grinders for mower knives. Tool and saw gumming wheels extra. McCormick-Deering Shredder Knife-Head Grinder.

RAKES (All Types) TEDDERS, McCormick-Deering Self-Dump Rakes, 8, 9, 10, and 12-foot; cornstalk rake, 11-foot. McCormick-Deering

POTATO PLANTERS AND DIGGERS. McCormick-Deering one and two-row Potato Planters, picker-wheel type, plain and fertilizer. Two and four-horse Potato Diggers, elevator type, rod-link and bar-grate. Walking Diggers. Farmall Power Drive Diggers, 1 and 2-row.

CULTIVATORS. McCormick-Deering, for all crops. One and two-row, riding or walking, disk and surface cultivators. All varieties of shovels and gangs. Lister Cultivators, single row, sled, and wheeled. Two and three-row wheeled. Field Cultivators, 6, 7½, 9, and 12-foot sizes.

CORN BINDERS AND PICKERS. McCormick-Deering Corn Binders, 1-row vertical and horizontal, 2-row power-drive. McCormick-Deering Corn Pickers, 1 and 2-row Farmall and pull type.

ENSILAGE CUTTERS. McCormick-Deering, four sizes with capacity of 3 to 25 tons cut ensilage per hour. Force feed, large throat and boiler plate steel flywheel. Six to 25 horsepower required. McCormick - Deering Running Ensilage Harvester and McCormick - Deering Ensilage Blower.

RAKES (All Types) TEDDERS, McCormick-Deering Self-Dump Rakes, 8, 9, 10, and 12-foot; cornstalk rake, 11-foot. McCormick-Deering Sweep Rakes, three styles. McCormick - Deering Side Rakes and Tedders, 7¼ and 8-foot sizes. McCormick-Deering Tedders, 6 and 8-fork.

HAY LOADERS AND STACKERS. McCormick-Deering Windrow Loader, 6-foot. Double Cylinder Loader, Cylinder-Rake Loader, 6-foot. All unhitch from top of load. McCormick-Deering Stackers, two types, overshot and special high lift.

HAY PRESSES. McCormick-Deering one and two-horse type and power presses. Three sizes, 14x18, 16x18, and 17 x 22 bales. Power presses run either by tractor or engine.

PLANTERS AND LISTERS. McCormick-Deering Corn Planters: 100 Series, checkrow, drill and hill-drop drill, flat-, edge-, or full-hill-drop plates. McCormick-Deering Cotton and Corn Planters, walking and riding, single and two-row. Fertilizer attachments. Horse and Tractor Listers, corn, cotton and corn, and Wheatland.

McCormick - Deering Ensilage Blower.

HUSKERS AND SHREDDERS. McCormick-Deering Steel Husker and Shredder. Large capacity, all-steel construction, combined snapping and husking rolls, all moving parts protected by shields, large and convenient feed tables.

CORN SHELLERS AND FEED MILLS. McCormick - Deering Shellers. Spring type, hand or power, mounted or down, 4 sizes. Cylinder Shellers, 2 sizes. McCormick - Deering Feed Grinders, 3 types in various capacities. McCormick-Deering Hammer and Roughage Mills.

FARM WAGONS AND TRUCKS. Weber Wagons; Keystone and Monarch Trucks; standard and wide track. One-horse wagons. McCormick - Deering All - Purpose all-steel, roller-bearing Truck. Wagon Boxes.

SOIL PULVERIZERS. Double Gang. Two machines in one. Cultivates the soil and crushes lumps. Finishes what other tillage tools begin. Made in eight widths for horse or tractor power. Also single gang soil pulverizers.

McCORMICK-DEERING LINE

PLOWS (All Types). McCormick-Deering Walking Plows and Middle Breakers, steel and chilled. Two, three, and four-furrow moldboard and disk Tractor Plows. Sulky and gang, moldboard and disk Riding Plows. Farmall Plows. Orchard and Vineyard Plows. Harrow-Plows. Special plows for every purpose.

TILLAGE IMPLEMENTS (All Types). McCormick-Deering Disk Harrows, seven sizes, with or without tandem. Special orchard disk, and reversible types. Tractor Disk Harrows, Offset Disk Harrows, Spring-Tooth Harrows, Peg-Tooth Harrows, One-Horse Cultivators with 5, 7, and 9 shovels, also 7, 9, and 14 teeth. Ridge Busters, for horses or tractors. Rotary Hoes, Soil Pulverizers, Field Cultivators, Rod Weeders, Land Packers, and Plow Packers.

KEROSENE ENGINES. McCormick-Deering, operate on kerosene as well as gasoline. Sizes 1½ to 2½ and 3 to 5 horsepower. Equipped with high-tension, rotary-type Wico magneto. variable-speed throttle governor, replaceable bearings, automatic splash lubrication, and enclosed crankcase. McCormick - Deering 4 and 6-Cylinder Industrial Power Units.

TRACTORS. McCormick-Deering, Models W-12, O-12, 10-20, W-30, WA-40, WD-40 (Diesel). Also Industrial Tractors with rubber tires, including Diesel types. Power Take-Off for tractor binder, ensilage harvester, corn picker, rice binder, etc. Tractor Hitches for all drawbar machines.

FARMALL TRACTORS. McCormick-Deering, 2- and 3-plow sizes, operate on kerosene or gasoline. Also F-12, the new Farmall for smaller farms. Fast, economical power for seed-bed work, planting and cultivating row crops, haying, harvest, and belt work. Special Farmall machines.

TracTracTors McCormick-Deering T-20, TA-40 and TD-40 (Diesel) for farm, highway and industrial work. Rugged construction; compact, powerful engines, readily accessible steering clutches, convenient controls, a variety of speeds to meet all requirements.

MOTOR TRUCKS. International Motor Trucks, ½ to 10-ton capacities, including ½-ton pick-up and panel delivery, 1, 1½, 2, and 3-ton speed trucks, and heavy-duty models in 3, 3½, 4, and 5 to 10-ton capacities. Also six - wheel trucks (trailing and dual-drive axles) of various sizes. A variety of wheel bases and suitable bodies for all hauling purposes.

THRESHERS. McCormick-Deering, 22 x 38 and 28 x 46. Ball-bearing cylinders. Roller bearing stacker fan. Can be equipped with self-feeders, wind stackers, grain-measuring elevators and loaders, Pea and Bean Attachments and Rice, Alfalfa and Clover Threshers.

CREAM SEPARATORS, McCormick-Deering Ball-Bearing Separators with stainless steel disks are easy to keep clean. Hand, engine, and electric driven types. Capacities, 350, 500, 750, 900, 1200, and 1500 pounds of milk per hour. McCormick-Deering Cream Separator Oil, a specially prepared light-bodied lubricant for cream separators.

MILKERS AND MILK COOLERS. McCormick-Deering Milkers, single and double units, single and double cylinder vacuum pumps, engine and motor drive. No-oil, no-spring pulsator assures satisfactory performance in hot and cold weather. McCormick-Deering Milk Coolers, 2 to 10-can sizes.

CANE MILLS, McCormick-Deering. Powerful three-roll mills that "get the juice." Upright, horsepower mills in four sizes, capacities from 35 to 90 gallons of juice per hour. Belt power mills, three-roll, horizontal, capacities 175 to 250 gallons per hour. Juice pumps.

GRAIN DRILLS AND LIME SOWERS, McCormick-Deering Grain Drills; sizes 5 to 57-furrow openers; 4, 6, 7, and 8-inch spacing. Press drills and press wheel attachments. Also fertilizer drills, beet drills, alfalfa drills, one-horse, endgate and broadcast seeders. McCormick-Deering Lime Sowers, Endgate Lime Spreaders, Fertilizer Distributors, and Crop Dusters.

MANURE SPREADERS. McCormick-Deering horse-drawn, 60 to 70 bu. capacity, all-steel construction, eight roller bearings, five conveyor speeds. McCormick-Deering Power Spreader, 130 to 150 bu. capacity; entire mechanism operated by tractor power transmitted through the power take-off.

STALK CUTTERS. McCormick-Deering. Single row, 7 or 9 blades. Has steel wheels, non-clogging knife head, angle steel frame, dust-proof bearings, shock absorbing hitch. Two-row, 14-knife. Separate cutting cylinder for each row. The cutting cylinders on these stalk cutters are spring-suspended, greatly reducing vibration.

"Good equipment makes a good farmer better"

More pages from the catalog show the complete McCormick-Deering line during the horse era. **$50**

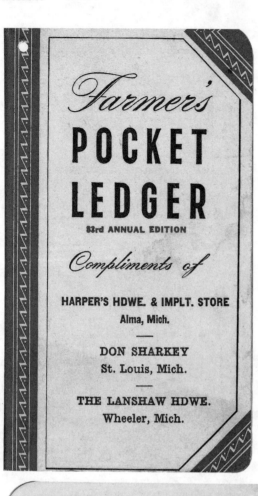

Farmer's **POCKET LEDGER**

83rd ANNUAL EDITION

Compliments of

HARPER'S HDWE. & IMPLT. STORE
Alma, Mich.

—

DON SHARKEY
St. Louis, Mich.

—

THE LANSHAW HDWE.
Wheeler, Mich.

JOHN DEERE TRACTORS LEAD THE FIELD

IN ADAPTABILITY

There's a size and type for every farm, crop, purpose. Six power sizes in general-purpose tractors . . . three sizes in standard-tread tractors . . . a variety of special single-front-wheel, adjustable-front-axle, and orchard models. Power for every job—drawbar, belt, power take-off, and hydraulic power lift or Powr-Trol for controlling equipment. A complete line of specially-designed integral, drawn, and belt-operated equipment. These are the reasons why a John Deere Tractor is more adaptable.

IN ECONOMY

Unequalled simplicity with fewer wearing parts, plus unequalled strength of parts means lower maintenance costs, more years of trouble-free service. Two-cylinder engine design means top efficiency, maximum savings in burning the fuel of your choice.

IN DEPENDABILITY

Simple adjustments, easy accessibility enable owners to keep a John Deere in perfect running order. Safeguarded, quality design and construction with automatic full-pressure engine lubrication . . . automatic oiling of transmission and differential . . . automatic engine temperature control, plus such safeguards as oil-wash air cleaner . . . replaceable oil filter . . . oil and dirt seals . . . ventilated crankcase . . . anti-friction bearings . . . fuel strainers—all make John Deere Tractors more dependable.

IN MODERN DESIGN

John Deere developed the tapered fuel tank for unexcelled view to either side . . . the centered seat and standing platform . . . hydraulic power lift . . . positive, shock-proof steering, and other outstanding ease-of-handling features. In the new models, you'll find such advancements as Powr-Trol for finger-tip control of both integral and drawn equipment . . . new engines with *cyclonic* fuel intake in both all-fuel and gasoline types . . . Roll-O-Matic "knee-action" front wheels for easier steering, greater comfort, increased safety, and longer tire life . . . adjustable, deep-cushion seat . . . roomier platform . . . automatic crankcase ventilation . . . starter and lights standard equipment . . . and many others that make John Deere Tractors the forerunners of a new age in farm power.

3

JOHN DEERE GENERAL-PURPOSE TRACTORS

Model "B"

Here is a new, more powerful tractor for medium-sized farms. Available with either all-fuel or more powerful gasoline-burning engine. More than twenty advanced features, including Powr-Trol, automatic crankcase ventilation, deep-cushion seat, make the "B" the outstanding value in its class. Complete integral equipment available; starter and lights standard equipment.

Model "A"

The new "A" handles two- or four-row equipment. Available with either all-fuel or more powerful gasoline-burning engine. Like the "B", the new "A" has Powr-Trol, automatic crankcase ventilation, deep-cushion seat and many other advanced features. Wide variety of integral equipment available; starter and lights standard equipment.

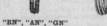

Model "G"

The Model "G" is a heavy-duty row-crop tractor for the large-acreage farmer who wants to burn heavier fuels. Available with a wide variety of integral equipment, including four-row bedders and cultivators. New features include adjustable deep-cushion seat and roomier platform. Powr-Trol and Roll-O-Matic Front Wheels are optional.

4

SINGLE FRONT WHEEL AND ADJUSTABLE FRONT AXLE MODELS

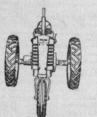

"BN", "AN", "GN"   "BW", "AW", "GW"

Higher clearance to handle tall crops without damage . . . wider wheel adjustability for planting and cultivating on beds or flat land in practically **any** combination of row widths . . . and **interchangeable** front-end assemblies which offer you the advantage of a single-front-wheel or an adjustable-front-axle in **one** tractor—these are the features you get in these special general-purpose models in addition to all the new features of the regular Models "A", "B" and "G", previously described.

The new single-front-wheel models ("BN", "AN" and "GN") are ideal for irrigated land and for work in narrow-row crops where maximum clearance between rows is desirable in order to avoid damage to growing plants.

The new adjustable-front-axle models ("BW", "AW" and "GW") meet the needs of farmers everywhere who want the advantages of standard-tread design in a row-crop tractor—for straddling beds . . . planting and cultivating without splitting the centers . . . traveling over soft and friable soils . . . or working in rough ground conditions where an oscillating front axle is desirable. They have adjustable wheel tread both front and rear.

Model "M" One-Row Cultivating Tractor

Complete power for the smaller farm . . . ideal "helper" on the large farm. Full line of "Quik-Tatch" equipment, all hydraulic-controlled. Pulls two 12-inch plow bottoms in normal soils; handles a 6-foot double-action disk harrow or a 7-foot power mower.

5

INTEGRAL EQUIPMENT FOR
JOHN DEERE GENERAL PURPOSE TRACTORS

PLOWS

Integral plows in disk and moldboard types are noted for good work, long life, and ease of adjustment.

BEDDERS AND MIDDLEBREAKERS

One-, two-, three-, and four-row bedders and middlebreakers for blank listing, bedding, middlebreaking, sweeping beds, and reworking middles.

PLANTERS

One-, two-, and four-row integral planting and fertilizing attachments.

LISTERS

Two-row listers for bedding, listing, middlebreaking. Plant corn, cotton, peanuts, kafir, and other seeds.

COMBINATION UNITS

These outfits, for all Southern crops, bed or furrow, plant, and fertilize once over. Substitute shovels and you're ready to cultivate.

CULTIVATORS

One-, two-, and four-row "Quik-Tatch" cultivators. Power lift or easy hand lift. Simple, strong, easy to attach or detach. Big daily capacity.

VEGETABLE CULTIVATORS

Special double tool bar cultivators in 90-, 120-, 136-, and 168-inch widths for beets, beans, lettuce, and other narrow-row crops. Two-row potato hoes.

HAY TOOLS

John Deere Mowers do a better job of cutting in all conditions. John Deere Sweep Rakes, power or hand lift, shorten haying time, slash costs.

HARVESTING EQUIPMENT

Includes two- and four-row bean harvesters and two-row peanut pullers either as complete machines or attachments for cultivators. Beet harvester. One- and two-row beet lifters.

CORN PICKERS

One- and two-row push-type corn pickers do a fast, clean, low-cost job of picking in all field conditions.

8

STANDARD TREAD TRACTORS

For the big farm, the medium-sized farm, the small farm, John Deere supplies you with the right size of power in standard tread tractors. In the field, the performance of these tractors is outstanding. They are easy to handle. They give you maximum traction at all times. On belt jobs all the power of the engine is delivered to the belt, because the belt pulley is mounted on the crankshaft.

MODEL "D"

The John Deere Model "D", the "daddy" of all John Deere Tractors, pulls four bottoms in many soils, three bottoms in practically all conditions, and supplies ample belt power to operate a 28-inch thresher.

MODEL "AR"

The Model "AR" Tractor, the ideal outfit for medium-sized farms, pulls two 16-inch or three 14-inch plow bottoms, depending upon conditions, and operates a 22-inch thresher in heavy crops.

MODEL "AO" ORCHARD TRACTOR

With its individually-controlled differential brakes for short turns, special orchard fenders, side exhaust, and air intake flush with the hood, the Model "AO" is a favorite with owners of orchards, groves, and vineyards. Has the same engine as the "AR" and delivers power from drawbar, belt, and power take-off.

9

PROPER HITCH MEANS BETTER, FASTER, EASIER, MORE ECONOMICAL PLOWING

It takes but a few minutes to check the hitch of your tractor plow in accordance with these instructions but it is time well spent. The ideal hitch is a straight line from point of load (center of draft) on the plow to point of pull on the tractor, both horizontally and vertically.

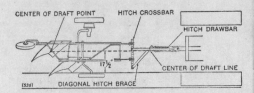

Proper adjustment of hitch, *horizontally*, is important in securing full width of cut of each bottom and steady running of both plow and tractor. Finding the center of draft on any size plow is simple if above illustration is followed. First, find total cut of plow. Half of total cut is *center of cut*. Measure to left of center of cut 1/4 the width of cut of one bottom to get *center of draft*. In the illustration two 14-inch bottoms are used. One-half the total cut is 14 inches (center of cut). One-fourth the width of one bottom is 3-1/2 inches. Measuring 3-1/2 inches to left brings the center of draft 17-1/2 inches from the furrow wall.

The center of pull of the tractor is a point approximately three inches ahead of the rear axle, at a point midway between the wheels, *regardless of their setting*. Any difference in distance from furrow wall between center of draft and center of pull must be offset by adjusting the hitch on the hitch crossbar.

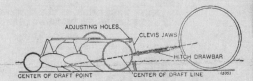

To obtain proper vertical hitch, adjust hitch point so it falls upon a line from *center of draft* to *point of load*, as in this illustration; bottoms run level and pull light; wear is reduced; and fuel consumption is decreased.

10

JOHN DEERE TRUSS-FRAME TRACTOR PLOWS

Truss-Frame design is a feature of all John Deere Moldboard Plows from the single bottom, integral type to the big capacity, five-bottom, heavy-duty No. 77.

Truss-Frame design, introduced originally in the heavy-duty John Deere Plows built for California's toughest plowing jobs, is field-proved in every plowing condition.

JOHN DEERE TRUSS-FRAME PLOWS FOR STRENGTH, CLEARANCE, LONG LIFE

Strength and clearance are two outstanding features of Truss-Frame Plows. Truss-Frame construction binds all parts into one husky, shock-resisting unit. Shocks of hard work are absorbed by the entire plow rather than by a single bottom. By eliminating the conventional curved beams, greater throat clearance is gained; bottoms are spaced fore-and-aft for maximum clearance; share-point to frame clearance is greater—independent jointers and eighteen-inch coulters, essential in clean plowing where corn borers are a menace, may be used with all John Deere Truss-Frame Plows. All are available with equipment for hydraulic power control.

JOHN DEERE TRACTOR DISK PLOWS

John Deere builds a full line of disk plows with features that offer all 'round satisfaction and full value. The angle steel frame bars with disk standards bolted between, make a rigid, sturdy unit. Roller bearing disk bearings mean lighter draft, longer life. *Heat-treated* steel disks last longer. Width of cut changed by simply angling the frame.

In John Deere Disk Plows ease of correct and lasting adjustment and ability to hold to their work in difficult soil conditions are combined with the strength and clearance you need for lasting satisfaction on the job.

In addition to the full line of drawn disk plows, integral disk plows in two-disk size are built for John Deere General-Purpose Tractors.

11

JOHN DEERE POWER-LIFT DISK TILLERS

John Deere Power-Lift Disk Tillers are famous as cost-reducers for preparing wheatland, for working fallow, destroying weeds, and for many other tillage jobs. Heavy-duty power lift, of the field-proved John Deere type, raises disks quickly for turning or transporting. Semi-floating hitch insures easy control of both tiller and tractor. Self-aligning bearings are easily oiled, strong, long-wearing, and light-draft. *Heat-treated* steel disks are correctly designed for good penetration.

The Disk Tiller is built in a wide variety of sizes to match the power of your tractor and the work for which you want to use it. Angle of gang is variable to meet conditions.

JOHN DEERE INTEGRAL PLOWS

With a John Deere Integral Plow for your John Deere General-Purpose Tractor, you can do a complete job of plowing—utilize every available bit of ground for profitable production.

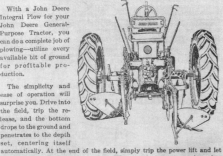

The simplicity and ease of operation will surprise you. Drive into the field, trip the release, and the bottom drops to the ground and penetrates to the depth set, centering itself automatically. At the end of the field, simply trip the power lift and let the tractor engine raise the bottom. When turning or transporting, plow is carried on tractor—plow and tractor are as easily handled as tractor alone.

John Deere power-lifted two-way plows are available for the "A", "B", "G", and "M" Tractors. Integral one-bottom plows, power-lifted, are available for the Models "A", "B", and "M" Tractors. In addition to the integral moldboard plows, integral disk plows are built for many John Deere General-Purpose Tractors.

JOHN DEERE MODELS "J" AND "JB" DISK HARROWS

These modern standard-weight tractor disk harrows not only work at full angle in plowed ground or other light disking jobs without clogging, but also do excellent work when weighted down for penetration in tough conditions. The Model "JB" is a double-action harrow; the Model "J", a single-action machine.

Simple, positive tractor control speeds up disking, makes good work easy. Easy adjustments provide just the right setting for practically any soil condition, any tractor speed.

Great strength assures years of low-cost service. Equipped for Alemite grease-gun lubrication. Scrapers are standard equipment. Trailer hitch available.

JOHN DEERE "K" SERIES DISK HARROWS

Entirely modern in design and performance, the John Deere "K" Series represents the very latest in double-action disk harrows designed and built for the tough disking jobs.

Deep, uniform penetration over the full width; simple, positive tractor control for angling and straightening gangs; elimination of gouging or ridging on turns; simple adjustments for good work under varying field conditions; great strength and a low frame construction are just a few of the many features of these new harrows. Available in two weights—heavy-duty and extra-heavy-duty—in a size to meet your requirements and a type with just the right spacing and size of disks for your particular disking jobs.

JOHN DEERE MODEL "S" DISK HARROW

The Model "S" is a big-capacity, single-action tractor disk harrow, made in 15-, 18-, and 21-foot sizes, with folding gangs, and in the 11½-foot size without folding gangs. Larger size single-disks up to 125 acres a day. Or, you can double-disk by lapping half. Tractor does all the work of angling and straightening the gangs. End gangs fold over, reducing the 15-foot size to 10½ feet, the 18-foot to 12½ feet, and the 21-foot to 14 feet.

KILLEFER 200 SERIES DISK HARROW

The 200 Series is a rugged, heavy-duty, offset disk harrow for deep disking in the toughest soil conditions of field, orchard and vineyard. It penetrates quickly and easily to the proper working depth . . . works deep and level . . . offsets to the right or left . . . makes right- and left-hand turns without gouging or ridging the soil . . . backs straight without buckling . . . is low to the ground . . . completely controlled from the tractor seat . . . and built with extra strength for many years of service.

Nine sizes ranging from 5-1/4 to 12 feet wide—a size to match your tractor power and your acreage. Disk blades are 20, 22, or 24 inches in diameter. Disk spacing is 9 inches. Squadron hitches are available for working two harrows together in a single unit as large as 24 feet wide.

16

JOHN DEERE SPRING-TOOTH HARROWS AND WEED DESTROYERS

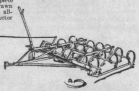

John Deere builds a complete line of tractor- and horse-drawn spring-tooth harrows for all-around seedbed work. Tractor harrows have trip-rope or lever control. For destroying weeds, simply change the type and spacing of the teeth.

John Deere *special-process* heat-treated teeth—individually tested and inspected—insure dependable, efficient field performance.

Eccentric tooth-bar construction—a feature exclusive on John Deere harrows—assures better clearance, greater working depth and, because the eccentric bars *drive* the teeth into the ground, much better penetration. Smoothing attachment available.

JOHN DEERE-VAN BRUNT MODEL "CC" FIELD AND ORCHARD CULTIVATOR

For making seedbeds; killing all kinds of weeds; cultivating orchards, alfalfa and certain row crops; summer-fallowing; "roughing" stubble land; and for other tillage jobs.

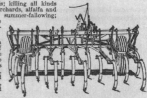

Can be used with either spring or stiff teeth. Shovels available in types and sizes to fit your needs. Wheels are set inside frame. Depth regulator and power lift. Sizes: 5-, 6½-, 8-, 10-, 11½-, and 14½-foot.

JOHN DEERE TOOL-BAR FIELD CULTIVATOR

Routine jobs for this versatile, big-capacity, heavy-duty implement include weeding, mulching, preparing seedbeds, sub-surface cultivating, working fallow land, conserving moisture, reducing wind and water erosion, and renovating alfalfa and pasture.

Furnished with 8- or 12-foot tool-bar . . . for hand lift, power lift or Powr-Trol operation . . . for field cultivating with 4- to 16-inch sweeps, deep work with heavy-duty chisel points, or sub-surface cultivating with 30-inch overlapping sweeps.

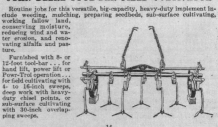

14

JOHN DEERE-VAN BRUNT GRAIN DRILLS

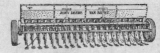

The John Deere-Van Brunt Model "B" Grain Drill is equipped with adjustable-gate fluted force-feeds which feed all crops in any desired quantity per acre. Plants cultivated crops in various row widths.

All-steel construction, crank-type axles, enclosed roller-chain drive, dustproof hubs with Timken tapered-roller bearings, low, automotive-type wheels, direct-reading land measurer, improved power lift, and non-spill box covers—these are construction features that assure better seeding and longer life.

Single-disk, double-disk, hoe-, or lister-type furrow openers can be furnished. Extra equipment is available. The Model "B" Grain Drill is built in a wide range of sizes.

JOHN DEERE-VAN BRUNT FERTILIZER-GRAIN DRILLS

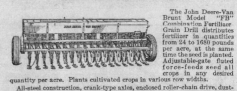

The John Deere-Van Brunt Model "FB" Combination Fertilizer-Grain Drill distributes fertilizer in quantities from 24 to 1680 pounds per acre, at the same time the seed is planted. Adjustable-gate fluted force-feeds seed all crops in any desired quantity per acre. Plants cultivated crops in various row widths.

All-steel construction, crank-type axles, enclosed roller-chain drive, dustproof hubs with Timken tapered-roller bearings, low, automotive-type wheels, direct-reading land measurer, improved power lift, and non-spill box covers—these are construction features that assure better seeding and longer life.

Single-disk, double-disk, hoe-, or lister-type furrow openers can be furnished. Extra equipment is available. The Model "FB" Combination Fertilizer Grain Drill is built in a wide range of sizes.

JOHN DEERE-VAN BRUNT LIME AND FERTILIZER DISTRIBUTORS

Cover 8 feet of ground; carrying capacity, 10 bushels. Direct wheel drive —each wheel drives half the machine. Steel or rubber-tired wheels. The Model "A" Fertilizer Distributor has star force-feeds for distributing fertilizers and

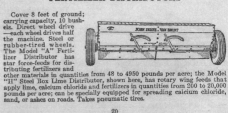

other materials in quantities from 48 to 4950 pounds per acre; the Model "H" Steel Box Lime Distributor, shown here, has rotary wing feeds that apply lime, calcium chloride and fertilizers in quantities from 200 to 20,000 pounds per acre; can be specially equipped for spreading calcium chloride, sand, or ashes on roads. Takes pneumatic tires.

20

JOHN DEERE No. 290 TWO-ROW CORN PLANTER

The John Deere No. 290 is an entirely new, high-speed, two-row corn planter that check-plants accurately at 5 miles an hour—as high as 30 acres in a day. The No. 290 has been built from the ground up for tractor operation. Thoroughly field-proved, it's a complete, self-contained machine that works with practically any make of tractor and can be hitched or unhitched "in a jiffy". Its many new features include high-speed valves, automatic markers, automatic wire release, and delayed-action power lift. Each runner floats up or down independently. Safety fertilizer attachment can be furnished. Special plates are available for the many grades and varieties of hybrid corn.

JOHN DEERE No. 490 FOUR-ROW CORN PLANTER

The new John Deere No. 490 is "tailor-made" for the large-acreage corn grower. Operating at 5 miles an hour, this big-capacity machine check-plants more than 500 hills of corn a minute—as high as 60 acres in a day—with unfailing accuracy. Here's capacity that saves one day in every three over the conventional 3 or 3-1/2 mile-an-hour four-row planter.

Like the No. 290, this John Deere four-row has many new safety and ease-of-handling features that make planting as foolproof as possible. Available with safety fertilizer attachment and a wide variety of other equipment.

JOHN DEERE No. 999 CORN PLANTER

For many years the John Deere No. 999 has been the world's fastest-selling corn planter—recognized by farmers everywhere as the most accurate and dependable on the market. Natural-drop seed plates for handling the many grades of hybrid corn and other crops; simple, positive valves; variable-drop for planting 2, 3, or 4 kernels to the hill merely by shifting a lever; enclosed clutch and gears running in oil; equipment for every need—these are the features that adapt the No. 999 to your every requirement. Available with tongue truck, tractor hitch, safety fertilizer attachment, pea and bean planting attachment, and a wide variety of opening and covering equipment.

18

JOHN DEERE COTTON, CORN AND PEANUT PLANTERS

John Deere Cotton and Corn Planters plant cotton, corn, beans, peas, sorghum, and many other seeds with outstanding accuracy. John Deere sawtooth type steel picker wheel for cotton and John Deere natural-drop seed plates for corn and other crops insure accurate, uniform planting under all conditions. Seed plates are available for practically all crops. Variable-drop mechanism gives twelve drilling distances from 5½ to 26 inches without changing plates. Clutch and gears fully enclosed and operate in bath of oil. No. 536 Two-Row is for drilling only. No. 535 is for checking, hill-dropping, or drilling. Both are adjustable to plant in rows from 32 to 48 inches apart. Automatic marker is regular. Tongue truck and safety fertilizer attachment and tractor hitch are some of the extra equipment available.

John Deere No. 536 Cotton and Corn Planter

JOHN DEERE No. 730 TWO-ROW LISTER

A two-row lister that embodies a field-proved principle of design. In place of full-length beams, the No. 730 has stub beams easily shifted along the tool bar to the desired row-spacing (42 to 54 inches) and locked to position by clamps. Forward wheels carry front of lister and act as gauge wheels. Available with shovel or disk coverers.

ROLLING STALK CUTTER FOR TRACTORS

The John Deere Rolling Stalk Cutter is simple, strong (all-steel), cuts more than 3 acres per hour, two rows at a time. For greater capacity, a special hitch can be furnished to make a 4-row hook-up of two cutters. Knives are of heavy, tough steel. Drawbar extends to rear of frame where an eye is provided for attaching disk harrow, if desired—no strain is put on the cutter frame. Illustration shows the cutter equipped with transport skids, which are regular and gathering rods which are extra. Special stalk straighteners can be furnished and are recommended for best work in corn.

19

JOHN DEERE BEET AND BEAN TOOLS

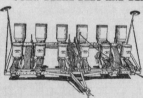

No. 66 Drill with Fertilizer Attachment

No. 88 Cultivator

Integral Beet Harvester

Beet Loader

The complete and modern line of John Deere tractor drills, cultivators, lifters, harvesters, and loaders is the climax of nearly 50 years of service to beet and bean growers.

Drills

No. 64 Four-Row Drill and No. 66 Six-Row Drill are designed for accurate planting, simplicity, strength, light-draft, and easy control from tractor seat. Natural-drop seed plates handle whole or segmented beet seed plus a wide variety of other seeds.

Cultivators

The No. 88 multi-row cultivator forms an integral unit with John Deere general-purpose tractors. Famous for big daily capacity, ample clearance, easy handling, good vision, and quick, easy adjustments for close, clean work.

Harvester

The John Deere integral beet harvester tops, lifts, cleans, and windrows the beets in one operation.

Loader

The big-capacity John Deere No. 6 beet loader loads 5 tons of beets in 6 minutes, making a big saving in time, trucks and manpower. One-man operation.

54

JOHN DEERE POTATO PLANTERS

Ideal for use with tractors because these latest-type planters with 12-arm picker wheel will plant accurately at rapid tractor speeds. With a new John Deere you can now plant up to 15 acres a day with the 2-row (illustrated); up to 7 acres a day with the 1-row. Simple. Strong. Easy to operate. Light draft. Large hopper. Fertilizer placed in approved band-type method.

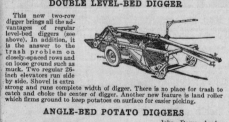

LEVEL-BED POTATO DIGGERS

The John Deere Level-Bed Diggers—one- and two-row for tractors—offer the very latest features for clean digging with gentle handling. Features include low, level line of travel—no long drops . . . straight-line transmission of power . . . renewable and reversible sprockets . . . safety release clutch . . . steel roller drive chain . . . fully enclosed and automatically-lubricated

John Deere One-Row Level-Bed Tractor-Drive Digger

main drive gears . . . and long-wearing, clean-scouring shovels of forged plow steel. Adaptable to all conditions.

DOUBLE LEVEL-BED DIGGER

This new two-row digger brings all the advantages of regular level-bed diggers (see above). In addition, it is the answer to the trash problem on closely-spaced rows and on loose ground such as muck. Two regular 26-inch elevators run side by side. Shovel is extra strong and runs complete width of digger. There is no place for trash to catch and choke the center of digger. Another new feature is land roller which firms ground to keep potatoes on surface for easier picking.

ANGLE-BED POTATO DIGGERS

John Deere Angle-Bed Diggers are "old favorites" for the way they handle tough digging conditions. Available in one- and two-row sizes with wide variety of equipment to meet any special needs. Rear rack is easily convertible from continuous elevator to extension elevator to meet varying digging conditions.

55

JOHN DEERE FIELD HAY CHOPPER

With the John Deere No. 62 Pick-Up Hay Chopper you can chop green hay for ensilage and field-cured hay for economical storage in barn or stack; salvage combine straw economically.

The John Deere picks up the material to be cut direct from the windrow, chops it into proper length and loads it onto the wagon or truck. You eliminate loading in the field and the hot, tiring, time-consuming job of "mowing back" at the barn—yet you preserve the feeding value of the hay in palatable form.

Row-crop unit which converts this chopper to a field-proved field ensilage harvester is available, to make the John Deere an all-around forage harvester.

JOHN DEERE AUGER FEED BLOWER

The John Deere No. 2 Blower is "tailor-made" for the man who has a silo to fill, chopped hay to stack or store in the mow, or any other job that requires moving chopped green or dry material. Sturdy in construction, simple in design, operating at big-capacity with low power requirements, it's the all-'round blower for general farm use. With such features as auger-type feed, full roller chain drive, heavy-duty fan, the John Deere is built for years of low-cost, satisfactory, profitable performance on your farm. And what's mighty important on the farm the John Deere gives you this big capacity with comparatively moderate power requirements; another advantage due to simplified design which makes use of power to get the work done rather than to drive complicated parts of the blower.

Hinged conveyor or hopper may be raised for easiest spotting of wagon for unloading. Capacity: 10 to 20 tons of silage per hour; 6 to 10 tons of dry material per hour.

JOHN DEERE TRACTOR CULTIVATORS FOR LISTED CORN

Follow trenches perfectly when tractor is on the ridges. Great variety of tillage equipment fully adjustable for all conditions. Four-row is available as hand-lift or with built-in power lift for operation with any tricycle-type tractor. Two-row is available in drawn type and in integral type for John Deere Models "A" and "B" Tractors.

60

JOHN DEERE No. 200 TWO-ROW CORN PICKER

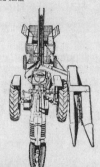

The John Deere No. 200 Two-Row Picker is a new pull type corn picker built for operation with two-plow tractors under most conditions. Modern in every respect, the No. 200 Picker is outstanding in design and construction, and incorporates features found in no other picker. Light-weight and light-draft—corn delivery is direct from the snapping rolls to the husking rolls—ears are snapped and husked with a minimum amount of travel through the machine—elevator throw-out clutch and corn deflector controlled from the tractor seat—snapping roll spacing adjustments easily and quickly made by hand crank—improved wagon hitch keeps wagon under the delivery spout making the No. 200 the ideal picker for either straight-row or contour planted corn.

JOHN DEERE No. 101 ONE-ROW PICKER

The John Deere No. 101 One-Row Picker is built for operation with one-two-plow tractors and is the choice of small or medium acreage corn growers. Hook-up equipment is available for John Deere Models "H", "B", "A", "G" and "GM" Tractors as well as most other tricycle-type tractors.

This new light-weight, light-draft picker is wheel and drawbar mounted with quick-on, quick-off features. Here's a picker you can attach or detach in less than thirty minutes. Its entirely new and exclusive design gives you many advantages found in no other picker.

JOHN DEERE No. 226 TWO-ROW MOUNTED PICKER

The John Deere No. 226 Two-Row Mounted Picker works with John Deere Model "B" Tractor on rubber or the Model "A" on steel or rubber. Corn is handled in a straight line all the way through the picker. Ease of attaching, light weight, wide, long, gently sloping gatherers, big-capacity snapping rolls, deep first elevator, clean-stripping husking rolls, safety slip clutches on all important drives, and high-grade bearings throughout are outstanding features.

63

A recent field find was this 1949-50 Pocket Ledger, also shown on the previous pages, from a nearby John Deere dealership, actually sponsored by three local dealers. I paid $35 for this and value it at that or even double, given the great illustrations of 1949 John Deere tractors and implements. I purchased it from a friend and told him it was worth at least $50. But he sells me a lot so he discounted it a little. The unique thing is that it is pristine, a little dirty on the outside covers but never used, and the inner pages are crisp and clean. The book shows the complete line of 1949 John Deere implements and the A, B, G, and M tractors. It also displays the narrow and wide wheel arrangements available on the A, B, and G tractors that then become the AN, BN, GN, AW, BW, and GW tractors by letter designation. What a great little find for the John Deere collector. .**$35-$50**

JOHN DEERE MANURE SPREADER

Your first look will convince you that the John Deere Model "H" Spreader tops the field in everything you've been wanting in a tractor-drawn spreader. Strong, yet light in draft, the Model "H" can be used with either small or large tractors. Proper weight distribution for best traction . . . enclosure of all drives . . . low, easy-loading box . . . handy operating levers . . . big-capacity beaters geared for tractor speed—these important advantages, plus a price tag that will surprise you, are but a few of the reasons why the Model "H" is your best buy in tractor spreaders.

JOHN DEERE TRACTOR MANURE LOADERS

The new John Deere Push-Type Manure Loader works with John Deere Models "A" and "B" Tractors. Power for operation of loader is taken from flywheel of tractor and controlled through unique foot clutch. Parallel arms keep bucket level at all times. This permits a shorter, easier drop of manure into the spreader—puts less strain on spreader box

Push-Type

and frame. Bucket can be dumped at any desired height by means of a trip rope. Easy penetrating bucket tines can be tilted down for positive penetration or leveled for cleaning a yard without leaving holes.

JOHN DEERE-LINDEMAN LANDSHAPER

Maximum, uniform yields from irrigated fields require a smooth, level seed-bed—the kind you get in fewer trips with the revolutionary John Deere-Lindeman Landshaper. Its shaping blade is mounted well toward the rear—an exclusive feature that provides 1/3 more span to "bridge" uneven ground, more efficient leveling. It also means less weight and lower power requirements. Side-tilting of the blade, caused by conventional wide-spaced front wheels rolling over uneven ground, is eliminated in the Landshaper by exclusive three-point suspension. The LS400 (40-foot) has center-mounted dual front wheels; the 20-foot LS200 (shown here) attaches directly to the tractor drawbar.

56

MILES TRAVELED IN PLANTING AN ACRE—3' 6" ROWS
1-Row Planter . . . . .2.34 miles
2-Row Planter . . . . .1.17 miles
3-Row Planter . . . . .78 miles

ACRES PLANTED IN TRAVELING ONE MILE—3' 6" ROWS
1-Row Planter . . . . .42 acres
2-Row Planter . . . . .84 acres
3-Row Planter . . . . 1.26 acres

There are 10,667 stalks in an acre planted in 3' 6" rows, three stalks to the hill, hills 3' 6" apart, or drilled one stalk every 14 inches. There are 3,556 hills in an acre planted in 3' 6" rows, hills 3' 6" apart.

GESTATION TABLE

Date of Service	Date Animal Due to Give Birth							
	Mare		Cow		Ewe		Sow	
Jan. 1	Dec.	6	Oct.	10	May	30	April	22
Feb. 1	Jan.	6	Nov.	10	June	30	May	23
March 1	Feb.	3	Dec.	8	July	28	June	22
April 1	March	6	Jan.	8	Aug.	28	July	21
May 1	April	5	Feb.	7	Sept.	27	Aug.	20
June 1	May	6	March	10	Oct.	28	Sept.	20
July 1	June	5	April	9	Nov.	27	Oct.	20
Aug. 1	July	6	May	10	Dec.	27	Nov.	20
Sept. 1	Aug.	6	June	10	Jan.	26	Dec.	21
Oct. 1	Sept.	7	July	10	Feb.	25	Jan.	20
Nov. 1	Oct.	6	Aug.	9	March	27	Feb.	20
Dec. 1	Nov.	5	Sept.	9	April	26	March	22

CAPACITY OF SILO

A silo, properly filled—that is, if the contents are made compact throughout—contains one ton of silage for every fifty cubic feet of space. To illustrate the economy of a silo to store stock feed as compared with a barn, a ton of hay requires 400 cubic feet of space. A farmer can easily figure how much a silo will contain by the following rules:

Multiply the square of the diameter by 0.7854, that will be the area of the circular floor. Multiply the area of the floor by the height, that will give the number of cubic feet. One cubic foot of silage weighs 40 lbs. Multiply the cubic feet by 40, and the result is the number of pounds of silage the silo will contain. Divide that by 2,000 to find the number of tons.

Diameter	Depth	Capacity in Tons	Acres to Fill 15 Tons to Acre	Cows It Will Keep 6 Months, 40 Lbs. per Day
10	20	31	2-1/3	8
12	20	45	3	12
12	24	54	3-3/5	15
12	28	63	4-1/5	17
14	22	67	4-1/2	18
14	24	74	5	20
14	28	87	5-2/3	24
14	30	93	6	26
16	24	96	6-2/5	27
16	26	104	7	29
16	30	120	8	33
18	30	152	10-1/5	42
18	36	183	12-1/3	50

57

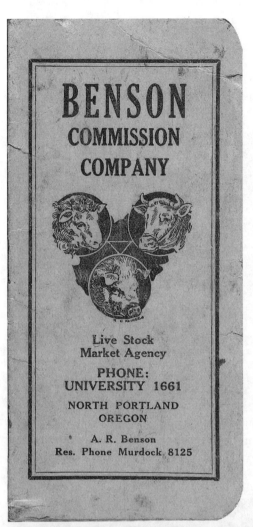

These two little pocket notebooks from 1939 were sent to me by a friend in Oregon, Tony Zazweta, in some of our lure trading deals. Both are worth between $5-$15. My preference is for the Benson as it shows whiteface sheep, similar to the ones we raise. .... **$5-$15 each**

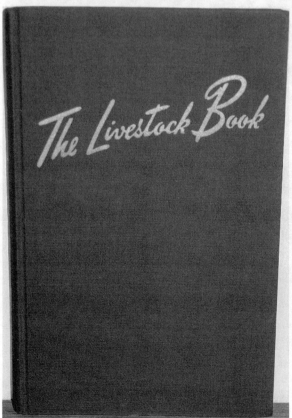

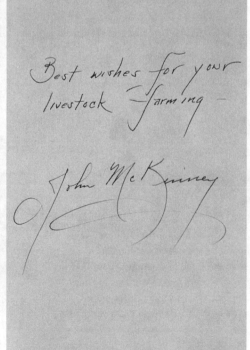

The two photos show a nice book for the farm collector and the inside page detailing the autograph of one of the two co-authors, a nice touch indeed. This book is from 1952. *Lewis Collection* .... **$35+**

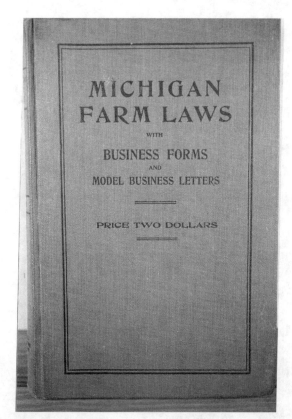

This 1943 item shows the patriotism of the farm community during the war era and is a wonderful buy at only $8 online. I purchased this for research on the book. The contents include a complete listing of all farm tractors and machinery companies in business in 1943 and all major equipment made, as it was needed for the lubrication guide furnished by Texaco. Also, the booklet has many fine line drawings of equipment and photos of the types of oil containers from the era. I purchased three of these Texaco guides from 1941, 1943, and 1947, and paid from $8 to $27.50 for them, all in excellent to mint condition. Not only are they colorful, but the data inside is worth a lot to the collector..$8

A 1908 First Edition of *Michigan Farm Laws* is of special interest to me as a lawyer/farmer. I purchased it years ago for a few dollars at an antique store. It is a nice example of a special interest publication that one can add to a collection. *Lewis Collection*......................... **$20-$30**

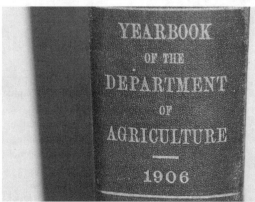

This 1906 *Yearbook of Agriculture* was printed in 1907 and followed predecessor publications detailing news and new developments in agriculture in America. A review of the Table of Contents shows that one can learn about everything from modern Game Wardens to Dairy Farming in the volume. My wife purchased this as a gift for me for $5 at a local antique store. Eventually, the Yearbook of Agriculture became dedicated to one topic per year. These are readily available and are an excellent source of data on farming and on what have become farm collectibles today. *Lewis Collection*.............................$5

A 1947 example of the Texaco farm manual, similar to the one shown above from 1943. This one shows many tractors, trucks, oil cans, and data for equipment from 1947. It is in mint shape. *Lewis Collection* **$17.50**

This great October 1938 *Farm Journal* shows a wonderful International Truck advertisement on the inside front cover and a Kalamazoo Stove advertisement on the rear cover. These are just two examples of product information available in early magazines. I would value this particular magazine at $20-$30, due to its age and its fairly clean condition. It does have some corner and edge wear, and a little soiling, but has been stored in a clean and dry environment.
Paulsen Collection .... **$20-$30**

NEW FARM MACHINERY

SUCH color! Blue, green, yellow, orange, red—all the colors of the rainbow except maybe violet. No wonder farmers are drawn to farm machinery exhibits at Wichita and Harrisburg, and at the state fairs in fall. No wonder they spend a half billion dollars a year for machinery and tractors.

This year, if you want a guess, they'll spend considerably more than that. Last year the figure was well over a half billion. The industry expects a gain of 5 to 10% over 1940 this year. This estimate is based on better moisture conditions in some of the states forming a part of the old dust bowl, and on an expected increase in farm buying power.

It isn't just color that farmers get for their half a billion dollars a year, and it isn't color alone that attracts them to the shows—though color helps. They buy labor, and time, and crop insurance, and various other things which come along with tractors and implements that enable them to get their work done when it needs to be done without having to depend on extra help to catch up.

A Big Implement Year

Farmers will buy more tractors and implements this year because they need the equipment. Labor is likely to be scarce. Machinery will be needed to keep production costs down. Some machinery, in use a long time, will have to be replaced. Some implements will have to be discarded in favor of newer ones which do the same old job better plus, maybe, some new jobs that didn't exist a few years ago. Farming methods are as changeable as that, despite the gags about farming "like granddad did."

A quick change in farming methods, if there ever was one, is the wide acceptance of the combine. All the manufacturers are now making the so-called "vest pocket" combine—the straight-

through type, cutting a swath five feet or less in width. Handling the straw after one of these small combines is still an unsolved problem.

The newest thing about combines this year is a gadget one of the manufacturers is putting on this year, to change the speed of the cylinder while the rig is in use. Some of the farmers who saw this feature on a combine at the Harrisburg Farm Show in January guessed they would "have to trade my old combine in" so as to get the new feature.

What it amounts to is a small crank; turn it, and you change the diameter of the cylinder pulley, which is driven by V-belt. A tightener takes up the slack in the belt as the cylinder pulley becomes smaller, and lets the slack out as the pulley grows again. Operators can change the cylinder speed at different times during the day, with such a quick and simple way of doing it. It is a matter of seconds, not minutes or hours.

In spite of the rapid advance of the small combine, the threshing machine is far from licked. Help for those who believe in the thresher method is found in a small, lightweight, low-cost rubber-

tired trailer thresher that can be pulled by an auto. Developed by TVA engineers, this thresher is now on the market at a cost under $400. An air-cooled gasoline engine (5 to 7 H. P.), mounted on the thresher frame, costs about $150 more. A five-horsepower electric motor will run the thresher. Users in the TVA area say it will out-thresh the larger rigs, because so little time is needed for moving from one job to another. It will travel the road at 50 miles an hour, if the auto wants to go that fast.

New in haying machinery is "ready-sliced" baled hay. The bale of "ready-sliced" hay falls apart when the ties are snipped, in contrast to the accordion-fold bale. This ready-sliced bale is produced by a continuous feed, blockless pick-up baler that takes the wilted hay from the windrow. A knife on the plunger slices off each charge as the plunger presses it into the bale. Instead of the usual divider blocks, this new baler has very light metal dividers automatically inserted.

Not exactly new, but gaining rapidly in use, is the ventilated metal building for storing chopped hay. It's a safe guess that 1941 will be the best year ever for sales of these buildings.

Another piece of haying equipment that has made farmers' tongues wag in the Mid-West is the tractor-mounted bucking and stacking tool. Several different kinds are already on the market, and some are still in the hands of farm-inventors. The implement is used in field stacking, rack loading, gathering straw after the combine, and loading grain shocks on bundle wagons.

Take a look at one of the farm-born rigs. It is essentially a sweeprake head (Continued on page 87)

FOR SMALL FARMS ★ This small all-metal balanced-load tractor spreader for herds under 12 cows has 16-inch rims; sells under $100 without tires; will go through a 5½-foot door; holds 35 or 40 bushels of manure; weighs about 430 pounds; can be pulled by a small tractor; height of box from ground, 34½ inches.

This issue of the *Farm Journal and Farmer's Wife* magazine from March 1941 introduces new farm machinery for the year and also has a nice advertisement for Case plows, showing one at work. Also note the Farmall Cub pulling a manure spreader. *Paulsen Collection*

.... $20-$30

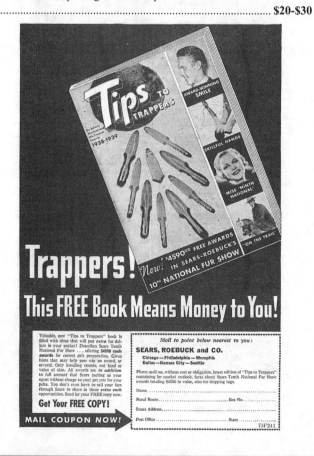

This nice cover shows a happy harvester of apples and a nice collecting basket in demand today by collectors. The inside front cover is a nice Farmall tractor advertisement. An ad on page 32 illustrates the importance of trapping to the farm family. Sears thought it important enough to run this large advertisement for trapping supplies specifically targeted at farmers. Trapping was a supplemental income to many farmers. *Paulsen Collection* .... $20-$30

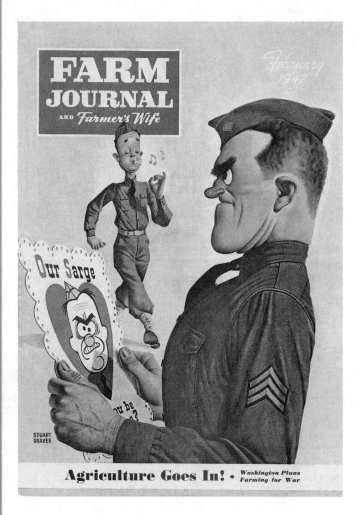

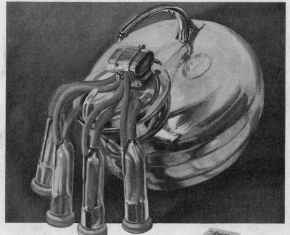

This great magazine, the February 1942 *Farm Journal and Farmer's Wife,* shows America in the middle of war. It has many interesting war related advertisements. The inside front cover shows the older and newer Farmall tractors, another page discusses the importance of only one man being able to harvest crops by himself with the All-Crop Harvester by Allis Chalmers (see page 37) and another page shows life goes on for children. The American Seed Co. Inc. of Lancaster, Pa., offered a number of prizes for selling seeds. The illustration of the seed company advertisement shows the Daisy Red Ryder B.B. gun, a Gene Autry holster set similar to the one shown later and other must-have items for the child of 1942. The rear cover is a great photograph of the Surge Milker by Babson Brothers. It also shows its free catalogue, an item much harder to find than the milking machine itself. This magazine is worth about the same as the others. *Paulsen Collection* .... $20-$30

Chapter Three:
Farming in Advertising

This is likely one of the hottest areas of farm collectibles and should remain so, given past trends in collecting. This section includes the non-print areas of advertising: tins, signs, give-away items, pencils, pens, anything that a company could plaster its name onto and get into the general public's view. It also includes many items that manufacturers supplied dealerships with for advertising their products. The most valuable of these items are likely the porcelain and tin signs made by the companies for dealers and users of the products. This is also an example of "crossover" demand and "general appearance" demand in collecting.

Tin and porcelain (porcelain generally being older and generally more valuable) signs are in great demand by collectors in general due to their display value and great colors. My wife and I have collected dairy-related signs for years. There is nothing to spruce up a dull corner more than a colorful DeLaval or Surge sign. These signs have gone from being a mere $5-$10 auction item to usually starting at $25 and going quickly up to $100, if in fine condition. Of course, it is to a large degree brand driven. An obscure company will not usually bring the prices of a commonly known company in farming such as DeLaval or Surge or Deere. Our favorite buy was a very early artificial insemination sign with a Jersey bull illustration that we found on an old barn door at a garage sale. The man wanted to give it to us and we insisted he take something for it. Finally we negotiated what we thought a fair price and the sign now hangs in our farm kitchen (see photo in this chapter).

The finding of items is often more fun than the item itself. Value is important, but so is history. It is amazing the things one finds that are "advertising items": barometers, thermometers, tape measures, yard sticks, yard sticks as walking sticks, tin signs in every size and shape imaginable, pens, pencils, patches, hats, knives, can and bottle openers, glasses, kitchen containers, utensils, mirrors, tins, boxes, counter mats, banners, neon signs, calendars, display stands, display racks, salesman's samples, salesman's sample cases, toys, cast iron animals, chalkboards, tools, key chains, and watch fobs.

The area of greatest concern to the collector of advertising items is the reproduction and manufacturing of fake items. Many of the signs have been recently reproduced and it is difficult to tell the reproductions from the originals. This shows the importance of provenance in antique finds. It is far safer to buy such advertising items at an auction with provenance than from an unknown dealer. However, some of the older reproductions (signs reproduced from the 1960s-1980s) are already taking on a collectible nature of their own due to their beauty. But the fake signs and reproduced advertising items are an area of concern that one should know about in this field. This happens whenever a collectible attains a high value. There is always someone in the wings waiting to rip off the unsuspecting buyer. Just be aware of your source, buy from reputable dealers only, buy at a sale where you know the item is original, familiarize yourself with the reproductions on the market, and have fun looking.

Values in this area are from a few dollars to thousands. It would be easy to spend a few hundred dollars on just one or two good signs. A neon sign advertising a local tractor dealership could cost more than $1,000 easily. Many small items, such as tape measures and measuring cups, would command only a few dollars. But the bullet pencils given away by dealerships bring from $25-$75, depending on brand name and location of dealership. Other items, such as display stands used for literature or small products, come up for sale so infrequently it is hard to judge their market value. However, the guides given in the previous chapter on paper collectibles apply to any advertising item concerning brand names and general appeal to other collectors. I have seen many an urban buyer go after a DeLaval sign because of its black/yellow color pattern who did not have a clue what a milking machine was, let alone a DeLaval brand milker.

Items of greatest value appear to be those that can be easily displayed in one's home. This includes any of the tin or porcelain signs that are smaller than 24" by 24". The really large signs are much harder to find display space for in the home. Thermometers and barometers with advertising are also popular, as they can still be used and displayed. Next in line would be the small items that can be placed on a shelf to be admired.

An entire book could be written on just dairy-related collectibles (one has been and is available from *Hoard's Dairyman*). There is collector interest in milk bottles, milk cans, cream cans, cream and butter crocks, butter cartons, crocks in general, and dairy bottle caps. Most of these items are valued in general collecting books but they are all farm collectibles in every sense. Many of these items have a regional "value-added" to them, bringing greater money within their own region than elsewhere. Of course, online sales have had an impact on this aspect. But as to antique store and farm auction sales, local bottles will always bring a premium. Also, the more colorful the bottle or butter carton, the more value in general.

Some signs found at a local dealership for tractors and implements are now being collected by the dealership. These include a very rare neon Minneapolis-Moline sign from my hometown. Shown is an older classic red/yellow New Holland sign along with the current New Holland sign in comparison. There is also a Ritchie waterer sign (newer). The neon sign is valued at well over $1,000. The neon Minneapolis-Moline is still in its storage crate. ......**$100-$1,000 each**

Values of Advertising Items

Rumely watch fob, triangular shape, shows threshing machine on one side and location of company, La Porte, Ind., on the other. **$32.50**

A tin sign from a farm stand that was about 16" long, simply stating "Celery" on both sides. This sign was a homemade sign by the farmer. **$22.50**

Two crate-end labels marked "Gay Johnny Fresh Vegetables," showing a Huck Finn type boy and bucking broncos. It was vintage 1930s-40s, and measured 5" x 7". Both labels were in mint condition (see similar examples later in this chapter).....................................**$10**

A USDA metal sign from the Federal Crop Insurance Corp., measuring 14" x 20", in very good to excellent condition. This seems a bargain to me but one wonders the provenance of the sign, as no details were given. It was the simple white background with a green leaf design. **$7**

Dairy equipment tin signs in our own collection. One of the very lucky finds for us was the black/yellow DeLaval sign that is virtually new from old stock found in an old hardware store in Bay City, Mich., in the past 20 years. The store was a DeLaval dealership and had a box of 12 of these signs still with the shipping paper attached new in the box. Signs such as these are selling for $50-$150 each at auctions and in antique stores, depending on the quality and the age and the color or patterns. *Lewis Collection*...................**$50-$150 each**

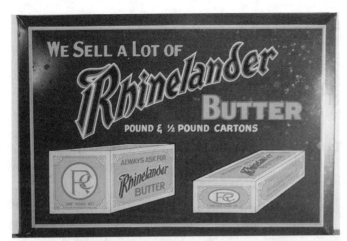

A related collectible consists of the signs provided by dairy companies to indicate one's loyalty to a creamery or milk company. These tin signs are much harder to find and would command a bit more money that the equipment signs. An example for butter is shown, valued at $100 or more. *Lewis Collection* .... **$100+**

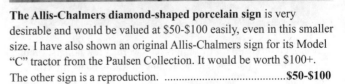

Some crate-end labels still on the crates, one older one and two a bit newer to show how these have evolved but are still being used by some producers. Although one can buy pristine end labels online, I find the ones on crates of greater interest due to the history of it actually being used and the known provenance of the item. Also shown is a local cherry box. *Nerbonne Collection* ....**$10-$20 each**

The Allis-Chalmers diamond-shaped porcelain sign is very desirable and would be valued at $50-$100 easily, even in this smaller size. I have also shown an original Allis-Chalmers sign for its Model "C" tractor from the Paulsen Collection. It would be worth $100+. The other sign is a reproduction. ....**$50-$100**

The large-sized Shell porcelain sign was a real find made at only $75 at a dissolution sale of a large hardware wholesaler in Grand Rapids, Mich. This sign is worth at least $400 to most collectors but was just one of those items that the auctioneer failed to advertise. As it happened, not many buyers were present who were interested in such a rare piece that day. This is a great example of why one should attend "live auctions" when given an opportunity. Great buys do occur and it is always a matter of timing. *Smith Collection* ...... **$400+**

A dealership sign cost me about $100 in 1998 at a dissolution auction for a local grain mill in Ladysmith, Wis. This sign would not be worth as much elsewhere but was in high demand by the local farmers due to their association with the mill. *Lewis Collection* .... **$100+**

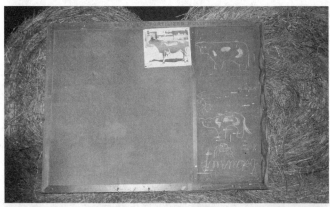

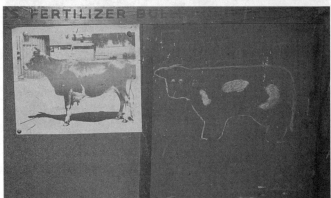

Half of a Goodyear Tire tin sign is only worth a few dollars. I found it at a garage sale but it is still interesting. It would be worth $100 at least intact. *Lewis Collection* .... **$100 if intact**

A very unique piece cost more than $200 at the same auction in 1998 in Ladysmith. This Smith-Douglass chalkboard, tackboard combination advertising sign is from the same grain mill. This piece still has the cow drawing on it, done by a local school child as she waited in the warm grain mill office for the bus to come during a cold Wisconsin winter morning. I have left the sign as found because I felt it was interesting. **$200**

A unique fertilizer thermometer cost about $240. This is an older item and many antique dealers wanted it, too. The same auction also had two old glass bulb liquid fire extinguishers, bringing more than $50 each, and many other nice advertising items. $240

An "O-So Beverages" thermometer is clearly food related. It is also my favorite pop from childhood. This clean thermometer would bring $100 on up at an auction and would likely be priced at nearly $200 in an antique store or mall. Pop, or soda or soda pop, depending on locale in the country, collectibles are very popular and can bring thousands of dollars if the piece is rare. I was once fortunate enough to find some very rare tin Pepsi signs from the Depression era that each brought more than $1,000 when sold. This is unusual, but people need to realize that some advertising items are some of the most valuable items in many fields of collecting. The reason is that they display well, are colorful, and then, if rare, are of even greater value. *Lewis Collection*..........$100-$200

Another pop-related item is the little "open-closed" sign for Squirt. This wax board sign is from the 1950s-60s. *Lewis Collection* $25

An antique tin for Mammoth Peanuts is another food-related item with great collector appeal. *Lewis Collection* .... $50-$75

Three corn planters are among items that fall into two or more categories of this book. They are all clearly small farm implements but, due to the pristine nature of the labels on them, they could also be kept for the advertising. The most interesting history is the Acme brand made in Traverse City, Mich., that a neighboring farmer purchased in an antique store in Nebraska for $37 a few years back. One never knows where one will find something of interest.
.... **$30-$40 each**

The typewriter tin is a fun and inexpensive collectible item. These three examples show a great Art Deco version in the center that would command at least $30 if in mint shape, but it has a hole in it. *Lewis Collection*.. **$5-$15**

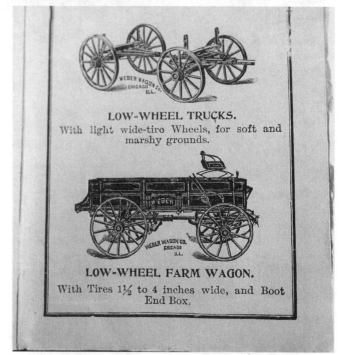

LOW-WHEEL TRUCKS.
With light wide-tire Wheels, for soft and marshy grounds.

LOW-WHEEL FARM WAGON.
With Tires 1½ to 4 inches wide, and Boot End Box.

A small pocket diary produced by Weber Wagon Co. of Chicago. It could be in many chapters but it is best seen as an advertising item. My wife's maiden name is Weber so this is especially fun for us. I purchased this online for $40. The photos show the cover, left, and one insert advertisement cropped to show two wagons, above. **$40**

This Farm Bureau Member heavy sign showing Michigan's Upper and Lower Peninsula has some corrosion but is still a fine addition to farm collectibles. It would bring $50 even in this condition. *Art Smith Collection* **$50**

A nice Master Mix Feed clock would be worth more than $25 at auction, even though it is newer than the Farm Bureau sign. I sold a similar clock at auction for $35. *Art Smith Collection* .... **$25+**

Clearly a reproduction sign, but interesting nonetheless, is this Moore's Wonderful Rat Destroyer sign. *Art Smith Collection* **$20**

Old feedbags make nice advertising items in a collection. This Larro Egg Mash bag was from Detroit. It has the added bonus of being a General Mills subsidiary, increasing its demand for collectors from two areas. Bags such as this in excellent shape sell for $5-$25, depending on quality, colors, graphics, and locale. *Art Smith Collection* ....**$5-$25 each**

DeLaval dairy collectibles have many followers. This can would command about $50 at most auctions. It is not perfect, but a nice enough early example of DeLaval Oil. *Art Smith Collection* **$50**

This full Maytag Multi-Motor Oil can was another great find. It is in very good shape and would be a nice addition to any collection. *Art Smith Collection*... **$75+**

A very rare can is this Standard Oil Company full can of Liquid Gloss furniture polish, shown being used by a properly dressed Victorian lady on fine furniture. Art Smith found this for very little at a farm auction but I should think it would command more than $200 if offered on an online auction or at a specialty auction of oil collectibles. The can itself is rare enough, but to find it full is very unusual. *Art Smith Collection* **$200**

The John Deere oil can is also rare. *Art Smith Collection* .... **$50+**

A nice porcelain Bell System sign should bring $75 easily at auction. *Art Smith Collection*..**$75**

Even a simple pressed board sign such as this tack shop sign is of some value, likely at least $10 at auction, as it is one of a kind. *Art Smith Collection*..**$10**

A beautiful old Cities Services 10-gallon can, likely used for kerosene, is on the VanAlstine porch. An item such as this would bring $50-$100 easily if oil company collectors were bidding on it. It is an unusual piece and in fine shape. .... $50-$100

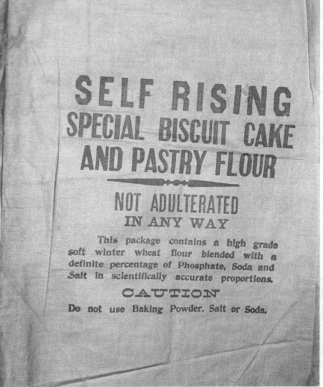

This nice Farm Bureau member sign from 1934 is displayed in the VanAlstine dining room. It was a real steal, purchased for a few dollars. It should be valued at $50 or better, even with the water stains, due to its age and fragility...............................$50

Harris Milling Co. flour bags were purchased by my wife at a local garage sale. They were owned by a former Harris employee, and she said they were from the 1950s. Both bags were mint and well worth the 25 cents each she paid. Two photos show the details. *Lewis Collection* ....$5-$10 each

These early Michigan license plates were found in the Nerbonne barn. These sell for about $50-$75 as examples from the 1930s.
.... $50-$75

A 1938 Michigan license plate is in the Paulsen garage, surrounded by two reproduction gasoline signs. Maybe the above plates were stamped out at Jackson prison, as shown on the walking stick in the tools chapter. Value of plate would be at least $50, the reproduction signs are worth about $20-$25 each, and the toy truck is one of the first Meijer trucks and would be worth at least $50 for the cab and trailer. It is shown in the next chapter. $50

A reproduction tin for Hershey's is a necessity for any dairy collection. It is not old, but is attractive. ....$5-$10

An original Keen Kutter Tools tin sign backed with material. *Lewis Collection* .... $75+

A Kent Feeds stocking cap from the 1980s is not an antique but will gain in value as time goes by. *Lewis Collection* $5

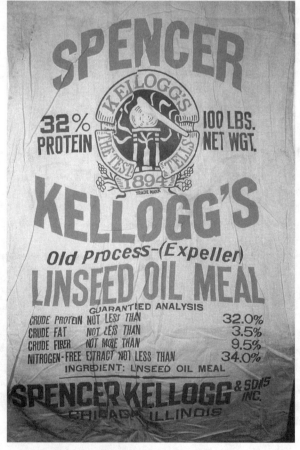

A large Kellogg's Linseed Oil Meal bag in near mint condition. *Lewis Collection*... $15-$20

Another crossover collectible increasing its value a little is this ashtray from Thorp, Wis., advertising a dairy bar and café. A nice little dairy collectible is worth at least $10, due to detailed advertising and demand by tobacco collectors as well. *Lewis Collection*.........**$10**

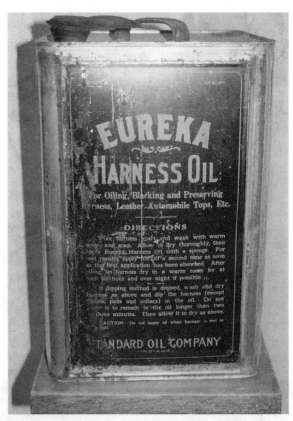

The Eureka Harness Oil can made by Standard Oil is one of our favorite collectibles. It is a very rare piece as it came in its original wooden shipping crate, so marked. It is in very nice shape and attractive for display purposes. We display it on the Mission Oak plant stand, sitting in a corner of our dining room. We paid $100 for this in 1995 and would not sell it for $300 today. **$300**

An older Ford tractor or truck emblem such as this will bring $10 easily at auction. It is a nice addition for a Ford collector. *Lewis Collection* **$10**

This Badger brand red clover bag shows nice graphics. It is one of a number of bags found in an old barn when we purchased our Wisconsin farm in 1997. Most were mouse eaten, but not this fine example. *Lewis Collection*.....**$10+**

The Mobiloil can was purchased for a few dollars in an antique store and has a missing top but is still worth about $20, due to its nice condition and large size. I use it as a little waste can. Because my dad was a Mobil dealer, this is a special addition for me. *Lewis Collection* **$20**

These Sealtest dairy recipe books make an interesting addition to dairy collectibles. From the 1940s-50s, they are not of great value but should trade for $2-$5 each. These were actually found in a large lot of similar materials and not purchased separately. *Lewis Collection* .... **$2-$5**

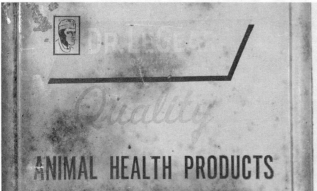

Advertising thermometers make nice collectibles. The Dr. LeGear Animal Health Products one was found on the side of a barn at a garage sale and purchased for $5. The Wisconsin Dairies one was purchased for $10 in an antique store. The dairy example is in excellent shape and the animal health example is well-worn. Both work. *Lewis Collection* .... **$5-$10**

The old butter and egg price sign hanging in the butcher shop, showing the day's prices on the two items, is another nice butter item. This example comes from an antique store in Wisconsin and I believe it to be an original. However, I also believe these have been reproduced. *Lewis Collection*.. **$40-$50**

Butter cartons are a very fine addition to any farm collection but fit in especially well with dairy collectibles. The photos detail three nice examples. One thing to do is try to find your favorite cow type (Jersey, etc.) or a local dairy to add to your collection. *Lewis Collection*..$20 each

A Roycroft egg carton from Sidnaw, Mich.(western Upper Peninsula), shows one cannot have butter without eggs to fry in it. The egg carton is a gift from a good friend and is in mint condition. Sidnaw was on the rail line to Minneapolis and at one time produced thousands of eggs for the city markets in Minnesota, Wisconsin, and Michigan. *Lewis Collection* ....$20+

An egg basket, a nice example from MoorMan's Feed, was once furnished to loyal MoorMan's users for their egg operations. We had a few dozen similar ones at one time to gather and wash our eggs. I recently traded a copy of this book (once printed) for this egg basket. The rubber coating on the basket was to protect the eggs in both gathering and in placing in the automatic washers we used in the 1950s and 1960s for egg washing. *Lewis Collection*......................$30

MoorMan's also produced a little hat rack of its trademarked cow. *Lewis Collection*..$25

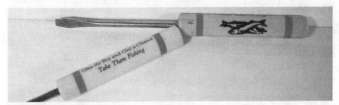

Two small screwdrivers from my fishing lure collectibles are examples of the types of items also given away by farm implement dealerships. These, along with small tape measures, yard sticks, and rulers, comprise an interesting area of collectibles. They bring anywhere from $5-$25 on most occasions. Again, the brand loyalty and geographical area are important considerations in pricing. Both of the screwdrivers shown are from a bait shop in South Bend, Ind., making them interesting as it was also the home of a major bait company. ....$5-$25

Milk cartons in mint shape, such as this Gibas' Dairy carton (shown folded), are a nice addition of more recent packaging. *Lewis Collection* $10

This Richelieu Mince Meat crock is another example of food advertising. *Lewis Collection* $10

A beautiful Pet Milk advertising tin sign hangs on our kitchen cupboards. This is a reproduction (painted on rear side) but is a nice example of a 1921 sign produced by Pet. It is likely about 25 years old, as we have had it for some time. But there is no printer information on the sign, other than the original 1921 data. *Lewis Collection* .... 35-$50

This Lansing Dairy Co. "Sunbeam Products" butter or cream cheese crock is a great example of a local dairy collectible. This was purchased at a farm auction years ago. *Lewis Collection* $50

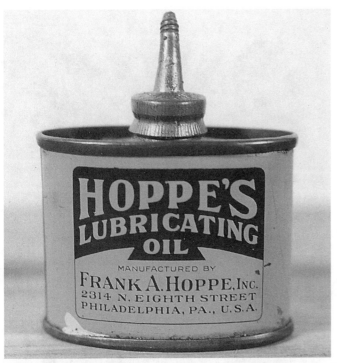

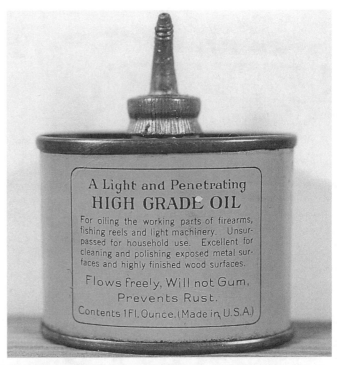

This Hoppe's Oil can could be in Chapter 10 instead, but I have shown it here as an example of a lead-top can. Most oil cans had lead tops until the post-war era, but some cans had switched to a plastic top on a lead spout even sooner. But a lead spout with a lead top is an earlier can. See my *Collecting Antique Bird Decoys and Duck Calls* recently published by Krause Publications for a complete history of similar items and photos of many oil cans. Values on oil cans vary by brand and age from a low of $25 to a high of about $500 for any of the pre-1950s cans. *Lewis Collection*... **$40-$75**

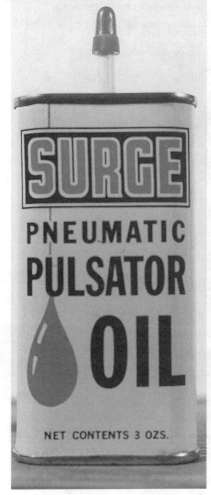

This is a newer Surge can (post-1950), as one can tell from the plastic spout. If one milks cows, one needs a little oil on the milking machine leathers, and this can provided the contents for the purpose. It is mint and makes a nice addition to one's advertising or dairy collection. *Lewis Collection* .... **$15-$25**

The rubber repair kit found in every farmer's tool crib is another advertising collectible. Flat tires and hay wagons just seem to go together and, when I was younger, it was my job to put on the patches and fix the tires. Bicycles also seemed to have flat tires very often. These little kits come in a variety of colors and brands and display nicely in a corner of a cabinet. This Camel brand is in excellent shape and still has its original content*s. Lewis Collection* .... **$15-$20**

A Wayne feed company patch for a jacket or hat is a nice little item for the farm collection. *Lewis Collection*.. **$5**

Health products for humans and animals alike are nice additions. This little ointment can is just one example. *Lewis Collection* .... **$10-$15**

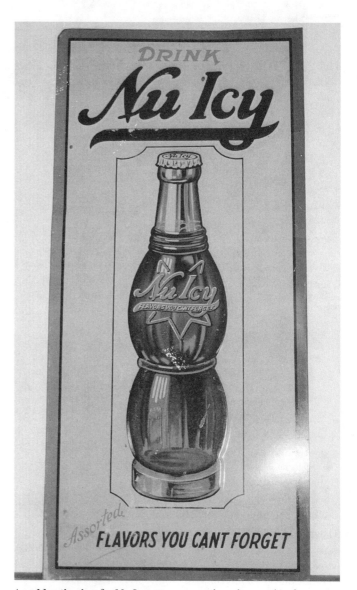

The Spear Head plug tobacco pouch will be especially appreciated by our tobacco-raising farmers. It was a give-away item of the company at one time. This nice old leather pouch was found in a Wisconsin antique store a few years back. *Lewis Collection* . **$15-$20**

An older tin sign for Nu Icy pop was purchased at auction four years ago for $35 each (two of them) and one was sold online two years ago for $65. *Lewis Collection* **$65**

Our rare and original ABS sign was found on the side of a barn. This sign is not mint but it proudly hangs above our kitchen phone and shows a Jersey bull. This is heavy gauge metal. *Lewis Collection* .... **$100-$200**

This DeLaval sign is a recent reproduction, showing many of the early separator advertisement examples. This is a nice addition to a DeLaval collection even if it is newer. *Lewis Collection*.............. **$20**

This Dekalb sign, a gift from a former student, is a newer version of the signs that seed growers place in the field or on the farmstead to show company loyalty. This is made of a Styrofoam type material and will not weather for dozens of years as the tin signs have done. But it makes a nice addition, especially for someone who won two Dekalb corn-growing awards as I did (see the pins in Chapter 11). *Lewis Collection*.. **$25+**

This Loyal Farm Equipment sign, at the edge of our era, was purchased at auction in 1998 for $25. The company went into business in 1956. But it is a fine example of a tin sign, similar to the ones by Surge and DeLaval from the 1950s, very thin tin. *Lewis Collection* .... **$25-$40**

This Grace sign was purchased at the same 1998 auction. It is very heavy metal and also from the 1950s. *Lewis Collection* .... **$75+**

This Jersey paperweight from the Jersey association in Canada is a breed loyalty item. It was purchased at an antique store a few years ago for $10. *Lewis Collection* .... **$10-$20**

Rural Route Box Holder
LOCAL

Sec. 562, P. L. & R.
U. S. POSTAGE
PAID
BUFFALO, N. Y.
Permit No. 237

This 1949 DeLaval Year Book, at left and above, is an example of the common yearbooks published by many companies and distributed free to rural route box holders. This one is not mint, as the cover is loose, but it is clean. It is of special value to us as it is from my hometown and from a classmate's grandfather's (and then father's) business. Also, it was a John Deere dealership as well. Photos show the covers and one advertisement for the separator related to egg production. *Lewis Collection* .... **$25-$50**

Chapter Four:
Small Scale Farming and Children's Recreation

This section includes the development of farm toys and related items designed for children that have now become collectible. Of course, there are many books already out on toys and even farm toys. This chapter will attempt to at least introduce the reader to the importance of farm toys and related child items in the field of farm collectibles.

Items which immediately come to mind include: coaster wagons, sleds, farm toys to be ridden, farm animal toys, Milky the Cow, early Fisher-Price farm sets, the Marx farm sets, Ertl tractors and all of the predecessors, Auburn tractors and trucks, Lionel farm-related train cars and accessories (my favorite item was the cattle unloader and stock cars), lunch boxes, cap guns and BB guns, "small scale" tools and tool sets, "small scale" household items, and anything else to occupy the time of a child on the farm.

This chapter is far more selective than others. I have simply illustrated some items that strike me as being farm related. I recommend that the reader consult any of the toy books or toy tractor books on the market for a detailed analysis of those fields. A good general pricing guide is *Dick's Farm Toy Price Guide + Check List* available from www.bioptik.com/dicksdesigns.com and other sources. Also very inclusive in its treatment but somewhat dated is the *International Directory of Model Farm Tractors*, 1985, by Raymond E. Crilley Sr. and Charles E. Burkholder, published by Schiffer Publishing. This is a massive work with wonderful photos of toy tractors up through the mid-1980s. I would recommend finding it and *Toy Farm Tractors* with text by Bill Vosler and photos by Andy Kraushaar, published by Voyageur Press, Stillwater, MN, 1998, as my starting references for toy tractor collecting. Additional online resources include www.toytractortimes.com and www.toytractorshow.com for both toy tractor and real tractor history.

One of my all-time favorite items, though of recent 1970s vintage, is "Milky the Cow." There was a similar cow toy in the 1950s that I recall but do not know the manufacturer. I purchased Milky for my children in the mid-1970s. It was a marvel that actually gave milk after inserting water and milky colored tablets. This cow was akin to the crying dolls and wetting dolls: toys that actually did what the real thing did. One of these cows in its original box would easily garner double its sale price of a few years ago, if not more.

Coaster wagons and sleds are two popular items with all collectors that have a special place in the heart of a farm kid. The coaster wagon allowed us to assist our parents in gardening chores or hauling product (eggs, milk, cream) into the home from the barn. On our farm, the wagon was a tool and a toy. I would have fun playing with it but also used it to help out. The day the coaster wagon was under the Christmas tree or wrapped as a birthday present with a single bow on the handle is a day well burned in every farm kid's memory! The same is true with the sled (or sleigh as originally called). The first Flexible-Flyer is remembered by all of us for the joy it would bring in the winter on the local farm hills. But it also served to haul that bale of hay to our pony in the wintertime while doing our own personal chores. Today, many of these items are purchased to hang in urban lofts, apartments, and homes for decoration, or they adorn the walls of a local restaurant. However, one can often find a nice wagon or sled for $25-$50 at farm auctions or even in some antique stores. We found a coaster wagon left behind in the dairy barn of our farm when we purchased it a couple of years ago. It had been used to cart things around while doing chores, and remained with the farm. It is a good demonstration of the functional use of some of the "toys."

The tractors designed for little folks to peddle instead of plow with are some of the most desirable of all farm collectibles originally made for children. Some of these sell for hundreds of dollars. The nicer the condition and older the item, the more it will bring. I find these items to be similar to Lionel trains. We all wanted one even if our parents could not afford them in the 1950s. I wanted so badly to have a riding John Deere tractor as a kid, but I never had one. So when my first son was born, I made a trip to the local John Deere dealer to purchase a riding tractor and pull-behind wagon. As soon as he could peddle, he was placed upon it with pride in suburban Evansville, Ind., to ride around the suburbs. At age four, we moved him and his tiny brother back to our dairy farm in Michigan. I still recall with great dismay the day one of my farm hands drove our brand new Allis-Chalmers 7000 over Justin's John Deere. It broke all of our hearts, especially Justin's. We replaced it with a riding Allis but it was never quite the same.

As an early parent, I always joked that we should all buy Fisher-Price stock because we all bought their toys. Well, I should have listened to my own advice. The Fisher-Price barns and related farm toys have held their value and increased, if they are the early versions. Fisher-Price is still making this line and has added many things to it. But the original little barn in which one placed all the fence and animals has become quite collectible, even though beyond the normal years of this book's coverage. In addition, the Marx farm sets are of great value, with the Roy Rogers and Dale Evans ranch being a closely related item of great value and interest. There were also many other barn kits and house kits available for farm children, and these are all now collectible. In communities in which the Amish live, many hand-made crafted barns and farm animal sets show up that are very collectible and desirable. At an estate sale, I recently purchased four cast iron farm animals that were either homemade or a small company's efforts to enter the toy market. There would be an endless quest to simply collect farm animals, barns and related items.

Toy guns always had a special place for farm kids. The Red Ryder BB gun is famous to all of us aged 55 or so. It was a recreational item for the vast spaces of the farm and a pretend hunting weapon, too. Many an hour was filled with target practice sessions to hone hunting skills. Also, many bad guys were disposed of with the Red Ryder and the holstered cap guns important to the kids of the 1940s-1950s. A Gene Autry cast iron cap gun, which cost a few dollars in the 1940s, is now worth $300-$500. My Roy Rogers double holster set would garner well over $100 if I still had it. See the interesting seed company advertisement, scanned in Chapter 2, illustrating both a Gene Autry gun set and a Daisy Red Ryder BB gun as "give-away" premiums for selling seeds for the American Seed Company. A Gene Autry is shown in this chapter.

There were also special toys marketed to farm kids, such as toy steam engines. All kids liked these, but farm kids knew steam engines were still being used by some "old-timers" to run antique threshing machines and mills. My older brothers spent many hours running their little steam engine and hooking it up with belts to mini-mills and machines.

Also, in our formerly more unabashed sexist past, many companies marketed small-scale household appliances to the farm girls. Tiny sewing machines, kitchen appliances, and related items were designed to occupy little sister's time and teach her those all important survival skills of a homemaker. The little cast iron stoves and utensils are quite valuable and collectible, as are the small Singer sewing machines from the 1950s.

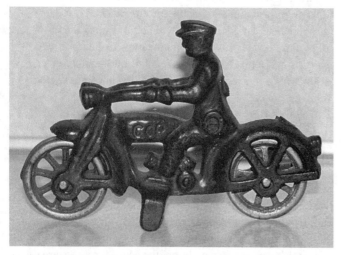

An Arcade motorcycle and rider. These motorcycles range from about $40-$120 in value, depending on the color and model. *Art Smith Collection*.. **$40-$120**

This is just a "remembering" of some of the many items designed for children living on farms, and in many cases elsewhere. It is not all-encompassing but it should serve to direct our attention to children on the farm when looking for collectibles. I have not even mentioned the special role of games and books for farm children, often far more important than for their urban counterparts due to the isolation of early farms. When one's playmates are three miles away, one finds games and books far more important to wile the time away than if the playmates live next door or in the same apartment complex.

Values of Small Scale Farming Items

Early 1960s Auburn Vinyl Farm Implement Set, complete with box, included a tractor, bulldozer, hay lifter, disc, mower, plow, and wagon. **$115**

1960s Slik Toy die cast aluminum manure spreader, about 1/32nd scale. This item, made in Lansing, Iowa, had worn edges but was complete and about a 7 on a 1-10 scale. **$5**

1990 CAT Farm Implement Challenger Set, New in Box..........**$25**

Farm implement 1/64th trailer hitch. **$5.50**

Unidentified A-C style combine. **$6**

1930s Arcade brand two-wheel farm trailer (cast iron) with one bad wheel. **$20**

A John Deere 4400 series Ertl tractor, well used and played with. **$10.50**

This "antique 1900s wood barn by Marx" was an attempt to trick bidders, mentioned earlier in the book. It sold for $100 and was a good deal at that price. But it was not "antique" nor was it 100 years old as claimed. It was a nice heavy board barn with lithographed sides showing doors, windows, hay/straw. It came with a number of the white plastic farm animals and plastic fence common in the late 1950s. There were also some Hubley implements and an Auburn tractor, making this a bargain. The funny thing is that a listing stressing the quality of the Marx items would have likely brought far more if targeted to the Marx toy collectors. **$100**

This 1/16th scale FFA John Deere Model A tractor was to promote the Georgia FFA in 2002 and was made by Ertl. The item was new in the box..**$35**

A 1/24th scale FFA John Deere NASCAR die cast car was new in the box..**$40**

A nice cast iron road scraper toy was found within the walls of a 1920s home. The seller thought it a type of plow and listed it as a "farm toy." It appears that it may have been an Arcade brand cast iron toy. It was in very clean condition, with only common wear marks on the paint..**$52**

A Hubley metal bodied, rubber tired, manure spreader 7" in length did not sell because the hitch was broken. **$10**

A **John Deere Model A** and driver from about 1952 in die cast. This is a nice old model in pristine condition and should be worth $300-$500. *Art Smith Collection*.. **$300-$500**

This small Hubley farm truck is another of Art Smith's items. He paid $80 for this mint item at auction. *Art Smith Collection* **$80**

Some skis were found in the Nerbonne barn. These older Nordic skis are for a child and a young teen. I have sold many of these skis for $25-$75 per pair, depending on condition and rarity. The small pair shown is worth the most due to condition and the presence of the bindings as well as the unique smaller size. ....**$25-$75**

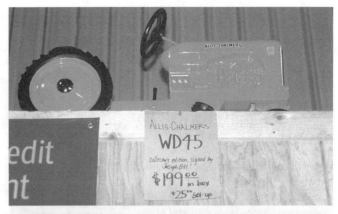

Farm dealerships are selling reproductions of older riding tractors made by Ertl such as the Allis-Chalmers and Ford shown. These are not collectible per se, but will likely become so due to limited production runs of the models. A conversation with the local dealer also raised the point that some individuals have reproduced the older riding tractors without disclosing the reproduction status to the buyer. So again: Caveat Emptor. According to one of my former tool and die clients, reproducing an early riding tractor using the modern CAD/CAM programming would be a simple matter. So if you are spending a few hundred dollars on an early John Deere rider, make sure it is real. At an auction, a fairly nice Murray riding tractor from the early 1960s sold for $75, a Kubota 6950 model brought $105, and a Kubota M9000 brought $125. Sorry to say, the rain made me leave my camera in the car. But the M9000 was like new and the earlier Kubota was about 80 percent, as was the Murray. I think these prices are about typical of what one would find at a farm auction but the Murray seemed a little low for the condition. Two photos show two reproduction models and the third photo shows an older 1960s version made for Sears, not in great shape but for sale for only $40.
.... **$40-$125**

Old sleds, called sleighs in some parts of America, can easily fetch up to $75 for a Flexible Flyer in great shape. The older sleds that truly look like a sleigh, with the upturned runners, will bring even more. Many sleds are sold for only $25 or so at auctions, but they are getting harder to find in great shape. At a recent visit to a nearby antique store, the least expensive sled was $50 and they were priced up to $125 for the older wooden runner models. Small and large toboggans usually do well at auctions too, selling in the same range as sleds. ....**$25-$125**

The little red wagon is usually present at a farm auction sale. It will bring from $10-$100, depending on the model and the condition. Most sell for around $20-$25. A few are shown as examples. An interesting thing to note is that one of the wagons could clearly be dated from the early 1960s due to its name, "Astronaut." A look at toys from the late 1950s to mid-1960s shows many names and marketing angles related to the space race between America and the USSR of the time period. At a large farm implement auction, a wagon from the 1930s with lights on each side sold for $140. It had original paint in fine shape but was used. This was one of the earliest of the wagons that I had seen sell recently............ **$10-$100**

The .45 caliber Hubley is valued at about $50, maybe a little more. *Lewis Collection*..**$50**

An Arcade tow truck purchased at auction in 1997 for $240 is likely worth about double that price today in its condition. It is model 2201, marked Freeport, Ill. *Lewis Collection* .... **$250-$500**

The Gene Autry diecast toy gun and holster is mine. It is valued at $400-$500, according to antique shop owners specializing in toy guns. .... **$400-$500**

The Red Ryder BB gun famous to all of us 50 years of age or better sells at farm auctions for $40-$80 in most cases if in decent shape: less if rough and more if pristine. The sleeper among the BB guns is the very rare double barrel made to look like a double barrel shotgun. Also, the silver Daisy pistols from the 1950s are a bit rare. .. **$40-$80**

Marx play sets have some very high values. Too many exist to detail here but collectors should be aware of the Alamo, Custer's Last Stand, the Roy Rogers/Dale Evans set, and others. Some of the Marx sets sell for thousands of dollars and most sell for hundreds of dollars if complete, new in the box, and pristine. Obviously, a set that is common and "play-worn" will only bring a few dollars in comparison. But some of the sets are very rare and I would caution you to do your homework before selling your parent's or grandparent's toys for a few dollars.. **$100+**

An early heavy die-cast Lindy airplane should bring about $150. *Lewis Collection*..**$150**

A Mobil tow truck, purchased from Mobil a few years ago, is simply to demonstrate the growing interest of toy and oil company collectibles. This currently does not have a great value. But it is the type of item current collectors buy in hopes of an increase in value. In my case, I purchased it because my father was a Mobil dealer and I simply liked it. *Lewis Collection* .... **$50 with box**

Model railroading toys show how farm toys were part of that line as well. I have a Swift's Premium #6050 Lionel "bank car" on my windowsill that is from the 1950s-60s. And a tin cattle car is from my personal Marx train set from the early 1950s. I also had many other cattle cars in my Lionel collection prior to selling it in the early 1990s. One could amass quite a toy train collection just collecting cars related to farming: cattle cars, liquid fertilizer cars, early logging cars, the cattle loading sets from Lionel, the sawmills from Lionel, and many other agricultural and natural resource related train toys. Prices on toy trains range greatly and many excellent guides produced by Greenberg's and others need to be consulted for values. However, at farm sales it is still possible to pick up nice Marx and Lionel items for a few dollars on occasion. At our farm sale, we sold some common items bringing decent but not exorbitant prices. But the rare pieces brought "book prices" or better. .... **$10-$50**

An earlier Ertl Allis-Chalmers round baler toy owned by Jerry Paulsen. **$100**

A Case 600 owned by Jerry Paulsen.............................**$100**

An early 1980s Allis-Chalmers D21 owned by Jerry Paulsen.
.... **$75-$100**

A very nice Precision model 8N that cost $120 new has a value that is simply going up. *Paulsen Collection* .... **$120+**

A WD 45 Allis-Chalmers, also made by Precision, purchased for $100 in the 1980s is now worth at least $400-$500, according to all the trade data. *Paulsen Collection* .... **$400-$500**

Almost any Ertl tractor or other collectible tractor is valued at $30 minimum, according to Jerry Paulsen, and the ones with metal wheels are worth about double that at a minimum. The addition of the original box increases the value twofold. I know this is also true with fishing lure and sporting collectibles too. Boxes are so often discarded that at times the boxes are worth more than the original items for the box. ....**$30+**

John Deere Precision models start at about $200 and go up from there. *Paulsen Collection* $200

A nice Farmall C.

A neat little tin lithography duck from West Germany is not a farm toy per se. But it may have been found on a farm as a child's toy. It is worth about $10-$25 in nice condition such as this. *Lewis Collection*.
.... **$10-$25**

An Auburn Farm truck. *Lewis Collection* $20

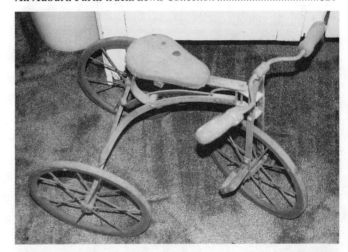

A very old tricycle. *VanAlstine Collection*.......................... $50-$100

An original Carom board from Ludington, Mich., an old dartboard, and a primitive checkerboard adorn the dining room wall in the VanAlstine home. As a Michigan youth, I can assure you that nearly every farm boy and girl owned a Carom board and spent hours playing. I recently saw two for sale in a small antique shop and they were each priced at $35 or more. **$35**

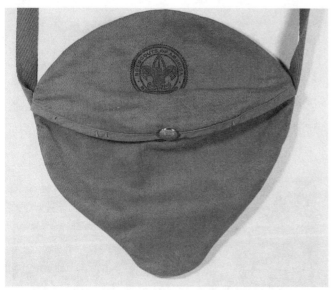

A Boy Scouts canteen holder has a personal family memory so it is special. It is my wife's brother's canteen holder, but all Boy Scout items are collectible. This would likely bring $5-$10 at auction. .... **$5-$10**

A neat little toy truck trailer from a box lot at an auction is missing its wheels and cab but has nice graphics. There is not much value as is, but maybe it is still worth $5. It would be worth a lot more to someone with the cab. **$5**

This Ertl BN Farmall, a recent gift from a friend, was purchased at a church bazaar for a few dollars. It will retain the value of $20+ for some time and go up from there. Boxes for the tractors increase their value, as mentioned earlier. .... **$20+**

A very collectible series of tractors is the FFA Collector Series made for different states and different FFA groups. The one shown is the third tractor issued by the Michigan FFA Foundation, issued in 1995 and sold only through Quality Farm and Fleet stores at that time. These tractors came in a completely closed cardboard box, with a certificate of authenticity and markings to authenticate the toy tractor. Due to the limited production of these tractors and the crossover interest generated by the FFA logo, they have really gone up in value. I have sold many online for up to $100, with most selling from $60 and up. Of course, the 8N is a very special little tractor in its own right and I know this would sell well. It is in our own collection. .... **$60-$100**

Some early pool balls are in the VanAlstine home. There are also a wonderful childhood game of Pick-up sticks, a tin lithographed top, a large spool, a crock, and an old pickle jar full of wooden blocks. My mother worked for Blockcraft Corp. in Cedar Springs, Mich., and may have painted some of the blocks on the table. I have sold individual wooden blocks for $5 each from our former antique store, and tops for $25. The Pick-up sticks should bring $10 if all present. The crocks are fairly common versions and would sell for about $10-$25 each. (Photo in color section) .... **$5-$25 each**

This lunch box is one of my personal favorite farm collectibles. It shows the romantic ideals of farm life around a barn. It is a fine example of tin lithography. .... **$50+**

This toy train car is not a farm collectible per se, but is special if you raise barley or hops for the brewing industry. It was a personal gift more than 35 years ago from my dear German friend, Gerd Dallmann, and has been cherished since. It used to be on my N gauge rail system but I have saved it since selling my railway interests to others...**$20**

A Marx Sparkling Tank is an exceptional example of colorful tin lithography. It winds up and sparks while traveling across the floor. It has the box, as well. *Lewis Collection* .... **$100+**

Structo brand was a huge manufacturer of toy trucks in the 1950s and most of us who are baby boomers owned at least one. I played with my Structo truck (a cab and a trailer) until it was nearly worn out. This nice example of a gas truck resembles my father's real truck from the 1950s. This one has a friction motor to drive the rear wheels. *Lewis Collection*.. **$75+**

A bicycle was one of the main items a farm child enjoyed. This one holds flowers in the VanAlstine landscape today. Most of the older bicycles still sell for a very reasonable price. One can often pick them up at sales for $10-$25 in decent shape. Of course, some of the early models command far more if a collector is bidding on it. ..... **$10-$25**

A reproduction of Barnum's Animals Crackers sand pail is not especially old, but is one of my wife's favorites. It is a fun little item and, of course, the original would be worth quite a bit. But this is still a colorful addition to a child's toy or tin collection. .... $5-$10

A nice safe rubber lamb kept the child company at times. This one was made by Rempel Enterprises of Akron, Ohio. *Lewis Collection* .... $10-$15

These little noise makers that sound like a sheep and a cow were sure hits for young farm children. The sheep version is older. *Lewis Collection* .... $10-$20 each

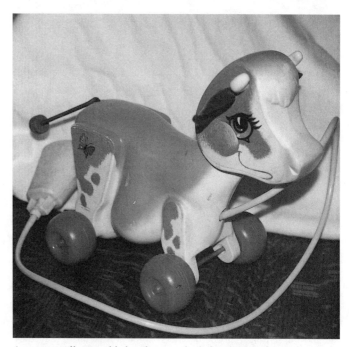

A cow to pull around is handy once the infant is out of the crib. I purchased this Fisher-Price cow new in 1974-75 for my first son. It has been used by both boys, and is now a favorite of our nieces and grand-nieces. *Lewis Collection* .... $20+

Some blocks will be used by children to build mansions and barns and such. These blocks likely were made in Cedar Springs, Mich., in the early 1950s by Blockcraft. Blocks sell for $1 to at least $5 each. *Lewis Collection*..**$1-$5 each**

These little stamped steel farm animals were a recent field find at an estate sale and are unknown to me. Likely made by a small tool and die operation or made in a home shop, they are nice folk examples of farm animals. One could build an entire collection on just farm animals from various companies and folk artists. *Lewis Collection*.......... **$10/set**

Chapter Five:

Farm Implements

This chapter is an introduction to non-tractor implements and their collectibility. Some of the early three-point and two-point hitch implements made for tractors from 1930-65 are also collectible but are only briefly covered in this book. I would refer readers to another book published by Krause Publications, the *Encyclopedia of American Farm Implements & Antiques*, by C. H. Wendel, published in 1997. This provides for a complete and detailed coverage of virtually every important farm implement of the same time period as covered in this book. However, this chapter shows in more detail how many of these implements are used by collectors and what makes certain items more or less valuable than other items.

Over the past 35-40 years, collectors have purchased cream separators to become garden flower pots, scalding kettles for the same purpose, windmills as decorations, one-row cultivators to set in the yard, scythes to hang on the garage wall, hog scrapers because they looked interesting even though most did not know what they were, and wool carders. Most of these functional items are not being purchased to be used, but simply to be admired.

Of course, some one-row cultivators get used and some implements are making a comeback, as others want to dabble in older agricultural technology. However, most of these things are now collectible due to their age and general difficulty to find in good condition. What makes a farm implement collectible? Like advertising items, ability to display the item is very important. A hog scalding kettle is easy to display in a rural setting by building a two-post mount for it in the front yard. Then throw in some potting soil (composted sheep manure in our case) and petunias, and one is all set for a nice flowerpot. Most urban households do not have the space for a hog scalding pot so they are doomed to be part of rural Americana. But do not buy one online or the shipping will drain your bank account in a hurry.

This leads to two of the biggest downfalls of many farm implement collectibles: weight and bulk. I have been involved in the dairy sector since birth (or a minute or two thereafter). I have always liked cream separators as a collectible, since dabbling in antiques and collectibles for the past 35-plus years. However, most of the separators are overlooked at farm auctions due to weight and bulk. People cannot easily haul them home from the sale. It is that simple. Last summer, my wife and I found a great fanning mill in nearly perfect shape and nearly bought it. But I realized that it could only be displayed in the barn and not the house (but see an example of one turned into a table later in this book). This is true of so many farm implements. Most are too large, heavy, or bulky to display in the home. It is exactly this reason that keeps the cost on most of these items under $100. I have passed up many $10 separators. Not if in perfect condition with all the goodies, but the common DeLaval models with parts or tubs missing.

But people who want larger farm implements are creative. They have certainly learned that an antique plow looks great in the rock garden or that a 1940s manure spreader makes a wonderful flowerbed if dirt is added. Large crosscut saws adorn the sides of many houses or garages. Large equipment simply sits proudly in the lawn, with landscaping all around it. My wife and her family totally restored a windmill for a yard decoration. It is functional, too, but was done mainly for the nostalgic reasons of keeping part of Americana alive. I have included a number of photographs from one great collection, owned by David and Kelley VanAlstine, showing creative decorating with farm implements.

Cost of transportation and space for display become the overriding concerns for collectors of these items. These implements do not often bring large sums of money, but instead remain one of the few bargains in collector circles. But they are only bargains if you have space for them, and can properly display them and keep them from further deterioration. A recent purchase by Kelley VanAlstine well documents the issue. She was at a local farm auction and purchased the New Idea hay loader shown in this chapter for only $2, the opening bid. The hay loader actually was in fully restorable condition and nearly usable as purchased. However, there were few people at the auction to purchase implements and it is such a bulky item most could not transport it. VanAlstine had access to an implement delivery truck, so she purchased the loader. It now is displayed at their home, amid a veritable museum of farm implements and farm collectibles.

Values of Farm Implements

A 26" steel wheel with eight spokes...$15.50

Two steel wheels measuring four feet in diameter, according to the listing, both rusted...$25

A pair of 43" wheels. $15

A pair of 44" wheels. $15

A single 26 1/2" wheel. $13

A gorgeous cast iron implement seat marked "Adriance Buckeye." This seat was in extra clean condition and I would question if these are being reproduced. The seat simply looked brand new. I recently sold a "forecart" for horse-drawn implements made in the 1990s with very similar seats. The seat was pretty but maybe not old. The seller claimed it was a true antique and very old...................................$100

An unmarked common steel implement seat with five holes in an "arrow design." Again, the seller claimed it was an antique tractor seat and that it may be iron or steel. It was clearly steel.................$10

A "Dains" cast iron farm implement seat weighing 12 pounds and measuring 14" across and 14" deep. The Dains was written on the back of the seat and it had been painted and was crudely cast. $60

A salesman sample single-bottom walking plow was a most unique item. The plow was 19 3/4" from handles to hitch, with 7 1/2" wooden handles and original paint. There were no markings representing any company or any proof of originality for this item. Some type of provenance would have likely increased bidder interest, as would a brand marking. $495

A salesman sample for an "antique hay baler," actually a hay compactor used prior to portable balers, was even more unusual. The seller claimed it to be from a mid-1800s estate and indicated the markings of "SW" were on the item. This is a lot of money to spend without some further documentation as to provenance and originality, but folks sure liked this item. $2,025

A pressed steel seat for a farm implement not marked but similar to many I-H seats. The shipping was high. $11

A seat claimed to be cast iron marked either 731 or 781. The seat may have been pressed steel instead of cast iron and it had a small crack in the metal. $10

This Studebaker No. 3 Farm Wagon was the real deal. This wagon frame also included a nice grain box with sideboard extensions. It was in nice condition and ready to hitch. I do not have shipping information but I am sure it was a "pick-up" only item. See a similar one in the final chapter showing advertisements for one from 1905. ....$1,225

An Ontario Drill sold first at a huge antique implement auction. It brought the low bid of only $10 "as the first item sold," something that often happens at farm sales. This was the Yoder semi-annual farm sale that always includes dozens of horse-drawn items and attracts hundreds of buyers, Amish and non-Amish, to compete for these items. The next items shown are from this sale. The sale was held for two days in Mt. Pleasant, Mich. $10

An Oliver Drill. $25

A nicely restored McCormick (IHC) corn binder, the "high of the sale" implement, sold for $950. (See the final chapter for a reprinted advertisement for this item). **$950**

Assorted eveners sold for $5-$32, and the neck yokes sold for $5-$15. The tongue with eveners only sold for $10. I sold one a year ago for more than $100 at my own farm auction. ......**$5-$32**

A dump rake. **$55**

An old bobsled and one-horse fills sold for **$120** and a John Deere Van Brunt steel grain drill sold for $75. ....**$75 and $120**

A Papec silo filler sold for $65. But see the interview with Art Smith about what a Papec sold for at one of his auctions when only one was available............. **$65**

A decent riding cultivator. **$65**

Two large steel wheels from "an Amish farm" measuring 25" high with double spoke design and 12 spokes each with a 5" tread.......**$70**

A seeder box marked American Harrow Co., Detroit, Michigan and Windsor, Ontario A 70, with a patent date of 1876 and 1878 did not bring any bids. This was a nice item but faces two problems: shipping costs and display space. **$25**

A small two-gang disk. **$75**

A multiple-hole implement seat (26 holes in two roles with a crossroad pattern in the center of the seat, typical for I-H). Shipping was $8.50 for this steel seat. **$20**

The set of old bobsled runners brought $35. An interesting item to the right is the "stone boat," designed to be pulled behind horses or a tractor to pick of stones in a field. This one sold for a surprising $110... **$35 and $110**

A small two-section drag sold for $60 and the old spring tooth drag sold for only $10. ....**$10 and $60**

The red cutter box in the background sold for $225; the New Idea corn shredder sold for only $120; the John Deere 2-row planter with missing parts sold for $55; and, the nice hand corn sheller sold for $45. Shellers always sell well as collectors like them for home display.
.... **$225, $120, $55, $45**

A very old bobsled brought the decent price of $250..................**$250**

A second bobsled sold for $90 with two tongues. **$90**

A Mohr walking plow from a Greenville, Mich., manufacturer sold for $125 ready to use and a spike tooth drag sold for $40............... **$40, $125**

A primitive spike tooth cultivator sold for only $10 and a primitive furrower to match sold for $5 with broken handles. These two items were well aged and likely on their way to a garden spot. ....**$5 and $10**

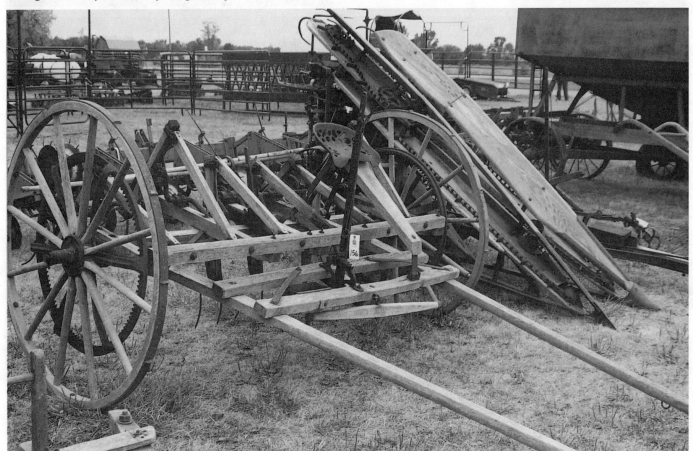

A beautiful old hay tedder with the left tire "flat" but in otherwise excellent working condition and with a cast iron seat sold for a mere $85. This same item is shown in the advertising items reprinted in the final chapter from a 1905 magazine. The seat alone was worth the price. **$85**

A nice older John Deere corn binder, above and right, was not restored but in working order. **$350**

A walking furrower sold for $15 and the beater cultivator shown behind it sold for $10..**$10 nd $15**

A Papec silo filler shows some information in close-ups, below.... **$100**

A nice riding McCormick (IHC) disk. **$180**

Close-up of Oliver Plow

A primitive forecart for horse hitch items. **$20**

An Oliver sulky plow may have been the "steal" of the day. In very nice original condition, the plow sold for only $125. Most of the time, these fetch a far better price, and $300-$500 is not uncommon. **$125**

A small Conestoga Manure Spreader was not old, but interesting.
....**$1,600**

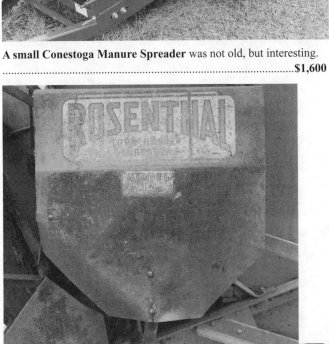

A red/gray bobsled with fills. **$140**

A Rosenthal Corn Husker/Shredder made in Milwaukee, Wis., was the most unique item at the sale. This nice old machine was a Model 40, Serial Number 22285 made in "Milwaukee 14, Wisc" by the Rosenthal Corn Husker Co. I thought this would be, and should be, the high selling item, but it only made it to $450 before the gavel went down. Of all the original condition items, this was the finest, waiting to be restored. But again, the price stayed down due to the size and weight of the item and the fact that most people cannot move such an item easily
...................................**$450**

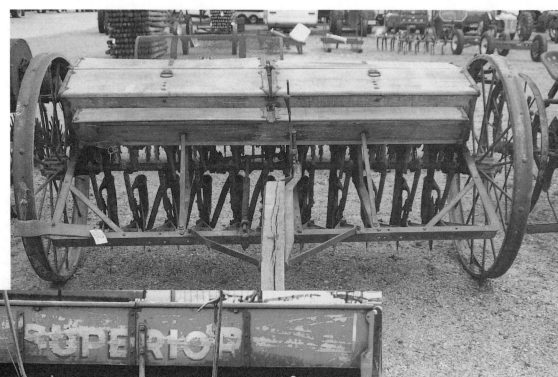

A Superior grain drill,
front and back. **$35**

A very rough McCormick (IHC) New Ideal mower...**$7.50**

This McCormick (IHC) riding cultivator was an item with many competitive bids, selling to an Amish buyer. **$435**

The favorite drill at the sale commanded $220 for this old Van Brunt on steel. **$220**

This Eagle brand silo filler sold for $195. It could be driven with either a power take off shaft or a pulley drive.
.... **$195**

An old New Idea ground-driven spreader on two wheels with original good paint......................... **$150**

A spreader on four steel wheels...**$100**

This International Harvester four-wheel Model 200 was prized by buyers. **$800**

Another good spreader was the two-wheel New Idea with original paint and good wood. **$410**

A repainted Case in nice shape sold for only $120. The gem of manure spreaders was this New Idea Model #8, selling for $1,750 and fully restored in working order. This is an excellent spreader and was nicely restored. .... **$120 and $1,750**

A David Brown four-wheel on rubber...$325

An early grading scoop for use with horses...............................$100

A John Deere sulky plow sold for $425, what the Oliver should have brought, too. $425

A McCormick #7 silage cutter was in great condition. $800

A John Deere No. 4 mower received a bid of $675 and was a no sale. $600

A McCormick (IHC) totally rebuilt four-foot cut mower (single horse) marked MA684 on castings that received a bid for $600 was also a no sale. In addition, a McCormick (IHC) totally rebuilt Model 9 mower received a bid of $925 and was a no sale. All of the foregoing mowers were returned to the shop in Ohio that rebuilds them. The single horse one is very rare and would make a nice mower for the hobby horse farmer. ....$500+

A four-wheel New Idea spreader on steel was owned by David VanAlstine's grandfather. The John Deere B in the background is shown in Chapter 12. The following few implement photos are all from the VanAlstine collection mentioned elsewhere in the book. **$75**

A John Deere two-row corn planter hides among the willows at the VanAlstine farm. **$25**

A Champion brand potato digger in the VanAlstine collection. **$100**

A John Deere Van Brunt grain drill, above and left, in the VanAlstine landscaping.
.... **$200-$300**

A nice old Massey-Harris side delivery rake at the VanAlstine farm was formerly owned by Kelley VanAlstine's grandfather, Hugh Strey of Remus, Mich. ....**$150-$200**

A New Idea hay loader was recently purchased by Kelley VanAlstine near Evart, Mich., for $2. No one came to buy implements at a general farm auction that day. This was actually in working order when parked in the yard. ....**$200-$300**

An Oliver two-bottom plow in the VanAlstine collection. ....**$75-$100**

Wheels from a John Deere Model 290 horse drawn corn planter at the VanAlstine farm.

A nice restored John Deere Sulky plow. The owner paid $450 for it a few years ago and it would bring up to $600 today. .... **$450-$600**

A cast iron implement seat in the Art Smith collection marked #147 with no other marks. .... **$100+**

Various items in the back of this pickup were sold at the Yoder consignment sale mentioned in the previous chapter. The large set of wheels brought $55, the small set of wheels brought $35, the buyer spent $8 on the cultivator and the grinding stone, above, sold for $45 .... **$8, $35,$55,$45**

A repainted furrower at the VanAlstine farm.
.............................$20-$30

A Wolverine Deluxe hand-powered walking cultivator made by Fuller Mfg. Co. of Swartz Creek, Minn. It is in fine condition. VanAlstine Collection................ **$100+**

A four-wheeled manure spreader on steel is used as a lawn decoration about two miles from our farm. This is one of a few I drive by daily on my commute.
....................................**$50**

A windmill without a fan on a farmstead near our farm. Since working on this book, I have noticed more than 20 windmills in the 19-mile drive from our farm to my office at the college. Most of them blend into the landscape similar to this one, or the fans are gone, or they have been built around, or trees have taken them over. Windmills often exceed $2,000. ....**$2,000**

An old pump head could go in the garden chapter. But I thought it was a nice follow-up to the windmill. VanAlstine Collection
....**$10-$15 in this condition**

A nice riding cultipacker on the Nerbonne farm. The seat, left, alone is worth at least $25 and the unit should bring $75 at a farm auction.
....**$75**

An American brand corn planter made in Burr Oak, Mich., sold at the Yoder sale, in fine shape.....................................**$17.50**

A nice pair of buggy lanterns (kerosene) also sold. ......**$27.50 each**

A tractor-mounted International mower on the Nerbonne farm. If all there, it is worth only about $25. These have little trade value and are not really too collectible, unlike the riding mowers. Of course, it would be a real find if needed to fill a collection for someone, and they would be willing to spend more in that case. **$25**

An early John Deere trailer-plow sitting behind the Nerbonne barn. Trailer plows normally sell for $50-$150 and are often used in gardens today. ....**$50-$150**

This unique walk-behind seeder that is on the Nerbonne farm is one of the finest farm implements I found. Terry bought it at a farm auction for only $25-$35 a few years ago and it is extremely nice. I would value it at a minimum of $100. The close-ups show the cog mechanism and the seeding chart. It works just fine. I would think it would be better pulled by a horse, full of seed, but there is no place in front of the wheel to hook it up. I guess an enterprising farmer would be able to use an evener and hook it to the frame of the stand but this seems awkward to me. This could go in the garden or implement section, but I put it here. ....$100+

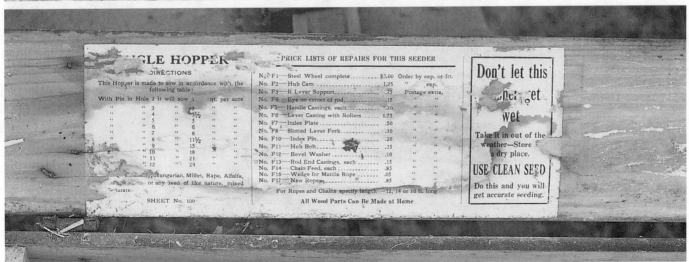

GLE HOPPER

DIRECTIONS

This Hopper is made to sow in accordance with the following table:

With Pin in Hole 2 it will sow 1   qt. per acre
"   "   3   2
"   "   4   3½
"   "   5   5
"   "   6   6
"   "   7   8
"   "   8   11½
"   "   9   15
"   "   10   18
"   "   11   21
"   "   12   24

... Hungarian, Millet, Rape, Alfalfa, ... or any seed of like nature, mixed separate.

SHEET No. 100

PRICE LISTS OF REPAIRS FOR THIS SEEDER

No. F1—Steel Wheel complete	$3.00	Order by exp. or frt.
No. F2—Hub Cam	1.25	" exp.
No. F3—R Lever Support	.75	Postage extra,
No. F4—Eye on center of rod	.15	
No. F5—Handle Castings, each	.20	
No. F6—Lever Casting with Rollers	1.75	
No. F7—Index Plate	.50	
No. F8—Slotted Lever Fork	.10	
No. F10—Index Pin	.20	
No. F11—Hub Bolt	.15	
No. F12—Bevel Washer	.10	
No. F13—Rod End Castings, each	.15	
No. F14—Chain Feed, each	.85	
No. F16—Wedge for Manila Rope	.05	
No. F17—New Ropes	.85	

For Ropes and Chains specify length—12, 14 or 16 ft. long

All Wood Parts Can Be Made at Home

Don't let this ... get wet

Take it in out of the weather—Store in a dry place.

USE CLEAN SEED

Do this and you will get accurate seeding.

An International-Harvester wood wheel grain drill is still used by Nerbonne and pulled with his John Deere 60. I have shown the drill and some close-ups of details. Value would be from a few dollars to a few hundred, according to sales data given earlier in this chapter. I would guess it would easily bring $300 at a good consignment auction of horse equipment. **$300**

Chapter Six:
Farm Tools

This chapter concentrates on the smaller tools of the farming trade: wrenches, hammers, shovels, rakes, and hoes. There are books dealing with some of these items on the market, However, there is nothing specifically about farming tools and some of the special wrenches and items needed to repair farm implements, such as the items needed to repair chains and sickle bars, and specialty items such as hay knives and hay hooks. Early advertising illustrations are often the only source of information about these tools. They are used liberally in Chapter 14 to show readers many of the possible finds in the tool category. Krause Publications has an earlier work written by C. H. Wendel, *Encyclopedia of Antique Tools & Machinery,* published in 2001, that details many of the tools included in this section. It is recommended background reading for the novice collector.

Wrenches from John Deere, Ford, Fordson, or DeLaval all bring a premium price to collectors of farm items, but are also in demand by collectors of tools and hardware items. This is a driving force in the pricing of tools. There is competition with other collectors for the same item. Add to that the brand value of an item, and the cost goes up even more. It is not unusual to find simple wrenches or pliers going for five to 10 times the normal value due to the presence of a brand name or trademark on the item, such as Winchester.

On the other hand, many tools are so uniquely suited only to the farm that most collectors do not recognize them or know what they were used for. That, in turn, keeps the values down. For instance, in researching this book, I was shocked to see the general utility fencing tool that I still use was invented in the late 1800s and looking almost identical. Yet, most urbanites would not know this is a fence tool or its history. Actually, many of the tools we still use on the farm were invented in the late 1800s or early 1900s and have been modified rather little over the past century. Fence stretching-tools are another interesting sideline to collect. Early stretchers have been around for more than 100 years commercially and most of these would be passed over at auctions.

One item I was thinking about the other day is the common grease gun. Oil cans and oilers are a common collectible and are gaining interest in many fields. I just paid $10 each for a collection of about 30 oilers for fishing reels. However, I do not know of any collectors going after early grease guns. How do you display them? For those of us still farming with a huge pole barn, an old grease gun on each post would be interesting, to say the least. The grease gun is such an important tool to the farmer. What implement does not need grease? A good grease gun has saved many a repair bill later by properly lubricating the equipment or implement. Also, some tractors came with a grease gun, such as the Farmall Cub, making it of interest to collectors.

Another item that is unique to farming, and only from the past 50 years or so, is the bulk tank wrench. Each bulk tank for milk had to have a wrench to couple and uncouple the bulk milk truck's hose for emptying the product of the dairy. I have had about five bulk tanks and all the wrenches were different. I am sure this would make an interesting "modern" collectible. It would be an item most people would overlook, as it is a rather bizarre looking large wrench unknown to all but dairy farmers or milk haulers.

Marked items will be of greater value than unmarked items, as a general rule. Many functional items also carried the brand name for the tool's intended use, and this adds greatly to collector value today. I have owned stainless steel buckets that say DeLaval, wrenches that say Fordson, pliers that say Winchester, Keen Kutter axes, Stanley planes, and New Idea tools. Any of these brand names would increase the item's value greatly.

Many of the above tools are listed in general collector price guides and some have even had complete books dedicated to them. The history of Winchester, John Deere, or Keen Kutter can fill many books. Please consult any of the general references for a general guide to tools. Then do the "value-added" for the brand names desired, usually doubling the value of an item if not adding even more value.

There are also unusual farm-related items gaining interest in more than one collecting field, such as early chain saws. Crosscut and buck saws have been collected for some time now. However, now folks are starting to collect early chain power saws and related items. The chain saw became a permanent fixture on every farm when it was invented and should be seen as a farm tool. As with many tools, this one is sought after by more than one group. But it is not real popular yet as a collectible, so the costs are still down on most items. Old saws themselves often go for a mere $5-$10 at farm auctions. Bargains will be had, if one keeps a watch for these items.

I had written the above paragraph not knowing that I would find the David VanAlstine collection of chain saws. It turns out that a neighbor has collected saws for some time now and a few of his saws are shown in this section. He informed me that even though the saws were invented in the 1920s, with even earlier attempts being made, the idea of power saws did not become popular in West Michigan until the 1940s and early 1950s. Thus, one will not find the earliest saws in all regions, due to different adoption rates of the technology by the buying public. However, his collection of chain saws and the way they have been displayed shows that some have already started a very serious collection of power saws and related items, such as the early weed whacker.

Not long after writing this section, I viewed an hour-long special on the History Channel about early power lawn and garden tools. It had an excellent segment on power saws and weed whips. The special also covered the growing interest in older equipment to a small degree. But it did a great job of covering the invention of all types of this common farmstead and suburban equipment. I would highly recommend viewing this segment if interested in older lawn and garden equipment, and the history of power saw development.

Tools and implements designed for barn use is another category to keep an eye open for, if you have a place to display the items. This includes everything from the common wheelbarrow to the feed cart used for delivering grain or silage to farm animals in the barn. Also the stanchions used to hold in the animals are collectible, especially if all-wood construction. Early watering devices, oiling devices, and cooling devices are also collectible. The problem, again, is space for display. I have shown some of these items in this chapter and also in the next chapter dealing with horse hardware and stable items.

Another item related to tools, due to its functional use, is the category of oils, greases, and sprays. As mentioned before, oilers are collectible, grease guns may become so, and early sprayers are also in demand. The actual oil can, grease tubes, and spray containers are in demand if the graphics are good and the container is clean. Pricing also depends on brand demand to a large extent, with Mobil and Standard Oil products in great demand. One thing to be aware of are laws related to selling and transporting cans with any liquids still in them, and the proper disposal of any contents. Most auctioneers will no longer sell these items, due to federal and state laws regarding insecticides and pesticides. However, a fine old DDT container (empty) from 1940 produced by Standard Oil makes a novel addition to any farm collection. An oil can will bring anywhere from $5-$50 or more, depending on age, rarity, and condition.

Going back in history, most of the major oil companies also produced harness oil for the horse trade. We own a fine example of a Standard Oil Eureka Harness Oil Can and shipping crate. It was shown in Chapter 3. I paid $100 for this item in an antique store in rural Michigan in 1997. I am sure it is worth at least three times that amount today. There were also little saddle soap cans and harness soap cans that make a nice addition to a farm collectibles collection, which also crosses over into our next category, horse hardware.

Values of Farm Tools

Rathbone's Farm Implement Wrench Book is one of the leading sources for information on early wrenches and is itself collectible. Online auction prices for this book usually are from $45-$60. This is a "must-have" item if you are trading significantly in wrenches and, as most of the listings say, "one wrench will pay for this volume." .... $45-$60

A dozen nice old wrenches, but not properly described in the listing, other than one I-H wrench. This lot of nice early wrenches sold for $10.50, a good deal for sure. This shows the value of properly describing items for sale and also the deflationary results of "multiple item listings." This is what I learned years ago listing fishing items for sale. I can buy tackle boxes online for a few dollars or a few hundred, and then break them up and triple my money. As a general rule, large lots lose money for the seller and are bargains. There are exceptions to this rule, of course, but it is something to keep in mind looking for things such as wrenches. Even the multiple lots of catalogs discussed indicate this same deflationary result. $10.50

Wrench marked D and #ED51, open end, one end angled. The listing person was quite knowledgeable but could not identify this particular wrench. It did not seem to hurt this item. $26

Farm implement clevis wrench, three openings, manufacturer unknown. $25

Vulcan Plow Company Clevis wrench No. 101. ....$22.50

J8 Frost & Wood implement wrench. $9

I-H F354 implement wrench. $4.25

No. 5 S implement wrench....$3

Frost & Woods implement wrench(Smith Falls, Canada) #378..$13

Unmarked pressed steel seat with round holes. The shipping would cost even more in most cases..$11

Another seat marked 731 or 781 on the bottom. Shipping costs really keep prices of implement seats down for online auctions unless the seat is very rare and clearly identified..$10

MM E13 implement wrench. $10

I-H R319R implement wrench...$15

A Vulcan implement wrench did not sell for its opening bid of $7.99, but the same seller received $7.99 for a Deering implement wrench the same day. $7

Rathbone's book sold for $47.55..$47.55

Unidentified wrench...$8

A large 1905 Keystone farm implement steel wheel did not sell or have any bids online due to the high cost of shipping such an item.....

Four wrenches. $7

Six wrenches. $5

A primitive hay knife brought $10.50 after being re-listed online for the second time, lowering the opening bid from $14.99 to $9.99. ....$10.50

Three corn dryers, early steel models for drying full ears of seed corn. $23.50

Five corn dryers sold after being viewed 111 times. These were of a wire construction and held 24 ears of corn, much lighter than the three in the listing above, which only held 10 ears of corn. $27

An old calf/goat collar and bell. The bell was 3 1/2" x 2 1/2" by 4" and appeared to be steel. $5

A set of cast iron ice tongs. $10

A nice tail docking device for sheep sold for only $2 with only one bid, as the seller did not know what the item was and listed it only as an unknown primitive farm tool. The tool had wooden handles and a cutting/cauterizing unit. $2

A pair of iron 12" sheep shears. The seller claimed them to be an antique, more than 100 years old, made of cast iron. But they were common steel shears. The seller also had some negative feedback, indicating past problems in selling. Actually, these same shears sell for a little more at many farm auctions.......................................$5.50

The "antique Amish farm wagon hub" was another example of exaggerated listings. It did not reach its reserve price and had a bid of $32. This hub had actually been turned into a lamp, which is something the Old Order Amish certainly would not be using. It was a common wooden hub, likely fairly old, but not Amish. It was the type of hub found on covered wagons, stagecoaches, and common farm wagons until the advent of steel hubs and running gears. $30

An early pair of steel ice tongs, 12" wide by 24" long. $4.25

Two beautiful metal and wood pulleys. They appeared to be in excellent shape and were fairly early examples of the type of pulleys used on hay slings. $6

A four-quart farm cream carrier, 11 1/2" high. It was steel, not stainless, and had one small dent. The handle was marked "Liquid 4 Qt."...$23

A nice little three-legged dairy milking stool made of steel, 12" high, new old stock. $20

A seamed Babson Bros. Surge milker unit without the cover. The seller mentioned it would make a nice planter. $5.50

Three nice farm tools. The lot included a small steel frying pan, a pair of blackened sheep shears made in England marked "27 England," and a common hay hook with a wooden handle...........$30

A "scrimshaw" whalebone corn husker and five buttons was a most unusual item. Our interest is in the corn husker. It did indeed appear to be a tool identical to manufactured corn huskers made out of bone, with a leather thong to hold the implement, even with adjustment holes. My guess is that it was not a corn husker but a knotting device for net making, similar to many I have in my own collection, and it came from Long Island, an area not known for its corn growing. I also am certain the bone, which was rounded somewhat, would have simply slid off the ear corn and not grabbed the kernels as the wood/metal huskers do. $50

A small calf/goat bell (3 1/2" x 3 1/2") was listed as a horse or wagon bell (horses do not wear bells, unless mounted on collars, normally). It appeared to be a simple steel bell. $5.50

A very nice farm hay spear to lift hay into the mow from the wagon (see illustrations in advertisements and a photo of my own version) did not meet a reserve price and only brought one bid. The problem was the shipping. The seller did a great job describing the item and had nice photos. It simply cost too much to ship a piece of steel 19" by 36". I did like the mentioning that the item would make a nice garden trellis, a neat idea for hay spears.

A 60" bull lead cane made by the James Manufacturing Co. came with an end loop that was used to lead bulls safely. It seems like a bargain for this unique item, dating from the early 1900s. $20

A simple galvanized pail. It was a 2 1/2-gallon pail with dents on the rim and bottom. These pails are very common at farm auctions and I was surprised it even sold. It just shows that items online go to such a wide audience that folks without access in one region will bid on common items from another region...$3

An unmarked milk-stripping pump sold with DeLaval equipment. This was a glass unit placed directly on the teat, and the metal pump on the other end would strip the teat of milk for testing for cream content..$5

A common hand scythe or sickle with a wooden handle. The handle was marked "Little Giant, North Wayne Tool Co., Oakland, ME USA." This was a sickle with a 12" blade. Postage on this item was $6.50, making its actual cost $18 to the buyer. **$11.50**

A 6" by 4" cow bell, common steel type. An interesting trick of the seller was to tie an old piece of baler twine to the bell to make it look older. But the twine clearly did not go "with the bell," as it was merely some frayed twine added for "color." **$15.50**

An antique grain measure from the 1870s, according to the seller, was a very nice item. The 1870 date on the side was likely a patent date, but still gives some idea of vintage. The wooden measure had metal strapping and was 14 1/2" across the top, 44" girth, and 7" deep. The item did not sell as reserve was not met...................... $12+

A "primitive dairy separator" listing was another attempt at duping the public. It was actually a simple, low quality, dairy strainer. This strainer was made of steel, not stainless, placed on top of the dairy can or milk tank opening to strain out hair or dirt, and not to separate cream. It sold for only $5, its value at a farm auction. By the time the buyer received the item, an additional $7 would be invested in shipping, making this item too expensive compared to farm sales...$5

Two nice wool carders marked "The Only Genuine Old Whittemore Patent Improved No. 8 Wool L.S. Watson & Co., Leicester, Mass." surprised me by not selling. I have shown some identical to these from our own collection. These received a high bid of only $9.50 on a reserve auction and did not sell. The reserve was $24.95, a fair value in my opinion. $25

A real corn husker, not whalebone, made of metal and leather. Many examples follow from the Art Smith Collection. $7

A hand flail made of a wooden handle and the flail piece of wood for dried beans. This was a beautiful item, with nice patina on both the wooden handle and the wooden flail piece. Shipping was $7.95, a bit high, it seems, for parcel post for this item....................................$9

Seven glass waterers for chicks. These waterers have become collectibles the past 20 years and were used to water baby chickens. These waterers were commonly used in chicken operations in the 1940s-1960s. They look like giant "juicers" at first blush. **$13**

An oversized oak nail keg, 19" high, 13" across, and 46" center girth. It was in nice shape and received the attention of 89 lookers. Shipping was $14 for this item, making it cost about $35. This is a bit higher than at farm auctions but still a fair price for this hard to find item (especially in clean condition). **$20.50**

A common hay saw or hay knife that is 37" long and 2 1/2" wide with two wooden handles (one on end, one on side). I sold two of these at a recent farm auction and they usually bring about this amount. This one still had paint on the wooden handles. **$15.50**

A bull ring bull-towing device the seller thought was a grabbing tool. This one was shaped like a gun with a trigger on one end and had two metal grasping claws on the opposite end.....................**$21.50**

The Cyclone seeder I mentioned, that the seller claimed was Amish, sold for $24. This was not Amish nor was it necessarily old. They are still available throughout the farm lands of the Midwest for grass seeding and spreading fall pasture mix, clover, and other grass crops (see details of one shown a little later). **24**

A "foot adz," an adz shaped like a foot on a 31" handle, was a bit older. These are still available and one cannot date anything like this without an examination of the item. This may or may not have been "primitive," as claimed. **$8**

Two hay hooks, a common red-handled one and a blacksmith version of an all-metal hook. Again, the listing seller called them primitive which they are not. However, they may be from the 1940s or 1950s. **$6**

A farm lot of items included two hog scrapers, a bull nose ring, assorted hog nose rings, and a hand held corn husker. **$7.50**

An old scythe anvil and hammer, made by a blacksmith known as Dengelstock, was a far different story. These beautiful wrought iron items received nine bids online. Amazingly, the shipping was only $6.50 for these two heavy pieces. These two items were used to sharpen early scythes by driving the anvil into a stump or log and then placing the scythe blade upon it for sharpening with the special hammer. The seller was very complete in the listing and very helpful in explaining the history behind these unique tools. Also, he had owned them for 40 years, giving them some nice provenance. **$46**

A pair of cast iron hand-wrought hinges over 24" long. This was a nice pair of hinges from a farm with the markings UB Co. cast into the hinge in small raised letters..**$22.50**

Two hay rope pulleys (wood and metal) sold for about what they bring at auctions or a little less. They were both in excellent shape. **$11.50**

Two vintage wooden milk stools (homemade). **$22**

A pair of horse clippers by Coates with a patent date of 1897. ......**$5**

A three-legged steel milk stool was in fairly rough shape, not bent but worn. **$29**

A long-handled, hinged two-piece wooden flail was well worn but had a nice patina. Frankly, this looks to me to be a $20 item, at least. I think the August date really hurts prices online.................................**$6**

A nice older hay hook, appears to be cast iron.............................**$15**

A two-man crosscut saw sold for $30 at the large Yoder consignment sale held in Mt. Pleasant, Mich., and a scythe sold for only $6 (in nice shape). Three three-foot levels, mainly newer ones, sold for only $8 the same day. ....**$6-$30**

A nice folding rule was purchased years ago in a "box lot" at a farm auction and is worth at least $20 today. **$20**

A common early box end wrench, showing details of markings. **$5**

A complete set of wrenches by one company: Walden Worcester. I recently purchased these from a collector friend for $5 each, and they should be worth that or even a little more each if sold as a complete set. It is unusual to find such a complete set of wrenches from one company. ....**$5 each**

Some additional wrenches of interest to a collector. The existence of a brand name such as Ford, John Deere, International, or Case increases the values greatly, often commanding up to $50 for certain wrenches. Only a thorough examination of current books on tools will give one a complete understanding of this complex area of farm collectibles. The wrench on the bottom is from "The Sharples Separator Co." and is for a cream separator. The middle wrench is from the Coe's Wrench Company of Worchester, Mass., and has the 1800 L. Coe's Patent. The top wrench is from R.O. Smith & Co. .... **Up to $50 each**

A nice wooden pulley similar to the ones described earlier in the author's collection. This would bring from $10-$20 at an auction, due to its excellent condition. .... **$10-$20**

A barrel-mounted "Black Beauty" corn sheller, in two views, was an easier way to shell ear corn than the hand method. A sheller such as this would sell for $25 or more at auction. .... **$25+**

Corn husking gloves and picks in auctioneer Art Smith's personal collection are shown here. These items are selling for $5-$20 on average, and some of the more unusual ones may command a bit more. The glove with all of the studs, above, is the most unusual one in his collection.**$5-$20**

A collection of old screw jacks.
These do not sell for much more
than $20 at most auctions, but make
for yet another interesting sideline
in collecting. Many have interesting
details and stampings to increase the
beauty of old functional items. *Art
Smith Collection* ....**$20 each**

A screw jack from our farm
and closeup at left. I use it
for its original purpose and
also as a weight to hold
open the chicken coop door
during the daylight hours. ...
.... **$20**

An old Model T jack from the Art Smith collection. **$20**

An early fence-stretching tool. Art Smith Collection...................**$20**

Marked pulley with brass trimming. Art Smith Collection
....**$25+ due to brass trim**

Spokeshave with nice wooden handles. Art Smith Collection ....**$10-$20**

A large one-man cross-cut saw. Art Smith Collection ....**$25-$35**

Saw set tools. Art Smith Collection ....**$10+ each**

An early fence stretching tool. Art Smith Collection .... **$10-$20**

Another milk can and a different version of a hay knife. ..... **$10-$30**

An American Standard corn planter and a hay knife leaning against a milk can at the Smith farm. The corn seeder is worth about $25 and the hay knives sell for anywhere from $10-$30. The painted milk can is only worth a few dollars at auction. Art Smith Collection..................**$10-$30**

A handmade creeper for auto, truck, and tractor repair on the farm. I wasn't sure where to put this, but it fits in the tools category. It is a neat old item, not worth too much, but it should bring at least $20, as it is unique. Art Smith Collection **$20**

A chain repair tool once found on nearly every farm made in Albert Lea, Minn., by Albert Lea Foundry. This is not of great value but is another reminder of how farmers had specialty tools to repair conveyers, manure spreader chains, and other similar items. **$10**

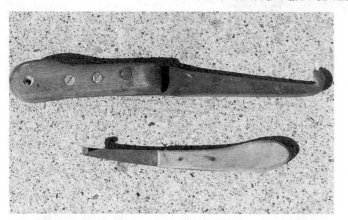

Older and newer hoof picks. The large version is older. Art Smith Collection .... **$5-$10 each**

An ornate old cast pulley from the Art Smith collection. .... **$20+**

Old machete. Art Smith Collection... **$5-$10**

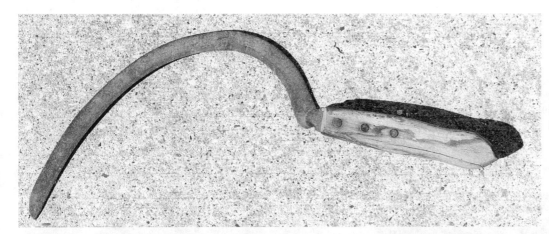

Small hand corn knife. *Art Smith Collection* .... $10-$15

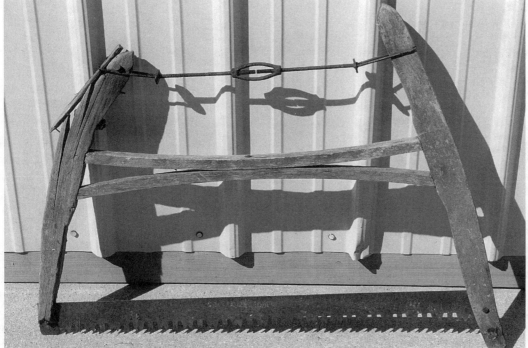

An example of a buck saw. *Art Smith Collection* ....**$10-$25** each.

A set of primitive pruners. *Art Smith Collection* $25

A **Dari-Kool brand bulk tank wrench** found in our old milk house. Lewis Collection .... **$10-$20**

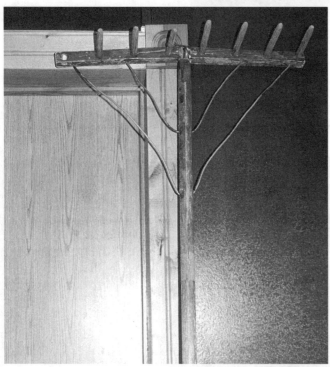

A very nice primitive wooden rake. VanAlstine Collection **$50-$75**

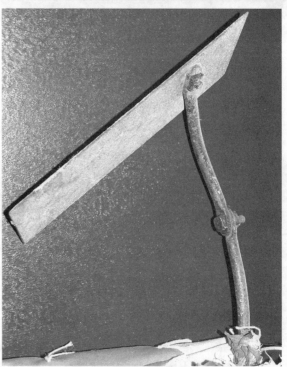

An early metal cement float for flat work. VanAlstine Collection .... **$10-$20**

A **handmade grain scoop** and/or dust pan? Nice primitive piece. VanAlstine Collection **$10**

A Lansing Co. grain bag/milk can mover. These were used for both moving cans and grain bags in the barn. Two photos show details of this collectible made in Lansing, Mich. This likely would bring $35+ at auction. VanAlstine Collection .... **$35+**

Primitive wheelbarrow for moving grain shocks, with a metal wheel. VanAlstine Collection .... **$50+**

Silage fork? An unusual farm fork has a metal band at the fork ends for scraping on cement. My guess is it is a fork designed to clean up silage in a cement manger, but it is smaller than any silage fork I ever used. It would be ideal for handling bark today by landscaping personnel. VanAlstine Collection...$25

This electronic "weed-whacker" is another early lawn tool in the VanAlstine Collection. Also shown is a 1950s chicken waterer. The waterer may bring $10 at auction. The weed-whacker is without trade data but I would expect it to fetch $10-$20 at this time. .... **$10-$20**

This cant hook is an older tool in like-new condition, made locally in Evart, Mich., by a logging tool company. This is not real old. But the company was local and is now out of business, so it makes a nice "local collectible" for someone interested in logging. VanAlstine Collection....................................$25

Early chain saws are displayed on the beams of the VanAlstine garage. David VanAlstine works for a John Deere dealership and is a specialist in small garden tractors and related farm and garden equipment. He developed an interest in chain saws some time ago. He has been saving them for years and picking them up at farm auctions whenever possible. Trading in chain saws is fairly recent, so there is not any real solid pricing information on them. However, the days of the $5 chain saw on the "jewelry wagon" at the farm auction are likely over for good. This is one development that I shall follow for updates in future volumes of this and any related works. The photos here show a wide variety of saws in David's collection, some dating into the 1940s. Some examples are a Mall from 1947 and a Hornet. .... **$10 and up**

A nice older shovel is shown with a totally wooden handle. These clearly predate the more common wood on steel handles on most shovels found today. I even have one with a solid wooden handle without the finger hole carved in it. These will command at least $25 at an auction due to their rarity, maybe more. VanAlstine Collection .... **$25+**

Two very old eveners from the Nerbonne barn. Nice aging and patina would make these in demand to a collector. Also much older hand wrought hardware makes them attractive. .... **$20 each**

Three nicely aged pulleys were found hanging in an old barn. These sell for $5-$15 each, usually. Nerbonne Collection .... **$5-$15**

A primitive sprayer for livestock insecticide and a can to add fluids to an engine. Nerbonne Collection **$5 each**

A very nice Myers brand hay grapple to grab the loose hay from a stack on a hay wagon and lift it up into the barn. This was in the Nerbonne barn when he purchased it years ago. Although these are unique and harder to find now, their value is not high, as there is not a good way to display one for most buyers. See the Art Smith interview for more value details on items such as this.

Another type of hay grapple also from the Nerbonne barn.

An old draw shave without its wooden handles. Hand wrought. Nerbonne Collection .... **$20+**

Nice older corn knife from the Nerbonne Collection. .... **$20-$25**

An even older corn knife and its stamping details from the Nerbonne Collection. .... **$30-$35**

Pulley mechanism from the top of the barn for hay loading into the mows. This mechanism ran on a rail (upside down from the way photographed) and would lift the grapple hooks full of hay and then release them into the mows for stacking. There is little market value but great historical value. Nerbonne Collection

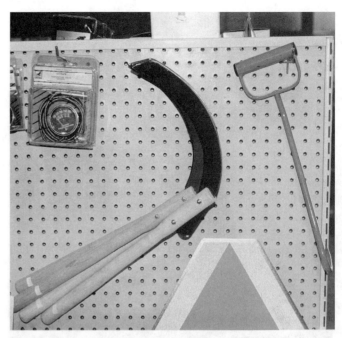

Modern corn knives and a hay hook demonstrate what one can buy at the local farm store. They have not changed much over the years.

A chain lever device found in the Nerbonne barn. .... **$15-$25**

A nice barn shovel, not as old as the pure wooden handled one shown earlier, is still a nice old shovel. *Nerbonne Collection*..... **$20+**

A hay knife found in the Nerbonne barn. .... **$15-$25**

An old fork with a handmade handle. *Nerbonne Collection* ...... **$35+**

A fairly old cant hook. *Nerbonne Collection* .... **$25-$35**

Unknown tool. This appears to be designed to clean a small trough, gutter, or eave. It may also be a cement tool. Please let me know. *Nerbonne Collection*

A very old hand-forged long handled hay hook. *Nerbonne Collection* .... **$25+**

A three-tine hay fork is shown to detail the metal reinforcement on the bottom of the handle. This type of tool is older than the ones with a straight insert into the tool tip. *Nerbonne Collection* .... **$15-$20**

This buck saw has a nice patina, making it worth about $25 at least. *Nerbonne Collection* **$25**

A beautiful old egg crate in its original paint. Photos show details on this nice piece. These sell easily for $25-$35, and one in this condition may bring a premium. *Nerbonne Collection* ...... **$25-$35**

A primitive rake with wood dowels as teeth reinforced with light wire braces. This rake was in the Nerbonne barn. .... **$50+**

Two very old hand-held hay hooks, hand forged, hand carved wooden handles, very heavy duty. *Nerbonne Collection* ... **$25+ each**

Old post hole digger, heavy pipe construction with tooled handle. *Nerbonne Collection* .... **$25-$35**

An older shovel. *Nerbonne Collection* .... **$25+**

A Leach Co. cant hook made in Oshkosh, Wis., in the VanAlstine Collection. .... **$30+**

A primitive barn scraper made by Terry Nerbonne's dad a number of years ago. *Nerbonne Collection* .... **$15-$20**

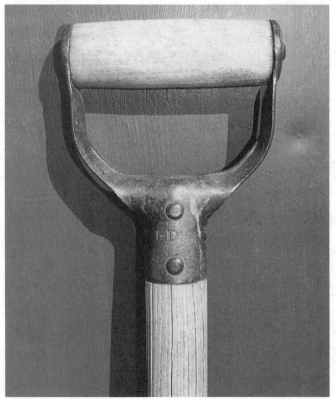

A nice fork, a chicken waterer, and a milk can adorn the porch of this small garden house at the VanAlstine farm. This fork is the reinforced type older than the straight-line insert type, and the details are shown.

A newer long handle shovel and spade are shown for comparison to the older fork. *VanAlstine Collection* .... **$10-$15 each**

A primitive hand-forged hay hook, an old hatchet, and a barn beam drill used to drill holes for the pegs in post and beam construction. The drills sell for $20-$35, the hatchet should bring about the same, and the hay hook from $10-$20. *VanAlstine Collection* .... **$10-$35**

Foot adze and details in the VanAlstine Collection. .... **$25+**

Old pick axe in the VanAlstine Collection. .... **$25+**

A primitive furrower selling at the Yoder auction. **$35**

A wheelbarrow used to carry shocks of grain or corn. *VanAlstine Collection*............. **$50+**

A walking one-row horse drawn cultivator. These usually bring $35-$60 in this condition. VanAlstine Collection...........**$35-$60**

A beautiful work bench, more than 100 years old, purchased by Jerry Paulsen at a farm auction for less than $100. What a nice addition to a workroom. He uses it as his base in restoration work on antique tractors, some of which are shown in that section of the book. **$100+**

A nice pair of woodworking planes in the Paulsen Collection. Planes sell for anywhere from $10 to well over $100, depending on brand, style, and model. These would likely start at $25 each and go from there. ....**25+ each**

A set of woodworking clamps in the Paulsen tool crib. .... **$50+**

A potato planter from the Paulsen Collection. .... **$20-$30**

A nice buck saw in original paint in the Paulsen Collection. .... **$35+ in this shape**

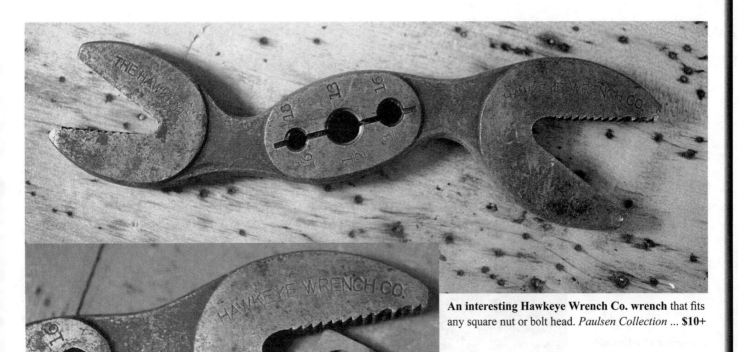

An interesting Hawkeye Wrench Co. wrench that fits any square nut or bolt head. *Paulsen Collection* ... **$10+**

Open end wrench number 677 with an H in a diamond on the other side. *Paulsen Collection* ....**$10+**

Small open end wrench number 25. *Paulsen Collection* .... **$5+**

A number 10 adjustable "Merit" wrench by Stillson Wrench, leaning on a plane on the Paulsen workbench shown earlier, and the details of the wrench. ...**$25**

An early electronic tool of some interest would be this "Guild Sander" made in Syracuse, N.Y. It is at least 40 years old already and would be a nice addition to a set of woodworking tools. As one can tell, Jerry Paulsen is still using this one. **$50**

A combination walking, measuring stick with great advertising on it for "Michigan State Industries" and all of the products made at Jackson State Prison located in Jackson, Mich. This is likely from the 1940s or earlier, when the prison system provided many market products, not just stamped license plates. At farm auctions, these types of measuring sticks usually bring $25-$35, more if a local merchant is advertised on it. *Paulsen Collection* ....**$25-$35**

A wrench marked "Reverse Gear Wrench." *Paulsen Collection* .... **$10+**

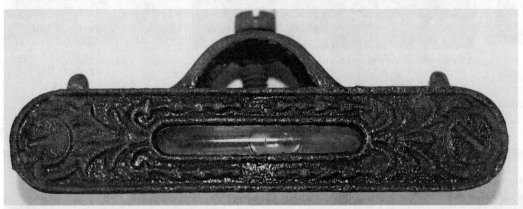

A large pair of wrought iron ice tongs similar to ones described before. *Art Smith Collection* .. **$35**

An ornate unmarked line level with nice casting. *Lewis Collection* .... **$10+**

This yard stick shows the name of the dealer for Jamesway Barn Equipment in Vassar, Mich. The nice part is that my wife's maiden name is Weber, so it is special. This is an example of the type of items that are collectible but even better when local or tied into a person's history somehow. *Lewis Collection* ....

An old shovel without a hand-hole in the handle, all wood top. This is likely a primitive hand-made replacement for the original. *Lewis Collection* ....$35-$50

A Conneaut #3 shovel and details. *Lewis Collection* .... **$25+**

Primitive sawmill at Yoder sale ....$300+

A fanning mill selling at the Yoder consignment auction. These normally sell for $50-$200, depending on the location and condition. Details below left. .... **$50-$200**

A feed bag cart.. $12

This unique Sears garden tractor was something I nearly bought for myself at the Yoder auction but could not carry home in our convertible. It is from the 1930s, a Series 38, Model 50B, #19951, 5 horsepower, made for Sears and called the "Handyman" tractor. It had a 12" plow and cultivators. I think it should have brought at least $600, but the buyers were not after it, as they could not haul it easily. The buyer told me he was prepared to bid it up to $800, but he got lucky and owned it when the gavel went down at only $300. This is the type of collectible that will likely increase in the future, as more collectors are developing interests in garden and lawn tractors. . **$300**

This wagon frame on steel sold for $85 at the Yoder auction.......**$85**

Examples of wheels sold at the Yoder auction. They are very similar to the steel wheels sold online that were detailed in this chapter.
.... **$25-$35 each**

A scythe for sale at a local antique shop. Similar ones sell for $10-$25 at most farm auctions and are quite common. This one was getting ready for the seasons.. $10-$25

This 1930s furnace motor, pulley, driveshaft, and crankshaft skewers has an unusual use as a hog roaster, with the drippings going into old water heaters, upper left. This is a Lefty Laughlin invention (see chapters 12-13 for more on Laughlin).

Chapter Seven:
Horse Hardware and Stable Items

This chapter covers the growing popularity of collecting what we term horse hardware: items related to horse harness. I have also included stable items related to other farm animals in this section. Of all of my favorite terms related to farming, this has to be tops on the list: "horse hardware." Most folks would not have a clue what this means. It includes old collars, hames, ivory rings, bells, buckles, decorative brass, tugs, and even complete sets of harness. It also includes antique tongues for farm equipment made by a particular company, such as Deere or International Harvester. It also includes tools to care for horses such as picks, combs, halters, brushes, and tack boxes.

Any animal used for draft purposes on a farm or in delivery of farm goods had to be harnessed to the equipment in some fashion. The various techniques used have not changed much in thousands of years. For the horse, it means the dressing with a collar kept in place by a set of hames, to which is attached the back bands and belly bands, and the surcingle around the middle to hold it all in place. Then, a set of tugs would be attached directly to the hames (often these were permanently attached) for the actual pulling. The tugs would then be hooked up to the eveners or wagon poles or whatever was being hauled. Of course, a long set of "lines" replaced the reins to control the horse and these were attached to the bridle in the same way as a set of reins.

For the oxen, usually castrated male bovines so called for their draft use and not their potential beef use as steers, the main necessity was a wooden yoke, to which would be hooked the necessary tugs. Harnessing a bovine was not nearly as complex, as all of the weight of the implement was directly on the front shoulders of the strong animals, transferred there by the yoke. In some regions, folks did actually harness cattle in outfits similar to horse harness. But, for the most part, one will find single and double oxen yokes in most farm country where cattle were used for draft purposes. A whip was often used to get the attention of the cattle and to control their direction.

The most obvious, and likely first, item in this field to be collected historically was the sleigh bell. These are colorful, well made, and sound nice, too. Also, all folks seem to know what they are. At one time, each family with a horse and a sleigh had some decorative or functional bells for the equine part of the equation. Early brass bells that were hand cast sell for $10 each, and complete sets can command up to $250 if in good condition. Many collectors will be bidding on sleigh bells, as they can be so easily recognized and displayed. This will keep the values increasing over the years in all likelihood.

The next area of popularity has been the horse collar and a set of hames that mounted the harness to the collar of a horse. Today, the hames often frame a mirror set within the collar. This is a nice way to display a functional piece of horse hardware in a modern home. The nicest and most valuable set of hames is a wooden set, or a set made of wood and metal with nice knobs on top of the framework. Metal hames in nice shape with good paint are collectible, but not in the same quality category as wooden hames with a nice brass knob ball atop. The collars do not make much difference, as people are buying them simply as a carrier for the mirror, but condition is important. No one wants a collar that has had a mouse nest in the stuffing or has been chewed on by mice. A collar with fancy double or triple stitching will bring more than one with simple single stitching. Also, deep solid black leather will bring more than a collar that has aged or has sun-burned leather.

Ivory rings (actually these are Bakelite) found on "spreaders" are likely the next category of interest because they hang fine from the hames around the mirror. The ivory rings for harness were designed for a dual purpose of decoration and to carry the lines (the leather reins from the bridle to the driver's hands), and keep them out of harm's way (the horse's hooves). Some farmers started adding ivory rings to decorate the harness even more. These rings have become very popular with collectors, due to their beauty and uniqueness. A few years ago, these were nearly free at an auction and now they command anywhere from $1-$10 per ring, depending on material, condition, and competition at the sale. A nice set of spreaders sold for $5 at the large Yoder consignment sale. That is inexpensive for the condition, but it was a huge sale with hundreds of horse harness items for sale.

Closely related to the rings is the category of rosettes and brass trim. Many farmers spending 10 hours a day behind a team of horses or mules decided to have a more aesthetic experience by decorating the harness with small rosettes or other brass hardware additions. They did not serve any functional purpose. They were simply to make the harness pretty. These rosettes and brass mini-horseshoes and floral designs first appeared on the horse's bridle, then spread back to the harness itself. The decorations were often a status symbol indicating the wealth of the farmer. The driving harness used to go to town was often decorated more than "work harness." However, some work harness had many ounces of brass added simply for decoration.

Related to the rosettes and decorations are all of the functional buckles and contraptions needed to make a set of harness work properly. Many of these older brass items are now selling for $1-$10 each, if in pristine shape and of vintage age.

Finally, whole sets of harness are sometimes bought to hang on the wall of a restaurant or family room. It is difficult to assign a collector value to sets of harness, as they also retain a "user value" regardless of age. I have bought and sold many sets of harness for as little as $25 a set to $800 a set, depending on condition of the leather, completeness of the set, trim, and age of the leather. Very old sets of harness found hanging in a barn that have not been oiled have little value other than to a collector. The leather is "dead" because it had not been properly oiled and cannot usually be brought back to life.

Collectors actively seek implement tongues. They include all of the major names in farm machinery manufacture. We sold, at last year's auction, a beautiful John Deere wagon tongue with original paint and a toolbox for more than $100. The tongue was found in our hayloft of our Upper Peninsula of Michigan farm when purchased in 1999. This demonstrates that these items are still out there waiting to be found. The tongue was perfect, stored out of harm's way for 70 years at least. Any tongue with a name on it will bring more than just a functional implement tongue.

Seats from early implements and tractors are also highly desired by collectors, and some of the early cast iron seats garner hundreds of dollars. These seats are used for everything from bar stools to implement restoration, driving up prices. Again, brand recognition is important to values. The pressed steel seats are not worth nearly as much as cast iron versions. So if buying from the Internet, make sure you know the seat material before shelling out a lot of money. I know of some factory reproductions of cast iron seats, so beware if not buying directly from the original owner.

Cow hardware is also important and fits in here. We sold a nice single ox yoke four years ago for $75 and a nice set of yokes could bring up to $500. Driving whips for oxen or horses are also collectible. Dairy cows also had their own special devices for training, including cow kickers and the little devices that transmitted a shock to the cow's back if she hunched too much while using her latrine facilities (cow trainers). Then there were the surcingles that hung over the cow's back to place a Surge brand milking machine in mid-air while the cow was being milked. Or, how about the three-legged milk stools now bringing $10-$50 at farm auctions?

Horse and cow care also included many specialized brushes and pieces of equipment, including tack boxes. Horses also had to have extensive foot care products, and many of the early hand forged devices are gaining value.

Veterinary products and home remedies related to horse and cow care also make nice additional items to one's collection. Many of these products came in colorful tins and jars that are desired by collectors in general, which drives the prices up. Some of these things have contents that one must be aware

could be dangerous, and need to dispose of the contents only according to law and recommended procedures.

Lastly, but not least, is the ultimate horse- or oxen-related item: the implements and carriages and carts. These also fit into our farm implement category (covered earlier). But I chose to place the carriages, carts, and sleighs here due to the direct relationship with this chapter (after all it is a "horse and carriage"). About the only high demand I ever see for horse-drawn (which includes oxen-drawn) equipment is by people with horses or oxen, not the general collector crowd. The only exception is the person that wants an item for their lawn.

Horse-drawn implements and conveyance devices have really shot up in value the past 20 years or so. When I bought my first team of horses in 1978 (Star and Stripe, three-fourths Belgian, one-fourth Quarter horse), it was not uncommon to find an old buggy or sleigh for $50 at a farm auction. The last two buggies I sold brought more than $500 each. The last sleigh (it was a dandy) brought about the same price and I cannot buy it back for $1,000 (I have tried). Old horse-drawn hay mowers were $10 about 20 years ago and now fetch a good price if still functional. Horse drawn manure spreaders are the same story. One could easily spend $5,000 for a decent carriage, sleigh, mowing machine, forecart, manure spreader, and riding plow. Of course, it would depend on brand names, age, attributes of the carriage and sleigh, and condition. But no one is going to walk away from a sale with a few bucks invested and get these items any longer.

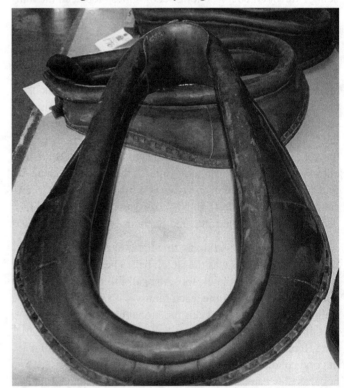

Horse collars at Yoder sale .... **$25-$70**

Values of Horse and Stable items

A Dakota farmstead cast iron hook found in the barn for hanging harness. This was a nice old item and I was surprised it did not do a little better. **$10**

A horse farm mirror of the type hung in a stable or mounted on carriages. **$53**

Broken hames pieces even garnered a $3.25 bid. Likely they were being purchased for the two brass knobs thrown in the deal. The hames themselves were broken and cracked and not worth much; however, one was the older wooden version. **$3.25**

Another cast iron harness hanging hook for the barn.................**$10**

An old "horse muzzle" or cribbing control device hanging on the VanAlstine garage.

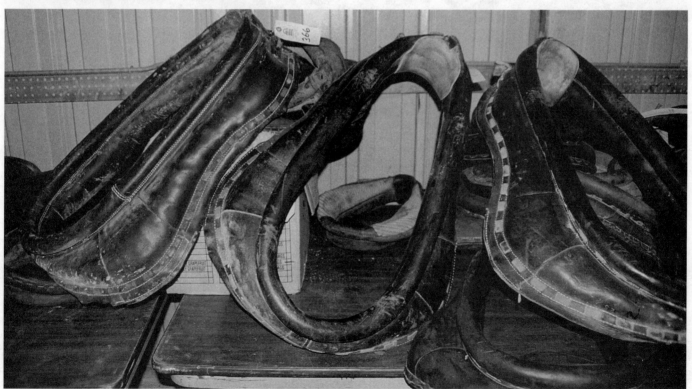

Thousands of items are sold in a two-day period related to horses and draft equipment at the semi-annual Yoder consignment sale. At a recent sale, collars sold as follows: A newer 24" sold for $70, a fancy 27" sold for $61, a plain 19" sold for $24 and another one sold for $40, an older 23" in nice shape brought $40 and a plain 18" driving collar sold for $26. Another fancy 25" sold for $55 and old/dirty 22" brought $22. A nice 25" sold for $47.50 and many collars sold in the $30-$35 range if usable. Small driving collars, 15" or 16" only fetched $5 each and some of the old work collars, even with pads only sold for $10-$15. A few of the collars are shown in the photos. ....**$5-$70 each**

Many eveners and neck yokes were shown in the Farm Implement chapter but here are some more examples. These sell for anywhere from $5-$40 usually, depending on the type of auction and demand for horse items at the auction.................... **$5-$40**

Harness sold at the Yoder sale for from a few dollars for the "piles 'o harness" shown to hundreds of dollars for quality working or driving harnesses. The values on harness at most farm auctions is quite low as often it was not stored properly and the leather is really "dead" and cannot be revived. I have purchased some examples for $5-$25 that, when taken to my local Amish harness maker, I found could be saved by a good soaking in his oil tank. But buying harness to use is risky business unless you have a lot of experience with it. I would advise buying something known to be complete and in good shape if you want to use it. The most value on many old harnesses is found in the rosettes and the ivory spreaders.... **$5-$25**

Dairy barn drinking cups selling for $6 each were placed in this chapter, as they fit best. These actually are newer ones. The older cast iron versions, as shown, above in our own dairy barn, should bring more and are in more demand. .... **$6 each**

Stainless steel milking machines and wash vats are also dairy-related. These buckets, mainly Surge but also a Chore Boy and some De Laval, sold for only a few dollars each at the Yoder sale. These milking machines normally range from $5-$20 each, depending on condition and model. Most of them had parts missing, broken handles, or something wrong with them (seams, welds, brazes) but would end up as someone's planter in the yard or on the farm house front porch. ....**$5-$20 each**

A wide variety of carriages, sleighs, cutters, buggies and vis-à-vis are shown in two photos. These were all sold at the Yoder consignment sale in Michigan. They included an old doctor's buggy, some nice old cutters, some Amish made buggies, and some new and newer models made by a Canadian firm. Prices ranged from a few hundred to a few thousand dollars depending on models. In general, old doctor's buggies do well, as do cutters and sleighs, stagecoaches, delivery wagons with markings, and any other unusual item on four wheels. With some good shopping, buggies can usually be found for $500-$800. .... **$500-up**

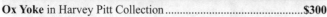

Ox Yoke in Harvey Pitt Collection $300

A Hasco brand cow number tag is made of brass. This number would hang from a chain around the cow's neck to identify her to a farmer or farm help. I still have the number tags from a few "great cows" that are very special memories to me. They also make neat collectibles. Wendy and I have purchased a few in antique stores for a few dollars each, some up to $15, depending on materials used to make the tag. .... $5-$15

A nice buggy seat selling at the Yoder auction. $50

A buggy seat is a most interesting adaptation of a horse item to a household. Art Smith uses the seat in his entryway to sit on while putting on boots and shoes. A buggy seat like this would sell for from $50-$100 at auction. .... $50-$100

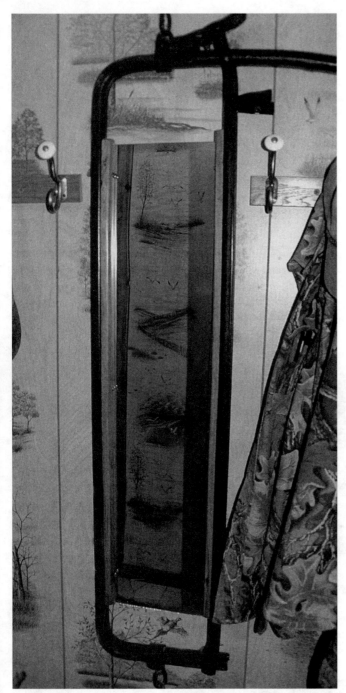

A lamp was necessary to go to the barn prior to electricity. This one is typical of what one finds in antique stores and at sales. It is a repaint and only worth about $10. I just sold a similar one for that online. Of course, marked original lamps are worth much more, many more than $100. ....**$10**

A cast iron cow stanchion is used as a mirror frame. This one was made by Art Smith after his wife Kim had seen a similar one in an antique store for more than $100. He only has a few dollars into this one. This is a nice use of a farm collectible. The stanchion by itself would be worth between $10-$25. Wooden ones could command double that easily. ....**$25-$100**

Some eveners and a neck yoke in a local antique shop and in the *Art Smith Collection*. (nexk yoke bottom left).....................**$5-$15 each**

A nice wooden stanchion adorns this tree at the VanAlstine farm. These wooden stanchions are in far more demand than the cast iron or steel varieties. .... $50+

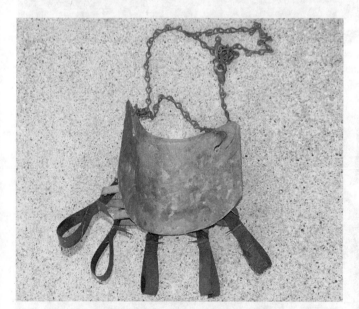

This unique calf trainer to wean a calf from nursing its mother is an unusual barn item. The little points went into the calf's nose and hurt when it tried to suckle its mother. *VanAlstine Collection* ...... $10-$25

A large simple steel cowbell hangs from a tree on the *VanAlstine property*. .... $10-$15

A nice primitive hog trough is shown. *Nerbonne Collection* .....$10+

An old cream can found in the Nerbonne barn. .... $15-$25

An old keg outside of the Nerbonne barn. The keg is worth at least $25 and was at one time full of doughnuts or dough for doughnuts. $25

A nice old tack box. *Nerbonne Collection* .... $40-$50

Original ropes and pulley found in the Nerbonne barn. Value of a pulley is $10-$20 at least, and the ropes would command at least $50 for ropes of this size and in such fine condition. ....$10-$50

Three neck yokes found in the Nerbonne barn. Nice patina and age on these should make them worth at least $10 each, if not more, even with tongue rings missing. ....**$10 each**

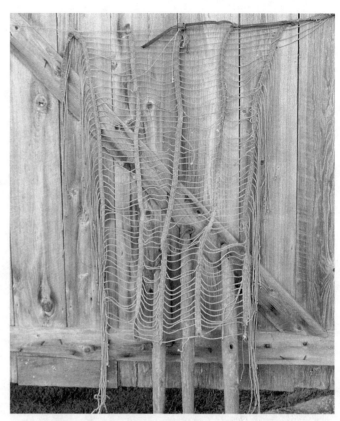

This set of "fly chasers" found hanging in the harness room of Nerbonne's barn is an exceptional find. A similar pair is shown on horses in some of the advertising items reprinted in that chapter. These certainly do not trade often but I should think something this rare would command a premium price to a harness collector. . **$300+**

Primitive four-leg milk stool from the Nerbonne barn. This nice milk stool would bring $25-$50 if offered for sale at auction. **$25-$50**

Two old fire extinguishers from the Nerbonne barn. A friend selling these online tells me they bring $25-$40 each. I have never sold one but have a few on our farm as well. ....**$25-$40 each**

This hay spear is from our dairy barn in Wisconsin and was made by Myers of Ashland, as was the large grapple shown earlier. This one we took with us for a memory of the farm. It would hang from the rafters on a track as seen in Chapter 14 from ropes as seen earlier. *Lewis Collection* .... **$25-$50**

Lights came to the farm along with electricity. This class act copper barn light came from a dairy barn near Coopersville, Mich. I have owned it and a mate to it for more than 30 years. I paid at least $50 for them then and should think they are worth $300 today. *Lewis Collection* **$300**

A larger and older brass bell. *Lewis Collection*......................**$25**

A Dari-Kool bulk tank wrench and a large metal bolus administrator is shown primarily to help identify them for people. They appear in online sales quite often as an "unknown" tool. This one is only about 20-30 years old but is worth at least $10, the cost of a new one. *Lewis Collection*........................ **$10**

Centennial Farm: This is our dairy barn, built by the Peters family in 1876 and still sound. Also shown is the original Centennial Farm sign, indicating the age of the farm. These signs are themselves collectible, as discussed in Chapter 3. The farm was in the Peters family from the time of a grant by the U.S. government in 1876 until they sold it to us in 2001. If it could only tell stories!

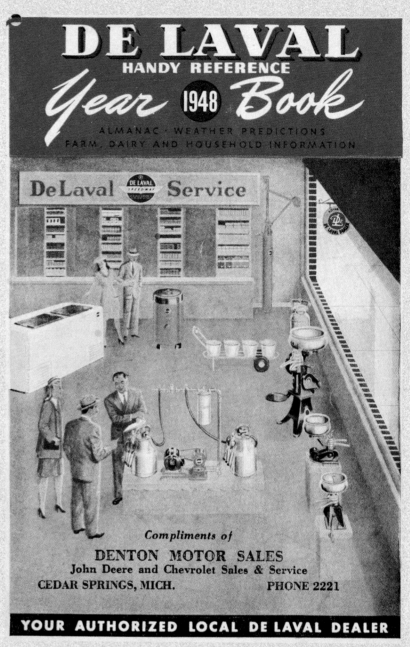

Paper Collectibles: The 1948 DeLaval Year Book, featuring articles ranging from milk house construction to "Time savers for the farm laundry," is a fine example of a paper collectible. Tractor and implement manuals are top sellers in this category. *Lewis Collection* **$25-50**

Magazine Rack: A 1938 issue of *The Country Home Magazine*, in mint condition, features a crowing rooster on the cover. *Paulsen Collection* .... **$10-$20**

Screwdriver Ad: This is an example of the types of items also given away by farm implement dealerships. These, along with small tape measures, yardsticks, and rulers, comprise an interesting area of collectibles. Brand loyalty and geographical area are important considerations in pricing. This screwdriver is from a bait shop in South Bend, Ind. *Lewis Collection* ....**$5-$25**

Oiler: The John Deere oil can is rare. And anything with a familiar brand name like John Deere brings added value. *Art Smith Collection*
....**$50+**

Crossover: A corn planter is clearly a small farm implement. But, due to the pristine nature of the label, it could also be kept for the advertising. *Art Smith Collection*...**$30-$40**

Butter Cartons: Three nice examples show why butter cartons are a very fine addition to any farm collection. One collecting method is try to find your favorite cow type (Jersey, etc.) or a local dairy to add to your collection. *Lewis Collection*...........**$20 each**

PURE JERSEY BUTTER

This butter is made from sweet Jersey cream, from a herd of registered Jersey cows, tubercular tested at regular intervals.

The herd is kept in a modern, sanitary dairy barn and the butter is made and packed under cleanly conditions at LA ROCHE VERTE FARM, GRAND DETOUR, ILLINOIS, owned by EDWARD J. BRUNDAGE.

Users of this butter are invited to inspect the conditions under which it is made.

'Good Results': An egg basket, a nice example from MoorMan's Feed, was once furnished to loyal MoorMan's users for their egg operations. We had a few dozen similar ones at one time to gather and wash our eggs. I recently traded a copy of this book (once it is printed) for this egg basket. The rubber coating on the basket was to protect the eggs in both gathering and in placing into the automatic egg washers we used in the 1950s and 1960s. *Lewis Collection* **$30**

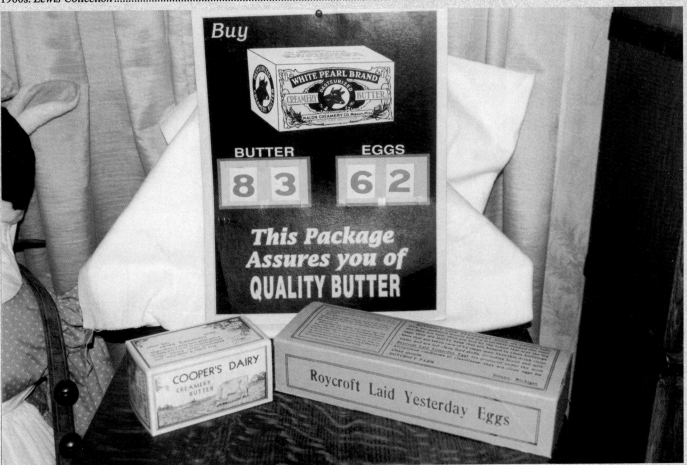

Butter and Eggs: A Roycroft egg carton from Sidnaw, Mich. One cannot have butter without eggs. The egg carton is a gift from a good friend and is in mint condition. Sidnaw was on the rail line to Minneapolis and at one time produced thousands of eggs for the city markets in Minnesota, Wisconsin, and Michigan. *Lewis Collection* .... **$20+**

Year Book: A festive scene right out of a county fair decorates this 1949 DeLaval Year Book, which was distributed for free to rural route box holders. Eager customers check out DeLaval milking products while the kids play outside the tent. *Lewis Collection*...**$25-$50**

Recipes Inside: These Sealtest dairy recipe books make an interesting addition to dairy collectibles. From the 1940s-50s, they are not of great value but should trade for $2-$5 each. These were actually found in a large lot of similar materials and not purchased separately. *Lewis Collection*...**$2-$5**

'King of All': A small pocket diary produced by Weber Wagon Co. of Chicago is best seen as an advertising item. My wife's maiden name is Weber, so this is especially fun for us.. **$40**

Ready for Winter: Old sleds can easily fetch up to $75 for a Flexible Flyer in great shape. The older sleds that truly look like a sleigh, with the upturned runners, will bring even more. Many sleds are sold for only $25 or so at auctions, but they are getting harder to find in great shape. .... **$25-$125**

Lunch Time: This lunch box shows the romantic ideals of farm life around a barn. It is a fine example of tin lithography. .... **$50+**

Little Red Wagon: These wagons may have seen their better days, but they will bring from $10-$100, depending on the model and the condition, at an auction. Most sell for around $20-$25. Two are shown as examples. The wagon below can clearly be dated from the early 1960s due to its name, "Astronaut." .... $10-$100

Autry Model: The Gene Autry diecast toy gun and holster is mine. It is valued at $400-$500, according to antique shop owners specializing in toy guns. .... **$400-$500**

Tractor Time: Collectible tractors range in value from $30 to more than $500, according to Jerry Paulsen. The addition of the original box can double the value. A selection of Allis-Chalmers models line up with a Case and a Farmall in the Paulsen collection, center and bottom. An Ertl Ford, top, is the third tractor issued by the Michigan FFA Foundation, issued in 1995. ....**$30-$500 each**

Horse-drawn: A beautiful old hay tedder, with the left tire "flat" but in otherwise excellent working condition and with a cast iron seat, sold for a mere $85. This same item is shown among the advertising items from a 1905 magazine reprinted in the final chapter. The seat alone was worth the price. **$85**

Plowing Ahead: An Oliver sulky plow may have been the "steal" of the day at the Yoder sale. In very nice original condition, the plow sold for only $125. Most of the time, these fetch a far better price, and $300-$500 is not uncommon. **$125**

Antique Lineup: An array of implements is ready for bidders at the Yoder semi-annual farm sale. The sale always includes dozens of horse-drawn items and attracts hundreds of buyers, Amish and non-Amish, to compete for these items. The sale was held for two days in Mt. Pleasant, Mich. **$10-875**

Yard Decoration: A John Deere dump rake has become part of the landscape at the VanAlstine farm. It fits in nicely with a wooden fence and wildflowers...**$50-75**

Low Bid: An Ontario Drill sold first at a huge antique implement auction. It brought the low bid of only $10 as "the first item sold," something that often happens at farm sales. **$10**

Deere Green: A nice restored John Deere Sulky plow looks ready to go. The owner paid $450 for it a few years ago and it would bring that to $600 today. ....**$450-$600**

Big Load: A New Idea hay loader was recently purchased by Kelley VanAlstine near Evart, Mich., for only $2. No one came to buy implements at a general farm auction that day. This was actually in working order when parked in the yard. **$2**

Auction: A typical farm auction scene finds many horse-drawn implements lined up at Mt. Pleasant, Mich. **$10-875**

End of the Rope: Brass trimming makes this marked pulley worth more. *Art Smith Collection* .... **$25+**

Jacked Up: An old Model T jack is from the *Art Smith Collection*.
.... **$20**

Specialty Tool: A chain repair tool once found on nearly every farm was made in Albert Lea, Minn., by Albert Lea Foundry. This is not of great value but is another reminder of how farmers had specialty tools to repair conveyers, manure spreader chains, and other similar items.
....**$10**

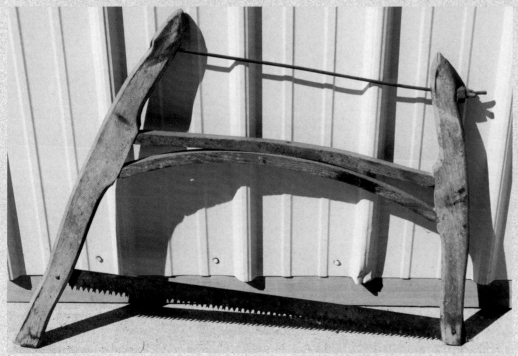

Pre-chain Saw: When a farmer had to tackle tree trimming, a buck saw was the tool to use. *Art Smith Collection* .... **$10-$25**

Early Chain Saws: The beams of the VanAlstine garage are the gallery for a collection of chain saws. David VanAlstine works for a John Deere dealership and is a specialist in small garden tractors and related farm and garden equipment. He has been saving them for years and picking them up at farm auctions whenever possible. The photos show a wide variety of saws in David's collection, some dating into the 1940s.
.... **$10 and up**

"Weed-whacker": They've progressed, but here is another early lawn tool in the VanAlstine Collection. The weed-whacker is without trade data but I would expect it to fetch $10-$20. .... **$10-$20**

Say Hay: Two very old hand-held hay hooks are hand forged, with hand carved wooden handles, very heavy duty. *Nerbonne Collection* . ... **$25+ each**

Plane Talk: A nice pair of woodworking planes is in the Paulsen Collection. Planes sell for anywhere from $10 to more than $100, depending on brand, style, and model. These would likely start at $25 each and go from there. ....**$25+ each**

Whatzit? A very nice hay grapple was used to grab the loose hay from a stack on a hay wagon and lift it up into the barn. This was in the Nerbonne barn when he purchased it years ago. Although these are unique and harder to find now, their value is not high, as there is not a good way for most buyers to display one........... **$10-$25**

Wrenching: Open end wrench number 677, with an H in a diamond on the other side, comes from the *Paulsen Collection*........... **$10+**

Fruity: Shown are a number of collectible crate end labels, most fairly common and valued at $5-$15 each. These are a most colorful collectible.
.... **$5-$15 each**

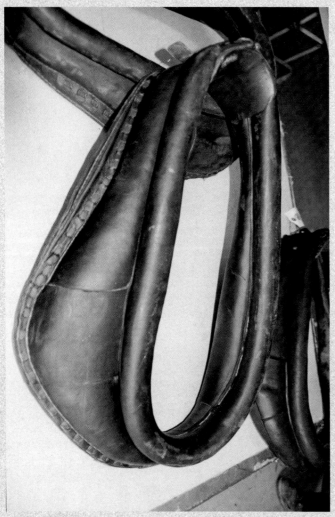

Collared: Horse collars at a recent auction ranged from $5 up to $70 for a fine example like this. .... **$5-$70**

Framed: This set of hames and horse collar, framing a pumpkin, was found hanging in Art Smith's garage. It would bring about $25 if sold together at auction, maybe even a little more as the brass knobs are present and in good shape. Many take a combination such as this, insert a mirror in the collar, and have a nice functional piece for the hallway. **$25**

Transportation: A wide variety of carriages, sleighs, cutters, and buggies are lined up at the Yoder consignment sale in Michigan. Prices ranged from a few hundred to a few thousand dollars, depending on models. **$500-up**

Rubber Tires: Altered for today's highways with rubber tires, a fancy buggy is restored and ready for use. A sleigh is in the background. **$500-up**

Plush: This horse-drawn carriage, with leather trim and red felt seats and lining, brings back the good old days of leisurely travel..**$500-up**

Rare: This set of "fly chasers" found hanging in the harness room of Nerbonne's barn is an exceptional find. These certainly do not trade often but I should think something this rare would command a premium price to a harness collector. .... **$300- up**

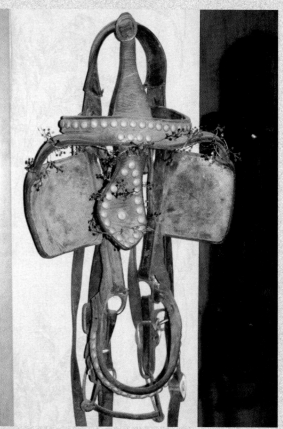

Take a Number: A Hasco brand cow number tag is made of brass. This number would hang from a chain around the cow's neck to identify her to a farmer or farm help. I still have the number tags from a few "great cows" that are very special memories to me. They also make neat collectibles. .... **$5-$15**

Memories: This horse bridle is priceless. It belonged to Prince, the king of the Percherons, that we owned for years. It hangs in his memory in a corner of our dining room, decorated for Christmas.

Ringing: Our maid Bossy is draped with a set of sleigh bells an Amish harness-making friend installed on new leather for me. This complete set of bells is valued at $250 (25 bells). *Lewis Collection*... **$250/set**

Sleigh Ride: Prince, the king of the Percherons, takes the author out for a ride on our former farm near Tony, Wis.

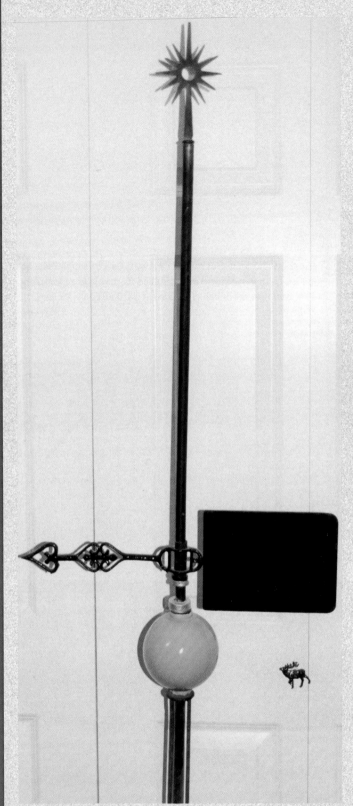

Have a Seat: A primitive four-leg milk stool is from the Nerbonne barn. This nice milk stool would bring $25-$50 if offered for sale at auction. .... **$25-$50**

Weathered: A beautiful cast iron weather vane and glass globe is from the *Art Smith Collection*. .... **$100+**

Ready for Milking: This three-legged milk stool from the Smith family is 50 years old at least. It is not for sale, but if it were, it would bring from $25-$50, depending on the day. *Art Smith Collection* .... **$25-$50**

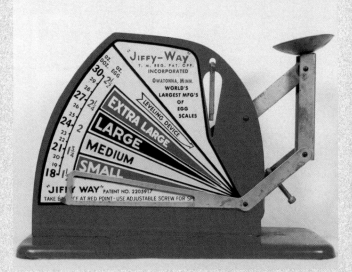

Weighty: A type of egg scale available for the farm collector. The Jiffy-Way scale was sold by Sears and Wards, and many show up at farm auctions today. This scale is worth about $25 minimum and may command more any given day, depending on competition at the auction. *Lewis Collection*.. **$25+**

Ding Dong: This No. 2 C. S. Bell & Co. bell from Hillsboro, Ohio, cast in 1938, is a fine example of a farm bell. It would command at least a $100 bid at any farm auction and may sell for far more. Of increasing value to collectors is the variety of bells found on old farmsteads. Again, beware of reproductions of cast iron products such as bells and seats. *Parker Collection* ....**$100+**

Quiet Corner: You never know what enjoyable collectibles might be found in the corner of a farmhouse. This grouping ranges from a toy tractor, box of wooden blocks, and quilt, to a crock of pool balls and some wooden signs. Values given earlier ....**$5-$100+**

Country Kitchen: A beautiful Detroit Jewel stove is the focal point of farm collectibles in the VanAlstine Collection. Also included are the butter churn from above, a second small churn in lower right, a very unusual egg crate on top of the stove, a nice small crock, a bird house, and some tin containers. Values given earlier **$25-1,500**

Rocking: A nice display of mixed collectibles blends with a creative use of wooden apple crates from nearby orchards. The photo shows an Amish bentwood rocker, the apple crates, some nice crockery pieces, quilts, and an old grate from a gravity-feed heating system. *VanAlstine Collection*. Values ....**$5-100+**

Colorful Collection: A colorful set of Ransburg canisters, made in Indianapolis, Ind., in the 1940s-50s are noted by their distinctive artist palette trademark on the bottom. Ransburg items sell well. My wife and I collect Ransburg and a number of interesting pieces are shown. Most of them were bought online, in antique stores, or at auctions the past 10 years. Prices for most cookie jars begin at $50 and usually only go to $125, depending on condition. Smaller pieces may even bring more if rare, but common salt and pepper sets sell for a few dollars to $30. *Lewis Collection* .... **$50-100+**

Crowing: A rare Ransburg Rooster Cookie Jar in the *Lewis Collection* .... **$200+**

Top Shelf: Even more crockery pieces adorn the VanAlstine cupboards, along with a "farm" rooster, a Maid-Rite scrub board, a granite ware strainer, a New Era chip container, two more wash boards, an old Quaker Oats container, and a Gold Medal tin tea box. **$25-200**

Front steps: Less valuable crockery and tins adorn the VanAlstine front porch and show a nice decorative touch near the garden, with the crockery holding flowers. ....**$5-$10 each**

Tub-thumping: A pair of old galvanized washtubs provide decoration on a garden fence. Galvanized washtubs are not high priced, usually only bringing $5-$20 depending on size, age, type, and condition. ....**$5-$20**

New Uses: A boiler is used as a garden decoration in the VanAlstine Collection, along with a steel wheel. Most copper boilers sell for $25-$50, sometimes higher at certain auctions, and the tin versions go for about half as much. ....**$25-$50**

Garden Party: The VanAlstines use a variety of farm collectibles and primitives to set off their beautiful gardens. These photos show their use of implement wheels and a pump head in the gardens. The gardens were toward the end of the season but still beautiful.
....**$35–50**

Fish Spearing: A winter pastime was spearing for fish in the north, from New York through Minnesota primarily. Collectibles related to spearing include both the fish decoys, such as this, and the spears. One needs a lot of guidance in this field to determine the value but the collector should be aware these little fish are valuable, ranging from a minimum of $25 to thousands for rare Oscar Petersens from Michigan (shown) and some of the very old New York decoys. ....$25+

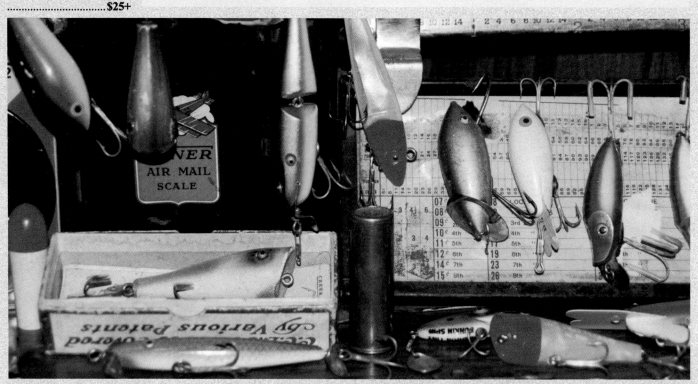

Fishing: A few lures and a neat old scale depict fishing on the farm. I received the scale when I purchased the Weber of Stevens Point fly fishing company archives. The company used it in its mailing operations. The lures include some rare colored CCBC plunkers, a nice rainbow Pikie, some rainbow Heddon River Runts, and some more common Bombers in rainbow. There is also a nice little Heddon Crab Wiggler. *Lewis Collection* .... $10-$300 each

Hunting Gear: A turkey call was useful when a farmer went hunting. Calls are often found at auctions for a few dollars and are usually a good buy. Many can sell for $25 to a few hundred dollars, depending on the age, maker, type, and rarity. Also, many calls are unmarked, making it difficult for the uninitiated to tell the value. *Lewis Collection*.................. **$75+**

Orange: A gathering of Allis-Chalmers tractors was in the front row at Hutchinson, Minn., in the summer of 1996. This shows some very nice A-C items, including the first truly successful commercial round baler, fourth item in the front row............................ **$1,500-up**

1935 Model: A nice F-12 McCormick-Deering from 1935 sold at a farm auction and it ran fine. This shows the low price these vintage tractors have reached. **$1,125**

Like New: A Farmall Cub glistens after restoration work was completed. The tires are original. And, you should hear it purr! A simple pull on the starter rod and it is off and running. *Paulsen Collection* **$4,000**

Green Machine: A John Deere Model 1010 from 1964 donned fresh paint and had a live PTO. **$3,050**

Deere B: A nice old John Deere B on spoke wheels could only muster a high bid of $1,500 and was a "no sale." ....**$1,500+**

Workhorse: Lefty Laughlin's 1948 Oliver 77 Row Crop is a working collectible. Laughlin found both of his Row Crop Oliver tractors with trees growing in front of both rear axles and had to "cut them out of the woods" before he could begin repairs. **$2,000**

Hit and Miss: John Deere hit and miss engines from the 1910s or early 1920s, 1 1/2 horse, are still usable. This one was used by a vendor to make ice cream at the Yoder consignment sale. What a great use of old technology! .... **$2,000+**

FARM JOURNAL

November 1938

Est. 1877

5 CENTS

THE NATIONAL NEWS—MAGAZINE FOR THE FARM FAMILY

SOILLESS FARMING • *By V. G. Frost*

Chapter Eight:

The Farm Kitchen/Household

This chapter covers items related to the preparation and preservation of food. They were not unique to farms but were of special importance to farm kitchens, given their isolation from "store bought" food in many cases. Also, most farms had an extensive farm garden for farm family use (see next chapter), making the preservation of goods even more important. There are many fine books on the market covering kitchen collectibles. This chapter will be an overview of important items to the farm family. It includes canning items, pie safes, Hoosiers, early refrigerators, small utensils, and other items of interest around the household and farmstead.

Many of the items in this chapter can be found in early advertising pieces touting the labor saving qualities of the item. Things that immediately come to mind are the old apple corers and cherry pitters used in preservation of those fruits. Related items include the famous blue Ball jars, and early tops and jars for preserving food.

Kitchen utensils with wooden painted handles are highly collectible and important to farm households and collectors. Also, cookie jars, breadboxes, and all the other odd and sundry items found in a kitchen are important to farm kitchen collectors. When I think of farm kitchen collectibles, I cannot help but think of all the miniature renditions of farm animals that adorn the kitchens of hundreds of thousands of Americans, farmers and urbanites alike. What kitchen does not have a rooster, a hen, a cow, a pig, a sheep, or some farm animal as a towel decoration, cookie jar, sugar bowl, or candy dish? The items related to the farm have spread everywhere due to the "general attractiveness" of the item. This increases demand and value.

Values of Farm Home Collectibles

A wire egg basket is a good example of a nice collectible. The seller juiced up the description by claiming it was an "Amish" egg basket. Maybe it was, but it was a common rubber covered wire basket used to wash eggs in automatic egg washers during the 1950s. These do sell well at farm auctions. Two examples are shown later in this chapter. **$13.75**

A nice egg carton with lithography from the 1940s. It was definitely from the war era, with references to turning the carton into money for the defense effort. The 1940s carton had a hen and rooster scene.. **$12**

The "kraut slicer," used to prepare cabbage for kraut processing, is an ever-popular item at farm auctions. A smaller version made of wood with a serrated edge was also sold for preparing fancy vegetables. One is shown later. **$10.50**

On a larger note, early iceboxes are very collectible, valued at $300-$1,000 if in great condition and made of oak. We had an antique wood cook stove, a Junger from Milwaukee, Wis., valued at about $1,500, in our last kitchen. Pie safes are a nice addition, representing the importance of preserving fruit in pies and a very traditional piece usually fetching at least $300. Hoosiers are great kitchen cabinets that were designed to store flour, spices, and needed cooking items. Today they are valued at $300 to more than $1,000, depending on condition, brand name, color, and completeness. The giant butcher blocks, once found in many farmstead butchering centers, are now fetching $300 or more and being reproduced across America.

In addition, there is the related area of kitchen and food preparation cutlery. This now brings in collectors of knives and Americana in general, increasing the value of good knives such as a Case. Some items such as kitchen steels are still very inexpensive (as little as $2 each). But many items of cutlery are worth more than $30 and some more than $100 each.

Now, one can add: flour sifters, egg baskets, porcelain funnels, specialty kitchen tools, early bowls, butter churns, crocks, egg scales, cutting boards, cast iron pots and pans, early kitchen appliances, dishes, bowls, cups, saucers, plates, sugars, creamers, ice cream scoops, salt and peppers, and spice sets to the above lists. Then one has a glimpse of the farm kitchen. It is the same kitchen as elsewhere, with a few more items usually added and none deleted.

Finally, there were items unique to a farm, such as extremely large tables and benches used for the threshing meals necessary to feed a hungry crew. In addition to the above items, I have included a sampling of things that simply strike me as either country or farm related that one would likely find on a farm in the past, and often still today.

A beautiful split oak gathering basket received lots of attention online with 15 bids. This basket was in excellent shape and was a fine example of early Americana. It was from an early estate in Philadelphia... **$210**

The wooden egg crate common until the late 1950s is another egg-related item. These 12" cubical crates were made to stack egg cartons for shipping and/or were provided with cardboard dividers to place the eggs directly into this crate. We had thousands of laying hens in the 1950s. We used these crates to ship eggs directly from the farm to the wholesaler, where they were then placed into cardboard cartons of one dozen each. One sold online with the cardboard dividers. It did not mention the wooden top that should have been present and must have been missing. The wooden top slid into the crate and had a wooden or metal handle for lifting the crates. See the one shown in detail in Chapter 6... **$10+**

An interesting "auctioneer's cane" claimed to be from the 1930s sold for only $5. Although not a kitchen item per se, I am including general household items in this chapter as well. I do not think the cane was that old. A common type of livestock cane still used today is likely why it had little bidder activity. **$5**

Another woven basket was likely a reproduction, given some newer screws in the handle noted by the seller. There were some older elements also, two cast-iron rivets and an iron hook. However, the newer screws were a problem for buyers. The photograph showed a basket not unlike many made in the 1980s when basket-making classes were "in vogue." **$17**

A European design farm print showed a thatched grass roof house and barn, a Percheron team, a terrier, and a man and a woman. The gilded frame was 47" by 33 1/2" and was very nice. This is a common print from the 1930s-40s found in many homes. **$50**

An old wire canning jar tote was one of the biggest "trick listings." The seller claimed the same tote to be a "farm find" over and over again, and sold many of them for between $9.99 to a high of $14.99. These were canning bath liners that held seven-quart jars. They can still be purchased today and quickly weathered outside with a little exposure. They are simple galvanized steel and pick up the "aged look" quite easily, even by simply canning. I still can tomatoes every year and mine looks just like the ones sold as "old." It is only a few years "new." These can be purchased wherever canning supplies are sold. Maybe the seller did not know they were newer and really thought them to be a "find." I simply know this does not look right when the same photo is used over and over again to sell an item such as this. .... **$10 or less**

A nice cast iron foot scraper was just a plain cast iron upright scraper with prongs to place it into the dirt outside of the back door. **$20.50**

Old six-pane windows were a surprise to me. These windows were found in every farm home in America in the early 1900s, until the remodeling craze of the 1960s removed so many in favor of double hung windows. I sadly left a number of these behind over the years and now wish I had them to sell. A six-pane version brought $30. Of course, shipping would be expensive too, making this easily a $50 investment. .... **$30 each**

A wooden carrier for a milkman to use marked "Lakeview Farm." It had a picture of a cow, was also marked "Farm Fresh" on one side, and was likely a reproduction or an item made to look old. Without physically examining the item I could not be sure. However, it did not appear old by the construction of the sides to the ends (no dovetail work). **$10.50**

A nice old farm rocking chair shows the problem of shipping for online auctions of large items. Shipping was from $90-$200, depending on location, and the item sold for $35. This was a nice vintage rocker from the 1930s or even a little earlier, but the shipping would deplete the savings of many. It only received one bid and was likely a local bidder who could pick up the item. **$35**

Four 19th century reprints of pigs and sheep were not old. There were two prints of each. They were clearly marked reproductions of

19th century prints. I included mention of them to show the interest in farm-related items and prints. **$12**

An original Belgian watercolor, showing a farmer plowing with horses. The frame was simple but it was a nice painting for the money, 29 1/2" tall and 23" wide. **$66**

A butter mold used from 1920-70 on the seller's family farm in North Carolina with a daisy pattern for the mold pattern. It had nice patina and had been cracked in the center and glued to restore it. **$20.50**

A kitchen table is an important item in any farm kitchen and many are found for sale online. A nice walnut 61" by 38" table, circa 1860, reached $86 but did not sell due to a reserve price not disclosed. Shipping is a problem, and this table had two significant cracks, deterring bidders. However, some online table sales reached four figures and many were in the $260-$500 price range. ....**$100-$500**

A watercolor signed by Herbert Jacob Gute (New York 1907-77) of a winter snow-covered farm landscape measuring 13" by 18" did not sell due to a reserve price. But the bidding reached $100. .... **$100+**

A simple old stool used in the kitchen to reach items out of reach that had been painted orange, dated from roughly 1900....................... **$42**

The lightning rod ball is one of everyone's favorite household items, but is a barn item in many cases. Indeed, some farm homes also had the glass balls on the rod, as did many large barns. These have been hot collectibles for at least 30 years and the cobalt blue ones easily reach $100 many times. One sold online for $100 with 13 bids. The same seller had two others online the same day and they sold for $51 and $54, which demonstrates a common problem facing sellers online. If one lists the same item in multiple lots at one time, the prices are depressed. If the seller would have listed the other two to end different days, they would have likely reached $100, or closer to that amount. Regardless, the lightning rod ball is always a good item to have to sell, as collector interest is high, has been high, and will likely continue. These are beautiful items that are limited in number and fragile. See the beautiful example included later in this chapter. .... **$100+**

A "firkin" was a pail, often painted, made of wood found in the northeastern part of the United States. An example painted in green was sold from a Maine farmhouse for $90 with seven bids. It measured 11 1/4" in diameter at the top and 12 3/8" at the bottom and was 11 5/8" high. **$90**

A nice screen door and matching porch door from an old farmhouse was a "pick-up" only item (e.g. no shipping). This was a nice set of doors but they had to be picked up by the buyer, likely keeping down the bidding. **$8.50**

A #2 16" antique farm dinner bell was offered for sale by a very honest seller. (Many of these are for sale in online auctions and most are reproductions.) The seller included all kinds of data and even included a Web site on old bells to learn more about the bells. The bell sold for $51, weighed 66 pounds to ship, and only had two bids. What I really liked about the listing was the openness of the seller to share information and assist the buyer in determining the value of the bell. See an example later in this chapter...................................... **$51**

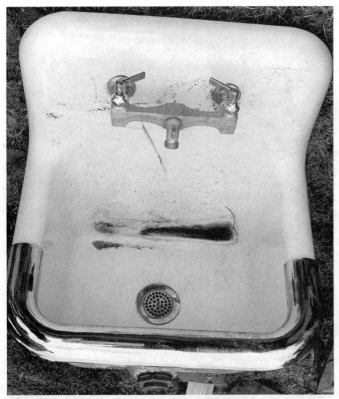

A cast iron sink from a dairy milk house sold for $35 at the Yoder consignment auction. This was a bargain given prices received online for the same items. $35

A Scandinavian Lefse wooden grooved rolling pin from the Dakotas. This was 21" long and turned from a solid piece of maple. Shipping was $8.75, making it a $50 + item. $43

An old Crane apron front cast iron/porcelain sink measuring 42" wide and 20 1/2" deep with a 14" high splashboard brought six bids. It had a couple of chips to the porcelain but nothing serious. The item could be picked up or shipped for $125. An example follows later. $290

A truly antique Bread Box brought home from England by Kelley VanAlstine while traveling on a John Deere dealer trip. ....$100+

A 30" Columbia single bowl kitchen sink of cast iron and porcelain with $100 shipping (or pick up). The Columbia sink was 30 1/2" wide and 19 1/2" deep. It, too, had small chips. $150

A nice primitive gateleg table did not meet reserve and ended at $81 with six bids. Shipping was likely the issue. It was a nice table covered with layers of paint and was 38" round. Shipping was only $45, but this likely deterred bidders...$80+

A nice stained glass window from a New York farmhouse measuring 19" wide by 52" long. $50

A beautiful square stained glass window measuring 28" by 32 3/4" received 12 bids. $135

A cast iron 13" weather vane found on an Iowa farmhouse. It was an arrow, heart, and knot design, with no animals. An example follows later.. $35

A six-pane window has an unusual use, designed by Kelley VanAlstine. $20+

A Daizy brand butter churn is an item that always sells well at auctions, normally commanding $100 and more. Art Smith Collection .....**$100+**

A colorful set of Ransburg canisters, made in Indianapolis, Ind., in the 1940s-50s are noted by their distinctive artist palette trademark on the bottom. Ransburg items sell well and these would likely fetch at least $100 in this fine condition and complete. My wife and I collect Ransburg and a number of interesting pieces are shown. Most of them were bought online, in antique stores, or at auctions the past 10 years. Prices for most cookie jars begin at $50 and usually only go to $125, depending on condition. Smaller pieces may even bring more if rare, but common salt and pepper sets sell for a few dollars to $30. Lewis Collection ....**$100+**

An enamel top four-legged table used for bread making, noodle making, or canning preparation is common at farm auctions. Many are painted and/or repainted. I do not know shipping on this item, but it would be costly. These are often found at auctions for this price or less...**$32**

A set of three antique gas-lights from an old farm house in South Dakota was one of the few true antiques I found under household goods. The lights, glass fixtures, and all parts were in excellent shape. **$105**

Roosters in the house! Many farm collectible homes are full of farm animals in the porcelain mode. We seem to have more chickens and roosters than any other type, even though we are former dairy farmers and currently raise sheep commercially. Some of the old glass roosters and hens were inherited from my wife's grandmother and have been in the family for many, many years. Other items just seemed to be picked up here and there until we had a flock. *Lewis Collection* ....**$10-$100+**

A clear green glass water jug is one of many types and colors that make an interesting collecting sideline for kitchen or household collectibles. I have seen one display of these water jugs covering an entire wall of a home and it is most impressive indeed. *Lewis Collection* **$10**

A water jug in a ribbed glass version. *Lewis Collection* **$20**

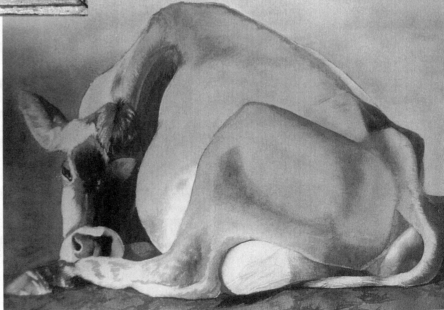

Farm paintings from our own home. Some of these are valuable, worth a few hundred dollars each, and some are fairly common prints. The reason they are shown is just to round out the category and to make collectors aware of another area to look for farm items. We like prints and paintings with farm animals in them, so we have bought a number over the years. I am also fortunate to own two originals painted by outstanding illustrators, one a gift and one earned as a legal fee years ago. Though of recent origin (less than 20 years old), original illustrations will increase in value and make great additions to a country home. One is an original painting of our former Jersey named Star as she was napping in the sun, painted by Doris Vinton, former National Society of Illustrators award winner and a good friend. The others are paintings and lithographs we simply enjoy. *Lewis Collection* .... **$50-$300**

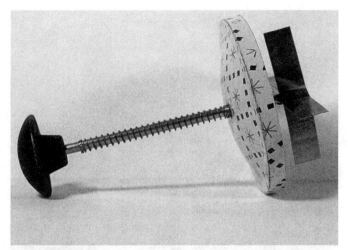

A neat little jar top churn or mixer found at a local estate sale for $1.50. This was placed upon a jar for an instant blending of items. It appears to be from the 1950s. *Lewis Collection* **$1.50**

A nice graniteware colander we use in the farm kitchen. It was purchased at a farm auction some years back for a few dollars. Chipping hurts its collector value but it is still a nice item to use in salad preparation and in washing vegetables and rinsing pasta. *Lewis Collection* .... **$10+**

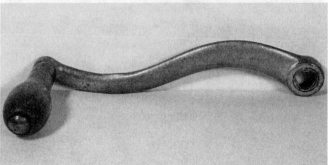

A Ward's brand meat grinder used to prepare meats for sandwiches and other purposes in every farm kitchen across America. This one is ours, purchased at a farm auction and used to make ground bologna sandwich meat. *Lewis Collection* **$35**

A type of egg scales available for the farm collector. The Jiffy-Way scale was sold by Sears and Wards, and many show up at farm auctions today. This scale is worth about $25 minimum and may command more any given day, depending on competition at the auction. I weighed many thousand eggs on a similar scale as a child when we had a few thousand laying hens. Of course, a related collectible would be the old egg candling machines, consisting of a simple light in a wooden box, to check for impurities in the eggs. *Lewis Collection* .... **$25+**

Farm kitchen scales are another interesting collectible. Here is a set of scales owned by Art Smith made for Sears, Roebuck & Co., and a set of scales from our kitchen made for Wards. At one time, I had about 10 sets of scales, as I found them colorful and interesting......................**$25-$50**

This three-legged milk stool from the Smith family is 50 years old at least. It is not for sale, but if it were, it would bring from $25-$50, depending on the day. *Art Smith Collection*.............................**$25-$50**

Multi-pane windows are now collectible and used for farm home restoration projects. Also very nice are the leaded glass windows found at auctions. The ones shown have been removed from the cabinet they once adorned and should bring more than $50 each, according to Art Smith. *Art Smith Collection* .... **$50 each**

A nice old sad iron. These used to sell for much more and rare ones still do. *Art Smith Collection*.. **$10-$20**

A typical 1950s egg basket from the Art Smith collection. These were made to serve two purposes: carrying the eggs and also to place them in the automatic washing devices developed in the 1950s to make egg processing easier. We had about 30 baskets on our farm for egg gathering and washing. The metal wires were covered by a thick rubberized/plasticized material to protect the eggs during washing. These have become very collectible and are used for everything from magazine holders to laundry baskets today. They commonly bring $25 or more at auctions, if in good shape. ....$25+

This die cast Black Americana item holds fruits or candies or other kitchen items. At auction, this would likely fetch $75+ without any trouble. *Art Smith Collection*...**$75+**

A nice washboard by the National Washboard Co., No. 862, with a hen on the reverse side. *Lewis Collection*...................................**$25+**

An old washing machine sold by Art Smith this past summer can be seen in the center of the photo. **$50**

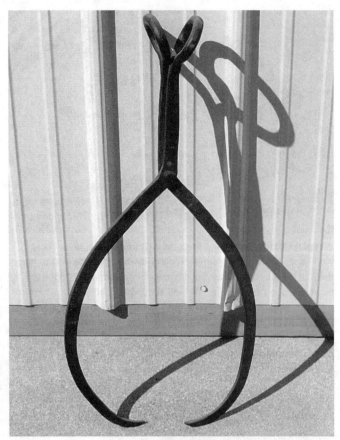

A large set of ice tongs in cast iron from the Smith Collection..... **$25**

A lightning rod and glass globe on a neighbor's barn in Western Michigan. As one can see, the globe is broken off the other lightning rod shown on the barn roof.

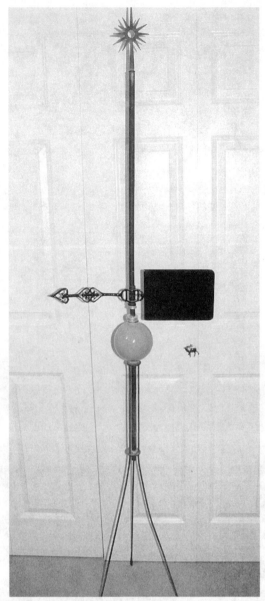

A beautiful cast iron weather vane and glass globe. Art Smith Collection .... **$100+**

A pump and handle serve as a modern mailbox post on a nearby homestead. Many hours were spent pumping water from a similar pump at our one-room country schoolhouse. Thank goodness we had running water on the farm, even in the 1940s when I was young. These pump heads and assemblies sell for anywhere from $10-$25 at auctions as collectibles and for even more if still operable, as many Amish farms still use them. .. **$10-$25**

This No. 2 C. S. Bell & Co. Bell from Hillsboro, Ohio, cast in 1938, is a fine example of a farm bell. It would command at least a $100 bid at any farm auction and may sell for far more. Of increasing value to collectors is the variety of bells found on old farmsteads. Again, beware of reproductions of cast iron products such as bells and seats. ......**$100+**

A Clipper Fanning Mill was available at a local yard sale but I did not have a place to display it. But the VanAlstine family found a use for one by displaying it as a coffee table in the living room. VanAlstine Collection..........**$200 at least**

A beautiful Detroit Jewel stove is shown in a close-up. **$1,500**

An extremely nice butter churn made by the Union Mfg. Co., Toledo, Ohio. *VanAlstine Collection*... **$300+**

The smaller butter churn is shown in a close-up. .... **$200-$300**

Details of the egg crate made of aluminum seen on top of the stove in photos. It held three dozen eggs in the little holders. I had not seen this crate previously and imagine it would bring $35-$50 at auction. *VanAlstine Collection*.. **$35-$50**

Tins and a small crock. The tins are a lard and a shortening tin, both of which would bring at least $25 at auction. We use a Farmer's Peet lard tin for our wastebasket in a bathroom. **$25**

Some of the nice crocks in the VanAlstine Collection.
..............................**$25-$50+ each**

A nice pie safe showing the crocks and a large clothing basket draped by a country quilt. Pie safes are selling for about $250 at most farm auctions. I am sure the basket would command $50-$100 at most auctions. **$250**

A Vail & Crane Cracker Co. tin from Detroit, Mich. This fine tin box would fetch $50 or better at any auction. **VanAlstine Collection**.
.... **$50+**

A nice detailed crock with extra graphics, making it worth at least $50, and a unique star that was one of the original city of Big Rapids Christmas decorations. *VanAlstine Collection* **$50**

A nice wooden berry basket holder worth $20-$30 is filled with older *Farm Journal and Woman's Day* magazines on display in the VanAlstine home. The magazines from the 1940s are worth about $5-$10 each as well. .... **$20-$30**

A crockery jug and a nice advertising pail with two pair of wooden skis. The skis are worth at least $25 a pair and the crock and pail would be worth the same or more. *VanAlstine Collection* **$25**

A nice antique English bread box, the skis and crockery jug again, and a beautiful old wooden ironing board. The ironing board should be valued at $35-$75. *VanAlstine Collection* ....**$35-$75**

Sunshine Krispy Crackers tin is colorful but not in perfect shape. It is of special local appeal as the crackers were made in nearby Grand Rapids, Mich. This tin is worth at least $25, even in less than mint condition. *VanAlstine Collection*.......................................**$25**

The pole insulator was once a very popular farm collectible. They have come out of favor and the value has dropped accordingly. But they are colorful and can usually be found at every farm auction. Rare ones are still valuable, the same as rare canning jars, but common ones are only worth about $2-$5 each. *Paulsen Collection*.........**$2-$5**

A Hoosier was adapted to modern function as an entertainment center in the VanAlstine home, surrounded by nice tin containers and crates. Hoosiers are selling for $500 easily at auctions in the Midwest. ....**$500+**

A water bath for cooling milk cans holds a hanging petunia plant on the VanAlstine front porch. This large tin should bring $25 or better at auction. **$25**

Advertising boxes and a water boiler sitting on an old table. The boiler should bring at least $30 in this nice condition and the boxes will fetch from $10-$20 each. *VanAlstine Collection*..................**$10-$30**

Earlier water jugs include a Hercules in a wooden box and a newer Shay Spring Water jug in a metal frame. The wooden boxed version should command at least $50 and the other one $25-$35 at least. They are both unusual but the Hercules is a little more in demand due to the wooden crate. *VanAlstine Collection* ....,,,,, **$25-$50 each**

An early wringing device on an old tub shows washday on the farm was never fun. It was made by The American Wringer Co. of New York and is their Horse Brand Clothes Wringer (trademark is a horse in a lucky horseshoe). *VanAlstine Collection* .... **$25-$50**

Graniteware and a country sign show a warm welcome to the VanAlstine country home. There is a neat little pair of child's boots, too. None of this graniteware is of great value, due to condition, but it shows a great way to display your graniteware with a chip or two.

A crock full of brass door knobs, a nice heater grate, a milk case, and a beautiful crock with flow blue designs sit next to the Hoosier entertainment center in the VanAlstine home. The flow blue piece would fetch better than $100 easily and most of the items in this photo are of significant value. The least expensive piece would be the milk case at about $20. The lady's shoes are gorgeous. .... **20-$100 each**

An old water boiler in rough shape was found in the Nerbonne barn. .... **$10-$15**

The Clipper Fanning Mill coffee table in the VanAlstine home and two more nice crocks are shown from another angle. Brown/white crock on left ....$35-$50
White #4..........................$75+

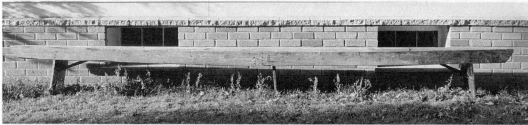

A nice old threshing bench shown in front of our farm home. We bought this for only $5 at a farm auction. However, attendance was very poor and so was the weather. I would value it at $25-$50 more realistically. .... **$25-$50**

A 1950s steel lawn chair in need of paint was purchased by my wife for a dollar at a garage sale. I think it was a steal and she actually bought three for $3. ....$1

A crock with blue trim, an antique candle mold and a large kraut cutter are shown in this photo, along with a couple of quilts. Kraut cutters usually sell for $50 or better, and the candle mold is nearly identical to one recently sold online for $65. The crock is about a $75 item. *VanAlstine Collection*..**$50-$75**

Some nice crockery jugs and USA Ware are shown in this photo, along with a large plastic crow. *VanAlstine Collection*.................**$50+**

My California Redwood hand-sculpted rendition of a Scottish Highlander bull was modeled after some photos of ones I had shown the artist. That was combined with the Texas Longhorns he had seen in the California foothills near Laguna Beach. No market value is available, as it is one of a kind and not for sale. But it is a neat little farm item made for me when I was far away from the farm, living in Laguna Beach...**Priceless**

Even more crockery pieces adorn the VanAlstine cupboards, along with a "farm" rooster, a Maid-Rite scrub board, a granite ware strainer, a New Era chip container, two more wash boards, an old Quaker Oats container, and a Gold Medal tin tea box. ....**$25-$100**

A weathervane, beautifully detailed but repainted, is from the original VanAlstine family barn a few rods east of the VanAlstine home. It is heavy cast iron. ....**$50+**

An evener is used to hold an American flag in the VanAlstine home. **$10**

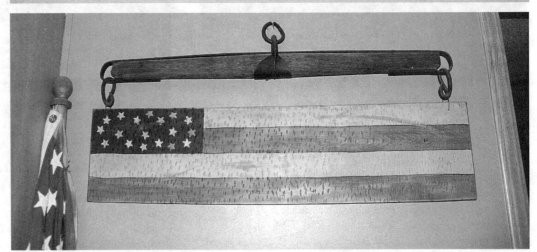

This crankshaft from a John Deere 4020 that holds up the mailbox at the VanAlstine farm is not old, but neat. ....**$10+**

My favorite cookie jar, a hen and her chick, was purchased for my wife in Ladysmith, Wis., in 1998 for $235 from an antique store. This is simply as country as one can find. It has a beautiful patina in the glazing and is mint. *Lewis Collection* **$235**

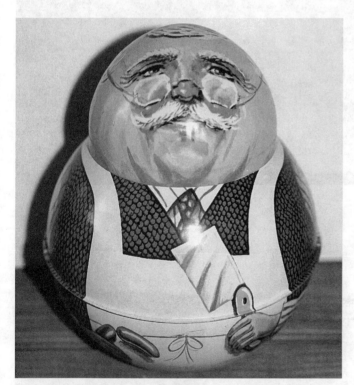

This butcher Roly Poly reproduction from Chien in 1980 is a nice collectible piece from a more recent production. Even the 1980 versions usually sell for $25-$50 depending on the figure. *Lewis Collection* ....**$25-$50**

This decorative crock is an heirloom kitchen piece that has been in the Lewis family for at least 100 years. It came with the farm my father purchased from my great uncle in 1946. The crock shows two cows, one standing, and in another field is some shocked corn. It is a beautiful light blue glaze, going to white in the center. Even with the two small chips, it would be worth $100+ due to age and also due to the unique details. *Lewis Collection* ....**$100+**

A reproduction Shredded Wheat recipe tin box from the early 1970s and an original pair of green checkered glass stove top shakers were given to me by my wonderful mother-in-law a few years ago. The tin was found at a garage sale for 50 cents and is worth 10 times that at least. The shakers are valued at about $30 a pair. *Lewis Collection*...............**$5-$30**

Wool carders from our own collection. They sit on a nice Hagar ashtray ($20-$30) and in front of a nice McCoy planter ($50). *Lewis Collection*.........**$25**

The wooden darning egg was a necessity to sew the socks on a farm. These tend to sell for $10+ at auctions. *Lewis Collection* ....**$10+**

Chapter Nine:

The Farm Garden

This chapter covers the one field still lasting into today's economy in large scale: the garden companies and their seeds, and the family garden. Each winter morning, one sits in anticipation of the seed catalog coming in the afternoon mail, bringing with it hopes of spring and abundance in the garden. There are many items of interest in this field: advertising specifically related to seeds and gardening, early gardening tools, seed packages, catalogs, and the comeback of "heritage or antique seed varieties" in recent years. Seed display units from old hardware stores are in demand, as are calendars and "give-away" items from seed companies (see advertisement reprinted in Chapter 3).

No chapter in the book likely means more to me. I truly became a farmer with the assistance of a farm garden. In anticipation of joining the FFA in the ninth grade, my father allowed me to have 1 1/4 acres for a garden to raise some money to buy my first animals for an agricultural production project. With that garden, at age 11, I grew one acre of sweet corn and a variety of other produce, then sold it all wholesale to a man with a stand on the main highway 2 1/2 miles from our farm. I grossed $756 for my efforts and with the money purchased three bred gilts that each gave me 14 or 16 piglets. I then raised them, sold them, and purchased a dozen Holstein heifers and, as they say, the rest is history. At age 15, I talked my dad into buying a dairy farm with me (we had a small one but this one was bigger, with cows included). Off we went, a few miles down the road, with my 12 heifers and 25 cows already in place. By the end of high school, we milked 120 head and I became Michigan's Outstanding Dairy Farmer in the FFA for 1965. The proudest moment of my farming life all started due to a farm garden.

We raised more than 20 acres of pickles for Heinz when I was young. When I was four and my brothers were 13 and 14, my dad told us we could have all the money from all the pickles we could pick to buy a television set, the first in our rural neighborhood in 1951. So this is a big garden, but 20 acres of pickles is just a garden.

Today, we all still anticipate the first cucumber of the season, that first vine-ripened tomato, the early potatoes that taste so good from one's own earth, those fall crops as they mature, and the parsnips we leave in the ground to sweeten with age. There is something about hope lasting eternal when one gardens, and the seed companies know this all too well. The seed companies must hire illustrators from the Planet Unbelievable to design the covers and illustrations of the plants one gets from their seeds, and only their seeds. We all know it is not going to happen on our land, yet we buy the seeds in anticipation of giant fruits and vegetables appearing shortly after planting, and full size Sequoias growing within

one year. The carnival barkers have nothing on seed salesmen.

Many of the items in the seeds and gardening category are paper items. This includes such items as early seed catalogs, seed bags and boxes, advertisements for seeds, and cloth seed bags for the farm trade. I have placed the crate labels of fruits and vegetables in this chapter because it seems appropriate. Any of these items increase in value greatly if in pristine condition.

Most catalogs get tossed out, making early seed catalogs collectible and valuable. Anything from the 1940s or earlier is going to bring at least $20 in fine shape, just for the value of illustrations. Add to that the demand by a particular company collector and it will increase quickly, doubling in value. For instance, Funk's Seed Corn has been in existence since the 1800s. If someone collected Funk's signs and memorabilia, they would pay more for a 1930 brochure than someone just interested in illustrations of seed corn. If one was given an award by Funk's, collected Funk's, and had a shot at the same item, one would likely pay even more. That is how the "value-added" approach works with antiques and collectibles: the more personal an item gets, the more we will pay for it.

Tin signs are also important in this area of collecting. All of the farm seed companies, and many garden seed companies, produced tin signs for the farmer to place in the field (by the roadside) for the passing motorists to see the brand and type of corn or barley or alfalfa. These signs are a thing of the past. The seed companies now provide a sign made of composition board or material that is not going to stand the test of time (see one shown in Chapter 3). However, some of the early seed company signs bring the same price as early tin dairy signs, $50 on up, depending on age and condition. Often these signs do not even come onto the market until a farm is sold. Even then they may not be sold, as they are often a part of the landscape and not in the barn or house to be found.

Early seed corn was shipped in wooden boxes. One of these boxes with the labels still intact would be worth more than $100. They are rare indeed. Then seed corn companies started shelling their corn and shipping it in the more common cloth bags that became popular with collectors, starting about 20 years ago. These bags are far more common, but condition is still often an issue. Nice ones with colorful graphics can still bring a decent price, but many can be found for a few dollars at auctions.

As with the seed corn, early garden seeds came in wooden crates and boxes, and then in both cloth bags and cardboard boxes. Some of the early cardboard boxes were very colorful items, with great illustrations of the fruits and vegetables one could expect from the seeds enclosed. These items are all very collectible and some are still found at auctions for reasonable prices.

The early seed companies also spent a lot of money on nice wooden display units for the hardware and feed stores. Many of these stands had outstanding graphic displays and beautiful lettering on them, and were well constructed. Though common at one time, with modernization of hardware and feed stores, many have been destroyed or tossed out. A few make their way to market. The prices vary widely and wildly, from a few dollars to a few hundred, depending on location and demand. It is far more likely that one will find one of the more common metal display units for sale. These bring up to $50, as they are usually adorned on top with nice tin lithography signs and illustrations of the vegetables and fruits.

Some groups, such as the Shakers, were shipping seeds very early in the 1800s and any of their items would be doubly valuable as a farm collectible and a piece of Americana. Items from the early communal societies such as the Shakers, the Oneida or the Amana colonies would bring a premium due to the wide appeal of these groups.

Fruit and vegetable shipping crates and labels have taken on a real interest with collectors in the past 30 years, and the demand is growing. The labels used on the ends of these crates were little works of art. They are in great demand for framing and display. Watch for fakes. Most labels still sell for only a few dollars so they are not being reproduced at the same rate as the porcelain and tin signs.

In addition, there have been ingenious and common garden tools around for more than 100 years that are worth collecting. These include: the old wooden-handled (no metal on handle at all) shovels and forks, early one-row cultivators for gardens, old hoes and spades, early row markers for planting, step potato planters, potato diggers, mulching devices, scarecrow devices, and special decoys of owls to scare away birds and pests. Many of these items have been shown in earlier chapters.

A Planet Junior garden seeder was a real bargain at the Yoder consignment auction at $15. It is in nice shape and all lettering is still visible.
.... **$15**

Some hive-smoking equipment. **$25**

Values of Farm Garden items

A seed identification display was made by Wendell Hester from Manilla, Ind. The display shows 24 common weeds found in Indiana, including wild lettuce, ragweed, and fox tail. This consisted of 5" x 7 1/4" unit with two panes of glass, bordered with a handmade galvanized metal frame. This is a classic gardening item as it identifies most of the gardener's enemies. **$26**

A lot of 33 wooden berry baskets consisting of old 1940s stock . **$18**

A 1930s-1940s vintage farm garden ornamental rooster (called a chicken) standing 19" high. Shipping was estimated at $14.50 to $35, hurting this item. Also, it was likely not as old as claimed. But it was a nice lawn type ornament with some age. **$25**

A nice hive-smoking set made by the Walter T. Kelley, Co. was in good working order and in fine condition. **$6**

A Simplex typewriter that was a give-away item from the Lancaster County Seed Co., Paradise, Pa. The Simplex was introduced in 1892 and this typewriter was an early model. It had an opening bid of $50 and, even though 55 people looked at the listing, there were no bids. I think this would have easily sold and brought far more if the starting bid was lower. This was a neat little item in its original shipping box and marked as a Seed Premium on the box. **$50**

A Louden's Cut-Out Form for High Curb Mangers was a neat adaptation of a tool to the garden. It was turned into a garden planter. The item was actually used to make curbs for one's dairy barn. See Chapter 2 for an example of a Louden's catalog available on CD-ROM. **$20**

A carrier for six berry boxes including the six boxes. The carrier is 18 1/2" x 12 1/2", large enough to hold six of the 6" berry boxes. **$10**

The hand corn planters were shown in Chapter 3 and in the tools section, Chapter 6. They were used normally to either inter-plant corn that did not come up in the field or as garden seeders.

Windmills were used to water animals in the fields, draw water for the home and barn, and water gardens. I have shown a windmill on Art Smith's garage. Another was shown earlier still standing near our current farm. Windmills are in great demand by collectors and restorers and can command up to $2,000 in decent condition. . **$2,000**

A farm garden decorative windmill is a common lawn ornament today, covered with vines. It stands near some traffic signs collected by their owner.

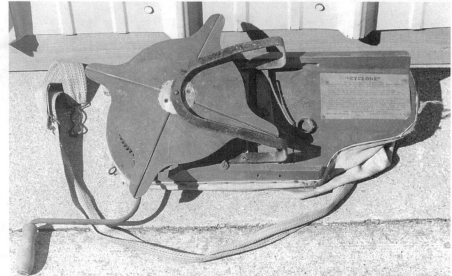

The "Cyclone" Seed Sower, described earlier in the book, from the Art Smith Collection shows the patent date and the original paper label on the bottom of the seeder. These are worth about $25 at most auctions, oftentimes far less. They are common and plentiful throughout the Midwest, where they were used to inter-seed crops and plant the garden. $25

This little flower garden, shown near the end of the season, adorns our farmstead and is lovingly crafted and tended by my wife (she gets me to weed once in a while).

These white pine stumps from more than 100 years ago, purchased for landscaping, were originally used in our part of Michigan for fencing. All of the ones shown are fairly small examples but still command $20+ when sold at auction. .... **$20 each**

A wooden hub wagon wheel sits in a hog trough. Both are very nice old pieces. These really break up the harsh lines of a foundation and add character to the entire homestead. The wheels would bring $35-$50 at auction. The trough is likely worth $5-$10. ....**$5-$50**

A wooden hub wagon wheel is used as a centerpiece in a neighbor's garden to set off a new tree planting.

A variety of farm collectibles and primitives are used by the VanAlstines to set off their beautiful gardens. The photos show their use of implement wheels, kegs, a buggy tire, and a primitive tool carrier in the gardens. The gardens were toward the end of the season but still beautiful.

Wheels..$10-$35
Tool Carrier.......................................$5
Bird house..$5
Keg..$20
Bob Sled...$75+

Some additional VanAlstine garden photos show a nice steel child's lawn chair, a tin water or grain tub, some barbed wire, and a wooden-handled shovel. ....**$5-$25**

An unknown very large wooden wheel I am guessing is a counter-weight from a mill or pump. It is a nice addition to the VanAlstine garden.

A hand pump is still in the ground but not functioning on the Nerbonne farm. ....**$100+**

A child's high chair and a galvanized bucket are on this corner of a small garden house on the VanAlstine property. ....**$5=$75**

Two metal chairs are found in the VanAlstine gardens. ....**$5-$10 each**

Boilers are used as garden decorations. These are all found in the VanAlstine Collection and have been used as decorating touches in the gardens. Most copper boilers sell for $25-$50, sometimes higher at certain auctions, and the tin versions sell for about half as much or less. ....**$25-$50 each**

The garden cultivator has seen better days but it makes a nice addition to this focal point in the VanAlstine garden. .... **$5-$15**

Tubs also make nice additions to the garden. The wash tub with the three holes in it was done for some sorting purpose to fit around a three-legged table. Also note the one tub on an original wash tub stand. All of these are from the VanAlstine Collection. Galvanized wash tubs are not high priced, usually only bringing $5-$20, depending on size, age, type, and condition. .... **$5-$20 each**

An early red wagon holds flowers and is displayed next to a neat roll of barbed wire at the VanAlstine farm. ....**$25-$50**

A nail keg serves as a flowerpot, a graniteware dish hangs, a silage shovel leans, and a child's "necessary" chair sits next to a well-aged barn wood door at the VanAlstine home. None of these items is valued at more than $20 each in the condition shown. But it is a nice way to use these items for display. .... **$20 each**

A primitive tool carrier, a graniteware frying pan, and an old wooden chair set off this garden scene at the VanAlstine home. None of the pieces are worth more than $10, but it makes a nice scene on the porch of this little garden house...................................... **$10 each**

This antique buggy is on the rear porch at the VanAlstine home. The funny thing about this beautiful stroller is that they found it at a home while visiting. The people were using it to cart wood into the house! I never thought I would see a nice antique being used as a wood cart but "one's person's treasures…" It is well-used and weathered. ....**$25-$35**

A square wash tub has been turned into a large flowerpot at another focal point in the VanAlstine garden. $10

These two pump heads were for sale at the Yoder auction. These brought decent money because they were both in working order.
.... $35-$60

A number of collectible crate end labels are shown. Most are fairly common. .... **$5-$15 each**

Chapter Ten:

Farm Recreation

Hunting and fishing were often necessary for the farmer to provide needed food. They were usually not seen as recreational activities in our earlier history, simply an extension of food production. Many companies marketed items to farmers in a different manner, including selling crow decoys and owl decoys to deter the crows as pests from the farm and garden, and the marketing of predator calls to eliminate those "bad" animals from the farm.

I covered the areas of hunting and fishing collectibles in my numerous books on fishing collectibles and a book on duck decoys and related collectibles. However, I thought it worth pointing out that some of these items had a special niche on the farm long before they were seen as recreational. Chapter 14 shows some special advertising to induce the farmer to buy a particular product that is now seen as recreational in nature. Also, there were games and recreational activities specifically marketed to farm families that will be covered here and in Chapter 14 as well. Clearly, many of these items are now in the field of general collector interest. But it is important to show their relationship to farming and farm family life.

Advertising items would be valued according to the same guidelines developed in Chapters 1 and 3 in this book. However, some of them would be far more valuable due to the high demand for sporting collectibles. Any of the calls, the decoys, the rods, reels, and lures are worth anywhere from a few dollars to a few thousand. It all depends on age, quality, rarity, and demand. These are the same factors as found for all collectibles. But, for the most part, many sporting related collectibles are available within a price range of $20-$50.

Other farm recreational activities of interest would be: the outdoor activities of sliding (sledding in some parts of the country), horse riding, things related to the showing of animals and the county fair, the role of baseball in agrarian America, and the numerous games and parlor activities developed to wile away the time prior to the advent of television and radio. Of course, many of these could be covered under children's games and toys also. But I have placed them here if more oriented to the entire family.

Values of Farm Recreational items

Current values can be found in a review of any of the books available. Values can be tracked online at www.ebay.com and other online auction services. I would recommend starting with *Collecting Antique Bird Decoys and Game Calls, 3rd Edition,* by Carl F. Luckey and Russell E. Lewis, Krause Publications, 2003, for an overview of the importance of bird decoys in collecting. In it, I show a number of crow decoys and crow calls, in addition to hundreds of duck decoys. Also, I discuss the importance of predator calls to farming and show examples. It is also an excellent source to examine photographs of related collectibles such as oil cans, shotshell boxes, knives, and advertising items. As to fishing lure collectibles, either of my books: *Modern Fishing Lure Collectibles, Volume 1* (2002) or *Volume 2* (2003), Collector Books, would be a good introduction to the field. See www.wwbait.net for more information on my fishing lure books.

Items to look for in this field include, in addition to hunting and fishing items, other farm recreational items, many mentioned earlier in the book, such as: croquet sets, badminton sets, Jarts, Carom boards, dart boards, BB guns, large farm play sets that may have been homemade (e.g., barns, fencing, even wooden animals made on band saws), outdoor play equipment, riding toys (horses, tractors, bicycles), toy wagons, sleds, toboggans, archery items, baseball and softball equipment, books on parlor games for children and families, and the list can go on.

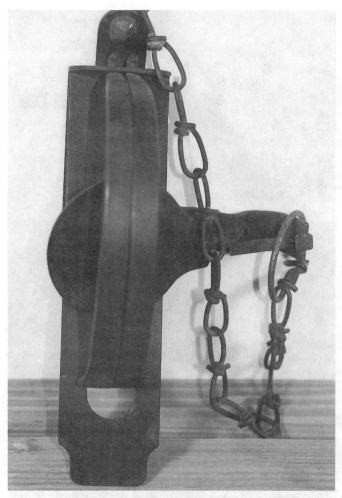

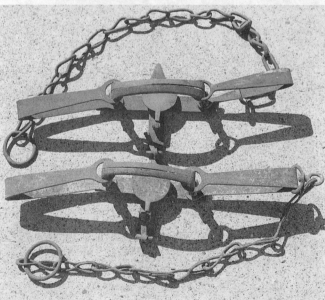

Trapping was part recreational and part economic for many farmers (see the large Sears advertisement reprinted in Chapter 3 directed toward farmers regarding trapping). Traps have increased in value recently, as have items related to trapping, such as trap identification, license tags, and scents. Some examples of collectible traps are shown. See the comments of Art Smith in Chapter 13 regarding trap values. Traps sell for $5 each to $500 or more depending on type, age, brand, and size. Art Smith Collection and Lewis Collection
.... **$5-$500**

Baseball is America's pastime. We all played it as children, rural schools had baseball tournaments, we watched it as we grew up, and most rural communities had teams. Softball was also a big rural pastime and most communities still have leagues. Of course, baseball cards were a part of all of our youth, and we all yearn for those Mickey Mantle and Al Kaline cards we used in our bicycle spokes to make the bicycle sound like an engine. In addition, one could spend a lot of time seeking out older items such as the "Official Clincher" giant softball from the 1880s shown. Lewis Collection...**20+**

**A common papier-mâché'
crow decoy** from the 1950s.
See my book on decoys for
hundreds of examples of crows,
ducks, and owls. Crows such
as this were often sold in a set
of two crows and an owl for
predator crow hunting. Lewis
Collection **$25**

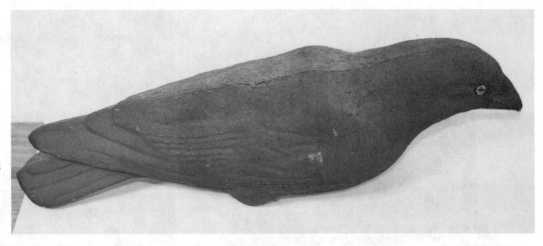

**Crow, duck, goose, turkey and
other game calls** are popular
collectibles. Farmers also used
fox and coyote predator calls.
Some examples are shown.
Calls are often found at auctions
for a few dollars and are usually
a good buy. Many can sell for
$25 to a few hundred dollars,
depending on the age, maker,
type, and rarity. Many calls are
unmarked, making it difficult
for the uninitiated to tell the
value. One simple guideline to
keep in mind is that most metal
reed calls are older than plastic
reed calls. Of course, the older
calls usually command more
money. Also, packaging is very
important and really increases
the value of the call. The photos
show crow, duck and turkey
calls. Lewis Collection
.... **$75+ each**

Bicycles, wagons, skis and sleds were farm recreational items for many of us. Additional related items would be skates and early snow coasters. Sleds sell for $25-$50 and so do the wagons.

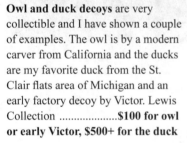

Owl and duck decoys are very collectible and I have shown a couple of examples. The owl is by a modern carver from California and the ducks are my favorite duck from the St. Clair flats area of Michigan and an early factory decoy by Victor. Lewis Collection ....**$100 for owl or early Victor, $500+ for the duck**

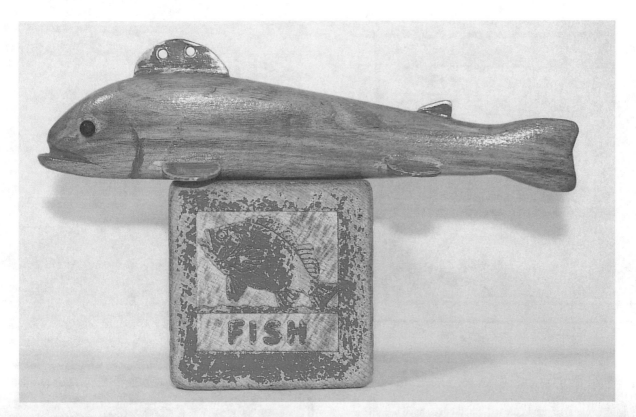

Spearing for fish was a winter pastime in the north, from New York through Minnesota primarily. Collectibles related to spearing include both the fish decoys and the spears. One needs a lot of guidance in this field to determine the value. But the collector should be aware of these little fish as being valuable, ranging from a minimum of $25 to thousands for rare Oscar Petersens from Michigan and some of the very old New York decoys. Often a spear sells for only $10 at a farm auction and would be a good buy at that price. A small decoy believed to be an Oscar Petersen is shown, as well as a typical Minnesota decoy and an unknown Michigan decoy. Lewis Collection

.... **$25-$500+ each**

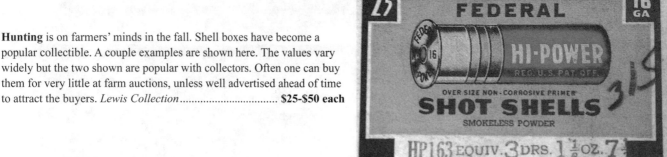

Hunting is on farmers' minds in the fall. Shell boxes have become a popular collectible. A couple examples are shown here. The values vary widely but the two shown are popular with collectors. Often one can buy them for very little at farm auctions, unless well advertised ahead of time to attract the buyers. *Lewis Collection* .... **$25-$50 each**

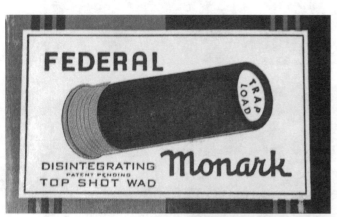

Trap and skeet practice helps prepare for hunting. The box shows some trap shells. Also shown is a Remington awards pin. *Lewis Collection* .... **$35+ for the box, $10-$15 for the pin**

Reloading shotgun shells was common in earlier times. Shown are a couple of reloading tools that are very collectible. These are often overlooked or unidentified at farm auctions but some command a decent price on the collectible market. *Lewis Collection* .... **$100 for reloading tool, $20 for measurer**

A Weber display piece ($50+), some nice reels and lures, and the head of a cardboard Dupe-A-Goose made in Seattle worth about $25 are shown in a closeup. *Lewis Collection* **Reels $100+, Lures $15-$100**

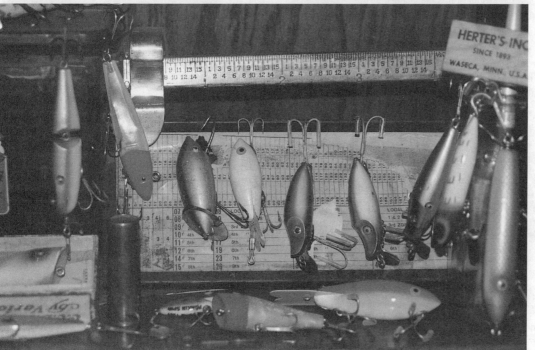

A few lures and a neat old scale received when I purchased the Weber of Stevens Point fly fishing company archives are shown. The scale was previously used by the company in its mailing operations. The lures include some rare colored CCBC plunkers, a nice rainbow Pikie, some rainbow Heddon River Runts, and some more common Bombers in rainbow. There is also a nice little Heddon Crab Wiggler. These lures range in value from $10 for the little red/white L & S lure hanging on the scale to more than $300 for the rare plunker in the box, because of its rare color. *Lewis Collection* **$10-$300 each**

FINE FISHING TACKLE by Shakespeare

CATALOG NO. 38 A

TOMORROW

Good Management—plenty food—plenty cover—plenty fish

A rare Perdew crow call seen at the top of the case on the second shelf from the top ($300-$500) and a reproduction Winchester lure in the box on the bottom shelf ($100) are part of my collection. Many nice three-hook Heddon and Pflueger lures are shown in the case, some common and rare fly rod baits, reels rare and common, and a very old Skinner box. Also shown is a Weber display piece from the 1950s. The items shown range in value from a low of about $20 to nearly $1,000 for some of the rare Vom Hofe reels. *Lewis Collection*. ....**$20-$500 each**

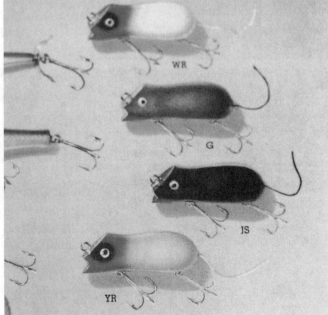

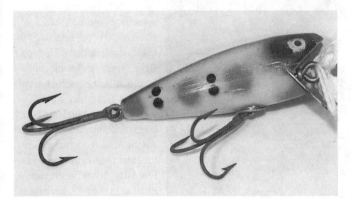

A 1950s Shakespeare Glo-Lite Pup hard plastic lure. **$20**

Advertising items are very valuable, and this 1938 Shakespeare Catalog mint in its mailing envelope is no exception to the rule. This is worth about $300 in this condition, due to its early date and mint condition. I have also shown a color chart for the famous Shakespeare mouse lure as an example of one lure to collect. *Lewis Collection*...**$300**

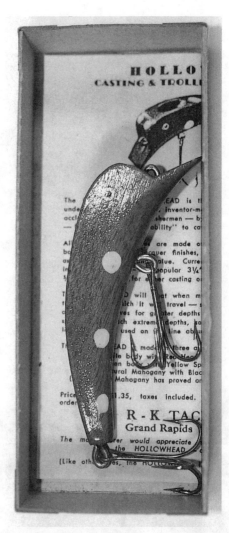

An early Lowe's spinner with the famous Buffalo trademark from the early 1900s. *Lewis Collection* .... **$50+**

This Hollowhead lure has an interesting history. It was manufactured of mahogany wood from the Baker Furniture Factory in Grand Rapids, Mich. It was made by an employee, using scraps, in about 1946-1949. I was fortunate enough to buy all of the remaining stock of the company that had been stored in the maker's garage for nearly 45 years. I have sold many of these for a low of $35 to a high of $65, all new in box. *Lewis Collection* **$65**

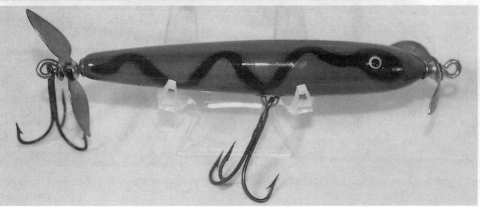

This early Paw Paw wooden lure has one of my favorite color patterns and is in mint condition. The torpedo shaped lure is from the 1940s or early 1950s. *Lewis Collection* **$75**

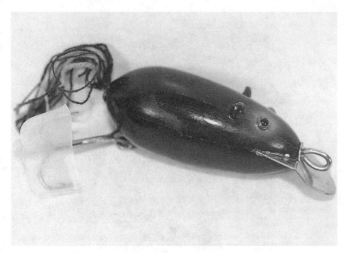

Another old Paw Paw is this valuable mouse lure. *Lewis Collection*.
.... **$100**

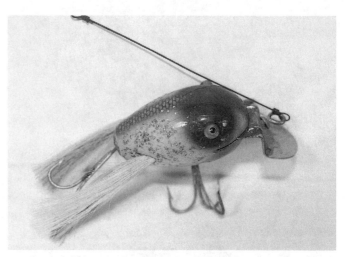

Creek Chub Bait Co., from Indiana, was famous for its Silver Flash color as seen on a Dingbat lure. The Dingbat lure is quite collectible and in this fine condition will sell for $40-$75, more for some colors. *Lewis Collection*... **$40-$75**

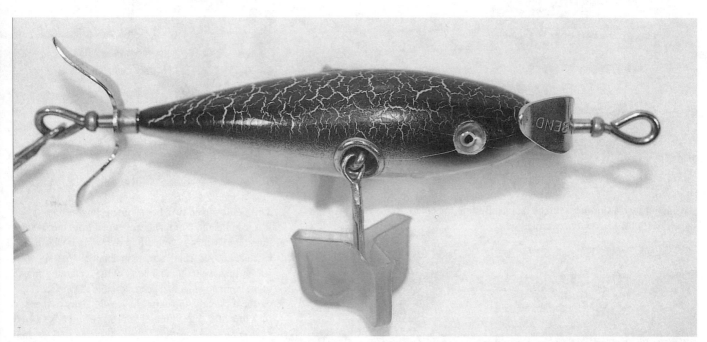

South Bend is one of the "big five" lure companies. This nice three-hook minnow with glass eyes in a crackleback paint pattern is a very nice addition to any collection. *Lewis Collection* .... **$150-$200**

Bud Stewart, a famous maker of fish decoys, also made lures and sold them nationally by advertising in sporting magazines. Bud Stewart lures are shown, not mint but excellent lures to find. *Lewis Collection* .... **$100+ each**

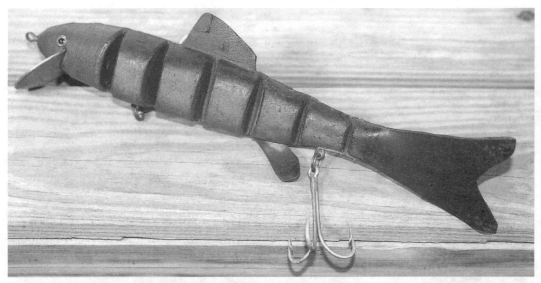

One of many rubber Musky baits offered in Wisconsin. This jointed Musky Sucker Minnow from the 1950s is valued at about $30. *Lewis Collection*..........................**$30**

Even empty boxes are valuable if in clean condition. Here are early 1950s Shurebite and Wood's boxes. *Lewis Collection*...**$20 each**

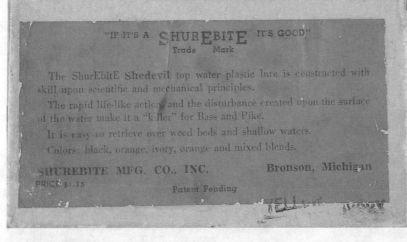

These little advertising screwdrivers are nice to add to a fishing lure collection. *Lewis Collection*..................**$10 each**

An early Fred Arbogast Tin Liz lure. *Lewis Collection* $35

A Pflueger "Speede" oil bottle, in mint condition, makes a nice addition to either a fishing or oil collection. *Lewis Collection* $15

Fly fishing collectibles include a reel such as my original Pflueger Medalist, purchased new in the 1960s ($50+), and the leather trimmed creel. *Lewis Collection* .... $50-$150

A group of collectibles includes a nice early fly reel, a fish knife and a Remington pocket notebook. The reel is valued at $100+, the knife at $15, and the notebook at $20. *Lewis Collection* .... $15-$100+ each

Collectible reels abound. They vary in value from $5 each for common baitcasting reels from the 1960s to hundreds and even thousands of dollars for early and/or rare versions. Shown is a common, but collectible, red Ambassadeur from the 1950s to rare early models. The Ambassadeur is worth about $100, as is the Paul Bunyan. The Heddon has been selling for $350-$450. The others are in the $150-$250 price range. *Lewis Collection* ....**$100-$450 each**

Chapter Eleven:

Farm Organizations

This chapter includes collectible items from organizations such as The Grange, 4-H, and the FFA. Most American farmers have been a member of an organization or cooperative. Each of these groups has produced items that have become collectible by their scarcity or by design (such as the toy tractors endorsed by the FFA discussed in Chapter 4). At this time, many of these items have little known market value. But as our demand increases for farm memorabilia, it is anticipated that we shall see an increase in the trading of pins, awards, and certificates in much the same way as similar fraternal society and military items have increased in value over the recent years.

This chapter is the most speculative of them all due to the little data we have on many items and the fact that many of them are very personal by design. In other words, someone's blue ribbon from the state fair is valuable, but how does one place a dollar value on it? Only time will tell which items become most collectible. But if an examination of fraternal and military items has any bearing, and I think it does, the pins, medals, and awards will increasingly valuable as fewer and fewer people are actively involved in agricultural production. I have included a number of my own awards as examples of what to look for and how these would be valued as to rarity. Clearly, a pin that is given to one of 22,000 is worth more than a pin given to each chapter member of the FFA. This is a beginning way to value such items and will help collectors be more knowledgeable at farm auctions. I have also given some online sales data prices and shown some of Art Smith's FFA memorabilia.

Some farm granges used tin or porcelain signs to mark their location, as found in other areas of collecting, and these would be of similar values. Again, values are still being developed but this is another area that should not be overlooked. Also, closely related are such cooperatives as the Farm Bureau and the hundreds of local co-ops that produce electricity and provide fuel for farmers. These co-ops gave away pens, pencils, clocks, thermometers, water gauges, calendars, and many of these items have advertising value as discussed in Chapters 1 and 3. Two examples of Farm Bureau signs were shown earlier in the book.

I hope that by the time I do a second edition of this book, this area is better known and patterns are more developed for these important personal pieces of farming history. In the meantime, I hope this is a guide for you.

Values of Organization Collectibles

Older FFA officer indicator for the president brought seven bids. This was the desk sign that we always placed out in front of the appropriate officer at chapter meetings, in this case the president. As chapters cease to exist, look for items like this being offered for sale by local school systems.. **$51**

A common chapter farmer pin did not bring any bids at $5.... **$2-$3**

A similar pin did sell for $5. ....**$5**

FFA members often had a metal sign in front of the farm that said "FFA Member Lives Here." This sign was in nice clean condition with no major bends or dents and paint was solid. It measured 13 1/2" x 9 1/2"...**$31**

A 1950s felt FFA pennant sold after receiving eight bids. This 22" banner was common among members and not at all rare, as the listing indicated. However, most of these old pennants have been tossed away, or folded, or damaged in some way. This pennant appeared to be in excellent shape. **$37.50**

Two FFA jackets with officer's pins still on them, both in great shape, were a real bargain. The pins alone were worth the price. **$12.50**

U.S. stamps commemorated the 25th anniversary of the FFA in 1953. A beautiful stamp and plate blocks of this stamp sell usually for around $10. ....**$10**

Four pins, including two FFA pins. **$5.50**

Six 4-H pins and three FFA pins. **$47.50**

Eleven 4-H and FFA pins sold after receiving only two bids. This lot included four award pins, a Gold Star pin, and others....................**$13**

Another FFA jacket without pins..**$8.25**

A Schrade Commemorative single blade knife, model SCH-LB8 Papa Bear 5" closed locking clip blade with brass bolsters and Staglon handles with the FFA insignia on the blade. **$33**

A 10-year vocational agricultural adviser pin from 1956 marked 10K gold. It was presented to Lloyd Thor in 1956 for his service to the FFA..**$26**

Another FFA jacket without pins from Missouri....................**$13.50**

A large sterling-silver FFA men's ring. **$25**

My personal trophies for outstanding agricultural production projects for the Cedar Springs, Mich., Chapter, awarded two years in a row, 1964 and 1965. *Lewis Collection* .... **$50+ each**

Two of my personal officer pins for the FFA. *Lewis Collection* .... **$10 each**

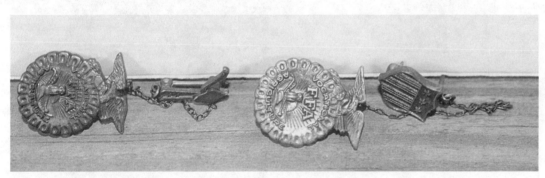

My personal pins for a Regional award and the highest honor available at the State level, Gold Star State Farmer in Dairy. Also shown are two Dekalb corn awards for highest corn yields for two years. These all date from 1964-65. *Lewis Collection* .... **$25-$100 each**

My personal pins for Chapter farmer, a record keeping award, and a pin from Funks' seed corn for outstanding corn crop. *Lewis Collection* .... **$5-$25 each**

My personal FFA pins from 1958-60. *Lewis Collection.......* **$5 each**

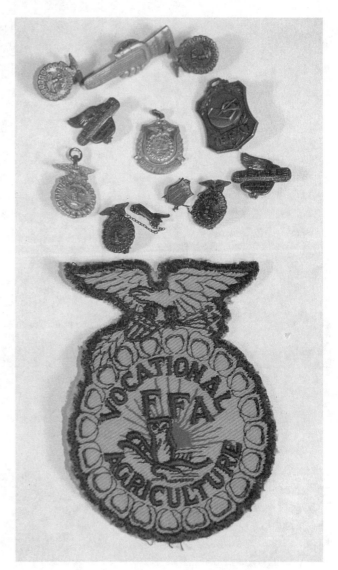

A commemorative knife made by Schrade for the FFA and sold through farm stores in the early 1990s. Value would be $25 in decent condition, likely double if still mint on the card (it came in a clear plastic card with a small FFA patch). The one shown I use to cut strings on hay bales on our farm. *Lewis Collection* .... **$25-$50**

Art Smith holds his FFA jacket from Coopersville, Mich., circa late 1960s. .... **$25+**

The pins and a nice patch from my personal FFA jacket, circa 1961. *Lewis Collection*.. **$10**

My most significant award from the FFA was this 1 of 22,000 award for being the best dairy youth in the State of Michigan for 1965. The odd thing is that the actual award was an inexpensive plaque that broke. So I removed the leather award emblem and have shown it here with the gold pin and the FFA emblem from my jacket. The leather patch has little trade value but the pin is very rare and should bring $100 or more if ever sold. *Lewis Collection* **$100**

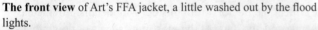

The front view of Art's FFA jacket, a little washed out by the flood lights.

Art Smith's State Farmer trophy for 1970, one of the chosen few to be best in the entire State of Michigan FFA organization for 1970. ....**$50-$100**

Art Smith's Star Green Hand award, meaning the best of the new members of the FFA in the Coopersville, Mich., Chapter that year. *Art Smith Collection*.. **$50+**

Chapter Twelve:

Collectible Tractors

When selecting the title for this chapter, I could not help but think that some might view the title as "fighting words." What is collectible to one person may not be to another. I have made a somewhat arbitrary selection of tractors that are the most recognized to my generation of farmers, those of us in our 50s and 60s. Not that the other tractors are not collectible, as they certainly are. However, we all recognize a John Deere A or B, and few of us recognize an old Rumely or even a very early green Allis-Chalmers. I have also had to select only a few of the major producers of tractors. And I have slighted some, only because I did not have access to all types or because some types were more popular than other types in our region. Thus, the lack of your favorite tractor being shown is not meant to indicate it is not valued, only that I did not have time to cover them all.

Our interest in collecting tractors stems from either what we had as children on the farm or what we wanted to have on the farm but could not purchase. I have documented this process well in my sporting collectible books and I certainly believe the same process is at work with farm collectibles. My earliest recollection of a tractor on our family farm was a Farmall BN. I not only rode on its square axle but actually fell off once while my dad was plowing. Of course, today we all see the dangers of that practice. However, at the time, there was no greater thrill than riding along with dad while he did his chores. After the incident, I was relegated to following behind in the plow furrow and was no longer allowed to ride along while plowing. A lesson was learned and farm safety then became more important to all of us.

Our family also had some early Allis-Chalmers tractors, and my Uncle Ray had only Allis-Chalmers products. Eventually we purchased the powerful John Deere A and B (non-electric start). One of our early "modern" tractors was a Case low profile. When a Ford dealer came to town, we bought a Ford 5000 as our first ultra modern tractor with newer hydraulics, live power, power steering, and all of the modern conveniences. Somewhere along the way, there were a couple of 8Ns and 9Ns used on the farm and in the woods for skidding logs. We also had some Oliver tractors in the family, with one great uncle relying on only that brand. Some neighbors thought that the Minneapolis-Moline brand was the only way to go while others had the more unusual Cockshutt or Co-Op tractors. Regardless of the brand or brands, I am certain that many of my readers had similar experiences and memories based upon family and neighborhood usage.

I think the "big names" in tractor collecting from the vintage era of 1930 through about 1965 are as follows (in alphabetical order to avoid brawling): Allis-Chalmers, Case, Farmall, John Deere, and, Oliver. Some would add to the list Massey-Harris,

Massey-Ferguson, and Minneapolis-Moline. Others might want to argue that Cockshutt, Co-Op, and others should be added. But, from my observation, the "big five" are the first five listed. I believe they have the greatest brand recognition to the non-farm community as well. John Deere undoubtedly has the greatest non-farm recognition due to its important role in history and its vigorous advertising in recent years for the lawn tractor market. Yet, most non-farm folks will still recognize any of the other big five brands as being important in the horse to tractor transition era.

I could spend an entire book on just this section but others have already and I am not going to repeat their efforts. I shall direct you to view their books. Also, there are a number of great Internet sites dedicated to antique and collectible tractors that should be on your favorite site lists. I would begin by viewing the following Internet sites and then selecting any number of excellent books to read on the subject. Sites to view include, but are not limited to: www.ssbtractor.com (a great source of history, parts, manuals, etc.); www.atis.net (claims to be the original Internet site for antique tractors since 1993, this site has an excellent bibliography of 23 different periodicals related to antique and collectible tractors and links to many of them); www.tractorshed.com (this is The Antique Tractor Shed and has photos, history and information on antique tractors, also a guide to upcoming shows and events); http://my.voyager.net (this Farm Life Page on the Internet has many links of interest); www.antiquetractorsonline.com/webring (this page links one to many, many interesting links on antique tractors and farm collectibles in general); and, last but not least www.antiquetractors.com (another complete site offering history, parts, discussion groups, show guides, events, and links to many other sites of interest).

Included in this chapter are a number of photos of some of the collectible tractors from this era with details provided as to value and age. One of the most fun aspects of doing this book was my encounter with "Lefty" Laughlin, a fine old gentleman from whom we purchase hay for our sheep farm. I am certain that there is a book in the life story of Laughlin. He was a flight engineer on the Outlaw, one of the planes in the 509th that tested the atomic bomb in the Pacific and was the right wing guard on the flights to Japan of historic importance during the war. But he is also a man onto himself in the tractor business. When I first purchased hay from him he mentioned that his **newest** tractor was a 1950 John Deere B. I knew I was in for a treat. Laughlin currently uses seven "antique" tractors in his daily farm operations. He is the only person I know who can state with authority that he has invested less than $1,000 in buying and repairing these tractors. His line includes: a pair of Oliver Row Crops, a 1948 Model 66 and a 1948 Model 77;

two 1946 John Deere As and a 1950 John Deere B; a 1941 Farmall H; a T5 International crawler from the early 1940s; a 1945 Oliver Model 60 baler and an older Massey-Ferguson Model 12 baler; an Oliver 77 and Oliver 70 waiting to be repaired, and an Allis-Chalmers B in the restoration stage.

How many collectors of antique tractors could state that they only use their collection? Laughlin thought it was funny that I should consider his accumulation of tractors as antiques but fully understood the value of his prized possessions to the collector. I have to share one story that is too good not to pass on to you. After a tour of his farm and his tractor collection, while driving by a neighbor's place, he told me about the time his neighbor wanted him to bale some hay but was unsure if Laughlin could do it "with such old equipment." Laughlin assured him that he had already baled thousands of bales that summer with the same equipment. Laughlin was so insulted by his neighbor's demand to use newer equipment to bale his hay that the offer to bale hay was withdrawn at that point. The moral of the story is many of us collect and use our equipment,

and its age is not a reflection of its inability to perform. I used my wife's Cub to rake hay each year while doing at least two cuttings of 40 or more acres of hay. It used a cupful of gasoline and was fun to drive for such a job. A Cub cannot do everything on a modern farm but it still performs fine for some jobs and should be used if available. Every tractor owner will have to decide the proper role for his/her collectibles but, for me, I will drive and use my tractors as part of my farm. They will not just be placed in "retirement row."

The photos selected for this section are somewhat arbitrary. They are ones that were easily available to me. I thought it better to show what is commonly found than what is the rare or difficult brand to find. I hope that the selection is enjoyed. Thousands of photos and dozens more models could have been shown if I would have unlimited space in the book and unlimited time to fill it. I do think the photos are representative of vintage tractors that are in high demand by collectors and I hope that it helps the beginner learn what people are seeking for their collections.

Values of Vintage Tractors

A gathering of the "orange" at Hutchinson, Minn., during the summer of 1996 shows some very nice Allis-Chalmers items. Included is the first truly successful commercial round baler. Also, note the All-Crop. A friend took a B to the show and sold it for $4,000, even though it was not for sale. ....$3000-$5,000

A small gathering of the "orange" at Millpond, near Blanchard, Mich. This shows a rare adaptation of a common Allis-Chalmers B into a road grader used by the road commission in the 1940s-50s in Michigan. The photo also shows a 1953 or 1954 WD-45 Diesel. It is easily recognized because the front cowling goes over the front axle only on that WD-45. .... $3000-$10,000

The mid-1940s Allis-Chalmers B with the road grader and a 1948 or 1949 C with the two-way plow.
.... $2,000

This 1951 WD-45 was owned and restored by Jerry Paulsen. Note the front end difference between this and the diesel shown on the previous page.
.... $3,000+

This wide front 1952 Allis-Chalmers CA was owned and restored by Jerry Paulsen and eventually traded for the 1956 Farmall Cub. Paulsen valued the CA at $3,500 at the time of the trade. $3,500

The Paulsen CA with another restored Allis-Chalmers B in the background at a tractor meet in Michigan. **$3,500**

The Cub that Jerry Paulsen received in a trade for the Allis-Chalmers mentioned, prior to any restoration work being done on it. **$4,000**

A 1946 John Deere A owned by Lefty Laughlin, waiting to be used. **$1,500**

The Cub after restoration work was complete, in three views. The tires are original to give one an idea of the excellent shape this tractor was in when found. You should hear it purr. A simple pull on the starter rod, and it is off and running. Paulsen would not sell this particular Cub for less than $4,000. ...
.... **$4,000**

Laughlin's 1948 Oliver 77 Row Crop, with engine shield removed, hooked to a 1960s New Idea manure spreader. This is a working collectible. Laughlin found both of his Row Crop Oliver tractors with trees growing in front of both rear axles. He had to "cut them out of the woods" before he could begin repairs. **$2,000**

Jerry Paulsen and his Cub.

A Case garden tractor for sale by a neighbor, with a nice snow blower on front. Asking price $1,200

An Allis-Chalmers 1965 garden tractor Paulsen is restoring at this time, showing two colors that will be corrected to the original when done. He estimates this tractor will bring between $600 and $800 when completed......................................$600-$800

Laughlin's 1948 Oliver 66 Row Crop next to a 1946 John Deere A............ $2,000

Laughlin's second 1946 John Deere A. .... $1,500-$2,000

Some of the implements that go with the A-C 1965 garden tractor, shown on previous page or similar Simplicity models. ....**Value: $25-$100 each**

Laughlin's nice 1950 John Deere B all tucked away for winter. A second photo shows the shift pattern on the 1950 B. All of his tractors will be stored in this or another shed for the winter. **$2,000**

A Ford 8N owned by a neighbor that was purchased at auction in Paris, Mich., and is used to mow the lawn. **$2,500**

Laughlin's 1941 Farmall H with a modified loader that is used to feed round hay bales to his Hereford cattle. He has increased the hydraulic pressure as much as possible and indicated to me that the tractor does just fine lifting the smaller 4x4 bales weighing about 800 pounds. It demonstrates that an antique tractor can be modified for modern needs. An interesting side note is that the chains seen on the tractor are from a 6x6 military craft that Laughlin retrieved from the Pacific when discharged in 1945. Yet another older item is still seeing use on today's farm. **$1,200**

A Massey-Ferguson Model 12 baler that Laughlin purchased for only $400 is in excellent working order. It was used all summer, baling hay. The baler did give him a little trouble until he discovered it was a simple spring on the hay dog that needed replacing, and then it only missed one tie in about 150 bales. Not bad for a baler at least 40 years old. **$400**

An early 1940s IHC crawler belonging to Laughlin. . **$3,000**

An Oliver Model 60 baler from 1945. This is also still used by Laughlin for hay baling. ..... **$600-$800**

An Allis-Chalmers B, with its front end already in the shop, being repaired by Laughlin. It is waiting to be pieced together and repaired. Value "in progress."

An Oliver 77 Row Crop waiting in the restoration department for care and repair, and an Oliver 70 also waiting for repairs by Laughlin. Value "in progress."

Laughlin's older Allis-Chalmers side delivery rake is in need of repairs. But it is still one that can be put into service when repaired. .... $75=$150

A couple of 1946 General Motors Corporation products, a ton and a half Chevy truck and a one-half ton pickup marked General Motors Truck on the plate. Laughlin is going to restore both of these items for use. The General Motors Truck is not marked GMC. Value "in progress."

A John Deere B purchased by David VanAlstine's father and still in the family on the farm in Michigan.
.............................$2,000

A **Ford 8N** that has been fully restored owned by Burnips Equipment of Burnips and Big Rapids, Mich. The tractor may be viewed in the dealership. ....$4,000+ **in this shape**

A **1946 Oliver** orchard model. Sold 2003 for.............................$850

A Ford 8N selling at the large Yoder consignment sale in Mt. Pleasant, Mich. All of the following tractors were from that sale and many were "no sale" tractors, bid back in by their owners. They are so noted, with the high bid also noted. This 8N was from 1948 or 1949 and the restoration job was noted by an obviously recent paint job. **$1,600**

A Ford 8N received bids of $2,400 and was still a "no sale." This should have been sold for that price, as that is about right according to my data. But some sellers put a premium on the restoration work they have done. **$2,400**

A nice F-12 McCormick-Deering from 1935 sold for only $1,125, and it ran fine. This shows the low price these vintage tractors reached. **$1,125**

An older McCormick-Deering.
....$1,025

A John Deere B............................. **$1,325**

A John Deere 70 Diesel sold for $1,225.
A John Deere AR sold for $1,400, a John
Deere wide front 720 Diesel sold for
$3,300, weights for the JD AR sold for
$550, and a three-point hitch for the JD
70 sold for $450. You can see these in the
background of the beautiful Ford 4000.
The Ford was all original and field-ready
with only 3,000+ hours. It only received a
high bid of $2,750 and was a "no sale."
.... **$450-$1,225**

A Farmall H with restored paint sold for $1,150 (shown) and a Farmall H, with original paint but the "H" painted on, sold for $975 (not shown).
....**$975-$1,150**

This 1949 Case VAC had frozen gears and still sold for $1,000. ....**$1,000**

A crank start Allis-Chalmers WC with spoke wheels received a high bid of $950 and was another "no sale." The 1940s Oliver Model 70 shown in the background sold for $950 and was original. ...... **$950+**

A rough John Deere B in original paint with a bad manifold sold for only $675, even though the new manifold was included. A repainted John Deere B received bids of $1,050 and it was yet another "no sale" that day. **$675**

A nice old John Deere B on spoke wheels could only muster a high bid of $1,500 and was a "no sale" also. **$1,500**

A Farmall Super H did not sell for $1,300, as the buyer wanted $1,800.
................................**$1,800**

An Allis-Chalmers C with single plow received bids of $1,250 and was a no sale, with a minimum of $1,800 needed. **$1,800**

A Farmall Super C with a "fast hitch" nicely restored. $1,800

A nice Ferguson Model 20, repainted with a nice engine. $1,750

A John Deere Model 1010 from 1964 sold for $3,050. It had donned fresh paint and had a live PTO...**$3,050**

An Allis-Chalmers B wide front.. **$900**

A Farmall C. $1,200

The Farmall Cub, used by my wife, next to its single bottom plow. My 8520 Case-International square baler is in the background on our Upper Peninsula farm. I used the Cub to rake all 50 acres of hay on the farm. **$2,500**

Four Farmall tractors were for sale in my neighborhood and they are all beautiful, nicely restored or original condition. I would buy them all but they are too high for the current market and they have already been reduced. Nevertheless, it shows the current state of the market. Photographs show all four of the tractors: an H, Super H, M and Super M. Close-ups are also shown. The Super M Farmall from 1952 is up for grabs for $2,600, a price they will likely get for a Super M. A Super MTA that was "show ready" did recently sell for $10,500, showing the demand for some of the more unusual Farmalls. This M is a 1939 for sale for $2,800, reduced from $3,800, far too high. This 1953 Super H is for sale for $2,800 and was also reduced. The prices reported at the Yoder consignment sale demonstrate that they will not likely sell for a while. A 1940 Farmall H is for sale for $2,400 and is again reduced, but not yet enough to sell quickly. .... **2,400-$2,800**

A blade for the Paulsen Cub.
.... **$100-$200**

**John Deere hit and miss
engines** from the 1910s or early
1920s, 1 1/2 horse each, being
used by a vendor to make ice
cream at the Yoder consignment
sale. What a great use of old
technology. .... **$2,000+ each**

Chapter Thirteen:

An Interview With "The Expert(s)"

In preparation for the final manuscript revisions, I was fortunate enough to spend a few hours with an old friend and expert in the field of farm collectibles and antiques, Art Smith. Smith is an auctioneer who has been specializing in "good old country auctions" since 1981. He is an award-winning auctioneer for his talents and is one of the most respected of all local auctioneers due to his honesty and his knowledge of the products. I have hired Smith for three major farm auctions during the past 15 years and have attended dozens of his auctions as a buyer. Smith and his son Noah are now in business together, along with wife/mom Kim. They maintain a great site at www.artsmithauctions.com that details all future and many past farm auctions. One can learn a great amount about values by going to this site and examining the excellent quality of photos and the values that items have sold for over the past few auctions.

We spent the morning going over recent and upcoming sales, and discussing the values on items and what items recently sold for at auction. We also discussed the fact that eBay and other online auctions have only helped the local auction markets, because now people attend farm auctions to buy items to re-sell online. Smith believes that farm auction prices have only gone up due to online sales. That is contrary to what was often believed when online auctions first began in the mid 1990s.

Smith was also kind enough to share with me for photo sessions some of his own farm collectibles and treasures. The photos have been integrated into the book. Regardless of one's experience, there are always surprises in valuation when speaking with someone with Smith's experience. My two big surprises that day were the values placed on "hit and miss" engines (see photos in last chapter) from the early 1900s, and the advertising pencils given away by farm dealerships known as "bullet pencils." Hit and miss engines bring upward of $3,000. Bullet pencils are currently selling for $25-$100, depending on condition, locale, age of dealership, and proximity of sale site to the former dealership.

I was also surprised to see that there is not as much interest in some of the horse hardware as I expected. Interest is present. It is just not as constant as on some of the major farm collectibles. Value on horse hardware items appears to have hit a valley at this time. Another thing to note is that values on old tractors have not kept up with the increased values on older implements. The valuation of horse hardware and tractors may have reached a temporary peak because these were some of the more obvious farm collectibles. Most interested had already purchased what they needed or wanted. It is likely that the values on old tractors and horse hardware will again increase, but it is difficult to anticipate when this may occur.

I would also like to note the assistance that Brian Taylor of Burnip's Equipment, my local New Holland dealer, has given me in terms of tractor valuation and trends. Taylor had a major sale in 2002. He noted with interest the high values on antique implements in his sale compared to the antique tractors. He had numerous examples of both and, by far, the biggest surprise was the high value assigned to many implements by the buyers. He indicated that prices for Ford 8Ns, 9Ns, Farmall Ms, Super Ms, Hs, John Deere As, Bs, and other common older tractors have really not gone up significantly during the past 20 years and may have even gone down recently.

The fully restored 8N located at Burnip's Equipment in Big Rapids, Mich., shown in Chapter 12 would be worth a little more than the normal top end auction price of about $2,500, due to its pristine condition. However, many 8Ns may be purchased for $1,500-$2,000 in the marketplace. Farmall Ms

Art Smith

now seldom bring even $1,500 unless exceptionally clean, an H may only bring $950-$1,200, and a Super M a bit more than an M. And so it goes with the John Deere versions. The exception is there seems to be a premium price paid because it is a John Deere, but even As and Bs are going for only $900-$1,500 in most cases. However, Taylor indicated how the prices of antique farm implements are only increasing in value at this time and items such as hit and miss engines are skyrocketing. Also, a rare tractor such as a Farmall MTA will still command a good price.

I should also like to thank the assistance of Jerry Paulsen and the hospitality shown by Jerry and his wife Carol. They welcomed me into their home for a photo session of some of his toy collection and related farm collectibles. Paulsen has worked his entire career in the farm tractor and implement field. He spent a number of years at both Allis-Chalmers and Ford dealerships, including the Ford dealership where we purchased our first Ford 5000 in Cedar Springs, Mich. He has also owned a store dedicated to farm toy collectibles and he has a large collection of Ertl and Precision tractors. Finally, he began restoring both tractors and garden tractors in recent years. Some of his restored Allis-Chalmers tractors and a nice A-C garden tractor in process of restoration were shown in the last chapter.

David and Kelley VanAlstine own one of the most phenomenal collections of general farm collectibles. I first noticed it when driving by their lovely home on my way to teach a couple of years ago. As I was writing this book, I dropped by to see if I could take some photos. They were kind enough to give me a guided tour and extended an invitation into their home full of country and farm collectibles and antiques. They allowed me the opportunity to photograph items for this book. The VanAlstine family owns literally hundreds of farm collectibles. They have also been very wise in their purchases, with many "bargains" being found by keeping eyes and ears open for items that others failed to value. Some of the prices paid for items were frankly shockingly low, due to their knack for finding "deals." But they also realize the value in the items. The photos from their collection have been shown throughout the book and without their contribution the book would be missing many rare items, such as the two early wooden butter churns.

Also, I want to thank my colleague, Dr. Terry Nerbonne and his wife Andy, for allowing me to photograph some of their antique and collectible farm items from their barn. Most of the items shown were present in the barn when Nerbonne purchased the farm. The pristine condition of some of the items was amazing due to the dry storage conditions in his barn. I could not believe the horse "fly-chasers," as I call them, found in the harness room. An item (fragile at that) from the 1920s-1930s in perfect shape! He also had a very rare walk-behind drill that he did pick up at a farm auction, as well as excellent examples of hay grapples and track mechanisms for hay storage. I took more than 100 photos at their home in one afternoon that have added greatly to the wide array of items shown in the book.

Jerry Paulsen

Wendy and friends

Lastly, but in no case least, I need to again remember the tolerance my wife has shown for once again invading our own country home to take photos of our personal items and to clutter the house with photos, items, and manuscript while working on this fun project. She has tolerated three years of fishing lures, duck decoys, and farm antiques being strewn throughout our home as I write away in the privacy of my den. Most spouses would not tolerate this with such compassion as she has shown. For this, I thank her. Maybe I need to build a barn just for collectibles and I seriously consider it from time to time. At any rate, without Wendy, this book could not have been completed.

Regarding your own education on farm collectibles, the best advice is for you to go to as many local auction sales as possible. You can see first hand what items sell for and make yourself aware of any local idiosyncrasies related to pricing of farm collectibles. By viewing a half-dozen local auctions, one will get the feel for the market, and the items described in this chapter will become easily recognizable if not already known.

I have organized this chapter according to the same categories as in the main part of the book and listed prices and item descriptions and dates sold, if known. Photographs of many of the items have been shown earlier in the book and many are also illustrated in the next chapter in advertising reprints.

Print Items

Farm Manuals ranged from a low of $12.50 to a high of $240 at a farm auction held in western Michigan. The high item was a manual for an International Harvester Corp. "hit and miss" engine from 1913. Many other manuals from the 1930s-40s sold for $40-$120 each, including manuals for Oliver, a Case 1952 D owner's manual, a 1932 DeLaval catalog, a John Deere 1937 Type E engine manual, many John Deere tractor and equipment manuals from the 1930s-40s, and an early AC combine manual.

Advertising Items for Ford and Massey Ferguson tractors and equipment, dating from the 1940s-70s, sold for $5-$40 per item at the same sale. Most of the advertising items sold for $12.50-$25 each. Included in these items were a number of "note book calendars," a popular give away by dealerships, grain companies, seed companies, and others.

Magazines of more recent vintage on collecting "Gas Engines" and "Antique Tractors" sold for $5 each in most cases at the same auction.

Books at an auction did not fare so well and most sold for only a dollar or two. Exceptional books from the 1800s still did well, but common farm books from the post-1900 period do not bring much at sales. However, a mid-1800s county atlas is expected to bring a few hundred dollars at an upcoming sale. So interest exists for the better, earlier, rarer books.

Postcards from recent auction and online sales reached prices of $10 with some commonality, and occasionally a card will sell for $35-$50. Only exceptionally early cards, rare scenes, or very detailed cards will exceed these figures.

Advertising Items

Oil Companies have produced many items now collectible. Many individuals collecting farm collectibles are also interested in early oil company labels and advertising. Chapter 3 had a fine example of an excellent buy made by Smith: an original Standard Oil Household polish tin. Also, oil cans with labels are collectible. A Mobil Oil can sold for $15, six oilers (household and farm type) sold for $95, and a New York Railroad lantern sold for $50.

A Stand from a hardware store used to measure rope sold for $25 and an Allis-Chalmers pith helmet sold for $140. Feed bags with advertising sold for $5-$10, depending on condition and area of mill. Cream and milk cans with local advertising sold for $15-$50. A Winchester calendar from 1899 sold for $130, and magazines and calendars sold in general for the same as sporting items: e.g. $10 each for items in the 1940s with prices quickly going up for each decade older. A John Deere bullet pencil sold for $75, as it had a local dealership advertised. Manuals such as DeLaval and others sold for up to $75. Wooden rulers and "walking sticks" used to measure items bring from $20-$40 each.

Children's Items

Sleds from the 1950s sold from $20-$40 at a farm auction in Michigan. A much older (1920s) red child's sleigh sold for $150, as did one from a large farm auction. A child's wheelbarrow sold for a surprisingly low $12.50. Common 1940s-50s sleds brought at least $35 at the same auction. A little wooden wagon, likely from the 1930s, brought $35.

Farm Implements

An Oliver Walking Plow sold for $140, an old ensilage cutter brought $40, a double beam potato plow brought $40, and steel wheels sold for $8-$12.50 each.

A Walking Cultivator brought $25, an old Oliver wooden wheel grain drill sold for $90, a Papec silo filler brought $300 (much more than another sale where a number of them were being sold at once), and IHC Model 7 hay mower brought $275, and a New Idea four steel wheel manure spreader brought in $975. A nice McCormick Deering grain binder sold for $775 (this is about what corn binders also bring), steel wheels sold for $12.50-$20 each, a corn binder sold for $900, a hammermill sold for $300, a dumpy rake brought $35, and a running gear on steel sold for $120.

A 1916 IHC hit and miss engine sold for $5,200 and a Fairbanks-Morse engine sold for $3,400 from the same era. A fanning mill only sold for $20 and platform scales brought

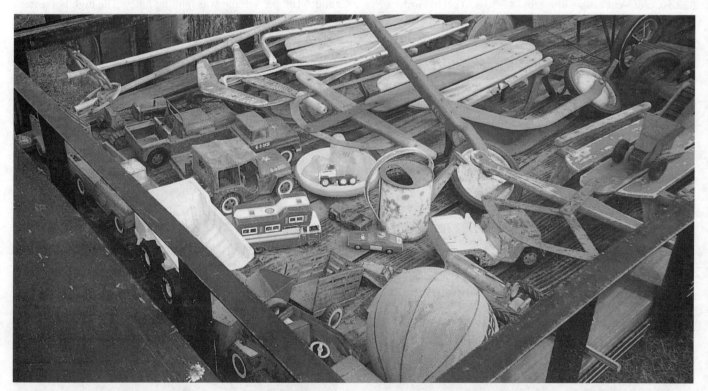

Children's Items. Arcade cast iron trucks are selling for $400-$500 at farm auctions and the Auburn rubber tractors usually fetch around $75, if decent. Farm toys vary too much in price to give a complete range, but toy tractors and implements are always in demand and create a lot of bidding competition. Good Ertl tractors always bring at least half of their book value, and sometimes more than book value if rare. The little cast iron Arcade motorcycles like the one shown in Chapter 4 are worth up to $75 each.

around $50. A primitive wooden two-section spike tooth drag sold for $40 and a most unusual item, an antique steam engine whistle, sold for $240 at the same sale. One-row walking cultivators sold for $75-$100, and riding cultivators sell for $150-$450 each, depending on brand and condition (high that I have seen was a McCormick for $450).

An American Seeding Co. (they made hand corn planters too) five-hole walking grain drill on wheels sold for $260. This is similar to the larger grain drill of Nerbonne's shown in the implement section. An Oliver cast iron seat sold for $225 at the same auction.

Farm Tools

An Antique Barn Beam Drill (to make the holes for the pegs in construction of barns, similar to the VanAlstine one shown earlier) sold for $70, many times what they were selling for a few years ago. At the same sale: a Cant hook sold for $12, two hand corn planters sold for $15 and $17.50, a hand potato planter sold for $22.50, old wooden planes sold for $40 each, a mattock sold for $7.50, nice old pulleys sold for $12.50 each, a clinker grabber (to remove unburned coal from a stove) sold for $12.50, a bean sorter brought $20, a Cyclone brand seeder sold for $15, a scythe sold for $35, a broad axe brought $30, a draw shave fetched $7.50, a bull leader (one grabbed the ring with this lead stick device) sold for $9, hay knives sold for $10-$20, and corn knives sold for $15-$30.

Additional Prices included: a lanyard scale selling for $22.50, cross-cut saws selling for $17.50-$30 each, Ford wrenches selling for $10-$30 each, a barrel mounted corn sheller selling for $40, milk cans selling for up to $150 in an Amish community (where they are still used to take milk to the local cheese factory) with ornamental type milk cans selling for $15-$30 each, cream cans selling for $40-$50, silage forks bringing up to $40 each (people are buying them to use on bark for landscaping), a saw set sold for $3, an IHC wrench sold for $20, hog scrapers sold for about $5-$10 unless exceptionally clean, hand held corn picks (hand huskers) sold for $5 most of the time, cream separators sold from $20-$220 for one in perfect working order that had been stored inside, a wooden 55 gallon barrel sold for $27.50, a hand sharpening grinder sold for $40, and hand cultivators, wheelbarrows, and mowers sold for a few dollars to about $25 each.

An Ashley milk can cooler sold for $100, a milk strainer sold for $25, and milk cans brought $20-$125 each. The glass chicken waterers from the 1940s sold for $75 each, and some interesting barn items included hay spears for $10-$15, a hay grappling hook for $35, a manure truck for $17.50, and barn roof rails for the hay track $5 per eight-foot section.

Horse Hardware

A Cowbell sold for $15 (steel, not brass) and a cast iron horse weight (used to tie horse down) sold for $45. Brass horse weights usually command more than $200 each. An ox yoke sold for $110 at the same sale.

A Set of Sleigh Bells brought $150 and collars brought from $5-$100, depending on condition. Some of the spreaders with ivory rings brought up to $40 each and harness sold for only about $100 per set, but was nothing fancy. The high horse item at the sale was an open top buggy selling for $900.

Two hit and miss engines	**$5,200**
1916 1HC	**$5,200**
Fairbanks Morse	**$3,400**

Fairbanks Morse Mod. Z

IHC Famous

Farm Kitchen

Ice Tongs sold for $10, an old egg crate for $7, wooden shutters for the home sold for $65 for four short ones and $180 for four longer ones, a No. 4 farm bell sold for $170 and another smaller bell sold for $100, and a canner sold for $10 (simple granite ware water bath).

Additional Prices included: sad irons now only bringing $5-$15 each unless very unusual, rug beaters bringing $10-$30, a gristmill for flour making in the kitchen selling for $80, old brass fans bringing $50, and kitchen scales selling for $15-$25. An unusual item was a kerosene powered slide projector selling for $400, wool cards bringing $20-$25 each, and lightning rod globes selling for up to $65 each at sales. A hand coffee grinder sold for $130, and two Hoosiers sold for $950 and $1,050. Pie safes are averaging about $225 each and old refrigerators (wooden ones) sell well, with a Leonard Oak Ice Box selling for $600 at a farm sale.

Always Popular are the colored-handle kitchenware items, selling for at least $5 each unless found in a box lot. Apple peelers sell for $50-$60 each, according to Smith, while cherry pitters with fewer moving parts only bring $25-$40 each. The once crazy high prices for green canning jars are all but gone, with jars selling for $3-$5 each, if old and in great shape. Some of the school size bells bring in $350 or better at farm auctions.

Farm Garden

A **Birdbath** from the 1940s sold for $170 at a sale. The lawn sprinklers made from die cast material on wheels sell for $75-$100 easily at farm auctions. The human neck yokes used to carry water to the house sell for about $5 each (not many good memories attached to these). Hog scalding kettles sell for $100-$150, and are now used nearly exclusively for planters.

Windmills are selling for nearly $2,000, in decent shape and complete. Smith sold one in 1992 that was about 75 percent complete for $650, and he believes that they would start at $1,000 today for the same condition. According to discussions with other collectors, 100 percent windmills start at $1,500 and go up quickly from there. Just two piles of windmill parts at a recent auction sold for $125 per pile.

An Interesting farmstead item was a Leader brand maple syrup evaporator selling for $1,850 at an Amish auction in Michigan. Maple syrup making is still fairly big business here and these items hold their value. The same is true for bee equipment, even if old and collectible, which is often still used.

Farm Recreation

Two Community Newhouse wolf traps sold for $150 each, and a homemade bear trap sold for $180. Bear traps often sell for $500 or more each, depending on make and condition. It is not often any more that bidders are not competing for traps, shell boxes, gun loading equipment, guns, fishing items, and snowshoes at farm auctions. Smith has sold individual fishing lures for up to $500 each and has a large following for his very competitive gun auctions.

Vintage Tractors

Tractors bring more at one of Smith's auctions than the current market value, due to the competitive spirit and the large following he has for his auctions. However, he did sell a Ford 2000 for $7,900 at one Michigan auction and a 1952 JD Model 60 (gas) for $3,100 at the same auction. He reports that the older tractors normally sell within the $1,200-$2,000 range, depending on the condition and models. This would be a little better than the current prices seen at many auctions but I would expect them to be higher at his auctions.

Summary

The foregoing is just a brief scratching of the surface of current auction values, according to what I learned speaking with Smith. Hopefully it shows the direction of items at this time, and will give the beginning collector an idea of values. Of course, what makes any auction fun is that one can sometimes find items really "cheap" and at other times, if caught in the auction frenzy, will pay "far more" than market value to beat out the other person or because the item is needed to fill a collection. Prices are sometimes volatile in collecting any item and this is true for farm collectibles as well. The prices given are for examples and general information. They should not be seen as a guarantee of future values, simply a guide based upon past performance.

The most often forgotten item is the importance of condition, condition, condition. Authors writing about collecting stress its importance but then buyers often forget how important it is when trying to sell their own items. An item in pristine condition will always bring a premium price, and one must remember that point. On the other hand, items in poor condition not only will not sell for much, they also will not go up in value. In my opinion, it is always better to invest more money in quality than in quantity. I hope readers will keep in mind the important role of condition when examining photos and prices in this book and when making purchases.

Chapter Fourteen:

A History Of Farm Advertising

This chapter is a review of many of the farm and agricultural items that are now collectible by reprinting a number of advertisements from farm publications dating from 1903 until about 1965. Of special interest are all of the detailed ads, reproduced from the 1903-05 period, that show most of the items found in this book. One should get an idea of how old many of the collectible items are. It will also become apparent that many farm items did not change greatly once invented in the late 1800s or early 1900s. For instance, fence-stretching tools, feeding equipment, and implements did not change significantly until the advent of the tractor in the 1920s.

A review of the *Montgomery Ward Farm Catalog* of 1964 demonstrates that many of the early 1900s items were still in use and demand in the mid-1960s. This should also assist the collector in dating items, to prevent them from buying "antique items" that are really only a few years old. I took photos of corn knives and hay hooks still for sale at the local New Holland dealership to demonstrate this point. Many of the items passed off online as "antique" are really only 30 years old and may not be all that rare. Of course, some of the more recent items are still highly collectible. But the buyer should be aware of how long many of the farm items of a collectible nature were actually manufactured. It is very difficult to tell a hoof pick from 2003 from one from 1965, for instance. This chapter is offered as a great way to familiarize oneself with changes through the ages of American agriculture.

I have selected items from catalogs from the 1930s, 1940s, and 1950s as well. They are reproduced as found in the catalogs. However, a careful study of the advertisements will result in viewing many items shown earlier in this book. For instance, kitchen roosters, the Jiffy Egg Scale, egg carrying

baskets, a calf muzzle similar to the cribbing muzzle shown, a calf weaning device like the one shown, calls and decoys, similar tools, barn track and pulleys like the ones shown, many early sleds, bicycles, and similar items.

I thought it better for layout purposes to show the advertisements as they actually appeared in the original publications. It is clear that the old magazines themselves from the early 1900s are now collectible. But the advertisements found in them are even more valued for the information provided to the collector and researcher. It was amazing to me that many of the advertisements found were then documented with the same item being sold. For instance a hay tedder advertisement from 1905 was found and the same hay tedder was sold at a horse-drawn farm implement auction in Michigan. A close examination of this chapter will show the reader many items that I did not have an opportunity to photograph but have been described in the previous chapters. Also, it will also show many items still to be discovered at those farm sales in the future.

I would like to give a special thanks to my wife, Wendy, for being the main researcher on the old farm advertisements from our collection of early 1900s *Breeder's Gazette* magazines. She spent many, many hours pouring over the pages of these great old magazines looking for interesting advertisements to help other collectors. We were fortunate to find two bound volumes of these magazines from friends in the Upper Peninsula that had had them for a number of years in their family. It is not common to find bound magazines from 1903 in nearly mint condition and it is lucky for us that we had these items for research purposes. Again, thanks Wendy for all of your help with this book, especially this chapter.

Breeder's Gazette 1905

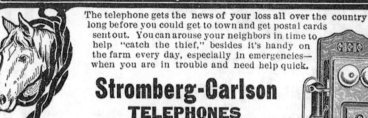

Don't Bind on the Track,

Can't jump off, don't break the fork pulley, trips easily—Bright marks of the

Louden Hay Carrier

A complete line and the only one that can be depended on for perfect working. We make a specialty of all hay tools, as Carriers, Steel Tracks, Switches, Pulleys, Hay Rack Fixtures, Feed and Litter Carriers. Our patent Flexible **Barn Door Hanger** is the best in the world. Save money by sending for our complete catalog of the above and other hardware specialties. It describes farm appliances that are adapted and that work. Mailed free for the asking.

LOUDEN MACHINERY COMPANY,
46 Broadway,   Fairfield, Ia.

GRAND PRIZE - ST LOUIS
DE LAVAL CREAM SEPARATORS

THE DE LAVAL SEPARATOR CO

74 CORTLANDT ST.
NEW YORK.

RANDOLPH & CANAL ST.
CHICAGO.

A BOY'S PLOW

"The Vacuna" Combined Riding and Walking, with new **Pivot Beam Guide.**

WHAT MR. WATKINS SAYS:
Petersburg, Ills., Dec. 15, 04.
Gentlemen:—I have one of your Vacunas, bought of your agent M. Kahn, which my boy Fred, who is only 10 years old, has used during the past season and he does as good work with it as it is possible for any man to do with any cultivator.   Yours truly,   J. G. WATKINS.
Nice catalogue of many styles of **Cultivators, Planters, Stalk Cutters, Wagons, etc.** mailed free. Ask for Catalog H.
We build high grade Farm and Threshing Machinery.

Avery Mfg. Co., 204 Iowa St., Peoria, Ill.

SEE!

With an **APPLETON WOOD SAW** you can rapidly and with ease and safety

SAW

your own wood and **SAVE COAL,** time, labor and money; or saw your neighbor's wood and make

$5 to $15 a Day

Strong, rigid frame, adjustable

dust-proof oil boxes, etc. We make five styles. Also the famous "Hero" Friction=Feed Drag Saw, Feed Grinders, Ensilage and Fodder Cutters, Huskers, Shellers, Sweep Horse Powers, Tread Powers, Wind Mills, etc. Write to-day for free catalogue.

Appleton Mfg. Co.   5 Fargo St., Batavia, Ill.

Sore Shoulders

and Galls guaranteed absolutely cured by the
Lankford Humane Cotton Filled Collars.
No stopping the plow—collar does its work while the horse does his. Lasts 5 years. Fits any neck. Collar and pad combined. Sold by dealers or sent prepaid for $1.25. Circular and memorandum book free.

POWERS MFG. CO.,
134 Sycamore St.,   Waterloo, Ia.

ACME Pulverizing Harrow
Clod Crusher and Leveler.
SENT ON TRIAL.

SIZES
3 to 13½ feet

Agents Wanted.

To be returned at my expense if not satisfactory.
The best pulverizer—cheapest **Riding Harrow** on earth. The **Acme** crushes, cuts, pulverizes, turns and levels all soils for all purposes.
Made entirely of cast steel and wrought iron —indestructible.
Catalog and booklet. "An Ideal Harrow" by Henry Stewart sent free.

. deliver f. o. b. at New York, Chicago, Columbus, Louisville, Kansas City, Minneapolis, San Francisco, Portland, etc.
DUANE H. NASH, Sole Manufacturer, Millington, New Jersey.
BRANCH HOUSES: 110 W. Washington St., CHICAGO. 240-244 7th Ave. S., MINNEAPOLIS. 1316 W. 8th St.,
KANSAS CITY, MO.   216 10th St., LOUISVILLE, KY.   Cor. Water and W. Gay Sts., COLUMBUS, OHIO.
PLEASE MENTION THIS PAPER.

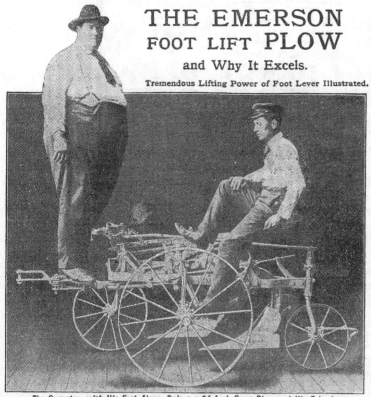

1904 **1904**
YEAR'S WORK of a BIG and BUSY FIRM

CLAY, ROBINSON & Co

	CATTLE	HOGS	SHEEP
Number of Head Sold	532,583	403,593	2,296,548
Number of Head Bought	51,264	2,021	330,561
Total Head Handled,	583,847	405,614	2,627,109

Grand Total Head of Stock Handled, 3,616,570

LONG-CRITCHFIELD-CORP.

445

ELECTRIC MACHINERY FOR FARMS.

Save Fuel. Save Power. Save Labor.
—— Never Freezes. ——
Always Ready —— Day and Night.

Northern Motor Driving Laundry Mangle—Motor Part of Driven Machine

POWER transmitted to any part of **your farm**, or to that of **your neighbors**, by means of a small copper wire which lasts forever. The **same wire** will, **at the same time**, carry electric lighting to your buildings and those of your neighbors, if desired.

THE MOTOR WILL NOT FREEZE—IS ALWAYS READY ⁄ ⁄ ⁄ ⁄ FOR BUSINESS WHEREVER NEEDED. ⁄ ⁄ ⁄ ⁄

Our system is simple and can be managed by any inteligent young man. Motor Booklet No. 4738 is free. For particulars address

NORTHERN ELECTRICAL MFG. CO., ENGINEERS, MANUFACTURERS, **MADISON, WIS., U. S. A.**

268

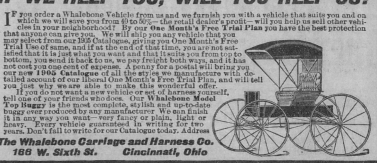

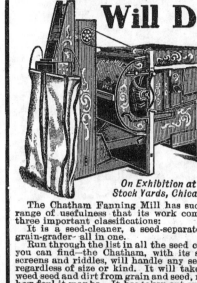

Look at the Big
Sprocket and Chain
Drive below.

Ours is the only Manure Spreader made possessing this advantage.

The Success Manure Spreader

is the one to buy. These are among the reasons why: It is the result of 26 years of continuous Manure Spreader making. It covers every requirement and every condition for the spreading of all kinds of manure, lime, plaster, ashes, salt, fertilizer, etc., broadcast or in drills. Spreads thick or thin as wanted. Apron returns automatically. Spreads largest load in 3 to 5 minutes. **Strongest, easiest to load, spreads most evenly and has lightest draft.** Made in 4 sizes to suit requirements of all sections. All about it and much more of value in our free book, "**Farm Fertility.**" Write for it.

KEMP & BURPEE MANUFACTURING CO., Box 67, SYRACUSE, N. Y.

Nine Tools in One

1 Wire Stretcher, 2 Wire Cutters.
3 Staple Pullers, 2 Hammers,
1 Wire Splicer.

BLACK BULL

the handiest tool ever made for
the man on the farm. Pays for itself in one month.
SEE WHAT THIS MAN SAYS:

Dear Sir: Joplin, Mo.
I think your Black Bull combination tool is the greatest all around farm and fence tool I have ever used.
                                          J. D. MORRISON.

Ask your hardware dealer to show you Black Bull tool. If your dealer doesn't carry the Black Bull, we will send it post paid to any address on receipt of $1.25. Address

UTICA DROP FORGE & TOOL CO.,
69 GENESEE ST., UTICA, N. Y.

RUMELY ENGINES

The Farmer's Favorite—every-day, every occasion engines. For pull or power their generating and traction qualities are unsurpassed. They are rear-geared, with single or double cylinders; burn wood or coal, or direct flue for burning straw. *The Rumely Separator* and one of these Engines make a *modern threshing outfit.* Free catalog fully describes them; write for it.
M. RUMELY CO., La Porte, Ind.

STUDEBAKER

WHEN A MAN GETS A STUDEBAKER

he is **satisfied**, because he feels sure that he is taking home the very best that money can buy.

He has nothing to apologize for.

And the longer he uses it the better he's satisfied.

There are a lot of little advantages about it, not found in most vehicles.

There's an **absence of repair bills** that's good for his pocket book. That's a **big** advantage.

There's the consciousness that he has in it the pick of the world's vehicle materials, with a half century's "know-how" in it, fifty years reputation behind it, and a **name on it that's a guarantee in itself.**

Studebaker superiority is the result of the strictest care in the selection of materials and in workmanship; the most rigid inspection of every part, and exceptional facilities found only in "the largest vehicle plant in the world."

If you are thinking of buying a farm wagon, a spring wagon, a surrey, a buggy, a family carriage, a vehicle of any kind for business or pleasure, or a set of harness of the sort that lasts—talk to the Studebaker agent. You don't make such a purchase very many times in your life—do it right while you're about it. Ask him for the Studebaker Almanac for 1905. If he can't supply you, send your name and address with two cent stamp to us and a free copy will be sent you. Address Dept. No. 15

STUDEBAKER BROS. MFG. CO.,
SOUTH BEND, INDIANA.

Agencies most everywhere. A dealer may make more by selling you some other, but **you** make most by buying a Studebaker.

WE WANT AGENTS

in every town to ride and sell our bicycles. Good pay. Finest guaranteed 1905 **MODELS**, with Puncture-Proof tires, Coaster-Brakes **$10 to $24**
1903 & 1904 Models of Best Makes..... **$7 to $12**
500 Second-Hand Wheels
All makes & Models good as new **$3 to $8**
CLEARING SALE at half cost. We *SHIP ON APPROVAL* and **TEN DAYS TRIAL** to anyone *without a cent deposit.* Write at once for **Special Offer** on sample bicycle.
TIRES, SUNDRIES, AUTOMOBILES.
MEAD CYCLE CO., Dept. B 82 CHICAGO

$52.50 RubberTire

TOP BUGGY. 2 year guarantee. Sold on 30 days Free Trial. It's a genuine Split Hickory. That means value. Guaranteed solid rubber tires. Worth 50% more than we ask. 192-page catalog free. Send now.
The Ohio Carriage Mfg. Co.
H. C. Phelps, Pres.
Station 7
Cincinnati, Ohio

Parties writing to advertisers will please mention The Breeder's Gazette.

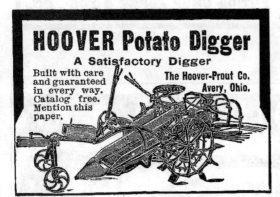

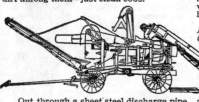

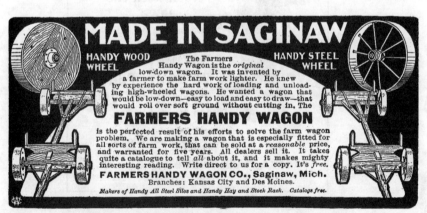

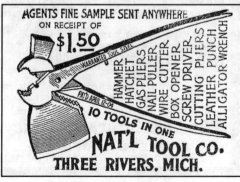

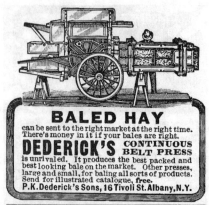

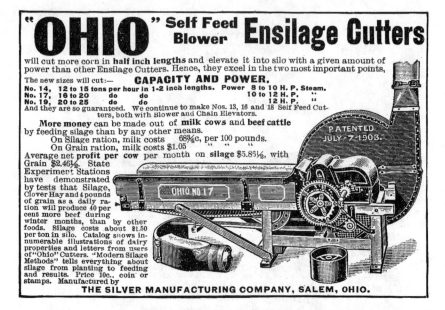

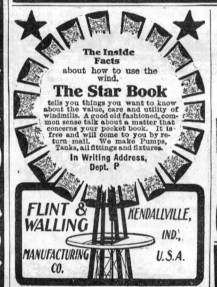

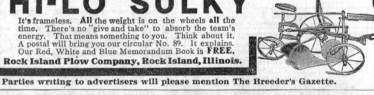

(Continued from page 543.)

public, sale June 7 are coming along nicely. I understand there will be a combination sale of North Dakota breeders in Fargo June 6, so that together we hope to get out the largest crowd of breeders that ever attended a sale in that part of the country." See page 555.

W. H. Miller & Sons, Mulberry, Ind., write: "THE GAZETTE is the paper to stay with and so far it is worth the price. We have decided to offer our Polled Durham herd bull Royal Abbotsburn for sale. He is just past three years old, a good dehorner, splendid breeder and we guarantee him in every way. He is a show bull in hot company. His calves are coming in his way and we offer him for no other reason. We also have a 20-months red polled bull out of a granddaughter of imp. Gay Monarch that is of the low-down thick meaty kind. He should head some choice herd. We also have a roan 12-months polled calf (out of a Scotch cow bred by F. Douglas, Canada) of the true Scotch type that will make a very valuable bull for some one. We have other younger ones that are very promising. All are sired by Royal Abbotsburn. Our herd numbers 75 head." See page 558.

ELDER LAWN SHORT-HORNS.

The reputation of T. K. Tomson & Sons, Dover, Kan., for breeding first-class Short-horn cattle is becoming widely known throughout the Middle West. They have recently made a very valuable sale to Mr. Nevius of Kansas on a choice bull and 10 females. However, they find themselves at this time with a splendid lot of young bulls on hand, both Scotch and Scotch-topped. They have at least 12 big strong useful bulls ready for service. They have issued a very neat little pamphlet giving the size and dam of each of these bulls, as well as a brief description of each. They will be pleased to mail this to all GAZETTE readers who are interested in the purchase of a good young bull. Their herd is made up of the very best representatives of Scotch and American families, particular attention being paid to the milking qualities as well as the thick flesh qualities of the Short-horns. They have been conspicuous in the show-rings in the hottest company for a number of years, having over 200 prizes to their credit won at State and National shows. The reputation gained by their chief herd bull, Gallant Knight, is certainly an enviable one of which any breeder could justly feel proud. This firm will furnish its stock with sufficient guarantees back of it. The announcement appears on page 553.

STEELE'S SHORT-HORN SALE.

On March 29 C. R. Steele, Ireton, Ia., will sell from his Willow Lane herd some 60 head of richly-bred Short-horns, including a large number of Scotch and imported Scotch cattle. He will be joined in this sale by C. F. Farrand, of the same place, who will sell 15 head. The cattle, however, are under the management of Mr. Steele, and it may practically be called his own sale. Mr. Steele has selected for this sale some of the best cattle in his herd, as well as some of the best from the Scotch standpoint. Since his last sale the herd has been very much strengthened in herd bulls. One of the best Scotch bulls in the West is Mr. Steele's chief herd bull, Grand Baron 2d, bred by A. & G. Davidson of Iowa. He was sired by Grand Baron, a straight Scotch bull by Glaucus. Grand Baron belonged to the famous Lavender family, having for his grandam imp. Lavender 38th by Dunblane. Grand Baron 2d's dam was the famous Duchess of Gloster cow, Duchess of Gloster 28th. She belongs to the best of this famous family, descending from imp. 12th Duchess of Gloster by Champion of England. This family in the hands of James I. Davidson of Ontario proved in all probability the most valuable family of Short-horn cattle that he ever owned. In Grand Baron 2d is found the typical old Baron Victor owned by Senator W. A. Harris, possessing practically all of Baron Victor's good points without its homely horn. This bull has a beautiful head and horn, is very low and thick, carrying a thick-bedded back and loin, an exceedingly wide hind quarter, and is as smooth a bull at the tail head as ever it was our pleasure to see. We speak of this bull at some length from the fact that a large percentage of the females in Mr. Steele's offering are in calf to him. Those not in calf to him, aside from a very few, are bred to Red Gauntlet 2d, which is included in the sale. He was sired by the Harris-bred bull Red Gauntlet, a son of Scarlet Knight, while his dam, Geraldine, was by the Cruickshank bull imp. Chief Baron. She is out of Gardenia by Cumberland. This is a splendid Scotch bull, low and thick, is a heavy flesh carrier and has proved himself an exceptionally good sire. Mr. Steele is selling him for no fault whatever, but simply because he has no use for so many herd bulls. He is a dark red, calved March 13, 1898. The females not bred to one of these bulls will be bred to two red sons of imp. Lord Banff. These two Lord Banff bulls are included in the sale. The choicest of the two was dropped July 15, 1903, and is out of imp. Contessa. She belongs to Mr. Cruickshank's famous Miss Gibson or Mary Anne (by Sittery) tribe. This bull is one of the choicest yearling bulls listed to pass under the auctioneer's hammer this spring. His stable companion is by the same bull and out of imp. Queen Elizabeth. This bull is perhaps not quite as attractive in all his make-up as his elder half-brother, but he is a corking good one. Either of them, however, is a choice bull and far above the average. Mr. Steele will offer a number of other good Scotch bulls, among which we note a son of H. J. Parsons' famous bull Victor Baron. This is a Mysie bull, royally bred, light red and is a very clever animal throughout. There are a number of other straight Scotch bulls of a little younger age, but the majority are ready for service this season. Mr. Steele is offering 19 long carrying heifers, the like of which is seldom offered by one breeder. They are bred to the Lord Banff bulls. Among Mr. Steele's straight Scotch cattle are two choice Orange Blossoms, two Mysies, two imported cows, one choice Canada-bred Scotch cow, two Louisas, one Spleenwort, one Sempstress, a richly-bred Secret and bull calf, and one beautiful daughter of Scottish Knight. She is one of the choice females. The Secret cow with bull calf at foot is one of the best-bred Cruickshank Secrets living, and her beautiful red bull calf is one of the attractions of the sale. The two will be sold together. There are too many good cattle in the offering to endeavor to individualize on any of them. It is sufficient to say that no one who attends this sale can possibly be disappointed in the quality of the offering. The cattle with few exceptions are in fine sale condition. These exceptions as a rule are cows that are suckling calves that sell with them. Mr. Steele has endeavored to cut out all drones, and every animal that would need to have an apology offered for it. The sale will be conducted by Auctioneers Woods and Jones, and will be held March 29, allowing time for breeders who attend this sale to reach the sale of John Lister at Conrad, Ia., on March 31. For catalogue address C. R. Steele at Ireton, Ia. See page 552.

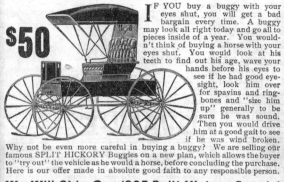

HOW TO BUY A BUGGY

Just as You Would a Horse—Look It Over Carefully and "TRY IT OUT" on the Road

$50

IF YOU buy a buggy with your eyes shut, you will get a bad bargain every time. A buggy may look all right today and go all to pieces inside of a year. You wouldn't think of buying a horse with your eyes shut. You would look at his teeth to find out his age, wave your hands before his eyes to see if he had good eyesight, look him over for spavins and ring-bones and "size him up" generally to be sure he was sound. Then you would drive him at a good gait to see if he was wind broken. Why not be even more careful in buying a buggy? We are selling our famous SPLIT HICKORY Buggies on a new plan, which allows the buyer to "try out" the vehicle as he would a horse, before concluding the purchase. Here is our offer made in absolute good faith to any responsible person.

We Will Ship Our 1905 Split Hickory Special Top Buggy, the Price of which is $50, Anywhere in the United States on 30 Days Free Trial. Guaranteed For Two Years.

We will tell you just how it is made, giving complete specifications, so that when you receive the buggy you can go over it part by part, and check up every item. You can compare it with the buggies sold in your neighborhood for nearly twice as much money. You can hitch up to it and use it just as though it were your own and if you do not find it just as represented, you can ship it back to us at our expense and your money will be refunded. *The Fourth National Bank of Cincinnati, Ohio*, will tell you we are responsible for our contracts and agreements and that you may be assured of fair and honest dealing.

Here are some points of merit of the SPLIT HICKORY SPECIAL.

Wheels are made of the very best selected second growth split hickory, with screws through the rims; axles are long distance, dust proof, best refined steel, with split hickory axle beds cemented and full clipped; oil tempered springs, 16 oz. imported all wool broadcloth upholstering; box frame spring cushion; solid polished panel spring back; water-proof top with No. 1 enameled leather quarters and leather back stays; 28 oz. water-proof rubber roof and back curtain; back curtain lined and reinforced; rubber side curtains; full length storm apron; padded patent leather dash; full length velvet carpet; split hickory, fully guaranteed, shafts. Painting, oil and lead process; all wood work carried 100 days in pure oil and lead, 16 coats, every coat rubbed out and dried before the next is applied.

Our 1905 Catalogue, containing 192 pages, is a regular Information Bureau on the subject of Vehicles and Harness. If there's anything you want to know about buggies you will find it there. We send it free and take pleasure in answering letters immediately.

THE OHIO CARRIAGE MFG. CO.,

(H. C. Phelps, Pres.)

STATION 7,   CINCINNATI, O.

MODERN COUNTRY LIFE

The rural mail delivery, the telephone and the suburban electric railway are working wonderful changes in the life of the farmer's family today. The former isolation which drove many of the young men and women from the farm to the city, has been banished by the many telephone lines now in use all over this country.

STROMBERG-CARLSON TELEPHONES

have brought the cost of building farmers lines within the means of every farmer. Time is near at hand when every farm will have its own telephone, and the farmer's family will be in close touch with the whole neighborhood, as well as the entire world. It is impossible to estimate the value, in dollars and cents, of the telephone to the rural home. Its influence on the boys and girls in keeping them contented and at home, is incalculable. The farmer will reap benefits every year worth considerably more than the entire cost to him—in keeping tab on the markets, in getting help in busy times and in many other ways. Write for free book F- 82 "Telephone Facts for Farmers"—giving information on how to organize and build a telephone line. Our book 82 tells how others have built rural telephone lines. Write today to nearest office.

STROMBERG-CARLSON TEL. MFG. CO.,
Rochester, N. Y.   Chicago, Ill.

STANDARD BOOKS

FOR THE FARMER AND BREEDER for sale at this office. Send for new catalogue. Address J. H. SANDERS PUBLISHING CO., Chicago, Ill.

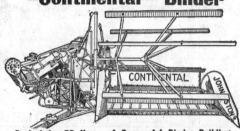

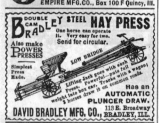

JOHN DEERE
MOLINE, ILL.

Cultivate two rows instead of one. Horses are cheaper than men. It will cost you less to buy a

Deere Two-Row Cultivator

and put the extra horses than it will to hire an extra man. You will need three horses under all ordinary circumstances, but if you want more, we can furnish a combination evener with which you can use three, four or five horses, as you like. There are things about this cultivator that will make you want it if you stop to think. No need to say much about the mechanical construction. Deere makes it. That is a good guarantee. But think of the work it will save. Take it on only forty acres. Working early and late, twenty days is the least time it will take to cultivate it three times. Twenty-four would be nearer the mark. You can put on an extra horse and do it in half the time with a Deere Two-Row. Are not those twelve days saved worth a dollar and a half a piece to you in the busy season? Or if you are hiring think of the extra work a man could do for you in those twelve days. It might mean the saving of a crop if the cultivating is late or the haying early.

If you would rather have it that way, we can furnish this cultivator with surface instead of shovel rigs, or with eight shovels instead of twelve.

Remember this. The Deere Two-Row has every advantage that any other cultivator has and some that no other has. Any how, you ought to find out all about it before you buy, and we'll be glad to have you write us.

Cutout this advertisement, write your name and address on the margin. We will mail you a beautiful little book and send you THE FURROW for a year free.

DEERE & COMPANY
MOLINE, ILLINOIS
F

Clean Sweep Hay loader:

Works equally well on swath or windrow. Divides a swath. It does not bunch, wad, tangle, pound or thresh the hay. Don't knock the heads off the clover. Works on ground hilly or level, in windy or calm weather. Will not wind or clog. Don't elevate trash and manure with the hay. It has an adjustable elevating carrier which raises as load enlarges. Loader detached from rack without men getting off load. Simple in construction, light draft, easy to operate, compact and durable. **Different from all others—Better than all others.**

Sandwich Side Delivery Rake

Leaves the hay in best possible condition to cure quickly. Rakes clean. Powerful in action and indestructible. Rides comfortably. No jerking or vibrating motion, strongly constructed. Popular with those farmers who employ advanced methods in haying. Best pair of hay making and saving tools on the market. Write for catalogue and colored lithographs.

SANDWICH MFG. CO.
148 Main Street,   Sandwich, Ill.

HANDLES HAY *Strickler* ANY WAY
BEST HAY TOOLS BUILT

THE HAY FARMER

is interested in the tools that will handle his hay in the easiest, quickest way and at the smallest expense.

Strickler Haying Tools

are the original and standard tools for handling hay and all sorts of forage crops. The Strickler Hay Sling puts away hay, corn fodder, Kaffir corn—a whole load at three trips. Our free catalog tells why the "Strickler" way to handle hay is the best way. Write for it.
STRICKLER HAY TOOL CO., Box 101, Janesville, Wis.

The Inside Facts
about how to use the wind.

The Star Book

tells you things you want to know about the value, care and utility of windmills. A good old-fashioned, common sense talk about a matter that concerns your pocket book. It is free and will come to you by return mail. We make Pumps, Tanks, all fittings and fixtures.
In Writing Address, Dept. O

FLINT & WALLING   KENDALLVILLE, IND.,
MANUFACTURING CO.,   U.S.A.

BOWSHER FEED MILLS

(Sold with or without elevator.)
Crush ear corn (with or without shucks) and Grind any kind of small grain at the same time, mixing in any proportion desired. Grind Kaffir Corn in the head.
Have Coni al Shape Grinders.
Different from all others.

LIGHTEST RUNNING
Handy to Operate.
7 Sizes. 2 to 25 Horse Power. One size for wind-wheel use. Also make Sweep Grinders, Geared or Plain.
V. N. P. Bowsher Co., South Bend, Ind.

A BOY'S PLOW

"The Vacuna" Combined Riding and Walking, with new Pivot Beam Guide.
WHAT MR. WATKINS SAYS:
Petersburg, Ills., Dec. 15, 04.
Gentlemen:—I have one of your Vacunas, bought of your agent M. Kahn, which my boy Fred, who is only 10 years old, has used during the past season and he does as good work with it as it is possible for any man to do with any cultivator.   Yours truly,   J. G. WATKINS.
Nice catalogue of many styles of Cultivators, Planters, Stalk Cutters, Wagons, etc., mailed free. Ask for Catalog H.
We build high grade Farm and Threshing Machinery.
Avery Mfg. Co., 204 Iowa St., Peoria, Ill.

Never Jumps the Track.
Cannot be pushed, hooked or blown off; don't bind or run hard. "The best hanger on earth" is the
FLEXIBLE DOUBLE TREAD BARN DOOR HANGER.
Double set of hangers. Absolute center draft. Carrier wheels are roller bearing. Always true and easy running, never out of order. Ask for free catalog of Hay Tools and field and farm hardware appliances.
LOUDEN MACHINERY CO., 46 Broadway, Fairfield, Ia.

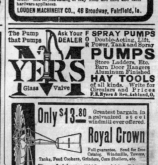

The Pump that Pumps
Ask Your DEALER

MYERS
Glass   Valve

FOR SPRAY PUMPS
Double-Acting, Lift, Power, Tank and Spray
PUMPS
Store Ladders, Etc.
Barn Door Hangers
Aluminum Finished
HAY TOOLS
of all kinds. Write for Circulars and Prices
F. E. Myers & Bro. Ashland, O.

Only $13.80
Greatest bargain in a galvanized steel windmill ever offered.
Royal Crown
Full guarantee. Send for free Catalog. Windmills, Towers, Tanks, Feed Cookers, Grinders, Corn Shellers, etc.
Winger & Johnson, 9154 Commercial Ave. Chicago.

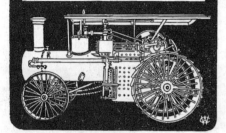

1930 L.L. Bean Catalog

L. L. BEAN
MFGR.
FREEPORT, MAINE
FALL 1930

1938 Western Auto Stores Catalog

Radios
Bicycles
Hardware
Sporting Goods
Auto Supplies

Western Auto Stores
See Back Cover for Address of Your Nearest Store

Western *Easy Roll* MOWERS
Superior Quality-Outstanding Value

SAVE ¼ to ½ !

The actual cost of building Western Mower is as much, or more, than other best quality mowers, even at double our prices. It's in cutting out middlemen's expenses and profits that we save you several dollars. When you can have as fine a mower that's built, in the size that meets your needs, why pay more?

Adjustable clamp screw keeps handle tight

Ball bearings 4 vital spots

Strongest known construction

Bed knife beveled for easier cutting

Strong, Durable! Quiet, Easy Running!

Light for their big size. Compact; cut close to any obstacle. Riveted cutting reel, 3 and 4 truss, with crucible steel blades that hold edge season after season. Permanently retained self-adjusting ball bearings, keep reel in perfect alignment. Easily adjustable cutting range ½ to 1½ inches. Big wheels with wide tread give positive traction and easier pushing, strong, sturdy, seasoned white pine handle, no slipping, long life.

Western Jr. "CHALLENGER"
X750—Four 14-inch blades. Light. Ideal for use by women and youths............. **$5²⁵**

"STANDARD"	"SENIOR"	"GIANT"
X751—4-16" blades... **$6²⁵**	X752—5-16" blades.... **$6⁹⁸**	X753—5-18" blades.... **$7⁴⁵**

Money Back GUARANTEE

We build into Western Mowers every desirable feature for easiest operation. Fast, true cutting and many years of efficient service. And in addition we guarantee complete satisfaction with any Western Mower you select—or your money back.

WESTERN *Rubber-Tired* DELUXE

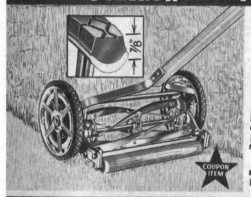

Quiet. Eliminates entirely that nerve-racking clatter on concrete. Heavy, solid, deep tread rubber wheels. Set so deep that they can't come loose or slip. Extra traction — no jar — no vibration. Protects sidewalk edges. Precision engineered throughout and rigidly braced to prevent twisting and strain. Strikingly handsome: Self-sharpening, crucible steel blades are oil tempered and hardened. Spring steel bed knife, adjustable ½" to 1½" cutting range.

X755—5 keen, self-sharpening 16" blades in perfect alignment... **$8⁶⁵**

COUPON ITEM

Handy GRASS TRIMMER

X871—Rugged yet light. Can be used with one hand. Swing it like a golf club. Double edge 9-inch tool steel blade. **c**

Fast! Easy!

65c

Double-edged Blade

WESTERN AUTO STORES
86

Revolving SPRINKLERS

X338
X339

X338—Rust-proof brass arms, 5½-inch sweep. Throws water up to 30-ft. according to pressure. Heavily enameled steel base.............. **29c**

X339—Three 7-inch brass arms, adjustable tilt. Sprinkles up to 54 ft. circle. Brass couplings and bearings............ **95c**

DELUXE
Fully Adjustable

X349

X349—Brass hose nozzles and head. Stationary, or revolving. Adjustable from spray to long stream. Sprinkles area from 8½ to 100 ft. in diameter.

Heavy cast iron base.............. **89c**

All-Brass SPRINKLERS

Coarse Spray

X337
X344

X337—"Spike" Sprinkler. Excellent for narrow places...................... **12c**
X344—"Round," 5" in diameter................. **59c**

All-Brass NOZZLES

X340
X341
X343

For all standard hose fittings. All adjustable to any degree of spray. Fully guaranteed.

X340—Dependable Service. Dress-molded sheet brass...................... **23c**
X341—Best ever at the price! Machine-turned from solid brass................. **35c**
X343—Big, heavy-duty. Machine turned brass. Extra large waterway............. **59c**

Grass CATCHER

X748—Heavy white duck on galvanized wire frame. Galvanized bottom slotted to fit more than one size mower. Strong hooks to attach included.

65c

Keen-Edged GRASS SHEARS and HOOKS

X874
X869

X874—Standard 5½" tempered steel blades. Spring steel bow. 12" long..... **29c**

X873 — Clippers 5½" forged cutlery steel blades. Malleable iron hdles... **42c**

X875—Level Cut Self-sharpening 5" blades parallel to ground. 3 adjustments. **89c**

STANDARD
X869 — Tempered 14-inch blade strong hardwood offset handle... **25c**

SCYTHE
X868 — Extra-quality. Ruggedly built. 12" tempered blade. Hand-fit handle. **39c**

X873
X875
X868

Electric *Bicycle* TAIL-LAMPS

FR686

FR666

STREAMLINE—Large oval lens flashes warning to rear; red jewel on left side, green on the right also gleam all the while the light is on. Operates from one small flashlight battery contained right in the case.
FR686—Brilliant chromium finish. Quick and easy to put on...... **65c**

"BRIGHT-BEAM"—Penetrating brilliance through a big 2-inch lens which makes an excellent reflector safety warning even when light is not "on." Adjustable bracket can be turned to any angle for installation at any point along the rear fender.
FR666—Ready-wired for easy hook-up... **49c**

TAIL-JEWEL Reflectors

STANDARD—Diamond-cut 1⅜-inch glass lens. Rust-proof mounting and bolt. A safety necessity! **FR653**...... **7c**

DeLUXE—Big 2-inch convex diamond-cut glass lens with light-catching polished metal reflector underneath. Famous "Tiger-Ey" super-reflector. Rust-proof mounting and bolt. **FR673**............ **15c**

HUB-JEWEL Reflectors

DeLUXE—Big 4-inch polished chrome disc with 2-inch "Tiger-Ey" reflecting jewel at the center. A vital safety need that also dresses up your bike's appearance.
FR617—Each.............. **32c**
     SET OF FOUR.............. **$1.22**

STANDARD—Flat polished steel disc, 3⅛ inches across with a 1-inch diamond-cut jewel. **FR535**—SET OF FOUR............ **55c**

FENDER FLAPS

Dress up your bike and at the same time protect from mud and gravel thrown by wheels. Reflector-jewels act as emergency tail-lights.

DeLUXE—Thick, shiny black rubber. Diamond-cut jewel set in big chromium ornament. Special non-scar bracket.
FR613—PAIR... **40c** Each... **22c**

STANDARD
Tough, black rubber with metal reinforced hole for bolting on.
FR612—
Each...... **9c**
PAIR....... **15c**

WESTERN AUTO
84 STORES

Increase Bike Enjoyment, Beauty and Safety!

FR594
FR593
FR665

New "Rocket" TWINS
Here's a pair of very handsome and useful teammates! Their beautiful, shiny polychrome finish and speed-lined design add a proud touch to any bike. No wires! Each operates from 2 flashlite batteries inside its own case. **THE PAIR**
FR665—Headlamp........ **$1.29**
FR594—Horn............ **$1.69** **$2.79**

Combination HORN and HEADLAMP
With Battery-Case, Remote-Control Button and Cable ALL Finished in Flashing Chromium!
Buck Rogers or Flash Gordon might have designed this Horn-Lite—it's that handsome and well-built! All wire encased in flexible metal tubing.
FR593—All hooked-up ready to go!............ **$2.49**

FR677
C538
FR540
FR541

ELECTRIC HEADLAMPS
"THE TORPEDO"—Unusually handsome streamline design. Chromium plated faceplate and shiny polychrome body. No wires! 2 small flashlight cells in the light itself supply current. You get both a red and a clear lens. Goes on handlebars or rear fender. **FR541**............ **98c**

"DeLuxe"—Beautiful chrome-plated oval head with excellent spread-light lens. Ready-wired to battery-case. Uses 4 flashlight cells. **FR677**—Complete, less cells...... **$1.49**

BATTERY-CARRIER CASES
For 4 Flashlight Cells. Exactly as shown and described above with FR677 DeLUXE headlamp. Switch at front end. Shining polychrome finish. **FR542**...... **59c**

For Common DRY CELL. Uses the regular 1½-volt No. 6 battery. Switch on front end of case. Gleaming polychrome finish. **FR664**............ **47c**

CHAIN GUARDS
Polished chrome-plate. Fit any bike.
FR616—Standard.. **45c**
FR608—DeLuxe........ **69c**
FR608

REAR-VIEW MIRRORS
10" long. Adjustable.
FR621—2¾" polished steel lens... **29c**
FR530—3¼" glass lens............ **36c**

FR616
FR530

Stewart-Warner SPEEDOMETER
Built like those for autos! Shows speed and records mileage, both! Beautifully finished in chrome and gray. Complete with fittings. **$3.49**
FR619—

FR622—PERSONS Speedometer by the famous maker of fine bike saddles and parts........ **$1.98**

FR620 — NEW DEPARTURE Cyclometer **35c**

Chrome Ornament 5 inches long. Mounts on fender or on its own bracket between truss-rods. **FR534**. **29c**

ELECTRIC MICRO HORNS
"DeLUXE"—A big, strikingly attractive horn with very loud blast and mechanism just like auto horns. Flashing chromium face. Full 4½-inches across. Ready-wired to hook up with same battery as your headlamp or to its own. Remote-control button mounts near your thumb on handle-grip. **C538**............ **$1.47**

"DeLUXE BANTAM"—(Not illustrated.) Very similar to C538 above in tone and mechanism, though smaller. Same wiring and control-button. **C537**...... **99c**

"LITTLE GIANT"—A lusty-toned horn operating from one flashlight cell in a polychrome-finish case just under the handsome polished head. Mounts near either hand. **FR540**............ **95c**

FR652
FR675
FR674
FR676
All Clamp to Handlebars

HAND HORN—Loud road-getting blast. **FR652**—Nickeled bell, face, plunger. **66c**
HAND SIREN—Entirely nickeled. **FR675**. **29c**
HAND BELL—Very loud. All nickeled. **FR674**—Continuous-ring mechanism. **19c**
BULB HORN—Polished nickeled, bell. **FR676**—10¼ inches long. Loud! **25c**

FR545
FR587
FR547

Wire Baskets
Rustless galvanized. Strong mesh.
FR661—11x6x4".... **39c**
FR662—15x10x4¾ ... **79c**

SUPER HEAVY-DUTY—For heavy deliveries. Braced from handlebars and front hub both. **FR545**.... **$1.29**

Luggage Carriers
STREAMLINED.
Heavy-duty. **FR587**. **66c**
FLAT STEEL.
Heavy-duty. **FR659**. **29c**
'SADDLE-BAGS'—Big roomy "bellows" pockets. Finest water-proof imitation leather, silver trim. Long strap. **FR547**. **89c**

PAINT Your Bike Yourself!
Wide range of colors. Finest Auto Enamels. Use WESCOTE! Page 76

Handlebar Grips
Big Diamond-Cut Jewels. Beautiful white rubber. **FR579**. **29c**
Other Grips, Page 83

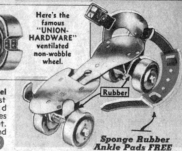

Casting Rods and Reels

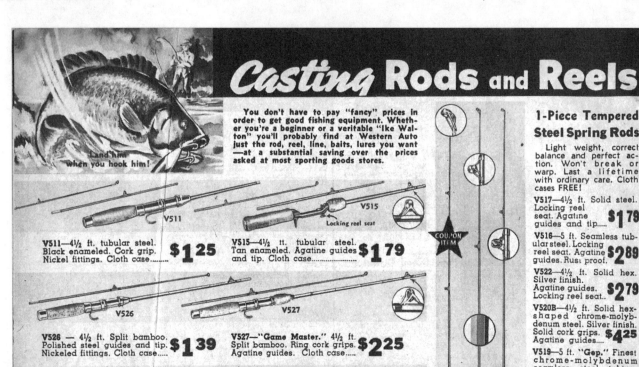

You don't have to pay "fancy" prices in order to get good fishing equipment. Whether you're a beginner or a veritable "Ike Walton" you'll probably find at Western Auto just the rod, reel, line, baits, lures you want—at a substantial saving over the prices asked at most sporting goods stores.

Land him when you hook him!

V511

V515

Locking reel seat

V511—4½ ft. tubular steel. Black enameled. Cork grip. Nickel fittings. Cloth case...... **$1 25**

V515—4½ ft. tubular steel. Tan enameled. Agatine guides and tip. Cloth case...... **$1 79**

V526

V527

V526— 4½ ft. Split bamboo. Polished steel guides and tip. Nickeled fittings. Cloth case..... **$1 39**

V527—"Game Master." 4½ ft. Split bamboo. Ring cork grips. Agatine guides. Cloth case..... **$2 25**

V524

V521

Agate tip and guides

Positive locking reel seat

V524—"Bass King." 5 ft. split bamboo. Agatine guides. Chromium locking reel seat. Solid cork grips. Beautifully finished. Bears comparison with most rods sold elsewhere at twice our low price...................... **$3 98**

V521—"Revelation." 5 ft. selected split bamboo specially processed for greater strength and flexibility. 1-pc. shaft for finest action. Agate guides. Chromium fittings. Solid cork grips. Multi-colored silk-wrapped. Cloth case. Expert's choice............ **$7 45**

1-Piece Tempered Steel Spring Rods

Light weight, correct balance and perfect action. Won't break or warp. Last a lifetime with ordinary care. Cloth cases FREE!

V517—4½ ft. Solid steel. Locking reel seat. Agatine guides and tip..... **$1 79**

V516—5 ft. Seamless tubular steel. Locking reel seat. Agatine guides. Rust proof. **$2 89**

V522—4½ ft. Solid hex. Silver finish. Agatine guides. Locking reel seat.. **$2 79**

V520B—4½ ft. Solid hex-shaped chrome-molybdenum steel. Silver finish. Solid cork grips. Agatine guides..... **$4 25**

V519—5 ft. "Gep." Finest chrome-molybdenum seamless steel tubing. Gun-metal. Agatine guides & tip. **$4 45**

COUPON ITEM

V520B V517

V519

*Ring Locking reel seats

Beginner's Casting or Bait Rod

2-piece rust-proof tempered solid spring steel with reel seat and wood handle.

V510............ **32c**

Anti-Backlash "Tru Form"

Spool stops as bait strikes water!

Usual $5.00 value..... **$3 65**

100-yd. Quadruple multiplying. Durable "bridge" construction. Wide spiral gears. Adjustable click and drag.

Adjustable jeweled caps, pillar-type rod-clip, reversible hardened "Duo-Pawl," attractive circle chrome finish, etc. **V486.**

New *Feather-weight* "Revelation"

Usual $8.50 Seller...... **$4 60**

Extremely light—yet strong—aluminum-alloy construction. Alumalite finish stays bright. Extra-heavy gears. Improved drag. Genuine agate spool caps, bronze bearings, cork spool arbor, other extra-quality features. 100-yd. capacity. **V492.**

V480—Special

29c

Level-Wind "Pelican"

95c

Strongly built. Quadruple multiplying. 100 yd. Adjustable click. Nickeled. **V482.**

Level-Wind "Cedar Lake"

$1 49 V481

Designed and precision - built for long faithful service. Adjustable jeweled spool caps.

3-piece easy take-down. Spiral gears. Reversible pawl. Adjustable click on tail plate. 100-yd. capacity. Quadruple multiplying. Beautiful chromium finish with attractively embossed end plates.

Anti-Backlash "Red River" **V484**— 100-yd. Adjustable drag, spool caps.

$1 95

"Western Warrior" **V493**—100-yard. Wide spiral gears.

COUPON ITEM

$2 15

"Thunder Hawk" **V491**—100-yard cap. Phosphor-bronze bearings.

$2 79

Pflueger "Akron" **V487** — 110-yard. Lightweight. Diamolite finish. Agate caps.

COUPON ITEM

$5 65

South Bend No. 550-C **V488**—100-yd. Famous anti-backlash device. Agate spool caps. c

$6 65

Complete stocks of **SURF and DEEP-SEA Fishing Tackle** at all seaport Western Auto Stores. Lowest prices.

All-Purpose Telescoping Rods

Just pull out here

Agatine guides

Strong tubular spring steel. Baked enamel finish.

V538

Equally fine for casting, fly or still fishing. Easily adjustable to length wanted. Reversible handle is adaptable for both casting and fly fishing. Strong, durable construction for long satisfactory service, yet light in weight for easy handling. Cloth case furnished with every one.

V538 — "Kastaway" (Shown). Extends from 38½" to 9 feet. Agatine guides and tip............... **$1 98**

V537—"Good Luck." Similar to above, but extends to 8½ feet. Metal guides........ **$1 25**

V539—"Bristol Hex." No. 45 (not shown). Extends 41½" to 9 feet. Hex shaft keeps guides always in perfect alignment. Chrome ring-locking reel seat. Extra-long cork grip.............. **$4 95**

Reversible handle. Attach either end to shaft, according to use

WESTERN AUTO STORES

90

Stream-tested Flies, Lures and Baits

(A) **Dry Flies.** 12 patterns.
V552-6-650-6—3 for **39c**; Ea... **14c**
V550—Four, with spinner... **22c**

(B) **Snelled Wet Flies.** 9 patterns. V580-8—3 for **25c**; Ea... **10c**
V590—Trout Flies. 5 for... **23c**

(C) **Bass Flies.** 6 patterns.
V592-7—3 for **39c**; Ea... **14c**
V578—Ass't, 2 with spinner... **35c**
V579—Pan-Fish size, 3 for... **22c**

(D) V635—"Fly-Oreno." 1⅛... **53c**
(E) V674-5-6—"Bass-Buster Jrs." **32c**

(F) V570-3—Bass Bugs. Each... **29c**
(G) V646-7-8—"Top-Sergeants" **39c**
(H) V661-2-3—"Hoodle-Bugs" **39c**
(I) V631—Helgramite... **24c**
(J) V670—Hair Mouse... **29c**
(K) V632—"Trix-Oreno." 1⅛... **45c**
(L) V621—"Tin Liz," fly size... **29c**

(A) V347—Creek Chub "Ding-bat" Frog (or Silver Flash) **89c**
(B) V370—S. B. "Babe-Oreno" **67c**
(C) V392—"River Runt"... **89c**
(D) V340—"Pikie Minnow" **1.10**
(E) V332—"Pikie Minnow"... **89c**

(F) V616—"Crawfish Crawler" **79c**
(G) V607—"Hawaiian Wiggler" **69c**
(H) V434—"Luminous Tandem" **55c**
(I) V430—Feathered Spoon... **16c**
(J) V604—"Shimmy Wiggler" **89c**
(K) V408—Casting Spoon... **12c**

Many other well-known and popular lures in our complete line are not shown here, including a large variety priced at only (V330).... **24c**

Best Quality **PORK-RIND BAIT**
V197—Bass size, 2-oz. bottle... **15c**
V198—Fly tips, 2-oz. bottle...

V603—GRASSHOPPER BAIT. **25c**
Natural coloring. Won't spoil

Silk and Wire LEADERS

V280—1-yd. finest Japan-silk knotless gut. 20-lb. **5c**
V281-7—Other lengths up to 10 ft. Lowest prices.
V275—6" Piano Wire, with snap and swivels **5c**
V277—9" Cable Wire... **8c**
V290-3—Snap Swivels... **3c**
V303-4—Connectors... **2c**

Leader, Fly and Bait BOXES

(A) V466—Leader Box. ⅝ x 4". Steel, aluminum finish, 2 felt pads... **19c**
(B) V472—Fly-and-Lure Box. Transparent "Pyra-Shell." Moth-proof... **79c**
V465—Snelled-Fly Box (not shown). Felt pads... **32c**
(C) V460—Bait-Box. Leak-proof. Wire belt fastener. Enameled steel... **16c**
(D) V473—Transparent Tubes for baits and lures. Size 1¼"x3½". **6c**

Save on Quality LANDING NETS

Elastic with Snap and Swivel

V448

V454—"Leader" (not shown)... **55c**
V449—Folding. (Not shown). Easy to pack and carry... **79c**
V448—"Game Getter" Laminated ash frame Silk net... **$1.78**
V450—Combination Hand-Boat Net. 2-pc. handle. **95c**

Rust-Proof MINNOW BUCKETS

V457—(Shown). 8-qt. Perforated inner pail. **72c**
V459—Same, 10-qt. **$1.29**
V458—12-qt. Oval. Floating type. Galvanized wire mesh on inner pail... **$1.55**

Jointed Cane "BANK" POLES

V540—(Shown). 8-foot. Genuine bamboo. 2-piece. Steel guides and tip. Nickeled fittings. Wood handle... **$1.25**

V545—(Not shown). 10-foot. 2-pc. Good quality cane. Wound ferrules. **42c**
V546—12-foot... **52c**   V547—16-foot... **72c**

Save on HOOKS of all Kinds

(A) V110—Assortment of 100... **19c**
V730-1-2—Carlisle. No. 6, 8 & 10. 10 for... **5c**
V740-4—Cinn. Bass. No. 26, 24. 10 for... **5c**
(B) V148-52—Snelled Cinn. Bass. Double-gut leaders. Any size. 6 for... **22c**
(C) V162-5—Snelled Carlisle. No. 4, 6, 8 and 10. 6 for... **14c**
V170—Snelled Carlisle. ass't of 6... **14c**
(D) V155-6—Treble Hooks, No. 5, 2, Ea. **3c**
Other sizes not listed—Similar low prices.

LINE, TWINE and TROT LINES

V246—"Holdwell" Braided Line. High quality long staple cotton. 50 yds... **10c**
V248-9-50—Select Cotton Twine. Small, medium and large. 8-oz. ball... **29c**
V257—Seine Twine. 2-oz. ball... **8c**
V469—Equipped Trot Line. 60-ft., with 20 Kirby hooks... **35c**
V468—Same, 150-ft., 50 hooks... **95c**

FLOATS and SINKERS

FLOATS—Complete stocks, celluloid, cork and quill. Money-saving prices as low as (V681)... **5c**

SINKERS—Complete stocks, Saranac, adjustable-end, split-shot, swivel casting, others—Lowest Prices.

Complete FISHLINE

V268—15 feet of line, float, hook and sinker... **10c**

FISH-BAG and STRINGERS

V175

V462—Fish Bag (Not shown). Heavy 1" mesh. Draw-strings. 36" long... **39c**
V175—Fish Stringer. 6-foot. Hook disgorger, scaler... **14c**
V174—"Ideal" Fish Stringer. Keeps 'em alive. 6-ft. stout cord. 10 rust-proof sliding hooks... **49c**

V174

Accurate FISH SCALE

V461—Scale. Weighs up to 15 pounds in ¼-lb. graduations... **49c**
V298—Fish Scaler. Cleans quickly, thoroughly Sharp steel blade... **8c**
V299—Fish Knife. Tempered blade. Scaler... **22c**

DIP-NETS and SEINES

V470—Dip Net. 42"x42" ⅛" mesh netting... **1.29**
Complete SEINES
V455—4'x4'... **42c**
V452—8'x4'... **85c**
Also 10 and 12-ft. sizes

Line and Fly Dressing, Rod Repairs

V305-15—Agatine guides and tips. Large or small. Choice... **15c**
V692—Line & Fly Dressing. Keeps lines soft and flies afloat. 1-oz. can... **19c**
V690—Floto Dry-Fly Solution... **23c**
V695—Ferrule Cement... **15c**
V697—Reel Oil... **19c**
V691—Rod Varnish... **19c**
V698—"Skeetrazz" Insect and Bug Repellant... **23c**

Limited space will not permit us to show many other items in our line of fresh and salt-water tackle.

WESTERN AUTO STORES

92

BASEBALL for Beginners

FREE 8-Page Book

"Finer Points of Baseball" Free with purchase.

PLAY BALL Better
With Equipment Endorsed By Stars!

When you can get equipment like this, at such low prices, why pay more? Sizes to suit every need. Satisfaction or Money Back.

X814—Heinie Manush. Full professional size. Selected top-grain horsehide; soft and pliable. Deep greased ball pocket. V-type back for snug fit. Wool padded strap on back. Double web straps............ **$2.79**

X815—Bill Rogell. Similar but with inner greased pocket; double tunnel loops.............. **$3.28**

JR. FIELDER'S GLOVE
X810—Thick, sturdy horsehide with leather lined palm. Well padded with felt. Also ideal for adult soft ball playing............ **49c**

BOY'S GLOVE
X811—Professional model. Genuine horsehide; leather lined palm and fingers. Spider-web lacing................ **95c**

CATCHER'S MITT
X803—Professional "Scoop" pattern. Correctly padded. Wine-colored sheep-skin on front and back. Leather-lined palm and fingers. Full-laced...... **98c**

29-Inch BOYS BAT

X793—Ash wood, 29" long. Choice of colors. Ideal for soft ball................ **25c**

Amateur League BALL
X775—Full-Size. Horsehide cover. Cotton yarn wrapped over rubber center. **19c**

BASEBALL CAPS

X765 to X770—Black felt. Flexible green-lined visor. Leather band. Sizes 6⅝ to 7¼. **22c**

X813—"TED" LYONS. Top grain horsehide inner greased ball pocket. Leather lined. Black leather welt seams. Leather laced heel for adjusting padding. Leather loops between thumb and forefinger. **$1.98**

X812—"AL" SIMMONS. Similar but with grease in inner ball pocket.............. **$1.45**

Star Model Professional BATS

Authentic reproductions of personal bats as used by Joe DiMaggio, Lou Gehrig, Hank Greenberg, Jimmie Foxx and other big league stars. Choice of 34, 35, 36".

X794—STANDARD. Selected ash. Handle taped...... **49c**

X795—PROFESSIONAL Fine grain ash........ **85c**

X796—AMERICAN Finest second-growth Northern Ash. Made by Hillerich & Bradsby, Louisville, Ky..... **$1.39**

Regulation Size FIRST BASE MITT
X800—'Lefty' Grimm model. Finest tan cowhide. Inner greased pocket, ready broke leather lined with inside fingers, double sewed for longer wear. Extra large thumb with adjustable leather thumb strap............ **$1.98**

CATCHER'S MITT
X805—Professional. Select cowhide. Inner greased ball pocket pad is stitched hair and felt layers. Leather lined and laced. Wool padded strap. **$3.45**

X804—"Eddie" Phillips "Scoop" model. Similar, smaller. **$1.98**

CATCHER'S MASK
X816—Regulation size. Heavy, welded steel frame. Comfortable hair stuffed leather pads. Adjustable elastic head straps. Removable green eye shade............ **$2.65**

SOFTBALL at Low Cost

Official BASEBALLS

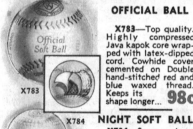

OFFICIAL BALL
X783—Top quality. Highly compressed Java kapok core wrapped with latex-dipped cord. Cowhide cover cemented on Double hand-stitched red and blue waxed thread. Keeps its shape longer... **98c**

NIGHT SOFT BALL
X784—Same as above but with white cover and threads for easy visibility..... **$1.10**

PLAYGROUND BALL
X781—Compressed sisal center. Yarn wrapped. Leather cover. Double hand stitched thread... **32c**

REGULATION BALL
X782—Official size. 100% Kapok center; Yarn wrapped. Horsehide cover. Double hand-stitched wax thread........ **59c**

Fielder's Glove

X809—Official. Tan horsehide. Leather-lined. No padding in palm and fingers. Outside padded from thumb to little finger, for easier catching. Adjustable leather laced at thumb.. **$1.79**

REGULATION BAT

X789—Smacko—she's out of the park with this straight-grained ash bat! Non-slip spiral tape grip............ **39c**

OFFICIAL BAT
X791—Built for long, hard hitting. Straight-grained seasoned hickory. New "Flox" grip; suede—for sure grip............ **69c**

Official size and weight; 9-in. in circumference. 5-oz. in weight. Finest horsehide covers. Double hand-stitched with wax thread.

CITY LEAGUE
X776—Strong yarn wound over Para rubber center. Will stand a lot of hard play and knocking around. Long wear at a low price.................. **49c**

MAJOR LEAGUE
X777—Cork and rubber center. Wound with high-quality mixed virgin wool and yarn. Holds up well under heaviest hitting. **79c**

OFFICIAL LEAGUE
X778—Similar to balls used by Major League teams. Cork and live rubber center wrapped with 100% Woolen yarns........c............ **$1.19**

WESTERN AUTO STORES 93

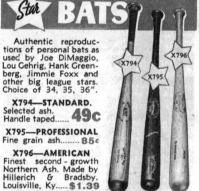

Galvanized Pails

All galvanized ware is made one of two ways: "Hot-Dipped" or the cheap "Sheet-Ware."

Western Auto Galvanized Ware is "Hot-Dipped." In this process we first form the raw sheet into the desired shape and submerge it in baths of hot molten zinc which seals all seams permanently. And in addition it gives a heavy uniform coat over all the surface.

Hot-Dipping means to you, **top-quality** durable galvanized ware with guaranteed **longer life** and a **rust-proof** high

G1205 **27c**
10-qt.

G1206 **32c**
12-qt.

G1207 **39c**
14-qt.

Lustre Finish.

Wash Tub

Heavy drop handles on spot welded lug-ears.
G1215—No. 2
14½
Gal.
Round..... **89c**

G1216—No. 3. Round.
17½ gallons........... **$1.05**
G1220—No. 2. Square.
14½ gallons........... **$1.15**

Garbage Can

Heavy vertical handle locks vertically against lids.
G1230—
6½ gallon........... **98c**
G1231—Same **$1.29**
10½ gallon.......

LOCK LID
RELEASES
WHEN HANDLE
IS LIFTED

Water Pail

Enameled
G1200 — 12 qts. Wood handle. 2-tone.. **89c**

ICE TONGS
SUPERIOR

Solid forged bows; duck bill points. Molded handles; solid forged bows.

Black japanned finish.

Each

No. 1200—No. 3 size, open 20 in., wt. each 6 lbs. **$3.95**

Open stock.

CLINKER TONGS
ADAMS

No. 2—Black Lacquer Finish
Opening and closing of tongs is controlled by a slight turn of the handle. Constructed of high grade steel and is light in weight. Red enameled handle.

Each

No. 2—52 in. long; wt. each 3 lbs. ...**$4.25**
Open stock.

SLAW CUTTERS
T & D

Plain, smoothly sanded bed; wide, smooth cutting surface.

Adjustable, polished and tempered steel knife; 45° shear.

Each

No. 625—6x16 in.; wt. per carton 25 lbs. **$1.50**

Twelve in a carton.

KRAUT CUTTERS
T & D

Plain bed; plain sliding box. Polished, adjustable, tempered steel knives; 24° shear.

Each

No. 673-W—9x25 in.; wt. per carton 20 lbs. **$5.95**

Three in a carton.

CHURNS
DAZEY ELECTRIC

Quiet, easy and efficient to operate; easy to clean and store.

Red enameled motor housing and chrome jar cap; aluminum rod and dasher.

Four leaf clover design jar makes easier churning and eliminates loss of unchurned cream in square corners; jar is easy to handle and clean.

Complete with jar, cord and plug.

110 volt, 60 cycle, AC only.

Nos.	4-ER	8-ER
Capacity, gals.	1	2
Churning, cap., gal.	½	1
Wt. each, lbs.	12	15
Each	$24.95	27.95

One in a carton.

DAZEY HAND

Four leaf clover design jar makes easier churning and eliminates loss of unchurned cream in square corners. Patented removable strainer eliminates need of removing gearing to test temperatures, remove butter milk or add wash water.

High speed, fully enclosed gears; streamlined, hardwood dashers.

Gear housing and crank handle finished in red lacquer, all other metal parts in aluminum paint.

Nos.	4	8
Cap., qts.	4	8
Churn. cap., qts.	2	4
Wt. each, lbs.	6¾	9
Each	$5.95	6.95

Four in a carton.

COUPON GOOD FOR ONE OR TWO DOLLARS

1 **2**

On the Purchase of Articles as Shown in this Catalog Marked with a Star
For Actual Coupon and Information See Page 103

COUPON ITEM

Here Are Some of the Articles on Which Coupons Can be Used!

COUPON ITEM

Western Auto Stores

105 E. Market St.

Corner, Market & Broadway   **Phone, Jefferson 3181**

Large, Convenient Drive-In Service Facilities—Free Parking for Customers

Open Daily (Except Sunday) 8 A.M. to 9 P.M.

AKRON, OHIO

1947 Firestone Catalog

Firestone

EXTRA VALUE MERCHANDISE

FOR CAR AND TRUCK
HOME AND FARM
WORK AND RECREATION

BROOKFIELD TIRE & BATTERY CO.

120 N. Main St.   Phone: 30

BROOKFIELD, MO.

INDEX

City, State or Federal
Taxes will be added.

*Prices subject to change
without notice.*

Fall
AND
Winter
1947

WEST

Be Ready For Sledding

(D) (E) SILVER STREAK SLEDS — There's a Silver Streak Sled at our store for youngsters of every age — from 3 years old up — in sizes from 38 in. up to 54 in. Come in and see these speedsters with their scientifically grooved runners, turned up and supported by strong curved steel brace. They're built for speed. Specially built yoke assures easier steering control. Runners and undercarriage made of special tempered steel for maximum service, securely riveted to body. The body and cross bars are straight-grained hardwood with extra heavy coats of weather-resistant varnish to withstand roughest treatment. All metal parts silver finish, attractive red and blue trim.

10-L-7 — 38-in. **4.98**
10-L-8 — 45-in. **5.95**
10-L-9 — 54-in. **6.95**

(F) 45-INCH ROYAL RACER SLED — A low priced, quality sled. Designed for easy steering with strong metal undercarriage supports, tempered flat steel runners. All metal parts are securely fastened together with heavy rivets. Bed, cross-members and steering handle made of hardwood, with weather-resistant varnish finish. Red baked enamel trim.
10-L-6 — 45-inch **4.45**

(A) (B) (C) YOUTH'S HOCKEY STICKS — When snow flies, and the pond freezes over, hockey is the sport every active boy enjoys. These sturdy, straight-grained, hardwood sticks are built for rough service. Easy to handle — proper weight and size. Attractively painted blade and lower shaft, smoothly sanded natural finish handle.
10-D-40 — Length 47 in. **1.29**

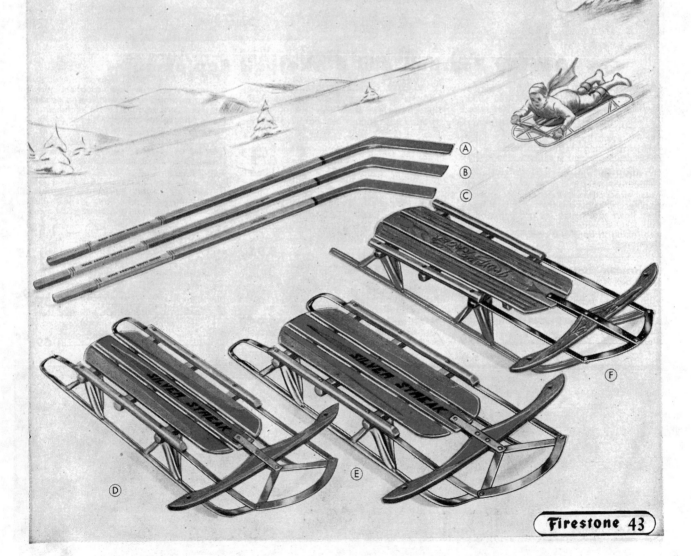

Firestone 43

Quality Football and Basketball Equipment

(A) FOOTBALL HELMET — Strong, rugged head protection for high school and sand lot players. Heavy top grain leather ears, front and back. Stiff, well-formed plastic fiber crown — thick felt lining. Carefully stitched seams provide long life. Adjustable snap button elastic chin strap.
10-J-24 .... **7.95**

(B) SHOULDER PADS — Designed for hard, competitive service — built to give maximum protection. Well-formed collar, shoulder and shock plates of stiff plastic fiber, lined with heavy felt and assembled with riveted wide leather straps. Strong web lacing in front and back, wide elastic arm bands.
10-J-22 .... **5.95**

(C) OFFICIAL FOOTBALL — The ideal low-priced ball for young players. It is cut- and scuff-resistant — DuPont Football Covering with pebble grain. Official in size and weight, sewed with tough waxed thread. One-piece molded bladder, leakproof rubber valve.
10-J-37 .... **3.95**

(D) VARSITY OFFICIAL FOOTBALL — Takes plenty of abuse on the sand lot or high school field. Double lined top grain, pebble grain leather, strong chain stitched seams. Official in size and weight. One-piece molded rubber bladder, leakproof rubber valve.
10-J-6 .... **6.95**

(E) SPALDING OFFICIAL FOOTBALL — A really fine ball — equal in quality to balls used by semi-pro and pro football players. Selected top grain leather, double vulcanized lined. Lock-stitched with tough waxed thread for rough use. Official in size, weight and shape. One-piece molded rubber bladder with leakproof rubber valve.
10-J-41 .... **8.95**

(F) OFFICIAL BASKETBALL — Easy to handle official size basketball, made with long-wearing, cut- and scuff-resistant DuPont basketball covering. Flat plastic laces eliminate bulging. One-piece molded bladder has leakproof rubber valve.
10-J-38 .... **5.95**

(G) "BLUE ARROW" BASKETBALL — For indoor or outdoor play. Tough, long-wearing rubber cover will take roughest playground service—resists scuffing on cement and unpaved surfaces. No stitches to break. Leakproof valve. Official in size and weight for accurate performance.
10-J-20 .... **8.95**

(H) MEN'S SWEAT SHIRT — Fine cotton yarns, fleece-lined. Jersey knit cuffs. Silver gray.
10-K-3 .... **1.59**

(J) KNIT "T" SHIRT — Attractive heather-tone colors — tan, blue and yellow. Full cut, hemmed bottom and sleeves. In sizes to fit.
13-C-4 .... **1.59**

(K) WHITE "T" SHIRT — Full cut — rib knit neck. Made of combed cotton.
13-C-5 .... **1.19**

(L) SPORT SOCKS — Good-quality combed yarn socks. Made of 50% wool, 25% cotton, 25% rayon.
10-K-8 — Pair **59c**

(M) ATHLETIC SUPPORTER — Elastic Neoprene synthetic rubber belt and leg straps. Rayon pouch has elastic edges.
10-K-1 .... **69c**

Firestone 44

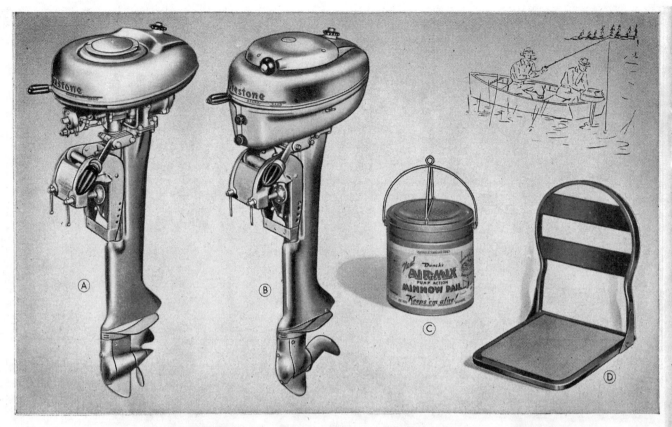

Everything for the Outdoor Man

(A) THE NEW FIRESTONE STANDARD 3½ H.P. SINGLE CYLINDER OUTBOARD MOTOR — Add hours of pleasure and convenience to your fishing and boating enjoyment. The new Firestone 3½ H.P. Single Cylinder Motor has new positive action water pump, drop-forged hardened steel connecting rods with roller bearings for friction-free operation. Scientifically designed counter-balanced crankshaft, high intensity magneto that gives hotter spark for quicker starting and lower idling speed. Positive non-flooding choke. New hydraulic jet silencer for quieter operation. Hardened, ground gears. Streamlined gas tank with full one gallon capacity. Handy carrying handle.

All castings especially treated for corrosion resistance. Weighs only 40 lbs.
10-A-1.................................... **99.50**
3½ H.P. DE LUXE QUALITY SINGLE CYLINDER OUTBOARD MOTOR — Same type as 10-A-1 above except has these added features: Self-winding starter rope; all enclosed mechanism to protect cylinder block, spark plug, gas lines from weather and damage. Weighs only 42 lbs. — easy to handle.
10-A-2 — (Not illustrated)............. **112.50**
Only 4.75 a Week on Budget Terms
(B) 7½ H.P. DE LUXE QUALITY TWIN CYLINDER OUTBOARD MOTOR — For maximum performance, smoothest operation, greatest speed and

life, choose this De Luxe Quality Twin Cylinder Motor. Has all the features of the 10-A-1 and 10-A-2 at left plus the following: Powerful 7½ H.P. twin cylinder motor; alternate firing for smooth operation at all speeds. Approved by the National Outboard Association.
10-A-3.................................. **164.50**
Only 6.75 a Week on Budget Terms
(C) 12-QT. MINNOW BUCKET — Keeps minnows alive longer without changing water.
10-M-155................................ **3.95**
(D) METAL BOAT SEAT — A safe, comfortable seat for fishermen.
10-A-5.................................... **4.49**

FIRESTONE IS FISHING HEADQUARTERS

SUPERIOR STEEL CASTING RODS — A fine quality casting rod — made of tapered, precision-ground, carbon alloy steel, oil-tempered and heat-treated. Stainless steel guides and tip, "Duo-Loc" reel seat. Screw type lock. Complete with cloth cover with protective wood insert.
10-M-195 — 5-ft. Length. Natural green finish. **8.95**
10-M-196 — 4½-ft. Length. Pearl gray finish. **8.95**

DE LUXE STEEL CASTING RODS — Solid taper, precision-ground silicon-chrome steel, heat-treated and oil-tempered. Cast-aluminum handle, comfortable cork grip. Finished in non-glare

cream enamel, red trim. Complete with cloth sack with wood insert.
10-M-224 — 4½- or 5-ft. lengths........ **6.45**
10-M-194 — 47-inch length............... **4.98**
STANDARD STEEL CASTING ROD — Solid steel, two-piece rod, with jeweled guides and tip. Cast aluminum handle has black ribbed grip. Removable reel clamp.
10-M-223 — 4¼ feet long................. **4.98**
INTERSTATE CASTING REEL — Handsomely designed, sturdily constructed fresh water reel. Satin chrome finish. Lightweight oilite cushioned spool and worm bearings permit greater yardage on casts with less backlash. Handy adjustable brake. Line capacity 100 yards.
10-M-169................................ **7.98**

NILE CASTING REEL — Highly polished chrome-plated finish. Adjustable drag and "S" shaped handle with tenite knobs. Oilite bearings and quadruple multiplying gears. Line capacity 100 yards.
10-M-170................................ **5.95**

FISHING FLIES, LURES, MINNOWS, PLUGS — Equip your tackle box with the proven flies, lures, minnows and plugs successful fishermen use. You'll find a quality selection of famous brands at our store, reasonably priced. Come in and look them over today — select what you need and be ready to head for that favorite fishing spot.

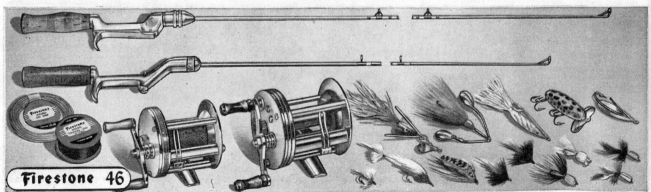

Firestone 46

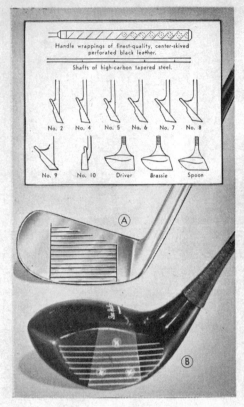

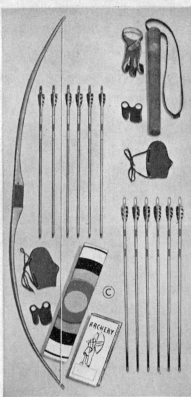

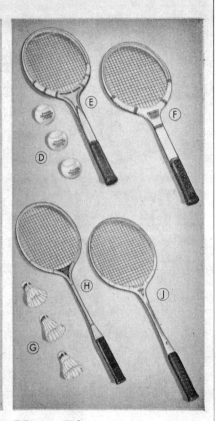

For Outdoor Fun That Keeps You Fit

(A) (B) FIRESTONE "DON MacDOUGAL" CHAMPION GOLF CLUBS — Designed to give you greater control, more power, a freer swing. Made from finest materials. Woods expertly designed, made of seasoned persimmon with Keystone fiber inserts on hitting face. Irons arch-back design, placing weight where it is needed most. Heads of irons are forged steel, chromium-plated over copper and nickel. All face scorings conform with P.G.A. specifications. All shafts of high carbon tapered steel. Shafts of woods chromium-plated, irons are hickory sheathed. Non-slip, perforated black leather handles. All clubs matched and registered, swing-weighted and balanced.

(A) 10-H-16 — Set of 8 irons (see illustration above)_____ **59.75**
(B) 10-H-11 — Set of 3 woods (see illustration above)_____ **29.75**

(C) SUPREME QUALITY ARCHERY EQUIPMENT — More and more archery enthusiasts are finding the many fine quality archery supplies they need at Firestone. Whether it's a complete target archery set you're looking for, a hunting bow, a set of arrows, gloves, finger tabs, quiver, target face or stand, see the exceptionally fine display and price range of equipment at our store before you buy.

(D) FIRESTONE CHAMPIONSHIP TENNIS BALLS — Approved by U. S. Lawn Tennis Association. Vacuum packed cans.
10-E-22 — White.....................3 for **1.79**

(E) PROFESSIONAL CHAMPION TENNIS RACKET — Truly the racket choice of those who demand the best. The eight-ply, laminated wood frame with its full flake overlay at the throat and six throat windings gives you the finest frame available. Strung with new, strong, red nylon. Leather handle grip.
10-E-21.................. **11.45**

(F) FIRESTONE "VICTORY" TENNIS RACKET — Nine-ply; laminated wood frame, tightly strung with clear nylon. Full-flake overlay and six throat windings. Perforated leather grip.
10-E-7 — Choice of weights............. **10.95**

(G) BADMINTON SHUTTLECOCKS — Selected white hand trimmed feathers.
10-E-19 — Indoor ....3 for **1.19**
10-E-18 — Outdoor. Weighted ....3 for **1.49**

(H) "VICTORY" BADMINTON RACKET — Five-ply laminated wood frame. Full-flake overlay at throat and shoulders. Clear nylon strings. Leather grip.
10-E-3................................ **5.75**

(J) "DRIVER" BADMINTON RACKET — Three-ply, laminated wood frame with "Pyralin" plastic overlay. Strung with clear nylon. Imitation leather grip.
10-E-11............................... **4.79**

(K) BASEBALL CAPS — 70% wool, 30% cotton. Size 6¾ through 7½.
10-F-34 — Royal Blue.................... **98c**
10-F-35 — Scarlet...................... **98c**

(L) SUPREME BASEBALL — Used by many leagues. Top quality cork and rubber center.
10-F-13 — Pearl horsehide cover.......... **2.19**

(M) SUPREME SOFTBALL — Official. 100% Kapok core. Triple-stitched, horsehide cover.
10-F-11............................... **2.29**

(N) "BOB DOERR" AUTOGRAPHED FIELDER'S GLOVE — Genuine horsehide leather. Welted seams. Fully lined.
10-F-15................................ **4.69**

(P) SOFTBALL MITT — Combination softball catcher's and baseman's mitt. Genuine horsehide leather, full laced except at wrist. Rawhide face webbing between thumb and ball pocket.
10-F-19................................ **4.49**

(R) "BOB DOERR" AUTOGRAPHED FIELDER'S GLOVE — A good quality, selected cowhide leather glove with tunnel loops. Hand formed. Fully lined. Rawhide lacing.
10-F-3................................ **5.29**

(S) SOFTBALL GLOVE — Genuine horsehide with half lined back. Raised padding.
10-F-18................................ **3.69**

(T) "RUDY YORK" AUTOGRAPHED BASEMAN'S MITT — Top-grain leather. Rawhide webbing between thumb and forefinger. Fully lined.
10-F-6................................ **5.95**

(U) BASEBALL BAT — Famous "Louisville Slugger" professional model.
10-F-33 — Assorted lengths and weights... **2.65**

(V) SOFTBALL BAT — Ash with taped handle.
10-F-9 — Assorted weights and lengths..... **1.59**

(W) SOFTBALL BAT — Good-grade ash.
10-F-10 — Red finish.................... **1.25**

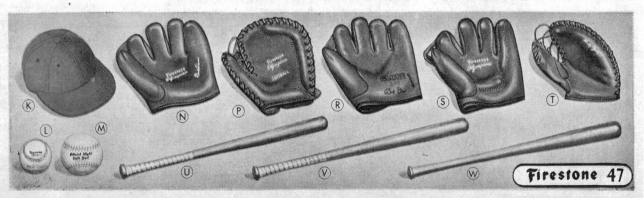

Firestone 48

PLENTY OF ZIP AND FLASH

(A) SUPREME QUALITY TRICYCLE — A new streamlined, chain-driven tricycle, built to last through years of rough-and-tumble service. The sturdy steel tube frame, ball-bearing wheels throughout, 1¾-in. semi-pneumatic tires — your assurance of trouble-free service. Handlebars are chromium-plated with rubber grips. The crank and sprocket are nickel-plated. Pedals are bicycle-type with ball bearings. Attractive, durable maroon finish with white trim.
9-C-68 — 16-in. rear wheels,
20-in. front wheel..........**38.95**

(B) STURDY VELOCIPEDE — Your youngster will get many miles of pleasure with this velocipede with its electrically welded 1¼-in. tubular steel frame and strong stamped steel rear platform. Seat is made of moulded rubber with double coil springs, shaped for comfort. Solid rubber tires, ball-bearing wheels all around. Bicycle-type spokes, deep front fender. Handlebars tubular type, double-adjustment to suit any rider. Rubber grips. Maroon and white baked enamel finish.
9-C-75 — 16-in. front wheel.. **19.95**

(C) DE LUXE TUBULAR VELOCIPEDE — Fun for growing youngsters. Strong 1¼-in. tubular frame and forged steel fork for long service. Full-size step plates and easy-to-steer handlebars with rubber grips. Moulded rubber saddle, formed for comfortable fit. Solid rubber tires, heavy machine spokes. Solid block rubber pedals. Beautiful baked enamel finish in meadow green with white trim on handlebars, seat, rims and spokes.
9-C-51 — 12-in. front wheel.... **10.95**
9-C-52 — 16-in. front wheel.... **12.95**
9-C-53 — 20-in. front wheel.... **14.95**

(D) SUPREME QUALITY VELOCIPEDE — A sleek, safe velocipede, built to last. The strong 1½-in. tubular frame with full size step plates and adjustable handlebars makes it easy to ride. Ball-bearing pedals and streamlined hub are designed for better performance. There's a new ride thrill, too, in the sturdy 1.75-in. semi-pneumatic punctureproof tires. Baked-enamel finish in maroon and white with green trim. Chrome handlebars, crank and sprocket.
9-C-13 — 12-in. front wheel.... **22.95**
9-C-14 — 16-in. front wheel.... **23.95**
9-C-15 — 20-in. front wheel.... **24.95**

(E) THREE-WHEEL SCOOTER — Low in price, yet sturdy and safe to ride. Ideal as a first scooter for children 2½ to 4 years. Bright finish. Solid rubber tires.
9-C-93.........................**2.49**

(F) STREAMLINED SCOOTER — Sturdy, all-metal construction for hard service. Wheels 7-in. diameter with solid rubber tires. Parking stand. Rubber handlebar grips. Fire engine red enamel finish.
9-C-38.........................**3.98**

(G) ALL-STEEL SCOOTER — A real riding scooter. Large size for children 4 to 8 years. Ten-inch "Artillery" wheels with solid rubber tires. Bright red, white and blue baked enamel finish.
9-C-94.........................**4.95**

For The Farm   For The Home   For Cottages

Heavy Gauge Steel Outer Jacket—Finished in White Baked Enamel

Three-inch Fiberglas Insulation—Will not Rot or Absorb Moisture

Heavy Gauge Steel Top Cover—Fits Tightly. Keeps Heat In, Dirt Out

ELECTRIC DAIRY HOT WATER HEATER

Designed for use in dairy barns to supply hot water for washing dairy utensils, sterilizing milking machines, furnishing adequate hot water when rapid milking system is used. Even though running water is not available, this heater will operate manually. With running water, heater can be made fully automatic. Extra-large water capacity — two sizes, 10- and 15-gallon. Special fill tank increases capacity to 12 and 17 gallons.

CHECK THESE EXTRA QUALITY FEATURES

Removable flange for easy cleaning. Brass swivel faucet — eliminates dripping caused by heated water expanding. Heavy gauge steel top cover — fits tightly — keeps heat in, dirt out. Steel outer shell and legs. Tank solid copper. Three-inch Fiberglas insulation, will not rot or absorb moisture; odorless and verminproof. Submersion-type heating element for quick, easy heating. Heavy-duty automatic thermostat turns current on when needed, off when water reaches correct temperature. Heavy-gauge steel bottom cover. Entire unit is easy to clean. Attractively finished in white baked enamel, trimmed in red. Heating element, rubber cord and plug, Underwriters' listed. Designed for 110-120 alternating current. Guaranteed one year.

16-A-41 — 12-gal. size.............**50.95**
16-A-42 — 17-gal. size.............**57.95**

FLOAT VALVE — Enables heater to be converted into a fully automatic unit. (Not illustrated.)
16-A-45.............**2.95**

(A) DAIRY FLY SPRAY—Will not taint foods.
16-A-77 — Qt.............**45c**
16-A-78 — Gallon.............**1.19**
16-A-79 — 5-Gallon.............**4.95**

(B) FILTER DISKS — Famous Johnson and Johnson.
16-A-6 — 6" Plain.............**49c**
16-A-7 — 6" Gauze.............**75c**
16-A-8 — 6½" Plain.............**55c**
16-A-9 — 6½" Gauze.............**85c**

(C) SUPREME DAIRY PAIL — 12-qt. heavy duty. Tin-plated sheet steel. Sides and bottom seamless. Dome bottom.
16-A-11.............**2.79**

(D) TIN DAIRY PAIL — 12-qt. Recessed bottom, riveted bail ears. Zinc base plating.
16-A-10.............**79c**

(E) PELOUSE DAIRY SCALE — Accurate. Seven-inch dial, graduating reading of 1/12 lb. up to 40 lbs.
16-A-24.............**4.19**

(F) DAIRY STRAINER — Heavy-gauge, tin-plated steel. Seamless construction — easy to clean. Perforated disc bottom and removable high-speed dome. 16-qt. capacity.
16-A-16.............**3.49**

(G) WOOD BUTTER CHURN — Three-gallon capacity. Sturdily built. Handle for manual operation. Platform base for stability while in operation.
16-A-38.............**4.50**

(H) ONE-GALLON DAISY BUTTER CHURN — Strong, durable glass withstands rapid temperature changes. Efficient washer, easy to clean. Streamlined gear case — makes churning fast and easy. Patented removable strainer.
16-A-13.............**3.25**

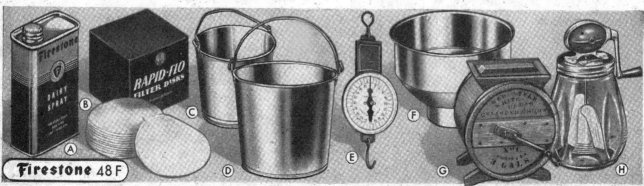

BE ASSURED OF PURE, SAFE MILK

High Speed Dome Perforated To Allow Rapid Flow

Electro-magnetic Agitation Means Constant Movement

Milk Automatically Heated To 143 Degrees

Firestone Electric Milk Pasteurizer

Farm families and families living in communities where pasteurized milk is not available can be assured of safe, pure milk for those growing youngsters, disease-free milk for the entire family. Avoid the danger of transmittal of undulant fever, typhoid fever, scarlet fever and diphtheria by pasteurizing your milk. Actual tests prove that the Firestone Electric Milk Pasteurizer kills or renders harmless all disease organisms which may be transmitted through milk. Meets pasteurizing requirements of the U. S. Public Health Service. Operates at the efficiency of large commercial units, yet priced within the reach of every farm family.

Pasteurizes two gallons of milk in one hour by simple water-bath principle. Electrically heated. Milk automatically heated to 143 degrees during pasteurization. Temperature and timing regulated automatically by timer and high-efficiency 4-inch Fenwall thermostat. Electro-magnetic agitator keeps milk and water in constant movement, assuring uniform pasteurizing temperature, avoids "cooked" taste.

Finished in snowy white, baked-on enamel with red trim. Water jacket coated with rustproof lacquer. Milk container heavy tinplated steel. Operates from 110-120 volt AC outlet; 1250-watt heating element. Complete with cord, plug and operating instructions.
16-A-43 _____ **47.95**

(A) SUPREME CREAM OR MILK CANS — Top quality, handy containers made of heavy gauge steel. Heavy tin coated after forming.
16-A-17 — 8-qt. **3.89** 16-A-18 — 12-qt. **4.49**

(B) STANDARD MILK CAN — Heavy gauge steel, sanitary seamless sides, durable rolled edges. Heavy tin coated after forming. Sanitary, seamless plug cover.
16-A-14 — 10-gal. capacity _____ **6.95**

(C) MILK STOOL — Sturdy construction—.065 gauge steel, torch-welded and practically "tip-proof" due to 3-leg construction. Circular brace on legs adds rigidity.
16-A-80 _____ **1.19**

(D) MILK STOOL — All-steel, tubular legs securely riveted to seat. Convenient height, no-tip design.
16-A-15 _____ **1.45**

(E) MILK CAN BRUSH — Winged-type. Bassine and Tampico fibers. Hardwood handle.
16-A-5 _____ **59c**

(F) MERCURY TUBE THERMOMETER — Finest quality, guaranteed accurate. Easy-to-read scale. Registers 10° F., to 230° F.
16-A-22 — 11-in. long _____ **69c**

(G) RED SPIRIT TUBE THERMOMETER — Reliable, good quality. Graduated scale from 30° F., to 230° F.
16-A-23 — 11-in. long _____ **38c**

(H) STANDARD MILK BOTTLE BRUSH — Horsehair bristles. Will not scratch.
16-A-4 _____ **29c**

(J) SUPREME MILK BOTTLE BRUSH — Fine quality. Horsehair bristles and end tufts.
16-A-3 _____ **79c**

(K) MILK BOTTLE CAPS — Strong, tab-pull, sprucewood cardboard. Fit all standard half-pint, pint and No. 2 qt. bottles. Paraffin coated.
16-A-2 — Tube of 500 _____ **49c**

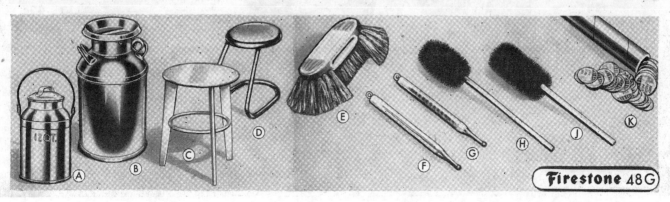

Firestone 48G

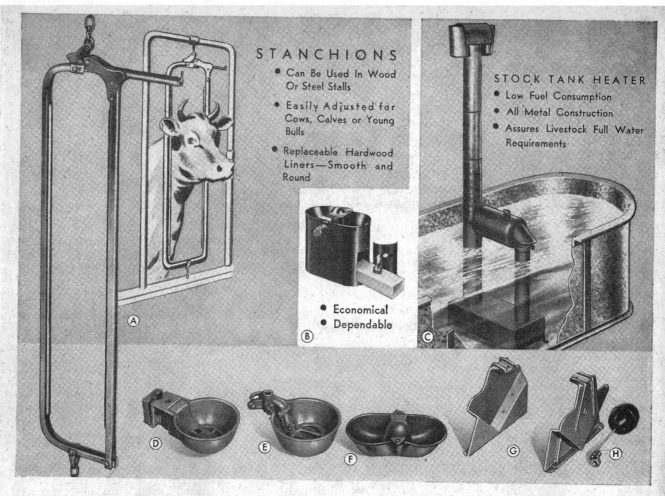

STANCHIONS
- Can Be Used In Wood Or Steel Stalls
- Easily Adjusted for Cows, Calves or Young Bulls
- Replaceable Hardwood Liners—Smooth and Round

- Economical
- Dependable

STOCK TANK HEATER
- Low Fuel Consumption
- All Metal Construction
- Assures Livestock Full Water Requirements

(A) OVAL-TYPE STANCHIONS — Fine-quality oval stanchions for use in either wood or steel stalls. Easily adjusted to needed width for cows, calves or young bulls. The steel bars, 1-5/16 by 7/8 by 3/16 in., have replaceable hardwood liners, smooth and rounded. Height inside 43 in., width at top 17½ in. Bottom adjustable to two widths for added comfort. Heavy malleable lock is cowproof — easily released.
16-J-3 — Stanchion.................. **3.95**

(B) HEATED STOCK WATERER — Removes chill from water during winter months — serves as water bowl year around. Heavy cast iron. Lead-coated kerosene or fuel oil reservoir holds 2½ pts. Easily connected to any tank or barrel. Over-all dimensions 15 by 12 in., drinking space 7 by 14 by 4½ in.
16-J-32 .... **8.95**

(C) STOCK TANK HEATER — Economical, efficient, all-metal kerosene-type water heater. Keeps water free from ice in coldest weather; encourages livestock to drink their full requirement of water. Low fuel consumption. Easily assembled.
16-J-23 — Instructions included...... **20.95**

(D) SUPREME DAIRY WATER BOWL — Regulates flow of water from either high-pressure or gravity water system — no splash, no overflow. Positive-acting, long-wearing, brass-type valve.
16-J-44.............................. **4.95**

(E) WATER BOWL — Trouble-free, simple valve mechanism operates by slight pressure of animal's muzzle. Easily mounted.
16-J-2 — Tapped for ¾-in. pipe....... **3.95**

(F) STOCK OR HOG WATERER — Cast iron drinking bowl. Over-all size 14 by 7 by 4 in. Automatic float and valve prevent overflow. Strainer prevents valve from clogging.
16-J-1 — Tapped for ¾-in. pipe....... **3.25**

(G) (H) HOG WATERER KIT — Farmers — Construct your own automatic hog water troughl Kit complete except for lumber. Includes cast iron trough ends (G), automatic float valve and float (H). Zinc-plated hinges and lock nuts, bolts, leather washers, door hooks and nails.
16-J-29 — Instructions included....... **5.49**

(J) CALF WEANER — Swings out of way when animal is eating or drinking. Rustproof, cadmium-plated steel. Malleable iron nose piece.
16-A-34.............................. **49c**

(K) YEARLING WEANER — Same as above except slightly smaller.
16-A-35.............................. **45c**

(L) COW HOBBLE — Copper-finished chain, with clamp on each end. Easy to adjust.
16-A-33.............................. **35c**

(M) GLASS ROOF WINDOW — Gives livestock and poultry much needed sunlight for better health and growth. Heavy, rust-resisting galvanized steel frame. One light. 20 by 28 in.
16-G-11 — Instructions included....... **2.69**

(N) REVOLVING HEAD ROOF VENTILATOR — Ideal for hog houses and poultry houses. Weather-resistant, aluminum painted, galvanized steel. Vent is 15 by 12 in. with grille to keep out birds. Base is 16 by 16 in., has 12-in. flue.
16-G-5 — With instructions........... **9.45**

Firestone 48 H

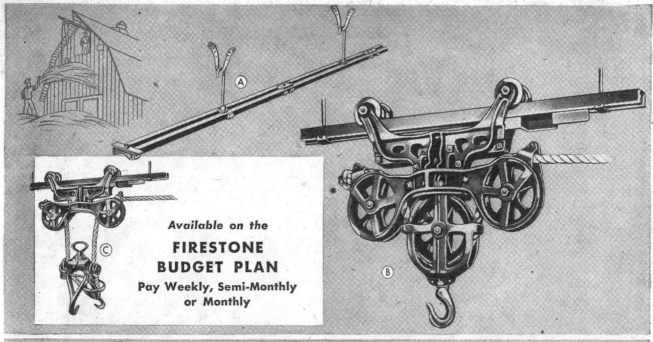

Available on the

**FIRESTONE
BUDGET PLAN**
Pay Weekly, Semi-Monthly
or Monthly

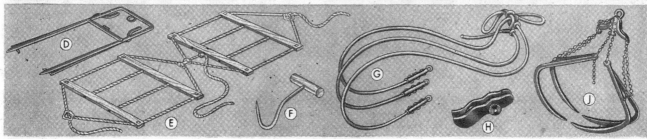

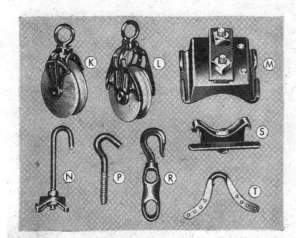

(A) **STEEL TRACK** — Smooth, positive joints permit easy movement of heaviest loads. 90-degree angle — steel 1 by 1 by 5/32 in.
16-J-10 — 10-ft.......................... **1.29**
16-J-18 — 5-ft............................. **59c**

(B) **HAY CARRIER** — Heavy duty, malleable iron with swivel base that permits reversing without removing from track. Large 7-in. pulleys are mounted on oilite bearings for long-life and easy operation. Fork pulley, 7-in. diameter, accommodates 1 in. rope or smaller. Long wheel base distributes load on track. Trip block furnished with each carrier to fit steel tracks.
16-J-9.................................... **19.95**

(C) **HAY SLING CARRIER** — Big 7-in. sheaves handle up to 1 in. rope. Double swivel and reversible, allowing complete reversal of direction while suspended. Pulley can be engaged from any angle. Constructed of heavy malleable iron, mounted on 17-in. wheelbase. Sturdy 3-in. track wheels, equipped with oilite bearings.
16-J-34.................................. **21.95**
Use Our Easy Budget Terms

(D) **HARPOON FORK** — Loads fast, trips easily. Long-tine, double-harpoon type. 17-in. wide, 25-in. or 31-in. long, as available.
16-J-17.................................... **4.25**

(E) **WAGON SLINGS** — Adaptable for 20-ft. racks but fully adjustable for shorter racks. Center trip permits easy removal of hay. Positive action trip will release when trip rope is pulled regardless of angle.
16-J-35 — 5-ft. wagon sling. 12-ft. 8-in. long. With 1/2-in. manila rope.................................... **7.95**
16-J-36 — 6-ft. wagon sling. 13-ft. 8-in. long. With 1/2-in. manila rope.................................... **9.45**

(F) **HAY HOOK** — Heavy-gauge; tough steel, 3/8 by 8 1/2-in. hook. Hardwood handle.
16-J-22.................................... **39c**

(G) **ROPE SLINGS** — Handle hay this economical way. Fully adjustable in lengths up to 20 ft. Equipped with 1/2-in. manila rope. Eyelets prevent fraying of rope ends. Malleable iron adjustment and pulley adapter.
16-J-37 — Two-Rope Sling. 20-in. long, iron adjustment and pulley adapter.... **2.19**
16-J-38 — Three-Rope Sling. 20-in. long.................... **3.19**

(H) **ROPE SLING HOLDER** — Malleable iron positive grip construction permits use with two- or three-rope slings.
16-J-39.................................... **1.49**

(J) **GRAPPLE FORK** — Simple, rugged, safe and fast. Spreads to full 6 ft. for faster loading. Four 1 1/2 by 1/2 in. high-carbon steel tines. Malleable iron pulley, chain-operated release. Malleable iron trip lock.
16-J-40.................................. **14.95**

(K) **REGULAR PULLEY** — Malleable iron frame, swivel eye, heavy axle. 5 1/2-in. maple wheel.
16-J-15.................................... **1.05**

(L) **WIDE-MOUTH PULLEY** — Flanged malleable iron frame. Large swivel eye permits splices to pass through easily. Heavy axle. 5 1/2-in. maple wheel.
16-J-16.................................... **1.19**

(M) **TRACK COUPLING** — Malleable iron with interlocking lugs.
16-J-19.................................... **37c**

(N) **TRACK HANGING HOOK** — Used with 16-J-13 Rafter Bracket to install steel track.
16-J-11.................................... **25c**

(P) **FLOOR HOOK** — For use when installing regular or wide-mouth pulleys.
16-J-12.................................... **25c**

(R) **SWIVEL ROPE HITCH**
16-J-14.................................... **49c**

(S) **END BUMPER** — Bolts securely to end of track to stop carrier.
16-J-20.................................... **25c**

(T) **RAFTER BRACKET** — Used with 16-J-11 Track Hanging Hook to install steel track.
16-J-13...................................... **9c**

Firestone 48 J

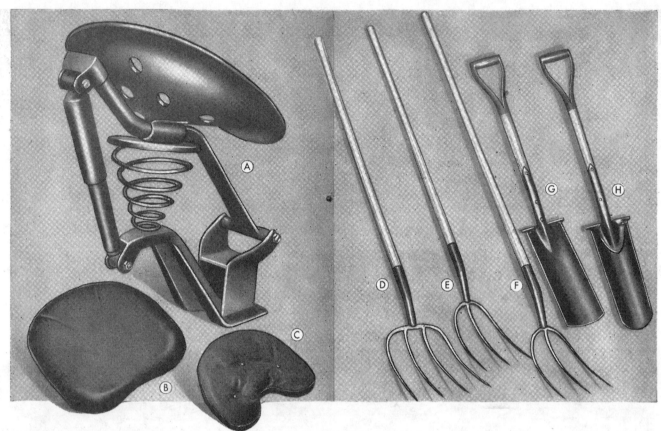

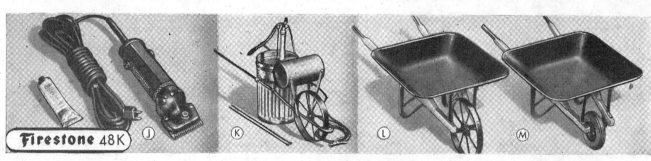

(A) **MONROE E-Z-RIDE HYDRAULIC TRACTOR SEAT** — Added comfort for the tractor rider. It cushions the jolts and bumps, makes your day easier. This tractor seat consists of a comfortably formed steel saddle mounted on one end of a lever bar supported by a special variable rate spring. Operating in conjunction with this is a Monroe Double-Action Hydraulic Shock Absorber to absorb jolts, jars and shock. The other end of the lever arm is attached through a pivot bearing to the stabilizer, minimizing side thrust and sway. Fits all popular makes of tractors from 1938. **29.95**

EASY BUDGET TERMS AVAILABLE

(B) **DE LUXE SEAT CUSHION** — Fits Monroe tractor seat and over 60% of all tractors. Waterproof fabric.
16-Z-20............................ **1.98**

(C) **STANDARD SEAT CUSHION** — Canvas duck covering waterproofed. Cloth lined.
16-Z-18............................ **1.39**

(D) **SUPREME QUALITY 4-TINE MANURE FORK** — Finest quality hot-rolled steel with polished tempered tines. Tested for strength and uniformity.
16-H-20 — 4-ft. handle............... **1.98**
16-H-26 — 4½-ft. handle............. **2.09**

(E) **SUPREME QUALITY 3-TINE HAY FORK** — Fine quality, hot-rolled steel with 12-inch oval polished, tempered tines.
(E) 16-H-25 — 4-ft. handle............ **1.79**
(F) 16-H-19 — 4½-ft. handle.......... **1.98**

(G) **DE LUXE QUALITY DITCHING SPADE** — Heat-treated steel blade 6¼ by 15¾ in. with two foot rests securely riveted to blade. Northern ash "D" handle, 27 in. long.
16-H-12............................ **2.49**

(H) **DE LUXE QUALITY DRAIN SPADE** — Heat-treated blade 4¾ by 15½ in. — rounded cutting edge. Northern ash "D" handle.
16-H-13 — Handle 27 in. long........ **2.49**

(J) **HEAVY-DUTY ELECTRIC ANIMAL CLIPPER** — Ideal for dairy farmers in removing excess hair from dairy herd udders for clean milk production. Designed for easy clipping. Simple to operate. Operates on 110-120 volt AC-DC, all cycles. Specially hardened cutting blades—highly polished. Plastic case.
16-Z-31............................ **29.45**
AVAILABLE ON EASY BUDGET TERMS

(K) **12-GAL. WHEELBARROW SPRAYER** — Heavy sheet steel tank, galvanized after forming. 16-in. by 2-in. steel wheel. Pressure tank 6⅜ in. by 12 in. Fitted with 300-lb. pressure gauge, 6 ft. of ⅜-in. spray hose, automatic shut-off with trigger "quick spray" lock and 2-ft. brass extension rod with nozzle.
16-Z-28 — 12 gal................... **27.95**
16-Z-29 — 18 gal................... **45.95**

(L) **GENERAL PURPOSE WHEELBARROW** — Easy to handle — strong, long-wearing. Heavy steel legs, riveted braces — smooth, comfortable grip wood handles. One-piece 16-gauge pressed steel tray, rolled edges. Capacity 3 cu. ft. Eight-spoke steel wheel, cold-rolled steel axle, 16-in. diameter.
16-H-6............................. **9.95**

(M) **PNEUMATIC-TIRED STEEL WHEELBARROW** —Same as 16-H-6 except with ball-bearing disc wheel with 10 by 2.75-in. pneumatic rubber tire for easy rolling.
16-H-30............................ **14.95**

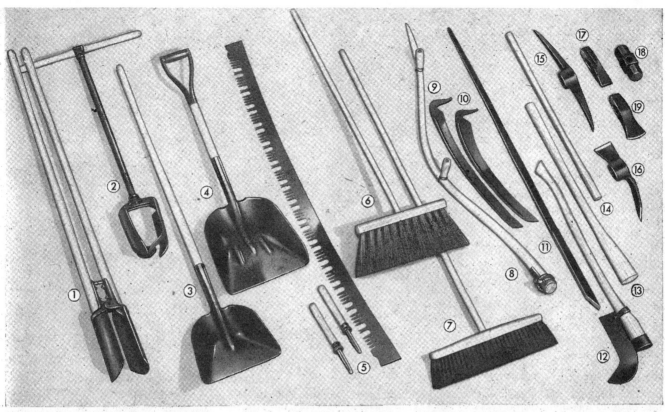

(1) **POSTHOLE DIGGER** — Hinged type. Malleable iron shanks, carbon steel blades. 10-in. length, 6-in. diameter.
16-H-28 — 48-in. handle.................... **2.98**

(2) **8-INCH POSTHOLE AUGER** — Sharp crucible steel blades interlock and twist into earth like a drill. Iron pipe handle. 47″ length.
16-H-29............................... **3.09**

(3) **UTILITY SCOOP** — Long handled barn and utility scoop. Stamped steel blade 11¾″ x 14¾″. 50″ straight ash handle.
16-H-10............................... **1.89**

(4) **"D" HANDLED GRAIN SCOOP** — Popular No. 10 size. Well balanced, light and durable. "D" handle attached by 6½″ ferrule and rivets.
16-H-11............................... **2.39**

(5) **DE LUXE NARROW CROSSCUT SAW** — 5½-ft. High-carbon oil-tempered steel blade. Smooth in action.
7-A-4 — Handles extra.................. **4.19**

CROSSCUT SAW LOOP HANDLES — Select hardwood.
7-A-5 — Pair.......................... **98c**

(6) **PUSH BROOM** — 14″ hardwood head — fiber bristles. 5-ft. handle.
16-H-15............................... **1.59**

(7) **PUSH BROOM** — 16″ extra durable broom. 60″ sturdy handle.
16-H-14............................... **1.85**

(8) **SNATH** — White ash, properly balanced snath. Malleable iron fittings. Fits grass or weed scythe blades.
16-H-3............................... **2.79**

(9, 10) **SCYTHE BLADES** — Special high-carbon steel to hold keen edge. Polished cutting edge.
16-H-4 — 28″ Grass Blade.............. **2.19**
16-H-5 — 26″ Weed Blade.............. **2.19**

(11) **60″ PINCH-POINT CROWBAR** — Hand-forged, high-carbon steel.
7-A-12 — Black finish.................. **3.39**

(12) **BUSH HOOK** — Curved, forged-steel blade, 2¾″ x 11″. Bolted with steel strips to 36″ handle.
16-H-24............................... **2.59**

(13) **PICK AND MATTOCK HANDLE** — 36″ white straight-grained hickory.
7-A-28 — Wax finished................. **75c**

(14) **SLEDGE HAMMER HANDLE** — 36″ white straight-grained hickory.
7-A-142 — Wax finished................ **49c**

(15) **DE LUXE 6-LB. CLAY PICK**
7-A-7................................ **1.55**

(16) **DE LUXE 5-LB. CUTTER MATTOCK**
7-A-8................................ **1.59**

(17) **DE LUXE 4-LB. SQUARE HEAD WEDGE**
7-A-9................................ **79c**

(18) **DE LUXE 8-LB. DOUBLE-FACED BLACK-SMITH SLEDGE**
7-A-11............................... **1.98**

(19) **DE LUXE 6-LB. OVAL EYE WOOD CHOPPER'S MAUL**
7-A-10............................... **1.98**

(20) **TRUCK AND TRACTOR FUNNEL** — Heavy gauge, galvanized steel, fine copper strainer.
16-Z-30.............................. **1.13**

(21) **HAND SPRAYER** — Delivers fine spray with easy operating long-life pump.
16-Z-27 — Capacity 2½ qts............. **3.19**

(22) **NEATSFOOT OIL** — Softens, renews and preserves leather.
16-K-40 — 1 pt... **69c**   16-K-41 — 1 qt... **1.09**

(23) **FLOODLIGHT** — Swivel base, die-formed highly polished aluminum reflector. Weather-tight seal and heat-resisting glass lens. 4-in. steel base with mounting holes. Uses 100-watt bulb.
16-G-6 — Six-ft. cord.................. **3.49**

(24) **BENCH SICKLE GRINDER** — Power operated, with two grinding wheels. Sickle holder included. Cone is 5½ by 3½ in., with ⅝ in. bore. For electric motor or gas engine.
16-H-9 — Motor not included........... **10.95**

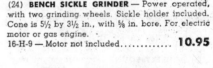

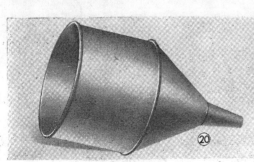

Firestone 48 L

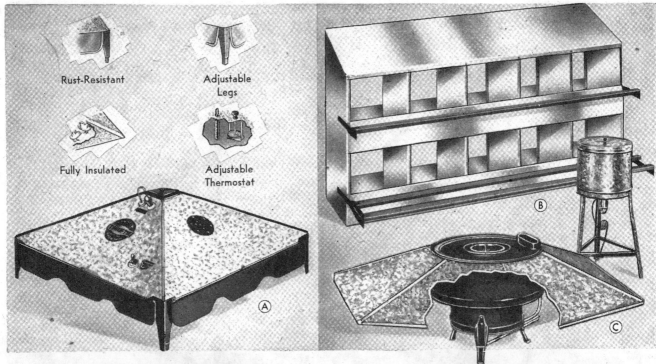

Rust-Resistant

Adjustable Legs

Fully Insulated

Adjustable Thermostat

(A) PREMIER ELECTRIC BROODER

Starts up to 400 chicks — efficient, trouble-free. Big electric heating element assures plenty of warmth when needed. Built for long-life operation. Adjustable thermostat maintains uniform temperature, turning current off and on as needed. Accurate thermometer. Legs are adjustable, permitting raising of canopy edge 7 to 12 in. off floor, to accommodate growing chicks. Galvanized, rust-resistant steel canopy. Securely bolted. Ventilators in top of canopy. Heavy denim drop curtains. Masonite insulation throughout.

16-B-31 — 200 chick size. 36 by 36 in............ **17.45**
16-B-34 — 400 chick size. 48 by 48 in............ **22.95**

(C) KEROSENE CHICK BROODER

400 chick capacity. Efficient drum-type brooder maintains uniform heat. Galvanized steel canopy easily removed for cleaning. Burns either kerosene or 34-40 distillate oil. Thermostatically controlled die-cast valve regulates flow of fuel, heavy cast-iron burner has draft equalizer. Six-gallon fuel tank is equipped with glass sediment cup, flexible copper tubing, metal stand.

16-B-33 — 400 chick capacity.................. **17.45**

> Buy the Farm Supplies You Need Now on the Convenient Firestone Budget Plan. Pay Weekly, Semi-Monthly or Monthly.

(B) ALUMINUM 10-HOLE HEN NEST — Can't rust. Cuts down cleaning time — easy to handle. Two decks—accommodates a flock of 50 hens. Removable nest trays. Wood perches are mounted on hinged steel supports. Sloping roof discourages roosting. Nests each 10½ by 13 in.
16-B-61_____ **12.95**

(D) POULTRY FOUNT — Rust-resistant steel, hot-dipped galvanized after forming, top-fill water fountain. Water released by brass spring shut-off valve; vacuum action controls water flow.
16-B-15 — 5-gal._____ **3.39**
16-B-14 — 3-gal._____ **2.49**

(E) STEEL FOUNTAIN—Five-gallon capacity, top-fill water fountain. Heavy-gauge gal-

vanized steel double walls hold the heat when used with Heater No. 16-B-12. Heavy strap steel carrying handle. Brass spring valve governs water level. Water for 100 full grown chickens for 24 hours.
16-B-11_____ **3.19**

(F) OIL HEATER FOR 16-B-11 FOUNT — With fuel tank that covers entire base. Holds three-week fuel supply. Brass kerosene burner.
16-B-12_____ **2.39**

(G) CHICKEN FOUNTAIN — Heavy gauge, galvanized steel walls and pan. Double walls. Top-fill type makes filling easy. Rolled edges. Vacuum action keeps pan at constant level.
16-B-7 — 3-gal. capacity_____ **1.89**

(H) GALLON GLASS JAR POULTRY FOUNTAIN — Sanitary. Easy to fill or clean. Galvanized steel drinking pan. Water remains at correct level.
16-B-10_____ **65c**

(J) CHICK FOUNT — For baby chicks. Hot-dipped after forming, galvanized. Top handle.
16-B-9 — 5-qt. capacity_____ **79c**

(K) GLASS FOUNT BASE — Heavy, clear glass base accommodates pint, quart or two-quart mason jars. Vacuum action prevents overflowing. Ideal when addition of chemicals to water is desired.
16-B-8_____ **10c**

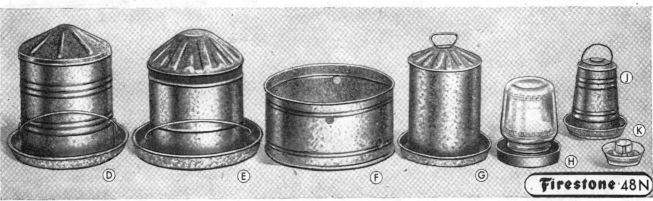

Firestone 48N

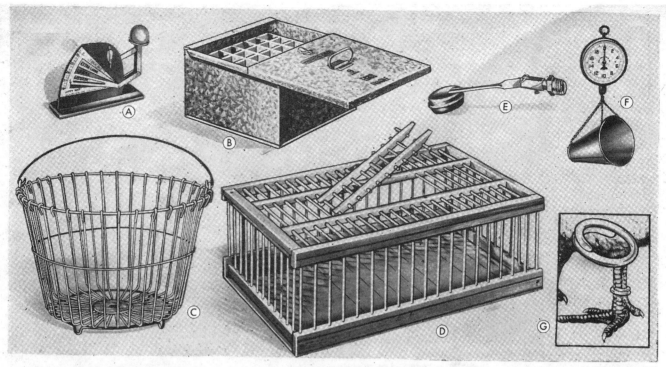

(A) JIFFY-WAY EGG GRADING SCALE — Dependable, accurate. Four-color dial, shows individual weight, weight per dozen and grade.
16-B-23 _____ **1.35**

(B) METAL EGG CASES — Sturdy, compact case of heavy galvanized steel. Slide-top cover locks securely. Strong carrying handle, address slot. Standard fillers and flats.
16-B-26 — 6-doz. size _____ **3.49**
16-B-27 — 12-doz. size _____ **3.98**

(C) EGG-CARRYING BASKET — Strongly built of heavy-gauge wire, spot-welded for durability. Extra-heavy wire handle.
16-B-40 — Holds 15 doz. eggs _____ **98c**

(D) COLLAPSIBLE POULTRY COOP — Thoroughly seasoned poplar frame, hardwood dowels, 3/8-in. floor boards. Easy to clean. Ends can be opened when stacked.
16-B-39 — Size 38 by 24 by 12 in. ____ **2.98**

(E) AUTOMATIC FLOAT VALVE — Construct your own automatic poultry founts. Long-wearing, rust-resistant. Made of brass throughout. Can be used with any watering device. Connects easily to 1/2-in. elbow or nipple with standard threads.
16-E-1 _____ **1.00**

(F) POULTRY SCALE — Weighs all poultry up to 20 lbs. Large steel funnel designed to weigh live fowl. Scale has 8-in. dial — graduated readings in ounces and pounds. Meets all state legal requirements.
16-B-57 _____ **4.95**

(G) LEG BANDS — Spiral celluloid bands. Assorted colors. Pkg. of 50.
16-B-17 — 1/4-in. _____ **11c**
16-B-18 — 9/16-in. _____ **15c**
16-B-19 — 11/16-in. _____ **19c**

(H) BROODER THERMOSTAT WAFER — Universal-type. Extra sensitive to temperature changes.
16-B-35 — Each _____ **35c**

(J) BROODER THERMOMETER — Accurate, reliable. Shows brooding temperatures for chicks of various ages on one side, other side calibrated 0 degrees to 120 degrees F. Guard protects bulb.
16-B-37 _____ **40c**

(K) RED ATTRACTION LIGHT BULBS — 7 1/2 watt, 1500 hr. life. Red color distorts chicks' vision — prevents cannibalism.
16-B-36 — Each _____ **20c**

(L) ELECTRIC EGG CANDLER — Serviceable all-metal. Multiple reflections in light chamber increase candling efficiency. Egg cups leather-padded for fast operation. Uses 110-120 volt AC. 25-60 watt bulb.
16-B-24 _____ **1.49**

(M) LIGHT CONTROL — Increases egg production. Automatic on-off operation. Hand-tripping switch does not alter automatic sequence setup. Designed for 115 volt, 60-cycle AC, rated at 30 amps., 3000 watts. Clock powered by synchronous motor. 16-gauge steel case. Underwriters' listed.
16-B-22 — Complete _____ **10.95**

(N) R-V-LITE — Flexible, plastic-coated, tough and transparent. Made with 1/4-in. waterproof green cord mesh.
16-G-2 — 36 in. wide. Per yard _____ **64c**

(P) FLEX-O-GLASS — Heavy, strong, 124-thread muslin, treated with heat-resisting wax. Not transparent but admits all beneficial light.
16-G-3 — 36 in. wide. Per yard _____ **35c**

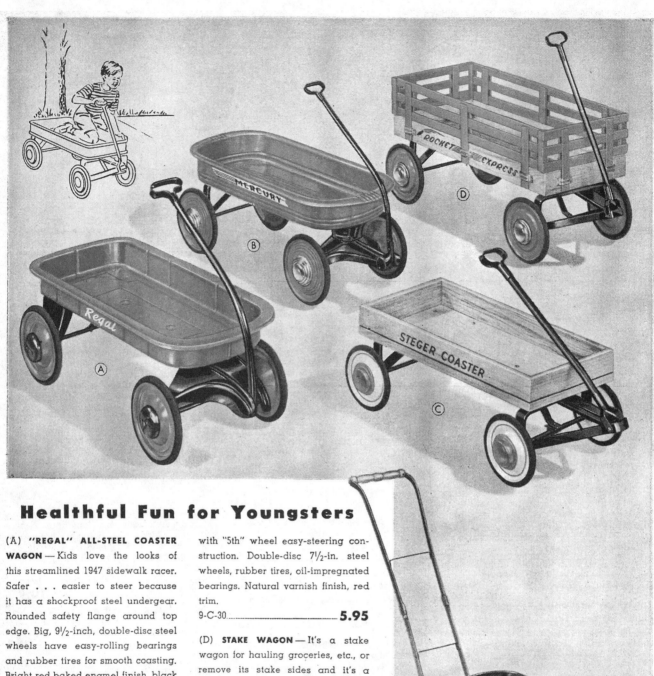

Healthful Fun for Youngsters

(A) "REGAL" ALL-STEEL COASTER WAGON — Kids love the looks of this streamlined 1947 sidewalk racer. Safer . . . easier to steer because it has a shockproof steel undergear. Rounded safety flange around top edge. Big, 9½-inch, double-disc steel wheels have easy-rolling bearings and rubber tires for smooth coasting. Bright red baked enamel finish, black undergear.

9-C-99 .... **12.95**

(B) "MERCURY" ALL-STEEL COASTER WAGON — Streamlined, speedy . . . and what a value! Built for miles of hard service, too. A full size, all-steel wagon with 10-in. double-disc steel wheels, free rolling ball bearings and solid rubber tires. Rounded safety flange. Flashy red baked enamel finish, black and white trim.

9-C-46 .... **8.95**

(C) JUNIOR COASTER WAGON — Right size for Junior! Smaller and lighter . . . strong laminated hardwood body with "5th" wheel easy-steering construction. Double-disc 7½-in. steel wheels, rubber tires, oil-impregnated bearings. Natural varnish finish, red trim.

9-C-30 .... **5.95**

(D) STAKE WAGON — It's a stake wagon for hauling groceries, etc., or remove its stake sides and it's a speedy coaster wagon. Strong, laminated hardwood body, steel undercarriage. Double-disc, 9¼-in. steel wheels have rubber tires, easy-rolling bearings. Weather-resistant varnish finish, red trim.

9-C-31 .... **14.95**

(E) BABY WALKER AND STROLLER — Use it as a "Stroller" or remove the footboard and push-handle and let baby "walk" it. Comfortable wooden seat, metal back. Ball-bearing wheels, rubber tires. Rubber bumper on front and back. Safety handle. Play tray for toys.

9-Z-3 .... **9.95**

Firestone 49

Only **2⁰⁰** A Week

Only **2⁰⁰** A Week

A Shiny New Firestone Bicycle

24-INCH JUNIOR SIZE BICYCLE

The ideal bicycle for youngsters 8 to 10 years old — 24-inch size gives them greater control, adds safety to riding. Strong tubular steel frame — double bar construction for long, rough service. New balloon-type fenders, modern styled chain guard. Well padded, coil spring seat, convenient kickstand. Ball-bearing, rubber treaded pedals. Balloon tires. Attractively finished in beautiful baked enamel. Handle bars, sprockets, crank and hubs all chrome-plated.

9-A-11 — Boy's Junior **38.75**
9-A-12 — Girl's Junior **38.75**

FIRESTONE PILOT BICYCLE

Sturdy, full adult size bicycle with strong tubular steel frame with double-bar construction. Streamlined with balloon type fenders, electric torpedo headlight, smart chain guard. Convenient kickstand, for easy parking — well padded, coil spring saddle for comfortable riding. Ball-bearing, rubber treaded pedals, rubber handle bar grips. Famous Firestone High Speed Balloon tires, size 26 x 2.125. Baked enamel finish in attractive color combinations. Handle bars, sprockets and crank chrome-plated.

9-A-3 — Men's **39.95**
9-A-4 — Women's **39.95**

(A) LUGGAGE CARRIER — Heavy chrome-plated carrier. Fits all 18-inch and 19-inch frames.
9-B-67 . . . . **1.79**

(B) DE LUXE CHAIN GUARD — Highly polished aluminum with safety reflector. Fits all standard bicycles.
9-B-72 . . . . **45c**

(C) SUPREME CHAIN GUARD — High quality chrome-plated steel. Attractive red reflector for safety.
9-B-71 . . . . **1.29**

(D) BICYCLE BASKET — Sturdy, heavy-gauge wire. Plated finish. Size 18 by 13 by 6 inches.
9-B-70 . . . . **1.39**

(E) "FLYING CARRIER" BICYCLE BASKET — Combines unusual strength with sleek streamlined appearance. Easy to attach. Weatherproof, finished in cadmium plating. Large capacity — 13½ by 18 by 4½ inches.
9-B-97 . . . . **2.98**

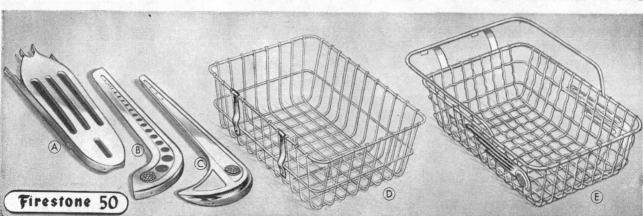

Firestone 50

313

Only **2²⁵** A Week

Only **2⁵⁰** A Week

To Suit Any Member Of Your Family

FIRESTONE PILOT BICYCLES — Same high quality construction as 9-A-7 and 9-A-8 at right. Big streamlined tank, sturdy luggage carrier, and smart, new truss rods. Electric torpedo headlight, attractive chain guard, sturdy kick-stand and safety reflector. Bright chrome handlebars, sprocket, crank and hub. Furnished in new, attractive color combinations.

9-A-13 — Men's **44.95**
9-A-14 — Women's **44.95**

(A) **"ROADLIGHTER" HEADLIGHT** — Throws a powerful beam. Operates on 2 flashlight batteries. Metal case. Baked enamel finish.
9-B-22 .... **1.49**

(B) **SUPREME HEADLIGHT** — Powerful light. Streamlined metal case, white baked enamel finish. A companion for 9-B-75 horn.
9-B-73 .... **1.79**

(C) **"WINNER" HEADLIGHT** — Uses 2 flashlight batteries. Metal case, built-in switch. Enamel finish.
9-B-21 .... **98c**

FIRESTONE CRUISER BICYCLE — If you want the latest in bicycle design, de luxe equipment, and trouble-free, effortless riding — be sure to see these bicycles. Full adult size with a streamlined tank and "built-in" electric horn with push-button control. Modern balloon fenders, distinctive chain guard. There's a de luxe type headlight and taillight or de luxe reflector, and a sturdy luggage carrier, convenient kick-type parking stand. Strong tubular steel frame, double bar construction. Comfortable coil spring saddle mounted on adjustable seat post. Firestone High Speed Balloon Tires and Tubes, size 26 x 2.125. Bright chrome trim. Beautiful contrasting baked enamel color combinations.

9-A-7 — Men's **49.50**
9-A-8 — Women's **49.50**

(D) **DE LUXE HEADLIGHT** — Torpedo shaped. White baked enamel finish.
9-B-80 .... **1.09**

(E) **STANDARD HEADLIGHT** — Torpedo styling.
9-B-74 — Baked enamel finish **89c**

(F) **SUPREME TAILLIGHT** — Streamlined white baked enamel finish.
9-B-82 .... **79c**

(G) **DIRECTIONAL SIGNAL** — Mounts on rear fender. Red arrow flashes direction of turn, at flick of handy switch. Easy to install. Aluminum finish case.
9-B-100 — Size 5 in. by 4 in. by 2¾ in. **2.59**

(H) **SUPREME HORN** — Loud clear tone. Streamlined design. Self-contained. A companion model to 9-B-73.
9-B-75 .... **1.98**

(J) **HAND HORN**
9-B-81 .... **1.69**

(K) **"CADET" SPEEDOMETER** — Sturdy, shockproof. Non-breakable lens. Sweep-action mileage pointer. Registers up to 50 m.p.h. Trip mileage registers in tenths. Complete with shaft and fittings.
9-B-90 .... **4.50**

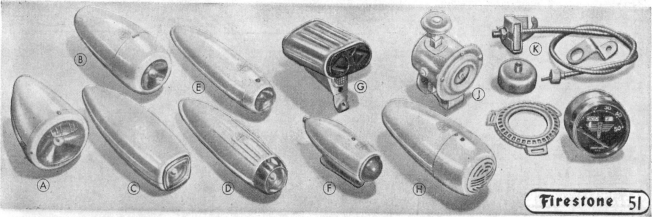

Firestone 51

1956 Missoula Mercantile Company Catalog

BLACKSMITHS' TONGS
STRAIGHT LIP

Solid Steel

Black japan finish.
For holding thin flat work. Heavy stock in jaws permits their being shaped by blacksmith to suit his individual needs.

Each
No. 10—18 in. long; wt. each 2¾ lbs. . **$3.60**
Open stock.

CURVED LIP

Solid Steel, Fluted Jaw

Black japan finish.
Used for holding bolts or other round work. The opening between the jaws and the hinge allows ample space for the head of a bolt.

Each
No. 12D—For ½ in. rounds, 20 in. long over all; wt. each 2⅝ lbs. **$4.15**
Open stock.

HORSESHOE

Solid Steel

Black japan finish.
Used for holding horseshoes. Recessed inside of face, giving them good holding power.

Each
No. 17—16 in. long; wt. per dozen 15½ lbs. **$3.15**
Open stock.

FARRIERS' TONGS
HELLER CLINCHER

Solid Steel

Useful on colts and nervous horses in clinching nails.

Each
No. 28—12 in. long; wt. each 1⅓ lbs. . . **$7.15**
Six in a box.

FARRIERS' PINCERS
HELLER J. I. C.

Standard Pattern

Forged from best quality refined tool steel, hardened and tempered, black finish, polished jaws.

Nos.	20	21
Length, in.	14 J.I.C.	12
No. in box	3	6
Wt. each, lbs.	3⅙	2¼
Each	$4.75	4.65

FARRIERS' NIPPERS
HELLER

Standard Pattern

Forged tool steel. Natural finish, polished head and handles, beveled jaws. Riveted joint.

Nos.	24	24A
Length, in.	14	12
Wt. each, lbs.	2¹³⁄₁₆	2¼
Each	$7.00	6.50

Light Pattern

Each
No. 25—15 in. long; wt. each 2⁹⁄₁₆ lbs. . . **$3.75**
Six in a box.

HOOF PARERS
HELLER

Standard Pattern

Forged steel, polished head, black finished handles.

Nos.	23	23A
Length, in.	14	12
Wt. each, lbs.	2¼	2⅛
Each	$5.75	5.50

Six in a box.

FARRIERS' PRITCHELS OR PUNCHES
HELLER

Octagon Tool Steel

For making or enlarging the nail holes in a horseshoe. Used also for handling the shoe.

Each
No. 30—12 in. long, ⅝ in. stock; wt. each 1 lb. **$1.20**
Twelve in a box.

FARRIERS' BUFFERS
HELLER

Forged Steel, Natural Finish

For cleaning nail holes in shoes and trimming hoofs.

Each
No. 39—6 in. size; wt. each 1⁷⁄₁₆ lb. **$1.85**
Twelve in a box.

FARRIERS' KNIVES
HELLER

Wood Handle

Hardened and tempered steel blade set in hand-fitting round wood handle.

Each
No. 50—⅝ in. blade; wt. per box 2½ lbs. **$1.95**
Twelve in a box.

FARRIERS' HAMMERS
HELLER

Rounding or Turning

Forged steel, black finish; polished face. Smooth hickory handle.

Each
No. 61B—2½ lb. size; wt. each 3⅛ lbs. **$4.50**
Four in a box.

Fitting

Forged steel, black finish; polished face. Smooth hickory handle.

Each
No. 62B—2½ lb. size; wt. each 3 lbs. . . **$4.60**
Four in a box.

Driving

Forged steel, black finish; polished face. Smooth hickory handle.

Each
No. 64B—14 oz. size; wt. each ⅚ lb. . . **$2.80**
Six in a box.

Heller Pattern Driving

Forged steel, black finish; polished face. Smooth hickory handle.

Each
No. 65B—16 oz. size; wt. each 1½ lbs. **$3.00**
Six in a box.

TIRE VALVES
DILLECTRIC

Rubber Covered

Standard valve for passenger car tubes.
Electric heating element furnished with each box.
Short valve, 1½ in. long x 2¼ in. base; for use on 4.00-12-15, 4.25-12, 4.50-12, 5.00-15-16, 5.50-15-16, 6.00-15-16, 6.50-15-16, 7.00-15-16, 7.50-15-16 tubes.

Each
No. 1415-10—(TR-15); wt. per box 1 lb. $0.60
Ten in a box.

Medium valves, 2⅞ in. long x 2¼ in. base, used where a slightly longer stem is required.

Each
No. 1425-10—(TR-25); wt. per box 1 lb. $0.60
Ten in a box.

RUBBER VALVE HEAT UNITS
CAMEL

For installing and vulcanizing rubber base tire tube valves.
Pre-roughed fuel board lights and burns easily in any weather.

Each
No. RX—Passenger car size; wt. per can 1½ lbs. $0.15
Twelve in a can, sixteen cans in a case.

Each
No. TR—Truck size, 3¾ in. diam.; wt. per case 18 lbs. $0.35
Fifty in a case.

TUBE VULCANIZING PATCHES
CAMEL

Made of 3-ply laminated natural rubber with Redi-light fuel board and Holla-tab protective backing. Easy to light. Each patch wrapped in moisture-proof paper.

Ideal for repairs on tubeless tires.

Large Round Patches
For use by service stations, garages, fleet owners, etc. Packed in moisture-proof sealed cans.

Per can
No. 12-X—2⅜ in. diam.; wt. per can 2½ lbs. $3.35
Twenty in a can, sixteen cans in a case.

Small Oblong Patches
Convenient size for motorist travel emergency use. Buffer top can.

Per can
No. 30—1x1⅞ in.; wt. per can 3 oz. $0.75
Three in a can, one-hundred cans in a case.

Diamond Shape Patches
In regular or king size.

Per can
No. 82-U—Regular, 1⅜x1⅞ in.; wt. per can 7 oz. $0.70
Ten in a can, one-hundred cans in a case.

Per can
No. 83-U—Regular, 1⅜x1⅞ in.; wt. per can 1⅞ lbs. $3.35
Fifty in a can, sixteen cans in a case.

Per can
No. 84-U—King size, 2¼x3½ in.; wt. per can 2¾ lbs. $3.35
Twenty in a can, sixteen cans in a case.

TUBE REPAIR KITS
CAMEL DELUXE

With Vulcanizing Patches
Especially designed for use by motorists and where ever a vulcanized repair is required. Deluxe clamp is made to lay on a fender or table without falling over on its side. Can of patches fits in holder which is part of clamp.
Each kit consists of buffer top can, three oblong patches and clamp.

Per kit
No. 7-X—Kit; wt. per kit 1 lb. $1.18
One kit in a carton, twenty-four cartons in a case.

VULCANIZING CLAMPS
CAMEL

Easy operating, quick acting heavy duty clamp for use on all shapes and sizes of vulcanizing patches.

With tube buffer.

Each
No. 79—Wt. each 9 lbs. $12.50
One in a carton.

TUBE REPAIR GUM
CAMEL

100% rubber, first quality, red, quick-cure gum for making vulcanizing repairs.

Per can
No. 26-A—1 lb. roll; wt. per can 1¼ lbs. ..$2.40
Twelve cans in a case.

BUFFER STICKS
CAMEL

Carborundum buffer stick for cleaning tubes before repairing.

Each
No. F-20—Wt. per carton ⅝ lb. $0.15
Ten in a carton.

MISSOULA MERCANTILE COMPANY

CHOPPING BOWLS
WOOD

Turned from hard maple; minor defects. Liquid-Proof finish is impregnated into the wood to seal out moisture and prolong the life of the bowl.

Nos.	PST6	PST9
Diam., in.	6	9
Depth, in.	1½	1⅞
No. in carton	24	24
Wt. carton, lbs.	10	20
Each	$0.75	.85

Nos.	PST11	PST13
Diam., in.	11	13
Depth, in.	2½	3½
No. in carton	24	6
Wt. carton, lbs.	32	14
Each	$1.90	3.30

SALAD BOWL SETS
WOOD

An attractive, hard maple salad set with Liquid-Proof finish.

Contents of Set
1—11 in. Salad bowl
6— 6 in. Salad bowls
1—10 in. Fork and spoon set

Per set
No. LPSM-9—Set, consists of the above items; wt. per set 5 lbs. **$7.95**

Twelve sets in a carton.

WOOD FAUCETS
REDLICH

Cork lined; finest wood, saturated with a protective solution.

Nos.	2	3	4
Length, in.	8½	9	9¾
Bore	⅜	7/16	7/16
For hole, in.	15/16–1⅛	1–1¼	1–1¼
Wt. carton, lbs.	4	5⅛	5¼
Each	$0.65	.85	.95

Twelve in a carton.

FLOUR SIFTERS
FOLEY

Made of aluminum with spring action handle. Single screen sifts as fine as triple screens.

Comes apart for quick and easy cleaning.

Each
No. 106—Cap. 5 cups; wt. each ¾ lb. . $1.69

Six in a carton.

FLOUR SIFTERS
FOLEY

Made of aluminum with spring action handle. Single screen; cone bottom sifts directly into measuring cup.

Each
No. 105—Cap. 1 cup; wt. each ¼ lb. . . $0.89

Twelve in a carton.

ANDROCK

One hand operated, spring action handle; lithographed golden wheat pattern in attractive colors on a solid background. Three screens.

Each
No. GW373—Cap. 4 cups; wt. each 1 lb. $1.25

Six in a carton.

One hand operated, spring action handle; red lithographed tulip pattern on white background and red enameled handle. Two screens.

Each
No. R792—Cap. 5 cups; wt. each 1 lb. . $1.20

Six in a carton.

ANDROCK HAND-I-SIFT JUNIOR

One hand operated, spring-action handle; red lithographed tulip pattern on white background and red enameled handle. One screen.

Each
No. R691—Cap. 3 cups; wt. each ¾ lb. . $0.85

Six in a carton.

FLOUR SIFTERS
PARKERSBURG

High quality tin plate; red enameled, embossed back handle. Three blade agitator; fine quality wire screen. Rolled top and bottom edge; red enameled knob.

Each
No. 50—Cap. 5 cups; wt. each ½ lb. . . **$0.55**

Twelve in a carton.

High quality tin plate; red enameled, flat back handle. Two blade agitator; fine quality wire screen. Rolled top and bottom edge; red enameled knob.

Each
No. 40—Cap. 3 cups; wt. each ⅜ lb. . . **$0.40**

Twenty-four in a carton.

NUT MEAT CHOPPERS
FEDERAL DELUXE

Chops nut meats fine or coarse; fully plated cutters.

Removable plastic cup has graduated measurements on side and opening for pouring.

Clear plastic measuring cup with red top; clear glass container.

Each
No. 572B—Cap. 12 oz.; wt. per carton 8¾ lbs. $0.59

Twelve in a carton.

A combination storage jar, chopper and dispenser.

Chops nut meats fine or coarse; fully plated cutters.

Clear glass container; red top.

Each
No. 572A—Cap. 12 oz.; wt. per carton 8¼ lbs. $0.49

Twelve in a carton.

MISSOULA MERCANTILE COMPANY

NUT MEAT CHOPPERS
FEDERAL

Chops nut meats fine or coarse; fully plated cutters.

Removable plastic cup has graduated measurements on side and opening for pouring.

White plastic measuring cup with red top; white plastic container.

Each

No. 572G—Cap. 5 oz.; wt. per carton 3 lbs. $0.59

Twelve in a carton.

ONION CHOPPERS
FEDERAL DELUXE

Heavy duty clear glass cup with graduated measurements; rust proof, nickel plated steel blades.

Snap-on aluminum cover with reinforced aluminum shaft; red wooden knob handle.

Complete with two chopping blocks.

Each

No. 294B—Cap. 12 oz.; wt. per carton 12 lbs. $0.65

Twelve in a carton

CHERRY STONERS
ENTERPRISE

Eliminates the distasteful task of stoning cherries by hand. All that is necessary is to feed the cherries into the hopper and turn the crank. The stones are ejected into one receptacle and the cherries into another.

Fitted with bracket and thumb screw so that it may be attached to any convenient table or bench.

Tinned finish.

Each

No. 16T—11¾ in. high, 3¾ in. hopper, 10¾ in. long; wt. each 4 lbs. $3.95

Twelve in a carton.

CHERRY SEEDERS
DANDY

Crank operated rotary plunger extracts seeds with least possible disfiguration of fruit; no springs; positive action.

Heavily tinned body and finger guard; wood grip on handle.

Each

No. 50A—9¾ in. high; wt. per carton 28 lbs. $2.90

One in a box, twelve in a carton.

Each

Extra Pads $0.15

Open stock.

CHERRY PITTERS
SPEE DEE

Knocks out the pit of both fresh or canned fruit.

Nickel plated finish.

Each

No. AU-78—8¼ in. long; wt. per carton 1½ lbs. $0.20

Twelve in a box.

CHERRY AND OLIVE PITTERS
KRASCO

A practical kitchen tool for use in the removal of cherry and olive pits.

Nickel plated, heavy gauge steel mechanism thoroughly tested and proven for efficiency and durability.

Assembled complete on standard pint jar. Screw top permits easy cleaning and inverting mechanism inside jar for complete storage.

Each

No. 101—Weight per carton 9½ lbs. . . $0.89

Twelve in a carton.

Each

Cherry Pitter Rubbers $0.05

Open stock.

STRAWBERRY HULLERS
SPEE DEE

Designed for the removal of hulls and soft spots from strawberries.

Nickel plated finish.

Each

No. AT-77—2⅜ in. long; wt. per carton 1 lb. $0.05

Twenty-four in a carton.

SPICE AND GARLIC PRESSES
MRS. DAMAR'S

An all-purpose press for garlic, onions, limes, lemons, herbs, etc.

Brightly polished, cast aluminum.

Each

No. 838—Weight per carton 3 lbs. $1.00

Twelve in a display carton.

POTATO CUTTERS
EKCO MIRACLE

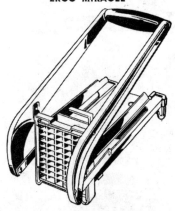

Sturdy, sanitary construction; tinned finish.

Quick and easy, one-hand operation; cutter unit is easily unlocked and lifted out for cleaning.

Cuts twenty-five French fries in one operation.

Each

No. T-5—9¾ in. long, 3¾ in. wide; wt. each 1¾ lbs. $2.98

One in a box, twelve in a carton.

MEAT AND FOOD CHOPPERS

UNIVERSAL TAB-L-TOP, HAND

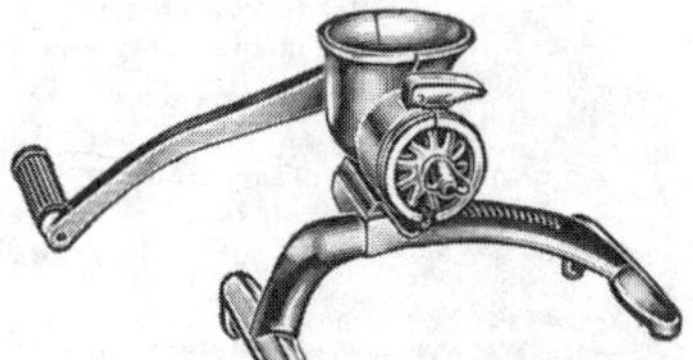

Heavily tinned, cast iron body, feed screw, base and crank handle; base has rubber padded feet to prevent slipping and marring. Hand pressure holds chopper firmly against edge of table or counter.

Precision made cutters stay sharp. Chops raw or cooked food and meat. Barrel swings apart for fast, sanitary cleaning; trough beneath barrel diverts excess juices into container. Extra long handle for leverage.

Complete with fine, medium and coarse cutters.

Each

No. 1590T—Cap. 3 lbs. per minute, hopper 3⅝x2¾ in., barrel 3¾x2¼ in., height above table 3 in.; wt. each 6¾ lbs. $6.95

One in a carton, six in a case.

EXTRA PARTS FOR ABOVE

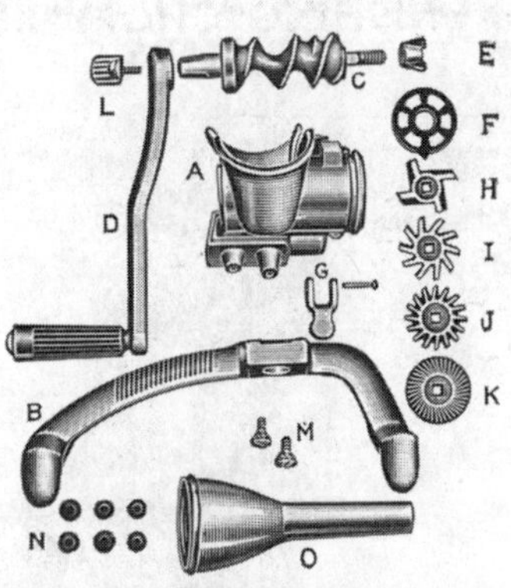

Prices are Each

Letter	
E—Wing nut	$0.15
H—4 tooth cutter	.35
I—10 tooth cutter	.35
J—16 tooth cutter	.35
L—Crank screw	.15

Open stock.

Note—In ordering extra parts, always give component part number and name, also number of chopper for which part is wanted.

MEAT AND FOOD CHOPPERS

UNIVERSAL, HAND

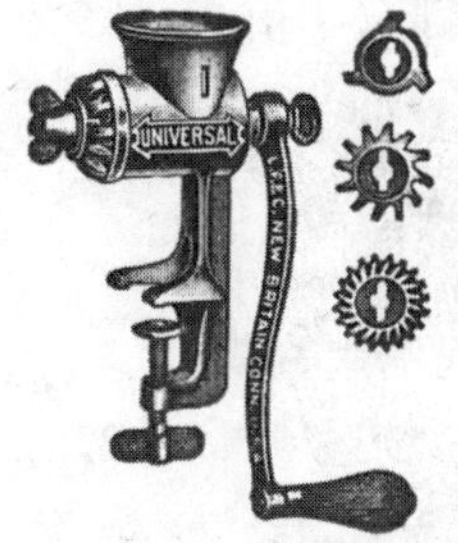

Self-sharpening, self-cleaning, shear-cutting cutters are beveled and concave ground.

Easily taken apart for cleaning and reassembled; smooth, interior, no rough places to catch food.

Cast iron, one-piece frame, accurately machined and beautifully tinned and polished; rustless, sanitary and durable.

Large throat increases capacity and eliminates mashing; long handle gives powerful leverage and saves labor. Liquids will not leak out as long as feed screw is turning forward, not back.

All sizes have three cutters, coarse to fine except No. 3 which has four cutters, very coarse to very fine. Stuffing attachment fits Nos. 2 and 3.

Nos.	1	2
Size	Reg. family	Large family
Cap. min., lbs.	2	2½
Diameter—		
Barrel, in.	1$\frac{15}{16}$	1$\frac{15}{16}$
Hopper, in.	2¾x3½	3¼x3⅞
Ht. above table, in.	2½	2¾
Wt. each, lbs.	4¼	4¾
Each	$4.25	4.50

No.	3
Size	Hotel, Market
Cap. min., lbs.	3
Diam. barrel, in.	2¼
Diam. hopper, in.	4x4¾
Ht. above table, in.	3¼
Wt. each, lbs.	8
Each	$6.00

One in a carton, six in a case.

EXTRA PARTS FOR ABOVE

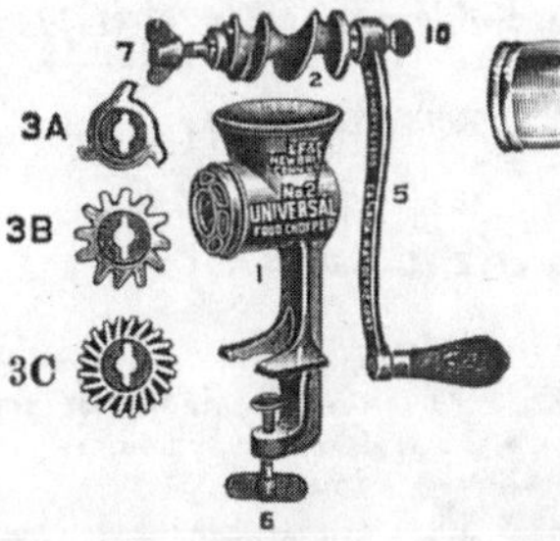

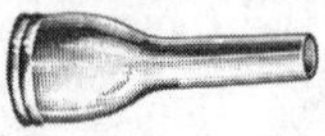

Seamless spun brass stuffing attachment, nickel plated.

Prices are Each

Part Nos.	For Choppers, Nos. 1	2	3
No. 2—Feed screw	$0.75	.75	1.40
No. 3A—Coarse cutter	.40	.40	.50
No. 3B—Med. cutter	.40	.40	.50
No. 3C—Pulverizer	.40	.40	.50
No. 4—Fine cutter	...	...	.45
No. 5—Crank comp.	.65	.65	.80
No. 7—Thumb nut	.15	.15	.15
No. 10—Hdl. screw	.20	.20	.20
No. 11—Stuffing attachment	...	1.30	1.50

Open stock.

MEAT AND FOOD CHOPPERS

UNIVERSAL SWING-A-PART, HAND

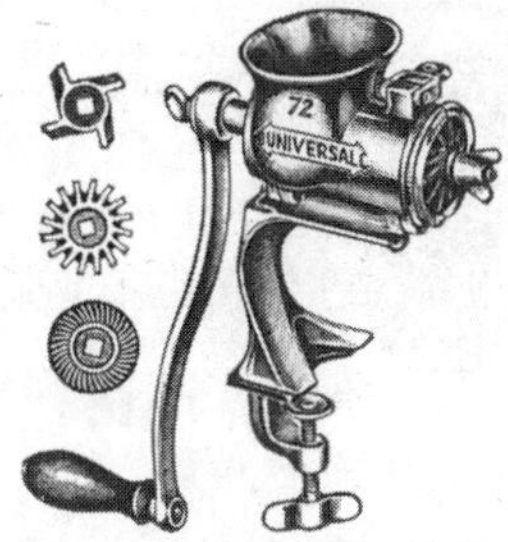

Cast iron, one-piece frame and spiral feed screw; accurately machined and finely tinned inside and out.

Knife blades, working constantly against the steel disc through which the food is forced, are kept honed to a keen edge; barrel swings apart by simply unclamping—exposing two halves that can be washed, cleaned and sterilized quickly and fully by simply plunging into boiling water.

Gutter below barrel carries all juices directly to receiving dish; rubber guard on upper part of clamp prevents marring of table when thumb screw is tightened. Powerful leverage of the long handle and the design of the feed screw forces the food through the cutter quickly and with almost no effort by the operator.

Complete with three cutters, coarse to very fine.

Nos.	71	72
Cap. min., lbs.	2	3
Diameter barrel, in.	3½x2¼	3¾x2¼
Diameter hopper, in.	3x2½	3⅝x2¾
Height above table, in.	2¼	2⅞
Wt. each, lbs.	5	5½
Each	$4.75	5.50

One in a carton, six in a case.

EXTRA PARTS FOR ABOVE

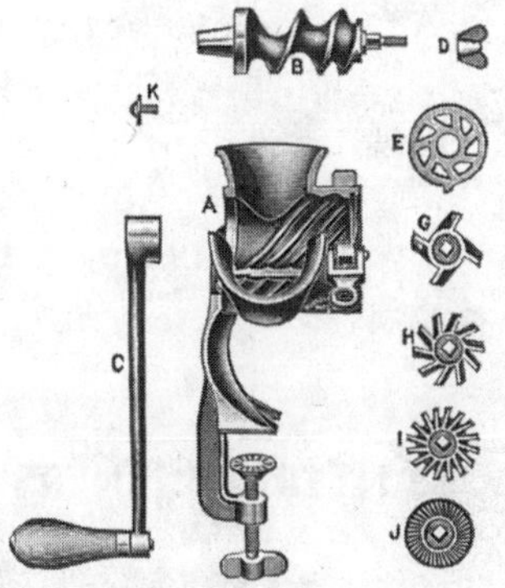

Prices are Each

Letter	For Choppers, Nos. 71	72
D—Wing nut	$0.15	.15
G—4 tooth cutter	.35	.35
H—10 tooth cutter	.35	.35
I—16 tooth cutter	.35	.35
K—Crank screw	.15	.15

Open stock.

MISSOULA MERCANTILE COMPANY 1011

LANTERN GLOBES

FITZALL LOCNOB

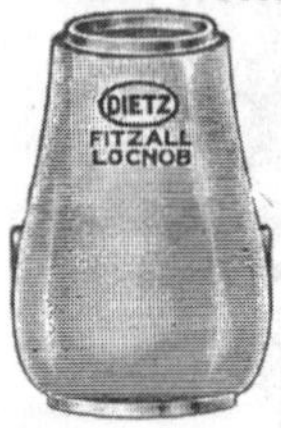

For use on Dietz Monarch, No. 2 Blizzard and Acme lanterns.

Height $6\frac{5}{8}$ inches, diameter top $2\frac{13}{16}$ inches, diameter bottom $3\frac{7}{16}$ inches.

Nos.	**2C-1**	**2C-3**
Color	clear	clear
No. in carton	12	36
Wt. carton, lbs.	9	27
Each	$0.40	.40
Nos.	**2R-1**	**2R-3**
Color	ruby	ruby
No. in carton	12	36
Wt. carton, lbs.	9	27
Each	$1.00	1.00

D-LITE LOCNOB

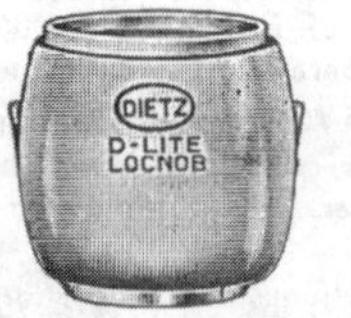

Short pattern, for No. 2-D-Lite cold blast lanterns.

Height $4\frac{5}{8}$ inches, diameter top $4\frac{1}{16}$ inches, diameter bottom $3\frac{7}{16}$ inches.

Nos.	**2DC-1**	**2DC-3**
Color	clear	clear
No. in carton	12	36
Wt. carton, lbs.	9	27
Each	$0.40	.40
Nos.	**2DR-1**	**2DR-3**
Color	ruby	ruby
No. in carton	12	36
Wt. carton, lbs.	9	27
Each	$1.00	1.00

LITTLE WIZARD LOCNOB

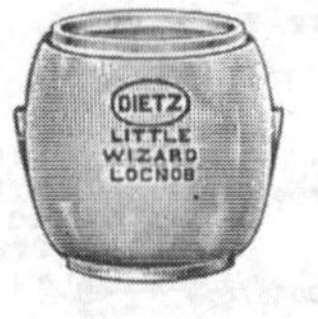

For use on Little Wizard, Little Giant, Roadster and Night Watch lanterns.

Height $3\frac{13}{16}$ inches, diameter top $3\frac{1}{4}$ inches, diameter bottom $2\frac{13}{16}$ inches.

Nos.	**LWC-1**	**LWC-3**
Color	clear	clear
No. in carton	12	36
Wt. carton, lbs.	6	18
Each	$0.35	.35
Nos.	**LWR-1**	**LWR-3**
Color	ruby	ruby
No. in carton	12	36
Wt. carton, lbs.	6	18
Each	$0.75	.75

LANTERN BURNERS

DIETZ

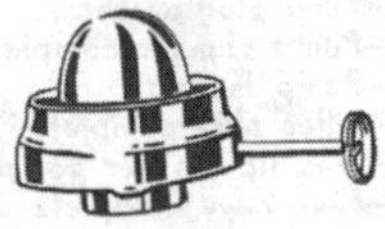

Wing lock type; steel finish.

For Roadster wagon lanterns.

Each

No. 201—For $\frac{5}{8}$ in. wick; wt. per carton 1 lb. $0.35

Twelve in a carton.

LANTERN BURNERS

DIETZ

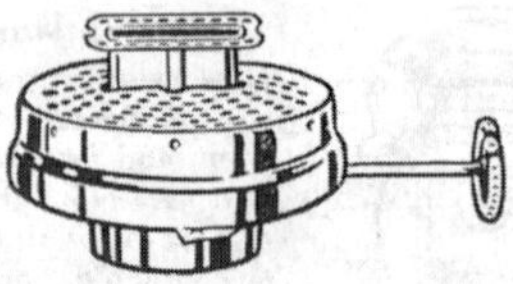

Rising cone type; steel finish.

For D-Lite and Blizzard tubular lanterns.

Each

No. 272—For $\frac{7}{8}$ in. wick; wt. per carton 1 lb. $0.40

Twelve in a carton.

DIETZ LANTERNS

DIETZ BLIZZARD, COLD BLAST

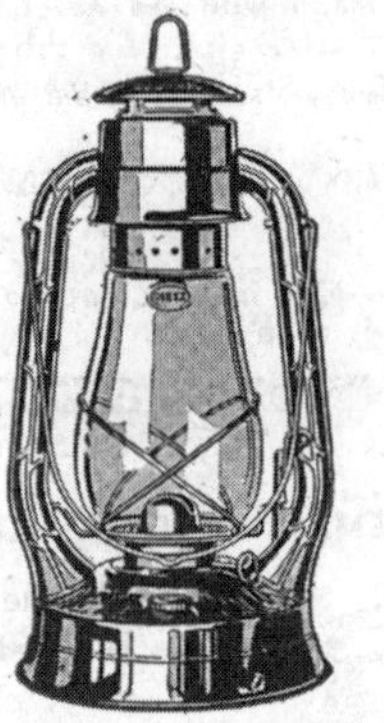

Made of cold rolled, terne coated steel, finished in blue-gray enamel.

Balanced draft of superior construction.

Globe cannot fall out when swung back for inspection; burner is locked on fount so oil cannot spill out if lantern is overturned.

10 candlepower; uses No. 272 rising cone burner; $\frac{7}{8}$ inch wick and Fitzall Loc-Nob globe. Burns 45 hours on one filling.

Each

No. 2-Blizzard—Clear globe, cap. 32 oz., $14\frac{3}{4}$ in. high; wt. per carton 18 lbs. .. $3.75

Six in a carton.

D-LITE, COLD BLAST

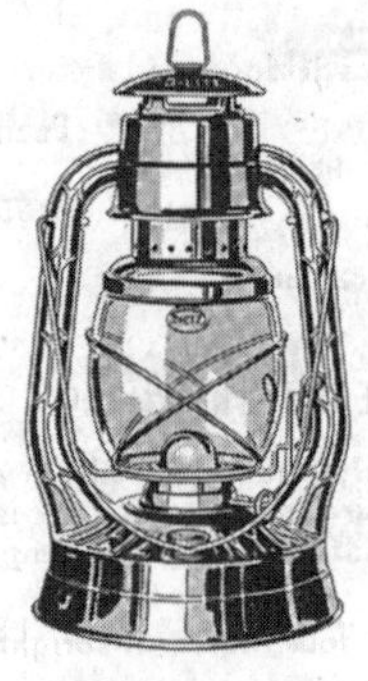

Made of cold rolled, terne coated steel, finished in blue-gray enamel.

Globe cannot fall out when swung back for inspection; burner is locked on fount so oil cannot spill out if lantern is overturned.

10 candlepower; uses No. 272 rising cone burner; $\frac{7}{8}$ inch wick and D-Lite Loc-Nob globe. Burns 45 hours on one filling.

Each

No. 2-D-Lite—Clear globe, cap. 32 oz., $13\frac{1}{4}$ in. high; wt. per carton 18 lbs. $3.75

Six in a carton.

DIETZ LANTERNS

LITTLE GIANT, COLD BLAST

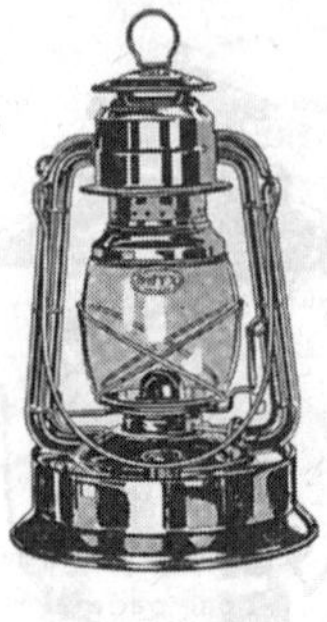

Made of cold rolled, terne coated steel, finished in blue-gray enamel.

Globe cannot fall out when swung back for inspection; burner is locked on fount so oil cannot spill out if lantern is overturned.

6 candlepower; uses No. 211 rising cone burner; $\frac{5}{8}$ inch wick and Little Wizard Loc-Nob globe. Burns 70 hours on one filling.

Each

Little Giant—Clear globe, cap. 32 oz., $11\frac{1}{2}$ in. high; wt. per carton 30 lbs. $3.45

Twelve in a carton.

COMET, COLD BLAST

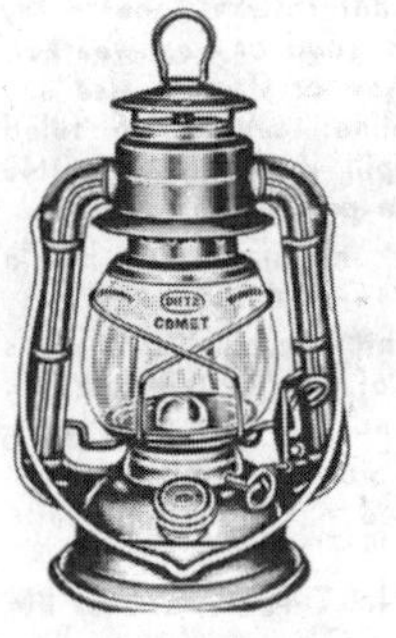

Made of cold rolled, terne coated steel, finished in red enamel.

Globe cannot fall out when swung back for inspection; burner is locked on fount so oil cannot spill out if lantern is overturned.

4 candlepower; uses Comet wing lock burner; $\frac{13}{32}$ inch wick and Comet globe. Burns 15 hours on one filling.

Each

Comet—Clear globe, cap. 5 oz., $8\frac{1}{2}$ in. high; wt. per carton 9 lbs. $2.95

Six in a carton.

LANTERN AND STOVE LIGHTERS

SPARKY

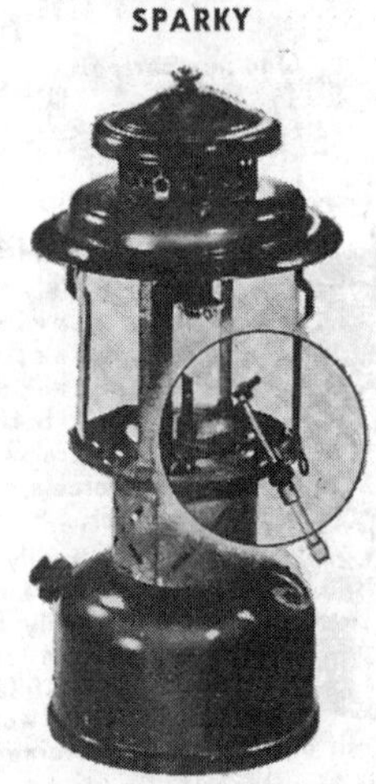

Lights gasoline lamps, lanterns, and stoves with a flick of the thumb in the wind or rain.

Installs permanently, no holes to drill, fool-proof, heat-proof, wind-proof and rain-proof. Quick reliable action lighter.

Each

Sparky—Wt. per carton 3 lbs. $1.40

One in a box, twenty-four in a carton.

MISSOULA MERCANTILE COMPANY

TARGET TRAPS
WESTERN HAND

A simple, inexpensive and easily used device which makes it possible to practice target shooting with the shotgun any time and anywhere and with any gauge gun.

Strong hardwood handle and leather wrist thong, with sturdy coiled spring flexible ferrule, fits readily into a hand bag.

Each
No. V1500A—Wt. each 13 oz. $4.85

One in a carton.

REMINGTON HAND

High or low, fast or slow, throw targets any way you want them with the Remington hand trap. Every type of wing shot, from woodcock to wild fowl, can be offered with this versatile little tosser. Light, springy, no effort to operate. Just the thing for vacation use.

Each
Remington Hand—Wt. each 1⅛ lbs. ..$4.90

One in a carton.

CLAY TARGETS
BLUE ROCK

Scientifically manufactured to rigid specifications, each target is balanced and uniform in weight. They are brittle and are easily broken by the shot pellets without being too fragile for easy handling.

Per carton
Blue Rock—Yellow dome or all black; **specify** when ordering; 135 in a carton; wt. per carton 31 lbs. $5.60

GUN CLEANING KITS
GUNSLICK

Contains all the necessary equipment and material to maintain gun in perfect shooting condition.

Packed in sturdy steel kit with baked enamel finish. Complete with handy removable tray.

Kit Consists of:

1—No. 600 Cleaning rod
1—Tube of Gunslick
1—Bottle of Nitro powder solvent
2—Bronze bristle brushes
1—Bottle of gun oil
1—Pack of cleaning patches

For Shotguns

Per kit
No. 478—Kit, 12 or 16 gauge; wt. per kit 2 lbs. $3.25

For Rifles

Per kit
No. 477—Kit, for .22 or .30 caliber; wt. per kit 1¾ lbs. $3.00

One kit in a box, twelve in a carton.

Note—When ordering specify gauge or caliber.

SHOTGUN CLEANING RODS
GUNSLICK

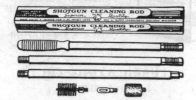

Three Joints and Interchangeable Tips

Made of first quality hard maple, lacquer finished. With slotted tip, wire scratch brush and swab. Superior quality throughout.

36 in. long.

No. 475—Wood Construction

For gauge	10–16	20–28
Each	$0.85	.85

Average weight each ⅜ pound.

Twelve in a carton.

Each
No. 475B—Slotted tip $0.10
No. 475C—Brush .... .10

Open stock.

SHOTGUN CLEANING RODS
GUNSLICK

Three Joints and Adjustable Tip

Made of strongest aluminum alloy. Palm rest handle; sleeve type joints; expanding tip provides positive contact.

Each
No. 625—For 12 to 20 ga.; wt. each ¾ lb. $1.65

Twelve in a carton.

RIFLE CLEANING RODS
GUNSLICK

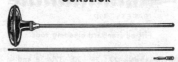

Three Joints and Interchangeable Tips

Precision machined of aluminum alloy. Extra long sleeve type joints for maximum strength. Palm-rest plastic handle with ball bearing for perfect swiveling. Three joints with one each jagged and slotted tips. Threaded to fit all standard cleaning brushes. 36 in. long.

Nos.	600	601	627
Caliber	.22	.30	.270
Each	$1.35	1.35	1.35

Weight each ⅓ pound.

One in a box, twelve in a carton.

MARBLE'S

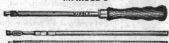

Three Joints and Interchangeable Tips

Brass construction. End of rod fitted with a roller-bearing swivel which will withstand hard pulls and thrusts and prevent unscrewing of joints. Furnished with combination jagged and slotted tip. Threaded to fit all standard size cleaners. 36 in. long.

Nos.	9622	9728
Caliber	.22 to .25	.28 and up
Diam., in.	13⁄44	¼
Each	$1.75	1.75

Weight each ½ pound.

One in a bag.

Each
Extra Tips $0.10
Extra Adapters .... .10

Open stock.

REVOLVER CLEANING RODS
MARBLE'S

One-Piece Solid Brass

Threaded hardwood handle and roller-bearing swivel tip. Fitted with combination slotted and jagged tip. Threaded for cleaning brushes.

Nos.	722	732
Caliber	.22 and .25	.32
Lgth., in.	11	9
Each	$0.90	.90

Weight each ¼ pound.

One in a bag.

SHOTGUN CLEANING SWABS
GUNSLICK

Wool bodied swab. Fits all standard shotgun cleaning rods.

Each

No. 474—12, 16, 20-28 and 410 gauge; wt. per carton ½ lb. $0.15

Twelve in a carton.

RIFLE CLEANING BRUSHES
BRASS WIRE

SAFETY TIP

Fits all standard cleaning rods.

Each

Rifle Brushes—.22, .25, .30, .32, .38 and .45 caliber; wt. per box about 3 oz. . .$0.15

Twelve in a box.

Note—When ordering cleaning brushes specify caliber desired.

GUN CLEANING PATCHES
HOPPE'S

Made of specially selected clean cotton flannel of proper weave. They a r e of correct thickness; will not wad up and jam in the bore; used for cleaning out all residue, fouling, corrosion and rust.

Round Shape

Per package

No. 2—For .22 to .270 caliber, 100 in a package $0.35

No. 3—For .270 to .35 caliber, 100 in a package 35

No. 4—For .38 to .45 caliber and 410 and 20 gauge, 75 in a package 35

No. 5—For 16 to 12 gauge, 50 in a package 35

Weight per carton about ¾ pound.

Nos. 2 and 3, twelve; Nos. 4 and 5, six in a carton.

NITRO POWDER SOLVENT
HOPPE'S

For cleaning high power rifles, shot guns, revolvers and firearms of all kinds. Removes and prevents r u s t and corroding. Removes m e t a l fouling and leading. Eliminates the use of the brass brush.

Each

No. 9—In 2 oz. bottles; wt. per carton 2 lbs..$0.45

Twelve in a carton.

NITRO POWDER SOLVENT
GUNSLICK

A modern solvent. Removes all metal and powder fouling and leading. Positively prevents electrolytic corrosion and pitting. Prevents rust. Not made with acids and will not injure finest steels. Maintains bores in original new factory condition, bright and true.

Each

No. 444—In 2 oz. bottles; wt. per carton 4 lbs. $0.45

Twelve in a carton.

GUN LUBRICANT
GUNSLICK

Used and recommended by largest metropolitan p o l i c e departments whose guns must never fail. Eliminates all friction, creates h a n d - h o n e d smoothness that gives shooter that sweet trigger pull so necessary for accurate shooting.

Each

No. 400—In m e t a l tubes; wt. per carton 1 lb. $0.25

Twelve in a display carton.

LUBRICATING OIL
3-IN-ONE, REGULAR

3-In-One oil is really three fine oils (animal, mineral and vegetable) in one perfect blend—that's why it gives triple service. Lubricates, cleans, prevents rust and tarnish.

Has no equal for carpet sweeper, s e w i n g machine, electric mixer, doors, guns, locks and skates.

In cans with non-refillable tops.

Nos.	8719	391
Size cans, oz.	1	3
No. in case	144	144
Wt. case, lbs.	18½	41
Each	$0.10	.25

Twelve in a box.

LUBRICATING OIL
WINCHESTER

For lubricating all parts of guns, machines or other metal work.

High grade lubricant of medium thickness. W i l l not become rancid in hot weather or harden while in use in cold weather.

Each

No. G1052V—In 3 oz. cans; wt. per carton 4⅓ lbs. . .$0.40

Twelve in a carton.

In Spray Can

New Winchester gun oil t h a t penetrates, prevents rust and lubricates. Neutralizes fingerprint acids a n d displaces water.

In n e w handy spray container.

Each

No. 1056V — In 5½ o z. cans; wt. per carton 5 lbs. $1.39

Twelve in a display carton.

TEXACO

Recommended as lubricant for machine tools, carpenter tools, electric motors up to ⅛ HP and fans. Excellent also for all types of sporting goods.

Light bodied lubricant.

Each

Texaco—In 4 oz. cans; wt. per carton 4½ lbs..$0.30

Twelve cans in a carton.

FINOL

Cleans and brightens brass, nickel, polished enamel, golf clubs, fishing tackle and guns. Softens leather.

Will not gum, c l o g or corrode. Purely a mineral oil.

Each

Finol—In 4 oz. cans; wt. per carton 5 lbs. $0.20

Twelve cans in a carton.

1354   **MISSOULA MERCANTILE COMPANY**

DUCK CALLS
SCOTCH

A revolutionary new call that makes anyone an expert. Simply shake or depress bellows and the Scotch call produces authentic, natural tones.

Neoprene bellows with a hardwood, hand finished sounding throat. Simply shaking or depressing the diaphragm-bellows produces the tones and imitation desired.

Each
No. 1401—Wt. per carton 1½ lbs. $7.50

One in a box, twelve in a carton.

OLT'S PERFECT MALLARD

Precision made of fine polished black hard rubber. Screw-in assembly makes it easy to take apart without loss or change of tone. With "mouth-fitting" mouthpiece.

Each
No. C3—4 in. long; wt. each 1 oz. $4.00

Twelve in a display.

OLT'S REGULAR

Molded of the finest polished black hard rubber. Special prepared composition reed, free from metallic or muffled wood sounds.

Each
No. D2—4¾ in. long; wt. each 1 oz. $2.50

Twelve in a display.

OLT'S JUNIOR

A small replica of Olt's No. D2 Regular Duck Call recognized by hunters as the standard shape of a duck call.

Made of black hard rubber.

Each
No. J15—3⅝ in. long; wt. each ¾ oz. ..$1.50

Twelve in a display.

DUCK CALLS
LOHMAN DELUXE

Shell made of carefully selected figured black walnut crotch wood. Turned and finished by hand.

Cherry insert; special waterproof treatment, composition reeds.

Each
No. 105—4¼ in. long; wt. per display 2⅝ lbs. $6.00

One in a box, twelve in a display carton.

LOHMAN

Black walnut shell with cherry insert; special waterproof treatment, natural finish. Special composition reeds tested by expert caller.

Each
No. 103—4 in. long; wt. per carton 1⅞ lbs. $2.00

One in a box, twelve in a display carton.

Each
Reeds—For No. 103 call $0.25
Shell—For No. 103 call .... .50
Insert—For No. 103 call 1.25

Open stock.

GOOSE CALLS
OLT'S PERFECT DELUXE

Hand made of the finest black hard rubber, nicely polished. Single, straight composition reed produces melodious double noted "her-onk." Can be taken apart, cleaned and reassembled without injury to tone.

Gold plated band with eyelet for attaching cord.

Each
No. A5—Deluxe, 4¾ in. long; wt. each 1½ oz. $5.50

OLT'S PERFECT STANDARD

Same as above, except without gold plated band.

Each
No. A5—Standard, 4¾ in. long; wt. each 1½ oz. $5.00

Twelve in a display.

GOOSE CALLS
LOHMAN

An all new goose call combining the simplicity of a single reed with famous Lohman quality, at a low price. Waterproof construction of the finest materials.

Each
No. 112—4 in. long; wt. per carton 2 lbs..$3.00

One in a box, twelve in a display carton.

LEE'S

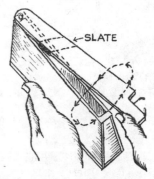

Excellent goose call; call must be kept dry. Illustration shows exactly how call should be operated.

Each
Lee's—Wt. each 3 oz. $3.50

One in a box.

CROW CALLS
OLT'S PERFECT REGULAR

Made of fine polished hard rubber throughout. Special prepared composition reed held securely in place between two hard rubber lips which constitute the mouthpiece. Wide groove in reed base eliminates possibility of reed sticking.

Each
No. E1—3½ in. long; wt. each ½ oz. ..$2.50

Twelve in a display.

LOHMAN

Black walnut shell; cherry insert. Waterproofed, natural finish. Special composition reed. Each call tested by expert.

Each
No. 104—4¼ in. long; wt. per carton 1⅝ lbs. $2.00

One in a box, twelve in a display carton.

ICE CREEPERS

NORLUND

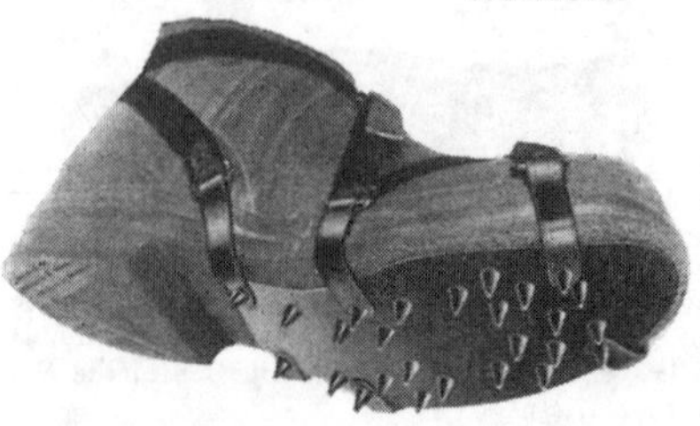

Detachable Calked Steel Soles

Made of flexible tempered spring steel plates, thickly studded with sharp, pointed, case hardened calks. Held securely in place by means of strong, durable straps.

Men's large size fits shoe sizes 8 to 11.

Per pair

No. 6035—Wt. per box 1⅜ lbs. $3.95

One pair in a box.

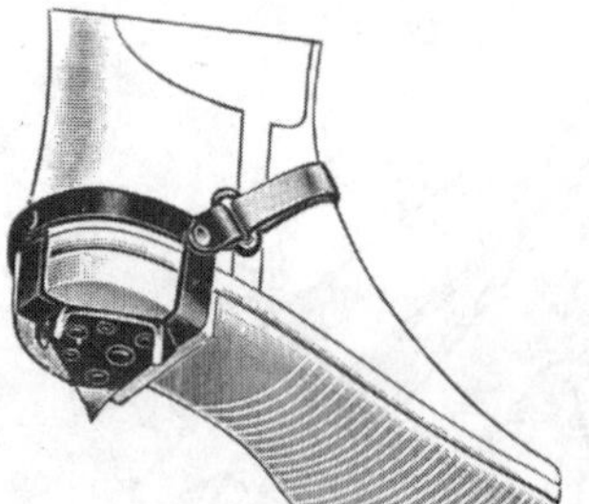

Detachable Heel Plates

Tempered steel plate with four points. Strong metal harness arrangement and good quality strap enables wearer to put them on or take them off as desired—the strapping arrangement is positive and comfortable. These plates will withstand hard usage.

Per pair

No. 6033-1—For arctics, 4⅛ in. wide $1.95

No. 6033-2—For overshoes, 3⅝ in. wide 1.95

Weight per box 5 pounds.

Six pairs in a box.

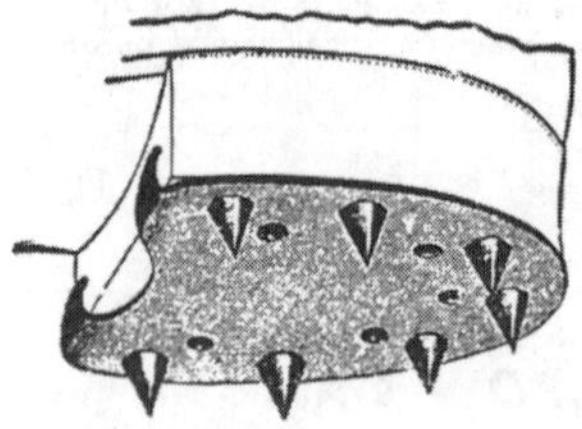

Calked Heel Plates

Seven ⅜ in. case hardened steel calks securely riveted to a 1/16 in. steel plate.

Suitable screws supplied for permanent attachment.

Per pair

No. 6031-1—For heels 2⅞ in. wide; wt. per box 3⅜ lbs. ..$0.60

Twelve pairs in a box.

STEERING SLEDS

YANKEE CLIPPER RACING MODELS

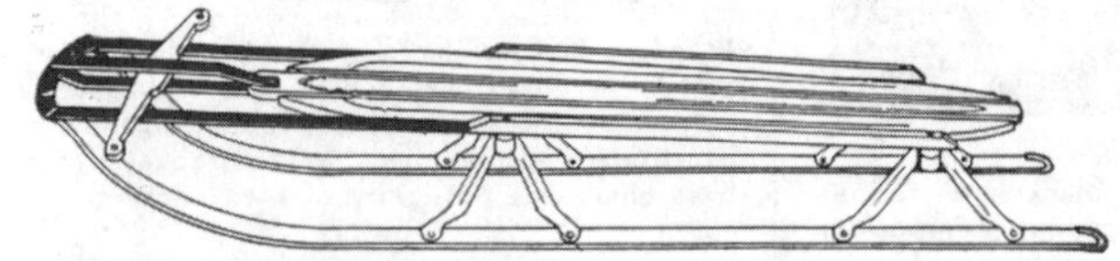

Streamlined, rakish and speedy, combining the most modern features of design and style with a proven construction for safety and dependability.

Spring steel runners are grooved for speed and safety, and turned over at the ends to eliminate sharp edges. Heavy reinforced standards absorb shock and side strain; the all steel front is strong and shock-resisting. All wood parts are selected white ash, smartly decorated and finished with clear varnish. Runners and standards finished in Chinese red; black enameled steel front.

All are racing models, lower in the back than in the front. Light in weight but strong and sturdy in construction.

Nos.	10	11	12	13	14
Length, in.	36	40	45	49	56
Width, in.	12	12	12	12	12
Height front, in.	6	6	6	6	6
Height rear, in.	5	5	5	5	5
No. of standards	4	4	4	4	6
Wt. each, lbs.	7	8	9	10	13
Each	$5.25	6.35	7.30	7.90	9.90

Two in a bundle.

STEERING SLEDS

FLEXIBLE FLYER

Streamlined, fast, good looking, light but very strong. All Flexible Flyers have the same safety construction features. All are streamlined, having curved bumper and steering bar, the "tear drop" deck, and the Airline Safety Runners.

All Flexible Flyers have "Super Steering" which by actual test permits turning fully twice as sharp as with other sleds. The strong steel front is made still stronger by the heavy patented bumper, almost as important as an automobile bumper, and affording the same protection.

The special analysis of the steel used exclusively in Flexible Flyer runners gives them tremendous flexibility.

RACING MODELS

Streamlined, fast, good looking—light but very strong, and above all safer. Super-steering and Airline runners, the two greatest safety features on any sled. Super-steering means sharp steering—quicker dodging. Airline runners help prevent accidents in case of spills.

All wood parts of selected second growth white ash; grooved runners of special analysis spring steel to stand terrific strain of Super-steering without "setting"; extra heavy standards are specially ribbed for rigidity; all steel front stronger than ever with heavy patented bumper. Streamlined seat, steering bar and bumper, and sloping and tapered deck for speed and beauty.

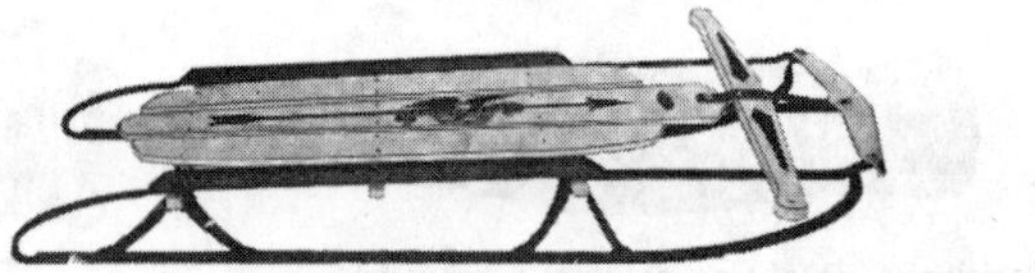

With Four Standards

Nos.	41	47	251	551
Length, in.	41	47	51	51
Width, in.	13¼	13¼	13¼	13¼
Height front, in.	6½	6½	6½	6½
Height rear, in.	4½	4¾	4¾	4¾
Wt. each, lbs.	9	12	12¾	12¾
Each	$11.20	14.65	15.80	16.80

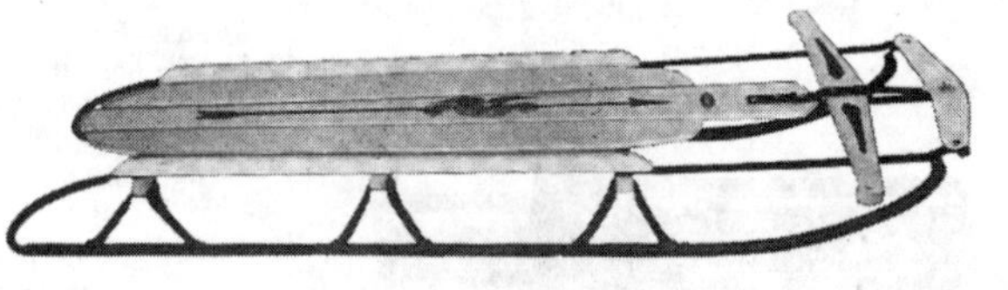

With Six Standards

Each

No. 60—Airline Racer; length 60 in., width 15½ in., height at front 8 in., at rear 5½ in.; wt. each 19 lbs. $19.10

STANDARD MODELS

Flexible Flyer Standard Models are constructed with the same high grade material and workmanship as the Racing Models; they have the same Super-steering and Airline runners, streamlined seat, steering bar and bumper. They are constructed a little roomier—higher and wider than the Racing Models.

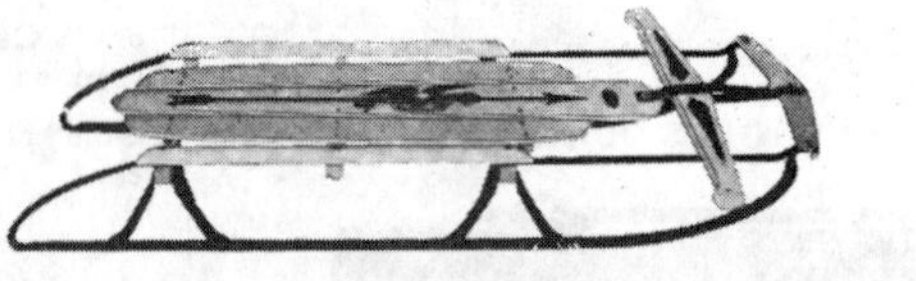

With Four Standards

Nos.	37	44	55
Length, in.	37	44	55
Width, in.	13¼	13¼	15½
Height front, in.	6¼	6½	8½
Height rear, in.	6	5¾	8
Wt. each, lbs.	8½	10	19
Each	$9.40	13.10	16.80

With Six Standards

Each

No. 65—Airline Cruiser; length 65 in., width 17¼ in., height at front 8½ in., height at rear 8 in.; wt. each 25 lbs. $28.40

All above, two in a bundle.

1378   MISSOULA MERCANTILE COMPANY

SNO-COASTERS
MIRRO

A new idea for coasting and sliding on snowy slopes.

This saucer shaped, fun conveyance works much like a toboggan; shift your weight and the Sno-Coaster turns and spins on its way down or goes straight as an arrow.

Completely safe and practically indestructible; all-aluminum construction prevents rust and eliminates painting. Bladed edge adds to saucer's rigidity.

Two reinforced tow rope holes enable it to be pulled like a sled; two strong, double riveted, heavy web handle loops.

One-piece construction.

	Each
No. 3589MT—27 in. diam.; wt. each 4 lbs.	$5.50

Six in a carton.

SNOW SHOES
TUBBS

Constructed of fine quality straight grain white ash. Finished with best quality sealers and varnishes.

Western rawhide lacing. All snow shoes rawhide wrapped for extra strength at toe and bars.

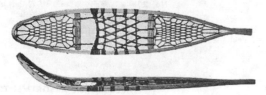

Alaska Trapper Model

With long curved up toe for use in deep snow or for trail breaking. Expertly balanced.

	Per pair
No. 100T—10x56 in.; wt. per pair about 4½ lbs.	$32.50

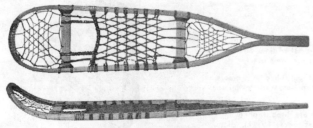

Cross Country Model

Narrow for greater ease in use; short toe for maneuverability; sharply curved up toe so that is will "track" well.

	Per pair
No. 200—10x46 in.; wt. per pair about 4½ lbs.	$30.50

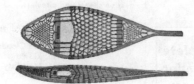

No. 74—Michigan Model

All-purpose model for use in any type of country.

Size, in.	12x42	14x48
Wt. pr., lbs.	4¼	4¾
Per pair	$29.70	30.95

SNOW SHOES
TUBBS

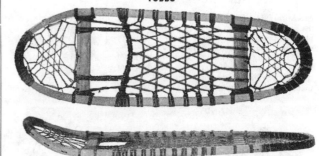

No. A—Green Mountain Bear Paw Model

Newly designed model. Correctly balanced, beautifully made.

Size, in.	9x28	10x36
Wt. per pair, lbs.	4	4½
Per pair	$26.50	29.50

One pair in a bundle.

SNOW SHOE BINDINGS
TUBBS

Made of best grade leather straps. Provides better control; adjusts easily to all sizes of boots. Snow does not pack under feet when in use.

	Per pair
No. H—Wt. per pair ½ lb.	$3.00

Open stock.

TUBBS KON-TROL

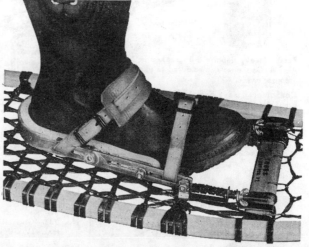

Gives complete and safe control over snow shoe. Nothing tight about shoes to cut off circulation. Ice cleats prevent slipping on ice or crust.

Adjustable to any size foot. Attaches to old or new snow shoes.

	Per pair
Kon-Trol—Wt. per pair 1 lb.	$10.00

Open stock.

KELLY-MANN

Made of heavy, tough latigo leather. Oil used in the tannage of leather makes it highly water resistant.

	Per pair
Kelly-Mann—Wt. per pair about 1 lb.	$3.50

Open stock.

HAND SPRAYERS
HUDSON ATO-MIZOR

Ato-Mizors represent high Hudson quality at the most moderate prices. Powerful Air-Pak plungers produce a fine spray of any oil-base insecticide. Plungers are high-grade synthetic. Oiled, like any other plunger must be, they last indefinitely and make any 1¼ in. diameter straight pumps deliver more air than 1½ in. pumps with conventional plungers.

HANDY

Pump: Heavy tinplate lithographed in 2 colors. Air-Pak. Container cap soldered to pump. Single atomizer nozzle.

Container: Heavy tinplate; lock-seamed. Leakproof. 1½ in. diam. mouth.

Each

No. 440—Capacity 27 oz., 4¼x3⅞ in. tank, 1¼x12 in. pump; wt. each ¾ lb. $0.59

Twelve in a carton.

VAPOR

Pump: Heavy tinplate lithographed in 2 colors. Air-Pak. Container cap soldered to pump. Single atomizer nozzle.

Container: Heavy tinplate; lock-seamed. Leakproof. 1½ in. diam. mouth.

Each

No. 222—Capacity 14 oz., 3⅜x3⅛ in. tank, 1¼x10 in. pump; wt. each ⅝ lb. $0.49

Twelve in a carton.

BANTAM

Pump: Heavy tinplate lithographed in 2 colors. Air-Pak. Recessed into top of cap. Single atomizer nozzle.

Container: Ribbed emerald green jar protects spray from deterioration; easy to see liquid level. 1½ in. diam. mouth.

Each

No. 205—Capacity 5 oz., 1¼x8 in. pump; wt. each ⅝ lb. $0.35

Twenty-four in a carton.

HAND SPRAYERS
HUDSON NEBU-LIZORS
Fewer Strokes Put Out More Spray with Finer Particles for Much Greater Insect Knockdown, Much Greater Insect Kill

The 4 jets on Nebu-Lizors are the reason why Nebu-Lizors give 20% greater knockdown, 25% greater kill, as proved by impartial laboratory-controlled biological tests.

The 4 jets break up insecticides into much finer particles that roll and billow, much like smoke—hang suspended longer in a room for greater effectiveness.

MISTY

Larger container and extra-size pump adapts the Misty for household, farm, restaurant, hotel and school use.

Pump: Heavy tinplate lithographed in 2 colors. Nu-Action. Container cap soldered to pump. 4-jet nozzle.

Container: Heavy tinplate lithographed in 2 colors; lock-seamed. Leak-proof. 1½ in. diam. mouth.

Each

No. 444—Capacity 27 oz., 4¼x3⅞ in. tank, 1¼x12 in. pump; wt. each ¾ lb. $0.85

Twelve in a carton.

FOG

Provides greater spray output of finer and more uniform particles. Popular for home use.

Pump: Heavy tinplate lithographed in 2 colors. Nu-Action. Container cap soldered to pump. 4-jet nozzle.

Container: Heavy tinplate lithographed in 2 colors; lock-seamed. Leak-proof. 1½ in. diam. mouth.

Each

No. 333—Capacity 14 oz., 3⅜x3⅛ in. tank, 1¼x10 in. pump; wt. each ⅝ lb. $0.70

Twelve in a carton.

CLOUD

Here for the first time, in a sprayer of its capacity is tremendous output with fewer strokes. A handy size for use around the home or office. Easy to see liquid level.

Pump: Heavy tinplate lithographed in 2 colors. Nu-Action. Jar cap rigidly soldered to pump. 4-jet nozzle.

Container: Ribbed green glass jar protects spray from deterioration. 1½ in. diam. mouth.

Each

No. 208—Capacity 8 oz., 3½x2 in. jar, 1¼x10 in. pump; wt. each ¾ lb. $0.50

Twelve in a carton.

SALES-MAKER ASSORTMENTS

An attractive, colorful display showing all three of the Nebu-Lizor sprayers fully described on this page.

Each assortment includes a 3-color counter display stand, window signs, merchandising suggestion sheets and circulars.

Contents of Assortment

24 No. 208 Clouds
12 No. 333 Fogs
12 No. 444 Mistys

Per assortment

No. SM3—**Assortment,** consists of 48 sprayers as listed above complete with display stand; wt. per assortment 37 lbs. $30.60

One assortment in two cartons.

Our large and complete stock enables us to render prompt and efficient service on all items shown in this catalog.

1514

MISSOULA MERCANTILE COMPANY

SCYTHE SNATHS
STA-TITE

Second growth Northern ash, varnished. All fittings are of malleable iron.

All standard blades fit and stay tight. Fittings reinforce the snath at point of strain and may be retightened after wood shrinks.

Sta-Tite Back-Saver; for Grass, Weed and Bush Scythes

Improved "Back-Saver" heel plate raises snath at its handles about 12 in.; eliminating stooping.

Each
No. 300—60 in. long; wt. each 4¾ lbs. . **$4.00**

Six in a bundle.

Improved Back-Saver; for Grass Scythes

Improved loop-bolt with "Back-Saver" heel plate which raises snath at its handles about 12 in.; eliminating stooping.

Each
No. 50-IBS—60 in. long; wt. each 4 lbs.. **$3.75**

Six in a bundle.

SCYTHE SNATH REPAIRS
STA-TITE

4X   No. 23

No. 10   No. 13

Note—When ordering, always give name and number of snath.

Each
No. 4X—Ring and set screw for No. 300 snath; wt. each 9 oz. **$0.60**

No. 10—Loop bolt and nut for Nos. 105-IBS and 105 snaths; wt. each 4 oz.   **.30**

No. 13—Loop bolt and nut for No. 50-IBS snath; wt. each 2¾ oz. . . . . . **.30**

No. 23—Nib complete for all snaths; wt. each 5¼ oz. . . . . **.50**

Open stock.

SCYTHES
SWIFT CUTTER

One piece of high carbon steel rolled to distribute steel in heel and point to attain perfect hang and balance. Forged under hammers, hardened and tempered; edge and point ground sharp and polished; beaded web. Top of web painted blue.

Dutch Grass

Each
Dutch Grass—Assorted 28 to 32 in. lengths; average wt. each 2 lbs. . . . **$3.20**

Six in a carton.

Weed

Each
Weed—Assorted 24 to 28 in. lengths; average wt. each 2 lbs. **$3.20**

Six in a carton.

Bush

Each
Bush—Assorted 20 to 24 in. lengths; average wt. each 2 lbs. **$3.20**

Six in a carton.

SCYTHE STONES
CARBORUNDUM

Aluminum Oxide

Fast clean cutting stone made from aluminum oxide. Made in just the right grit to give a proper edge.

Each
No. 188—10x1 5/16 x1 3/16 - 1 1/16 in.; wt. per box 6½ lbs. **$0.47**

Twelve in a display box.

CLEAR GRIT

A full oval shape stone of extra sharp Huron grit, sand bed finish.

Each
Clear Grit—9 in. long; wt. per box 20 lbs. **$0.18**

Thirty-six in a box.

BUSH HOOKS
LITTLE GIANT

Crucible steel blade; hardened and tempered, ground sharp; polished bevels, remainder painted red. 36 in. natural finish hickory handle.

Each
No. 19—3¼ lb. blade, straight blade edge 5 in. long, curved blade edge 6 in. long; wt. complete about 4 lbs. **$6.50**

Six in a box.

HAY KNIVES
IWAN'S THREE SECTIONAL

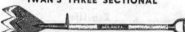

Solid Socket, with Step

Malleable casting composing blade and foot step in one piece. Hardwood handle fits into socket, requiring no rivets, making replacement of handle easy. Blade has narrow tapering rib in the center for greater strength.

Cutting sections have saw tooth edge and are set closely together to prevent clogging.

Blue enamel finish D handle with wood grip.

Each
No. 5—46 in. long; wt. each 5 lbs. . . . **$4.70**

Six in a carton.

Each
Extra Cutting Section—For No. 5 hay knife, complete with rivets **$0.35**

Open stock.

LIGHTNING

Weymouth Pattern

Blade forged from high carbon steel bars, tapering in both width and thickness toward point. 8 cutting teeth ground sharp, point and teeth polished, remainder painted red.

Hardwood handles with steel ferrule and natural varnish finish.

Designed for left or right hand use.

Each
No. 40L—36 in. long over all, 4 in. handle; wt. each 4¼ lbs. **$5.20**

Six in a carton.

MISSOULA MERCANTILE COMPANY

CORN KNIVES
ATKINS

Special steel curved black blade with polished beveled cutting edge. Sanded hardwood handle fastened by two tubular rivets.

Each

No. 2—15½ in. blade, 2⅞ in. wide, 22 in. long over all; wt. each 1 lb. **$1.25**

Six in a carton.

GRASS HOOKS
NOWATOCO SCYTHOOK

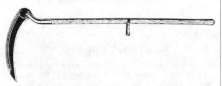

Combination Grass Hook and Scythe

Small enough for limited space; large enough for larger areas.

15 gauge high carbon steel blade, hardened and tempered; polished edge, green enameled back. Attached to high carbon pressed steel shank with 3 bolts. Shank securely riveted to 54 in. natural finish hardwood handle; nib attached for hand hold.

Each

No. 55—18 in. blade; wt. each 4 lbs. . . . **$2.60**

Six in a carton, KD.

LAWN KING

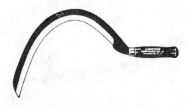

Exclusive concave design steel blade, hardened and tempered; highly polished double bevel; grooves, back and shank painted blue. Solid tang driven through handle and riveted firmly at end. 5 in. hardwood handle with black enamel finish; nickeled ferrule.

Designed for left or right hand use.

Each

No. 12—12 in. blade; wt. each 1 lb. **$1.30**

Twelve in a carton.

GRASS HOOKS
LITTLE GIANT

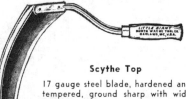

Scythe Top

17 gauge steel blade, hardened and tempered, ground sharp with wide bevel; turned-up back. Polished cutting edge; bead and back enameled blue, red strip on top. Drop forged shank, red finished; riveted for solidity. Natural grip, black enameled handle; ferruled.

Each

No. 8—12½ in. blade; wt. each ¾ lb. . . **$1.25**

Twelve in a carton.

Adjustable

Same construction as No. 8 shown above except blade is adjustable to 3 positions.

Each

No. 9—12½ in. blade; wt. each ¾ lb. . . **$1.40**

Twelve in a carton.

LIGHTNING

Sickle Type

Blade of fine cutlery steel, ⁷⁄₆₄ in. thick, 1⅛ in. wide, hardened and tempered, cutting edge ground sharp; offset shank. Natural finish hardwood handle, shaped to fit hand; attached to blade with two rivets. Blade enameled blue.

Each

No. 5—12½ in. blade; wt. each ¾ lb. . . **$0.84**

Twelve in a carton.

GRASS WHIPS
TRUE TEMPER, KELLY PERFECT

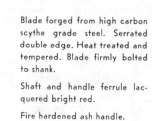

Blade forged from high carbon scythe grade steel. Serrated double edge. Heat treated and tempered. Blade firmly bolted to shank.

Shaft and handle ferrule lacquered bright red.

Fire hardened ash handle.

Each

No. 29—9x1½ in. blade, 38 in. long over all; wt. each 1½ lbs. **$1.85**

Six in a carton.

GRASS SHEARS
WISS

Long Handle

Backaches and sore knees are eliminated with this handy tool which enables the user to trim grass standing up. Two wheels provide steady, free moving operation. Lightweight, sturdy construction. Double spring action blades are plated and hardened.

Red and black enamel finish.

Each

No. 900—5 in. cut; wt. each 3 lbs. **$4.70**

Four in a carton.

Clipper

Up-and-down handle action takes the muscle strain out of grass cutting. Accurately adjusted for perfect cutting from heel to points.

Rust-resistant, plated, hardened blades, easily disassembled for repairs. Handles contoured for comfort and fitted with grip guard to prevent slipping. Closing latch.

Red and black baked enamel handles.

Each

No. 700—12 in. long over all; wt. each 1¼ lbs. **$2.15**

One in a box, thirty-six in a carton.

Quick Trim

Easy up-and-down handle action. Perfect cutting from heel to point. Rust-resistant bright plated hardened blades; easily disassembled for sharpening. Closing latch.

Green baked enamel handles.

Each

No. 801—12 in. long over all; wt. each 1 lb. **$1.95**

One in a box, thirty-six in a carton.

1516   **MISSOULA MERCANTILE COMPANY**

GRASS SHEARS
WISS

Grass Snip

Low in price yet high in quality; compact and sturdy. Up-and-down handle action; new riveted construction. Expertly adjusted for easy cutting action and dependable performance.

Comfortable handles, contoured to fit the hand; hardened and tempered electro-plated blades with beveled edges. Baked yellow enameled handles.

Each
No. 500—10 in. long over all; wt. each
1 lb. $1.50

One in a box, thirty-six in a carton.

Standard

The only grass shears that will cut certain types of tough wiry grass satisfactorily.

Entirely hot drop forged of cutlery steel with hardened, tempered, hollow-ground blades. Red baked enamel handles. Fitted with a closing latch.

Each
No. 5600—12 in. long over all; wt. each
1 lb. $3.00

One in a box, thirty-six in a carton.

MIRACLE

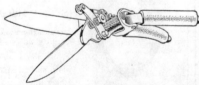

A drop forged tool, precision hollow ground, razor sharp. Hardened and tempered individually. Large bearing surface all around. Spring breakage unknown. Blister proof, soft cushion rubber handles, comfortable and easy operation.

Each
No. 2—4½ in. cut, 13 in. long; wt. each
1½ lbs. $2.75

One in a box, thirty-six in a carton.

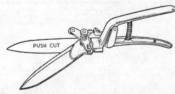

A drop forged tool, precision hollow ground, razor sharp. Hardened and tempered individually. Large bearing surface all around. Spring breakage unknown. Steel handles.

Each
No. 1—4½ in. cut, 13 in. long; wt. each
1½ lbs. $2.50

One in a box, thirty-six in a carton.

SHEEP SHEARS
BURGON & BALL

Straight Blades

High grade cutlery steel blades; polished, beveled and swaged. Double bow, oval grip.

Nos.	BBA-6½	BBA-7
Length blade, in.	6½	7
Length over all, in.	13½	14
Wt. each, lbs.	⅞	1
Each	$3.65	3.85

Six in a box.

FETLOCK OR ROACHING SHEARS
TREE BRAND

Curved Blades

Hot drop forged steel; nickel plated curved blades; black japanned handles.

Each
No. 165—8 in. long; wt. each ¼ lb. ...$5.00

Six in a box.

FLOWER SHEARS
WISS

Cuts and Holds Stems

Cuts the stem and holds it at the same time, with one hand. Ideal for picking flowers—roses particularly—and handy for cutting stems to just the right length and at the right angle in preparation for floral arrangements.

Fully chrome plated; stainless steel blades fitted with adjusting screw.

Each
No. FH4—6½ in. long; wt. each 4 oz. ..$2.50

One in a box.

FLOWER AND GRAPE SHEARS
WISS

Originally designed for thinning out thick growths of flowers or certain types of fruits, these shears are popular for garden thinning, flower picking and as a table accessory for selecting grapes.

Straight nickel plated blades; red enameled handles; fitted with a closing latch.

Each
No. C-4AR—8 in. long; wt. each 6 oz. ..$3.75

One in a box.

TREE PRUNERS
CLYDE

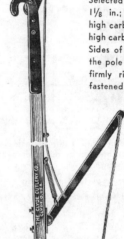

Selected spruce pole, 1¼x 1⅛ in.; two-piece riveted high carbon tool steel hook; high carbon tool steel blade. Sides of hook extend down the pole for 6½ in. and are firmly riveted. Steel lever fastened to pole 2½ ft. from trimmer head; extra long coil spring for holding blade open furnished with rope.

Lever trimmed in red, head enameled green.

Nos.	5421–10	5421–12
Lgth., ft.	10	12
Wt. each, lbs.	4¾	5½
Each	$5.25	6.50

Selected spruce pole, 1¼x1⅛ in.; two-piece riveted tool steel hook; high carbon tool steel cutting blade. Sides of hook extend 6½ in. down side of pole. Lever 13 in. long over all with ash handle grip and ferrule. Coil spring holds blade open.

Red trimmed lever, green enameled head.

Nos.	5407–6	5407–8	5407–10
Lgth., ft.	6	8	10
Wt. each, lbs.	3½	4½	5¼
Each	$3.55	4.05	4.40

All above, twelve in a bundle.

CALF WEANERS

IMPROVED SHAW

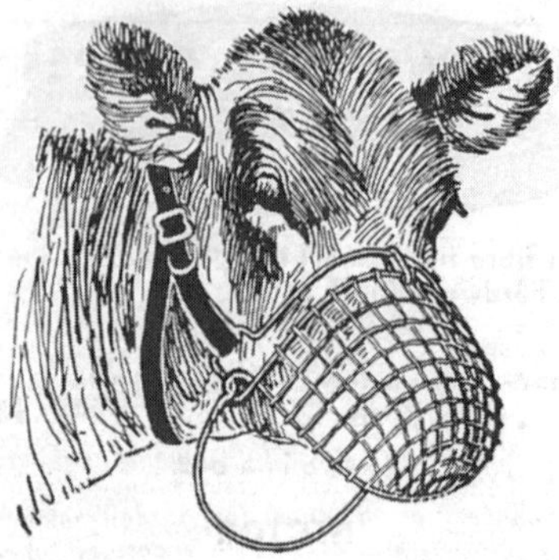

Safe and humane. Positively prevents sucking while at the same time permits the animal to graze.

Retinned after making, which gives added strength and prevents rust.

Nos.	1	2	3
Size	Calves	Yearlings	Cows
No. in ctn.	12	12	6
Wt. ctn. lbs.	7	9	7
Each	**$0.80**	**.95**	**1.15**

KEE'S IMPROVED

Four sharp prongs formed up in the plate make it more severe. The prongs can be dulled or bent down if they are not wanted.

Galvanized pressed steel plate, brass spring.

The most convenient weaner to put on or take off.

Nos.	525	626
Size	Calves	Yearlings
Plate, in.	$3\times4\frac{3}{4}$	$3\frac{3}{4}\times5\frac{5}{8}$
No. of prongs	3	4
Wt. ctn., lbs.	$2\frac{1}{2}$	$3\frac{1}{2}$
Each	**$0.25**	**.30**

Twelve in a carton.

WIRE GRIPS

KLEIN'S CHICAGO

For Messenger, Guy Strand and Heavy Conductors

Designed to provide in one tool a grip to handle almost every requirement. Forged from alloy steel, heat treated.

With Plain Jaw

Each

No. 1628-5—Approx. max. opening .58 in., takes No. 4 B & S solid copper to No. 4/0 B&S 7 strand copper and Nos. 6 to 3/0 A.S.C.R., safe load 8,000 lbs.; wt. each 6 lbs. ... **$11.75**

With Bronze Lined Jaw

Each

No. 1628-5B—Same as above except with bronze lined jaws to prevent slipping and consequent damage to conduction; wt. each 6 lbs. **$14.75**

Open stock.

KLEIN'S HAVEN'S

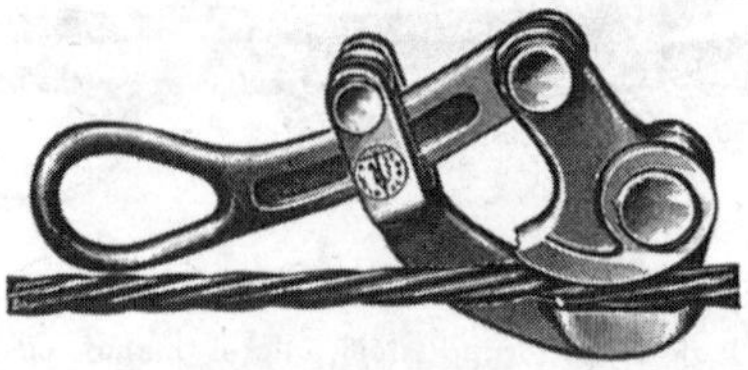

Eccentric Jaw

Improved; solid steel forgings; pear shaped eye. Roller fitted to body yoke permits free motion and smooth action. Holds instantaneously and will not slip, yet a shake on the tackle rope releases grip. All except eccentric is galvanized; hand cut serrations in face of eccentric.

Each

No. 1604-10—For No. 4 B&S wire and smaller; Max. opening $\frac{15}{64}$ in., Min. $\frac{1}{16}$ in.; safe load 2500 lbs.; wt. each 1 lb. **$4.05**

No. 1604-20—For $\frac{1}{2}$ in. wire and smaller; Max. opening $\frac{17}{32}$ in., Min. $\frac{9}{64}$ in.; safe load 5000 lbs.; wt. each $2\frac{1}{2}$ lbs. **5.50**

Open stock.

COW BELLS

BLUM "HOLSTEIN"

Brazed joint, steel loop, cast iron clapper with wire hanger. The special brazing process used in the manufacture of this bell produces a real bell metal with a tone quality that cannot be duplicated.

Heights given are without loops. No. 6 can be used as a sheep bell.

Nos.	6	4	3	1
Height, in.	$2\frac{3}{4}$	$4\frac{1}{8}$	5	$6\frac{1}{2}$
Length mouth, in.	$2\frac{5}{8}$	$3\frac{5}{8}$	$4\frac{1}{2}$	$5\frac{1}{2}$
Width mouth, in.	$1\frac{7}{8}$	$2\frac{1}{4}$	$2\frac{3}{4}$	$3\frac{1}{4}$
Wt. dozen, lbs.	5	8	12	22
Each	**$0.70**	**2.20**	**1.30**	**1.60**

Open stock.

COW OR TEAM BELLS

SWISS

Pure Bell Metal

Not tuned, without straps.

Nos.	1	2	3
Diameter, in.	3	$3\frac{5}{16}$	$3\frac{11}{16}$
Wt. each, lb.	$\frac{1}{2}$	$\frac{3}{5}$	$\frac{2}{3}$
Each	**$1.65**	**1.90**	**2.25**
Nos.	**4**	**05**	**5**
Diameter, in.	4	$4\frac{3}{8}$	5
Wt. each, lbs.	1	$1\frac{1}{3}$	$1\frac{3}{4}$
Each	**$2.50**	**3.60**	**4.95**

Open stock.

TURKEY BELLS

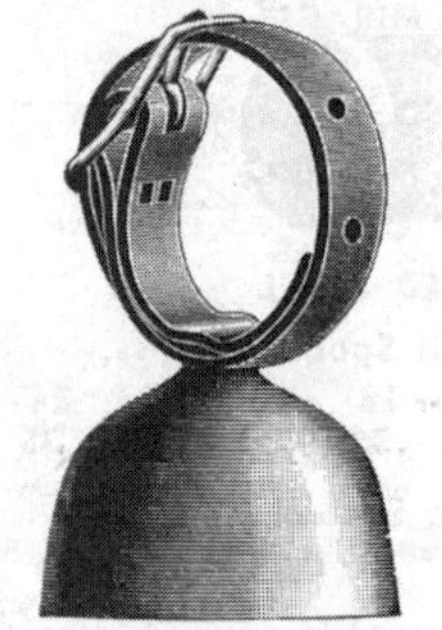

Bell Metal

Enables the flock to be easily located. A sure protection against animals and hawks. Polished finish.

Fitted with a good leather strap.

Each

No. 134-1—$1\frac{5}{8}$ in. diam.; wt. per dozen $1\frac{1}{2}$ lbs. **$0.40**

Open stock.

1964 Montgomery Ward Catalog

MONTGOMERY WARD

1964 **FARM** *Catalog*

HANDY INDEX

Complete Index, Page 96

Credit Information, Page 101

...able Grinder-Mixer Outfit.
...Feeds for Dairy and Beef
... Lambs and Poultry.
89 FB 25509 F— Listed on Page 23.
89 FB 25519 F—W

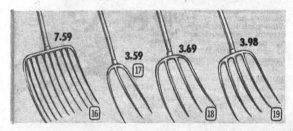

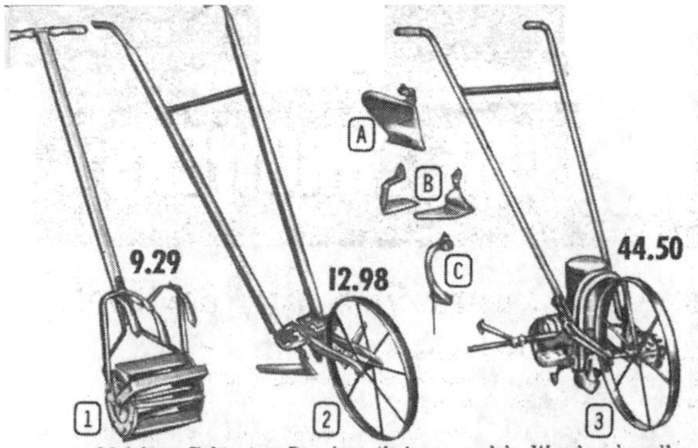

9.29 12.98 44.50

[1] Mulcher, Cultivator. Breaks soil, forms mulch. Wooden handle.
89 FB 1751Y—Ship. wt. 14 lbs. *Mail.* Eight 10-in. blades. .**$9.29**

[2] Speed Hoe. Use between rows. Large steel wheel. Includes 2 weeding hoes, 3 duckfeet, 1 turn plow, steel wrench.
89 FB 1766YO—Ship. wt. 21 lbs. *Mail.* Wooden handle. **$12.98**

[3] Seeder and Cultivator. Steel handles, rubber grips. Includes 2 weeding hoes, 2 hilling plows, 4 duckfeet, row marker.
89 FB 1755YO—Ship. wt. 57 lbs. *Mailable.* . . . . .Cash **$44.50**

[A][B][C] Tools for Speed Hoe [2] and Cultivator [3]. *Mailable.*
(A) Single Turn Plow. Right-hand, landslide bolt.
89 FB 1783—Plows 4 in. wide and deep. Wt. 3 lbs. . . . . .Each **$2.39**
(B) 6-in. Weeding Hoes. Staggered to clear trash, etc. With bolts.
89 FB 1786—Ship. wt. 2 lbs. . . . . .Pair **$2.39**
(C) Cultivator Duckfeet. 6 in. long. For roots, etc. With bolts.
89 FB 1785—Ship. wt. 8 oz. . . . . .Each **75c**

24-Inch High Wheel Cultivator

• Time-Proven, Efficient Tool for Row-Crop Gardening

[4] Cultivates Rapidly, Efficiently Between Rows. 24-in. wheel runs smoothly and easily. Over-the-axle drive lessens handle load—no wheel wobble. Hardwood handles. Includes 5-tooth weeder, turning hill plow, reversible shovel and wrench. *Mailable.*
89 FB 1771YO—Shipping weight 22 lbs. **$9.39**

Tools for Standard High Wheel Cultivators. Important: These tools fit only cultivators with a slotted foot.
[D] Reversible Shovel. Cuts 2- or 3-in. furrows.
89 FB 1777—Ship. wt. 1 lb. . . . . .Each **65c**
[E] Weeder-Scuffer. Reversible 4-tooth end; 8-in. wide blade cuts roots, forms mulch.
89 FB 1778—Ship. wt. 2 lbs. . . . . .Each **$1.69**
[F] Turn Plow. Hills and furrows. Plows 4 in. deep.
89 FB 1780—Ship. wt. 1 lb. 8 oz. . . . . .Each **69c**
[G] 8-in. Sweep. Triangular blade cultivates, hills, weeds.
89 FB 1776—Ship. wt. 1 lb. 4 oz. . . . . .Each **75c**
[H] Disc Hoe. Two 3 blade gangs. 4½-in. wide. 5½ in. diameter disc blades. Adjustable.
89 FB 1775—Ship. wt. 8 lbs. . . . . .Set **$5.89**
5-tooth Weeder. (Not Shown). Cuts roots 6 in. wide.
89 FB 1779—Ship. wt. 3 lbs. **$2.49**

Just Phone Your Order

Only **$9.39**

Ideal for Nurseries and Vegetable Gardens

Just Say "Charge It"
NO MONEY DOWN
See Page 101

7.79 [5] [6] 3.89 [7] 4.59

[5] Corn Planter. Double steel hoppers for seed, fertilizer. Divided steel jaws prevent fertilizer from contacting seed. Convenient adjustable drop. Sturdy hardwood frame. *Mailable.*
89 FB 2271M—Ship. wt. 7 lbs. 8 oz. **$7.79**
Single Hopper Corn Planter (Not shown). Like [5] above but with steel hopper for seed only—not to be used for fertilizer.
89 FB 2273M—Ship. wt. 6 lbs. *Mailable.* **$5.98**
[6] Potato Planter. Steel jaws, hardwood hdle. For home, trk. garden.
89 FB 2272M—Ship. wt. 3 lbs. 8 oz. **$3.89**
[7] Canvas Bag Seeder. Broadcasts grass seed 10 to 18 ft.; small grains 18 to 25 ft.—lever controls rate. Side crank; adj. strap.
89 FB 2274—Ship. wt. 4 lbs. 8 oz. *Mail.* About ½-bu. cap. **$4.59**

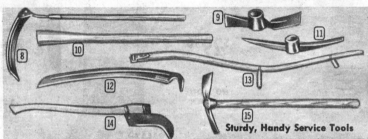

Sturdy, Handy Service Tools

[8] Long Handle Grass Hook. 11-inch high carbon steel blade with extra long, easy-to-work with 44-inch handle.
89 FB 812M—Ship. wt. 2 lbs. 8 oz. **$1.75**
[9] Mattock Blade. 3½-in. hoe blade and 2¾-in. cutter blade. Forged steel construction for long life. Use handle [10].
89 FB 1917M—Ship. wt. 5 lbs. **$3.29**
[10] Pick or Mattock Handle. Made from extra strong hickory wood.
84 FB 7095M—36 in. Ship. wt. 2 lbs. **79c**
[11] Railroad Pick. Heat treated, forged steel. Approx. 24 inches long. Ship. wt. 6 lbs.
89 FB 1916M—Use with Handle [10]. .**$3.15**

[12] Scythe Blades. Forged steel. Tempered—fit on handle [13]. Ship. wt. 3 lbs.
89 FB 1900M—Grass. Approx. 30 in. **$3.98**
89 FB 1904M—Weed. Approx. 26 in. 3.98
89 FB 1905—Bush. Approx. 20 in. 3.98
[13] Snaths. Ash. About 55 in. Fits Scythes [12].
89 FB 1907M—For Grass. Wt. 4 lbs. .**$3.29**
89 FB 1909M—Weed and Bush. Wt. 5 lbs. 3.59
[14] Bush Hook. Blade approx. 3¾x13 in.
89 FB 1910M—Ship. wt. 5 lbs. **$4.49**
[15] Cutter—Mattock. 3½-in., 1¾-in. forged blades. 54-in. fire-hardened wood handle.
89 FB 1914M—Ship. wt. 3 lbs. 3 oz. **$3.29**

7.59 3.59 [17] 3.69 [18] 3.98 [19] [16]

Farm Forks for Every Need . . . Low as $3.59

[16] Ensilage Fork. Finest quality 1-piece forged head with ten 16-in. tines. 15½ inches wide at points. 30-inch Ash handle with steel "D" grip. *Mailable.*
89 FB 1922MO—Ship. wt. 6 lbs. **$7.59**
[17] Hay Fork. Three 12-inch forged oval tines. 4-ft. select Ash handle. Sturdy—made to last. *Mailable.*
89 FB 1920MO—Ship. wt. 3 lbs. **$3.59**
[18] [19] Manure Forks. Finest quality. Strong 12¼-in. forged tines. 10 in. wide at points. 4-ft. selected Ash handle with steel ferrule. Choose either 4 or 5-tine fork. *Mailable.*
(18) 89 FB 1921MO—With 4 Tines. Ship. wt. 4 lbs. **3.69**
(19) 89 FB 1923MO—With 5 Tines. Ship. wt. 4 lbs. **3.98**

For Added Convenience Just Phone Your Order Or Visit Your Nearest Ward Catalog Store. Remember Too, No Money Down on Any of Your Purchases . . . See Page 101

4.85 [20] 4.85 [21] 3.49 [22] 1.61 [23] 4.39 [24] No. 10 Size 4.89 [25]

No. 12 Size 6.19

[26]

Husky and Durable Spades, Shovels and Scoops . . . Low as $1.61

• Solid Steel Shanks for Maximum Reinforcement Where a Shovel Needs It Most

[20] Post Hole Spade. 6¼x16-in. blade. 27-in. "D" grip handle. *Mailable.*
89 FB 1870M—Ship. wt. 5 lbs. 8 oz.**$4.85**
[21] Drain Spade. 4¼x16-in. forged tapered blade. 27-in. Ash "D" handle.
89 FB 1869M—Wt. 5 lbs. *Mail.* . . .**$4.85**
[22] Round Point Dirt Shovel. 8⅞x11½-in. forged blade. 47-in. straight handle.
89 FB 1831MO—Wt. 4 lbs. *Mail.* . .**$3.49**
[23] Good Quality General Purpose Shovel. Stamped steel blade. 46½-in. hardwood handle. 11½x13¾-in. blade.
89 FB 1832MO—Wt. 5 lbs. *Mail.* . .**$1.61**

[24] Dairy Barn Scoop. Deep bowl design. 10¼x15¼-in. blade. 44½-in. handle.
89 FB 1847MO—Wt. 5 lbs. 8 oz. *Mail.***$4.39**
[25] [26] Grain Scoops. "D" grip. Approx. blade sizes: No. 10—14x17½ in.; No. 12—14½x18½ in.; No. 14—15x19 in.
(25) Sturdy Steel. Steel blade. 27-in. ash handle. Ship. wt. 6 lbs. *Mailable.*
89 FB 1849MO—No. 10 Size. . . .**$4.89**
(26) Lightweight Aluminum. 27-in. handle. Ship. wts. 4 lbs. 8 oz.; 5 lbs. *Mail.*
89 FB 1852MO—Size 12. . . .**$6.19**
89 FB 1854MO—Size 14. . . . .6.59

CBAKS **WARDS 79**

GET MORE, DO MORE, SAVE MONEY WITH WARDS

Direct-Drive Roller Nose Saws

$159.50 8-HP*
NO MONEY DOWN

"Industry Rating"

Pressure-Type Oiler and Throttle Controls Grouped for Easy Operation

Extra-Heavy-Steel Tanks Located for Easy Filling

Button to Hold Saw at Fast Idle for Easier Starting

Handle for Perfect Balance... Minimizes Sawing or Poring

Convenient ON-OFF Switch

Large Positive Re-Wind Starter

Large Air-Intake Filter for Better Engine Performance

Heavy Step Plate, Wrap Around Handle Protects Carburetor, Air Filter

Power Products Double Diaphragm Carburetor for All-Position Cutting—Even Upside Down

Roller Nose Bar and Chain Cut 20% Faster

Included to Service Roller-Nose Tip
Handy Grease Gun

Buy Big Power 8-HP* Model WD-95 for Top Production

Compare These Prices!

$159.50 18-IN. SAW

$164.50 21-IN. SAW

$169.50 24-IN. SAW

No Money Down

- Cut 20% Faster! Roller saws make the difference—reduced friction and increase speed, automatic lubrication assures smoother chain operation with less operator fatigue.

(A) CutFaster, Better! A real powerhouse—gives you terrific output. A saw to handle heavy production cutting, yet for greater output. A saw to handle heavy production cutting, yet priced low enough for the budget-minded non-professional who wants top speed for quick, efficient cutting. Roller-nose bar and chain enables you for faster, smoother, uninterrupted cutting. Built to save wear and tear on chain, bar, sprockets. Long wear 7/16-in. pitch chain cleans sawdust to prevent binding and handling up.

High-efficiency 8-HP*, 8.1-cu. in. engine delivers top power in the cut. Direct-drive design gives maximum delivery of power for fast cut, long chain life and heavy-duty performance needed for top production and pulp cutting. Cuts close to ground—makes quick work of ground level stumps. Wear-resistant cast-iron cylinder liner retards lubrication for longer engine life, reduces maintenance costs for greater yearly savings. Triple Spike Bar anchors saw into tree bank so you can apply leverage for easier, faster cutting.

Ball and Needle Bearing Power Unit gives shaft extra "shock-load" support for smoother performance. Power Products Double Diaphragm Carburetor—one forces fuel feed, the other meters fuel to meet specific load requirements. Cuts in any position.

Cuts only when you squeeze throttle trigger. Automatic trigger release throttle and chain stops. Fast-idle hold button opens throttle to give engine more gas for quick, easy start. Heavy spring-ground chain keeps engine running slow when starting. Anti-spark fire controlled muffler minimizes noise.

Large Enclosed-Type Air Cleaner located up out of the way to keep dirt and rain out of engine. Polyurethane filter won't mat or tear, won't clog due to moisture, or puncture like paper filters. Easier to clean too, just wash out in gasoline or kerosene, squeeze edge out reinsert in position. Large air passage with plastic catches more dirt while letting more air through to engine. Blower housing designed for smoother air flow over engine to increase engine cooling needed with higher power delivery.

Deluxe Fuel and Oil Tanks with special loss-proof chained, plastic caps. Spark plug with protective rubber cap. Shipped by Freight, Truck or Express. Actual wt.: 29, 30, 31 lbs. No Money Down.

89 FB 24250R—18 in. Saw. Ship. wt. 33 lbs...........Cash $159.50
89 FB 24251 R—21 in. Saw. Ship. wt. 34 lbs...........Cash 164.50
99 FB 24252 R—24 in. Saw. Ship. wt. 35 lbs...........Cash 169.50

GUARANTEE: Wards Chain Saws are Guaranteed to be free from defects in materials and workmanship for 30 days from date of purchase, and will be repaired or replaced if returned within that period.

6-HP* Model WD-76

FOR AMPLE POWER, POPULAR PRICE

$144.50 18-IN. SAW

$149.50 21-IN. SAW

No Money Down

"Industry Rating"

NO MONEY DOWN

Handy Grease Gun Included to Keep Roller Nose Tip in Peak Operating Condition.

- Roller Nose Bar Tip cuts friction drag to a minimum—enables engine to deliver up to 20% more usable HP to chain.
- Cast-iron Cylinder Liner resists wear—means longer engine life

(B) Economical, Full 6-HP* Chain Saw with 5.8-cu. in. engine; "super performance"—roller-nose bar and chain. Roller nose supports cutting chain at point of greatest friction... increases cutting speed, saves wear and tear on chain and bar. Has the direct-drive heavy-duty efficiency of higher-priced WD-95 plus all the muscle-power that the average farmer, woodsman, resort—anyone who appreciates inexpensive power and dependable, trouble-free performance—wants and needs. Popular 7/16-in. pitch chain. Triple Spike Bar grips tree bank for better cutting balance.

Power Products Ball and Needle Bearing Engine—power is applied directly to chain to burn through more timber with greater speed. 1-piston rod; double diaphragm carburetor meters fuel and air to engine for sure starting, smooth running, cutting in any position. Automatic clutch prevents stalling. Just squeeze throttle trigger and cutting begins, release and chain stops. Large enclosed-type air intake filter has washable polyurethane filter—keeps more dirt out of engine for better performances.

Pressure-Type Oiler for easy chain lubrication. Thumb-plunger located on handle to instantly lubricate chain and bar whenever needed. Fast-idle hold button opens throttle to give engine more gas for sure starting. Anti-spark muffler. Large steel fuel and oil tanks. Convenient ON-OFF switch. Shipped by Freight, Truck or Express. Buy with No Money Down. See Guarantee above.

89 FB 24253 R—18 in. Actual wt. 26 lbs. Ship. wt. 29 lbs. ....Cash $144.50
89 FB 24254 R—21 in. Actual wt. 27 lbs. Ship. wt. 30 lbs. ....Cash 149.50

NO MONEY DOWN ON EASY TERMS
SEE DETAILS ON PAGE 101

See New "Low Profile" Gear Drive Chain Saw in Full Color on Back Cover

The modern look in Chain Saws. New laid-down design provides easier handling, better balance—really performs with greater lugging power at slower chain speeds. A combination hard to beat for heavy-duty cutting!

4-HP*, 16-In. Direct-Drive Economy Model WD-40

$106.50
NO MONEY DOWN

Dependable Cutting Power, Rock Bottom Price

USE A LIGHTWEIGHT ALL-PURPOSE CHAIN SAW

(C) A Full 4-HP*...does the greatest cutting power for the money, to the best of our knowledge. Plenty of power for the occasional user who wants ease of operation in cutting firewood, tree surgery, etc. Economical for farm use and farm budget, tool

Hard-nose guide bar withstands heavy cutting. Drop-forged steel crank shaft and connecting rod. Ball and needle bearings on power unit. Single-diaphragm carburetor assures adequate fuel supply for all normal cutting. Power is applied directly to chain. Pressure type oiler keeps chain properly lubricated. On-and-Off switch. Captive-mount handle permits better cutting balance—relieves operator fatigue. Triple Spike Bar.

Sturdy 4-HP*, 4.7-cu. in. 2-cycle air cooled engine. Single-diaphragm carburetor with vertically positioned. Fumble-free fast idle hold button for easier starting. Automatic clutch. Shipped by Freight, Truck or Express.

89 FB 24077 M—Actual wt. 12 lbs. Ship. wt. 14 lbs. Available......Cash $106.50

Guaranteed
See Opposite Page

Handy 10-In. Electric Chain Saw

$58.95
NO MONEY DOWN

Lightweight, Compact for Easy Handling

GET MORE CAPACITY, MORE POWER FOR LESS

- So Easy to Tote Anywhere—Weighs Only 12 Lbs. Complete.

(D) An efficient, convenient, low cost chain saw to do pruning work, trim bushes, small trees, cut cordwood, make boxing cuts into walls, joists, heavy beams, etc. with less effort than ever before! 10-in. long guide bar and chain handles volume of heavy cutting. Ruggedly built to industrial standards, yet can also do scores of jobs for the home craftsman. Well balanced.

Powerful 110.0 amp. universal motor, operates on 110-120 volt, 60-cycle AC-DC. Develops 3-HP. 6-ft. rubber-covered cord. 3-prong plug, adapter plug. Positive chain adjustment—no slack for smooth, efficient operation. Safety clutch prevents "kicking", reduces chance of motor burnout. UL Listed.

89 FB 24078 —Ship. wt. 1 lb. 6 oz. ....Cash $58.95

Replacement Chain for 10-in. Saw above.
89 FB 24078 —16in. Actual wt. 28 lbs. No Money Down..Cash $106.50...............$10.50

WARDS POWR-KRAFT
FAST ACTION SAWS

- Heat Tempered Steel—Designed For Rugged Use...Quick Cuts

1-2 **POWR-KRAFT Perforated-Lance-Tooth Saws.** Blades tapered from tooth edges to back, from both ends to center. Won't bind. 4 perforated teeth and 1 raker per section; hand-filed and set; deep gullets. Electric furnace steel, heat-treated and tempered. With set of handles. *Mailable.*

(1) 1-Man Saw. 16 gauge at teeth. *State size.*
84 FB 7051M—3 Feet. Ship. wt. 5 lbs........$8.95
84 FB 7051MO—4 Feet. Ship. wt. 7 lbs. 4 oz...10.99
(2) 2-Man Saw. 14 gauge at teeth. Tapers to 16 gauge to 20 gauge at back. *State size.*
84 FB 7060 MO—5 Feet. Ship. wt. 5 lbs.....$11.99
6 Feet. Ship. wt. 7 lbs......13.99

Flat Ground 2-Man Saw. 14 gauge. 3½-inch ends. 5¾-inch center. Wide pattern teeth. Shipping weights 5¾ and 7 lbs. *State size.*
84 FB 7057 MO—5-Foot Length............$10.99*
6-Foot Length............11.99

3 **Champion-Tooth One-Man Saws.** Economy, good quality model. Flat ground 14-gauge blade. Teeth filed, set by hand. Seasoned hardwood handles. Standard and auxiliary grip for two-hand control. Ship. wts. 4¼ and 7 lbs. *State length.*
84 FB 7052 MO—3-Foot Length............$6.50
4-Foot Length............8.99

4 to 7 **Hickory Saw Handles.** Extra strong, holds fast under rugged sawing jobs. (4) has wire loop clamp; (5) has wing nut; (6) has steel clamps; and (7) is main handle.

Catalog Number	For	Length Inches	Weight Lbs.	Price
(4) 84 FB 7069	2 man	9⅜	2¼	Pr. $2.95
(5) 84 FB 7070	2 man	13¼	2½	Pr. 2.55
(6) 84 FB 7072	1 man	6½	½	Ea. 69c
(7) 84 FB 7073	1 man	....	3½	Ea. 99c

*On saws marked with an asterisk (*) allow 10 lbs. postage because of Postal Regulations.

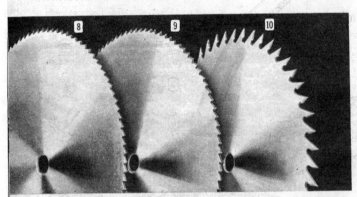

Cordwood, Rip and Crosscut Blades... Low as $11.95

8 **Cordwood Blades Are Tempered Steel,** hand filed and set for fast, clean cutting. Has polished finish. Standard 1⅜-in. holes. Bushings are furnished for smaller holes. For holes over 1⅜ inches to 1⅝ inches, send $1.00 extra, use Catalog Number 84 FB 6900F, shipped from Factory near Greenville, Miss. Pay from there. Holes over 1⅝ inches are not recommended for these blades. *Be sure to state the Catalog Number, Diameter, Hole Size, and Size Code Number.* Sizes 20 and 28 in. are Mail., others are Not Mail.

Saw Diam.	84 FB 6900 HB		84 FB 6900 R	
	20 in.	28 in.	30 in.	32 in.
Saw Code	20	28	30	32
Gauge Steel	13	10	10	10
RPM	1285	1285	1200	1200
Ship. wt.	12 lbs.	25 lbs.	28 lbs.	32 lbs.
Price Ea.	$11.95	$19.95	$21.95	$25.50

9-10 **POWR-KRAFT Master Quality Flat Ground Saw Blades.** Special analysis chrome-nickel alloy saw steel, heat-treated and tempered for longer teeth life. Precision tempered, filed and spring-set by hand. Polished finish—will not bind. Bore size 1, 1⅛ inches. 14 gauge. Shipping weights 4 and 5 lbs. *State Catalog Number, Diameter, and Code Number.* Mailable.

Catalog Number	Type	Diam.	Code	Each	Diam.	Code	Each
(9) 84 FB 6954	Rip	14 in.	1	$8.99	16 in.	2	$11.99
(10) 84 FB 6951	Crosscut	14 in.	1	8.99	16 in.	2	11.99

Saw Swage and Log Rule

20 **Mill Saw Swage.** Convex die spreads and flat die squares cutting edges. For 6 to 10-gauge saws. Shipped from Factory near Kansas City, Missouri, pay postage from there.
84 FB 7086 K—Shipping weight 12 lbs......$10.99

21 **Doyle Scale Folding Log Rule.** Shows board feet in 10 to 18-foot logs; also inches to 16ths. White with black numerals. End hook.
84 FB 7079—4-ft. length. Ship. wt. 6 oz.......$1.69

$1.69

112 WARDS CBASKDF2

BOW SAWS
$4.39 BIG 42 In.
Low as $2.74

11 **Big 42-in. Swedish-Type Bow Saw.** Tempered steel blade. Wing nut adjusting feature assures tight tension on blade. With fine cutting edge.
84 FB 7030 MO—With blade. Shipping weight 5 lbs......................$4.39
84 FB 7031M—Extra 42-in. blade for saw (11). Ship. wt. 1 lb. 8 oz........1.29

12 **Swedish-Type Bow Saw.** Teeth hand-filed and hand set. 4 cutting teeth to a section. Ship. wts. 2½ and 3 lbs. *State length. Mailable.*
84 FB 7026 MO—30 inches...............$2.74 *36 inches.........$3.15
84 FB 7027 M—Extra Blades for (12). *State length desired.*
30 inches. Ship. wt. 1 lb.........93c 36 inches. Ship. wt. 1 lb. 8 oz...$1.15

POWR-KRAFT Axes $6.35

13-14 **POWR-KRAFT Michigan Pattern Beveled Axes.** Bits are ground to correct bevel. Honed to keen lasting edge. 36-inch smooth Hickory handle is machine-driven into tapered head. *State size and size code no.*

(13) 84 FB 7118 M—Double Bit Axe. Ship. wt. 7 lbs. 3½ Lb. Head. (Code 7). $6.35 4-Lb. Head. (Code 8). $6.35
(14) 84 FB 7106 M—Single Bit Axe. Ship. wt. 7 lbs. 3½-lb. Head. (Code 7). $6.35 4-Lb. Head. (Code 8). $6.35

Make Logging Work Easier... Low as $1.98

15 **Peavy or Cant Hook Handles.** Made of top grade hickory. 2¼-in. diameter. 3½ feet long. *Mailable.*
84 FB 7090 M—Peavy Handle. Ship. wt. 3 lbs.....$3.16
84 FB 7091M—Cant Handle. Ship. wt. 3 lbs......3.16

16 **Dependable Socket-Type Peavy.** Easily withstands the rugged, everyday stresses of logging use. High carbon tool steel pick and hook. 3½-ft. hickory handle.
84 FB 7084 M—Shipping weight 10 lbs. Mailable. $10.22

17 **Cant Hook.** Dependable duty, takes the rugged treatment of logging use. Forged steel. 3½-ft. hickory handle.
84 FB 7083 M—Shipping weight 8 lbs. Mailable...$8.89

18 **8-Pound Splitting Maul.** Hardened bit. 32-in. handle.
84 FB 7082 M—Shipping weight 10 lbs..........$8.50

19 **Square Head Forged Wedge.** Hardened bit is heat-treated high carbon tool steel. Shipping weights 4 and 5 lbs. *State 4 or 5-lb. head.*
84 FB 7088 M—4-LB. Head....................$1.98
5-LB. Head....................2.29

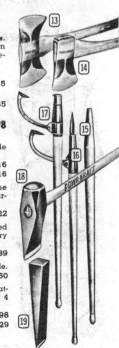

Protect Your Farm and Family
FIRE FIGHTER

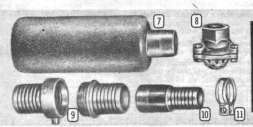

$7⁹⁵

$14⁹⁵

$37⁹⁵

Wards Hand Pumps
Serve You Efficiently . . . Economically

Proven in 1000's of fire-fighting applications protecting home, barns, livestock. Excellent for stand-by or direct use. Powerful performance—capacities up to 112 GPM at 60 lbs. pressure. Lightweight cast-aluminum body assures lasting service. Self-priming—built-in exhaust primer for quick priming.

(1) Finest Quality 9-HP Briggs and Stratton Engine . . . air cooled. Enclosed bronze impeller. Single-stage, centrifugal pump close coupled to engine. Check valve gives air-tight seal under adverse conditions. 2-in. suction and discharge tap. Rope-starter. Suction strainer and carrying handles. Cap. 6 qts. Ship. wt. 170 lbs.

Catalog Number	Performance at 10-Ft. Lift (pressure as stated).						Price
	20 lbs.	40 lbs.	60 lbs.	80 lbs.	100 lbs.	120 lbs.	
81 FB 3824F	146 GPM	135 GPM	112 GPM	88 GPM	55 GPM	30 GPM	$298.50

Hose and Fittings for Pump (1). 15 feet of 2-in. suction hose; 50 feet of 1½-in. cotton-jacketed discharge hose. Brass nozzle 12 in. long. 1½-in. female thread (National Fire Hose Thread), ½-in. orifice. Suction and discharge adapters. Order extra lengths of discharge hose below, if needed.
81 FB 3898 F—Ship. wt. 95 lbs. $99.00

Extra Lengths of 1½-in. Discharge Hose. 50-ft. lengths. Couplings included.
81 FB 3899 F—Ship. wt. 52 lbs. Per 50-ft. Length $42.95

"F" after Catalog Number means shipped from Mansfield, Ohio Factory; pay frt. from there. "R" means Shipped from Stock by Freight, Truck or Express.

(2)(3) **Lift Pumps** to 22 ft. Rugged cast-iron construction. Tapped for 1¼-in. suction pipe . . . order below. With 3-in. diameter cylinder.
(2) 81 FB 3807 M—Force Pump. ¾-in. discharge. Ship. wt. 21 lbs. $14.95
(3) Utility Pump. Sanitary swivel cap. Convenient pail hook.
81 FB 3805 M—Height 13 in. Ship. wt. 14 lbs. $7.95

(4) **Horizontal Force Pump** for small pneumatic or gravity tank systems. Rugged cast iron—painted. Moves 385 GPH at 1000 lbs. pressure. Forces water 230 ft. Large air chamber . . . delivers water on push or pull. 22-ft. lift. Tapped for 1¼-in. suction pipe . . . order below. 1-in. discharge.
81 FB 3821R—For cylinder, see General Catalog. Ship. wt. 65 lbs. $37.95

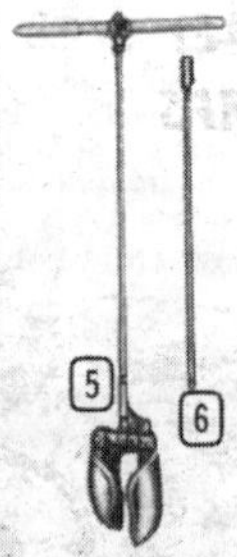

Well and Post Hole Borer $10⁹⁵

(5) **Sturdy Carbon Steel Blades.** Digs holes 7 to 14-in. diameter. Selected hardwood handle. 48 in. long. Bores to 30 ft. with borer extensions (6) below.
81 FB 3922 MO—Ship. wt. 16 lbs. $10.95

(6) **Steel Borer Extension** for (5). Length 49 in.
81 FB 3923 M—Bolts included. Ship. wt. 5 lbs. . . . . . . Each $1.79

JUST "CHARGE IT"
Take Up to 7 Years to Pay
See Page 101 for Details

WATER FILTER COUPLINGS AND HOSES

(7) **Water Filter.** Porous ceramic screw onto end of supply pipe. 1¼-in. pipe with male thread. Ship. wt. 6 lbs.
81 FB 3984—Diameter 3¼ in. Length 12 in $10.85

(8) **Combination Foot Valve and Strainer.** Cast iron. Aids in priming, maintaining of prime. For ½-in. pipe, order ¾-in. foot valve and reduce to ½ in. with bushing.
81 FB 3916—State Size and Size Code.

For Pipe Size, in.	¾	1	1¼	1½	2	2½
Size Code	30	40	50	60	70	80
Wt., lbs.	1¾	1½	2¼	3	5¼	7½
Price	$2.30	$2.45	$2.80	$3.40	$4.95	$6.95

(9) **Shank Type Coupler.** Cast iron. Bronze swivel ring locks coupler. Grooved hose end shanks for tight fit.
81 FB 3978—State Hose Size and Size Code.

For Hose Size, in.	1½	2	2½
Size Code	60	70	80
Ship. wt.	1 lb.	2 lbs.	2½ lbs.
Price, Each	$2.69	$3.65	$5.95

(10) **Combination Nipple** of galvanized steel for easier coupling of hose to regular fittings. Grooved hose end of shank gives tight seal into hose. State Size and Size Code.

Catalog Number	Pipe Size	Size Code	Fits Hose Inside Diam.	Ship. wt.	Each
81 FB 5113	1½ in.	60	1½ in.	1¼ lb.	60c
	2 in.	70	2 in.	3 lbs.	80c
	2½ in.	80	2½ in.	3½ lbs.	$1.98

(11) **Steel Clamps.** Use with couplers and hose at right.
81 FB 3981—State Hose Size and Size Code.

For Hose Size, I.D.	Size Code	Ship. Wt.	Price, Pair
1 in.	40	2 oz.	19c
1¼ in.	50	4 oz.	35c
1½ in.	60	5 oz.	49c
2 in.	70	10 oz.	59c
2½ in.	80	12 oz.	69c
3 in.	90	14 oz.	$1.35

(12) **Finest Quality Suction and Discharge Hose.** Synthetic rubber molded and braided to withstand maximum abuses. For all general purpose uses—hot or cold water, mild chemicals, air service. Lightweight and flexible for easy handling. Smooth bore. In lengths up to 50 ft. Order Coupler (9) and clamps (11) at left.
81 FB 3975 ½—State Length, Diam., Size Code.

Inside Diam.	Size Code	Wt.	Per Ft.
1 in.	40	9 oz.	98c
1¼ in.	50	11 oz.	$1.19

Standard Quality Suction and Discharge Hose. Braided rayon with wire reinforcement. Strong yet lightweight, flexible, easy to handle. Serves all general purpose uses. Smooth bore. Order Coupler (9) and Clamps (11) at left.
81 FB 3976H—State Length, Diameter, Size Code.

I.D. size	Code	Type	Per Ft.	Per Ft.
1 in.	40	Rubber	8 oz.	69c
1¼ in.	50	Heavy Rubber Reinforced	11 oz.	$1.25

(13) **Spring Steel-Lined Suction Hose.** Strong and durable . . . ideal for jobs where semi-gritty fluids are pumped. Synthetic rubber cover reinforced with cotton . . . galvanized flat metal spirally wound. Rough bore 1½-in. I.D. Ends enlarged to fit standard 1½-in. pipe. Order Coupler (2) and clamps (11) at left.
81 FB 3986 MO—State Length.

10 Ft.—Ship. wt. 11 lbs. $17.50
15 Ft.—Ship. wt. 17 lbs. 26.50
20 Ft.—Ship. wt. 22 lbs. 34.50
25 Ft.—Ship. wt. 28 lbs. 43.50

(14) **Wire-Reinforced Suction Hose.** Interwoven wire resists collapse. Rubber coated inside and out for added protection. Smooth bore. Lengths to 60 ft. Order Coupler (9) and Clamps (11) at left.
81 FB 3987 H—State Length, Diameter, Size Code.

Inside Diam.	Size Code	Wt. per Ft.	Price per Ft.
1½ in.	60	1 lb.	$1.69
2 in.	70	1½ lbs.	2.19
2½ in.	80	2 lbs.	2.70

(15) **Rugged Discharge Hose.** Built to take rough handling and use. 200-lbs. test pressure. Cotton jacket gives extra protection. Lengths to 50 ft. Order Coupler (9) and Clamps (11) at left.
81 FB 3977 M—State Length, Diam., Size Code.

I.D. Size	Code	Wt. per Ft.	Price per Ft.
1½ in.	60	1 lb.	79c
2 in.	70	1½ lbs.	$1.19

(16)(17) **High Volume, Multipurpose, ¾-in. Hose.** Delivers maximum volume of water under low pressure. Rubber or plastic. Garden hose fittings. State Length.

(16) **Two-Layer Heavy-Wall Green Plastic Hose.**
89 FB 514 M—50-ft. length. Ship. wt. 14 lbs. $6.49
Two 50-ft. lgths. Ship. wt. 28 lbs. 11.98

(17) **Five-Layer Heavy-Duty Black Rubber Hose.**
89 FB 560 M— 50-ft. length. Ship. wt. 16 lbs. $13.29
100-ft. length. Ship. wt. 38 lbs. 22.95

For more of the Best in Farm Equipment, see Wards General Catalog. Complete selections of Septic Tanks . . . Water Systems . . . Water Softeners . . . Pipe and Drainage Systems.

Phone Your Order . . .
Easiest Way to Shop

NO MONEY DOWN . . .
Open an Account at Wards Catalog Store

122 WARDS CBASKDF

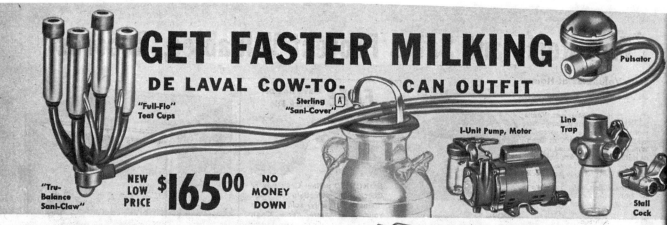

GET FASTER MILKING

DE LAVAL COW-TO-CAN OUTFIT

"Full-Flo" Teat Cups

Sterling "Sani-Cover" [A]

Pulsator

I-Unit Pump, Motor

Line Trap

Stall Cock

"Tru-Balance Sani-Claw"

NEW LOW PRICE $165.00 NO MONEY DOWN

- Milk Up To Twice As Many Cows in the Same Time with No Increase in Labor
- Easily Adapts to Any Barn Layout, Choose the Milker Operation You Want

Get Much Higher Milk Production, Bigger Profits with De Laval Cow-To-Can Milking. Cow-To-Can means fast, pleasant milking that gives maximum labor savings. For your present barn, it gives all benefits of mechanized milking without extensive alterations. For a new milk shed, it gives modern milking at lowest construction cost. Be sure to order De Laval Uni-filter with your outfit, for complete, modern, easy milk filtering. No milk pails needed, because milk flows from the cow to your 40-qt. cans. Simply transfer sani-cover to another can as can is filled.

[A] **Outfit with One Milker Unit.** Includes: FULL FLO TEAT CUPS—exclusive DE LAVAL cup with 1-piece tapered narrow bore neoprene liners. Automatically takes correct position on teat. Fits all size teats; TRU-BALANCE SANI-CLAW—perfect distribution, correct spacing of teat cups on udders of all sizes. 1-piece stainless steel. Brushes straight through for easier cleaning; STERLING OPERATING COVER—baffle keeps vacuum line milk-free. 1-piece stainless steel; STERLING PULSATOR—efficient, dependable, with only 2 moving parts. Never needs oiling. Pneumatically controlled. Plugs into stall cock, away from cow hair, etc.; DE LAVAL ¼-HP MOTOR AND VACUUM PUMP—engineered to give peak performance when needed. Provides large capacity, requires minimum maintenance. Starts easily; STERLING STALL COCK—automatic, designed for low cost installation, maximum efficiency; COMBINATION TRAP, VACUUM CONTROLLER—non-adjustable, maintains 12 to 13-in. vacuum. Outfit also includes rubber tube and plug for vacuum line. See "Ship. Note" at right.
89 FB 20042 F—Ship. wt. 63 lbs. No Money Down... Was $172.50; Now, Cash **$165.00**

Extra Cow-To-Can Milker Unit. With teat cup assembly, operating cover, pulsator.
89 FB 20044 K—Ship. wt. 15 lbs. No Money Down. .... Was $96.50; Now, Cash **$89.50**

Outfit with Two Milker Units. (See view at right.) Offers all the advantages of the more expensive milking systems, yet easily adaptable to your present setup. Outfit includes: Two TRU-BALANCE SANI-CLAW assemblies with FULL FLO TEAT CUPS, Two STERLING OPERATING COVERS, Two STERLING PULSATORS, Two STALL COCKS, ONE COMBINATION TRAP AND CONTROLLER A DE LAVAL ½-HP MOTOR AND PUMP (same as (C), right), and ONE RUBBER PLUG for vacuum line. See "Shipping Note", right.
89 FB 20043 F—Ship. wt. 107 lbs. No Money Down... Was $308.00; Now, Cash **$293.00**

Easy-to-Use DE LAVAL Uni-Filter $14.00

[B] Here's the really convenient way to filter milk. Simply install in milk line between teat cup assembly and operating cover. Preparing complicated filters is entirely eliminated with this modern up-to-date method. Saves lifting and pouring time without exposing milk to barn dirt and odors.
89 FB 20045 K—Ship. wt. 2 lbs. (Order Filter Tubes from Page 155) ...$14.00

DE LAVAL ½ OR ¼-HP MOTOR WITH PUMP

Make up your own outfits or replace worn pumps.

$150.00 2-Unit Pump, Motor

$85.50 1-Unit Pump, Motor

[C] De Laval ½-HP Motor and Pump for two milkers. Extra powerful, long lasting, engineered to provide large capacity and require minimum maintenance. *Not Mailable.* No Money Down, 89 FB 20047 R—Wt. 57 lbs. Cash **$150.00**

De Laval ¼-HP Motor and Pump to handle one milker, (pictured with (A) above). No Money Down.
89 FB 20046 MB—Wt. 38 lbs. Cash **$85.50**

Using Two Milker Units

IMPORTANT SHIPPING NOTE

De Laval Cow-to-Can Outfits and Uni-Filter shipped from Factory in Chicago, Ill. or Poughkeepsie, N.Y. You pay Freight charges from nearer. Pump-Motors above shipped from Stock.

LARGE VACUUM PUMPS TO SPEED MILKING TIME

Choose the Proper Size Pump to Assure Maximum Efficiency of Your Milking System

- The completely functional features incorporated in these pumping outfits assure you of sufficient vacuum reserve at all times to do a thorough job of milking.
- Get top vacuum per revolution with rotary vane pumps plus large vacuum tank.

[D] **Large Vacuum Tank with Belt Driven 1 or 1½-HP Pump.** Tank is hot dip galvanized inside and out for long, satisfactory service; 17-gal. capacity. Drain valve at bottom permits condensation to drain when pump is not in operation. Cleanout port with removable cover permits easy inspection and airing out.

Efficient Rotary Vane Pumps are precision products—vanes take up their own wear. Pumps are air cooled for efficient operation, longer life. Transparent oil reservoir automatically dispenses correct amount of oil to pump. Oil level is visible—check at a glance. Muffler reduces noise. Vacuum power assembly includes fan cooled pump, motor belt and pulley, piping from pump to vacuum tank, automatic vacuum controller, drain valve, motor insulator and vacuum gauge. Check valve between pump and tank keeps pump from running backward when switched off.

With 1½-HP Pump you can milk more cows faster or have reserve capacity for future expansion. For 110–120-volt or 220–240 volt, 60-cycle AC. Shipped from Factory near Springfield, Mass. You pay freight charges from there. Order your Dairy needs Today. No Money Down on Easy Terms—see Page 101 for further details.

$310.00 1 HP

NO MONEY DOWN

148 WARDS CBAKSDF

89 FB 20050 F—VACUUM TANK WITH 1-HP PUMP produces 11 cu. ft. air per minute—12-in. vacuum will handle 8 to 10 conventional units. Ship. wt. 170 lbs. Cash **$310.00**

89 FB 20051 F—VACUUM TANK WITH 1½-HP PUMP produces 16 ft. air per minute. 12-in. vacuum handles 10 to 14 conventional units. Ship. wt. 180 lbs. ..... Cash **$435.00**

RITE-WAY FLOOR MODEL PAIL-TYPE

Single Milking Unit

$139.50

NO MONEY DOWN

- Efficient Design, Quality Inflations
- Precision Built Pulsator—Smooth Action
- Gets Milk Without Hand Stripping
- Pulsator Control Regulates Speed

[E]

Speed Milking—Improve Quality

[E] Conventional Pail-Type Milker Unit of sanitary stainless steel, with scientific Rite-Way features that mean bigger yields—profits. Perfectly balanced pulsator has only 2 moving parts. Completely encased for smooth, uniform action. Calf-like action strokes—cow lets down milk naturally. 1-piece finest quality inflations; sanitary, well-balanced claw. Transparent milk tube shows flow—easy to keep clean. Precision built to do a thorough job in just 3 minutes without any hand stripping.

Unit includes stainless steel pail, pulsator, shells, tubing and all accessories. (Pump-Motor Units may be ordered separately, see numbers 89 FB 20047 R and 89 FB 20046 MB under item (C) above.) Shipped from Stock by Freight, Truck or Express. Ship. wt. 25 lbs. No Money Down on Wards convenient terms—see full details on Page 101.

99 FB 20030 R—Single Unit, 50-lb. capacity ..Cash **$139.50**

Bulk Milk Coolers
WITH 190, 250, 315 OR 420 GALLON TANKS

WALL-MOUNTED CONTROL PANEL

Sealed box you can mount in any convenient place—out of washing zone.

HEAVY DUTY CONDENSING UNITS

Electrically driven . . . attach to tank or use remotely . . . for specific needs.

A $1495.00 With 190-Gal. Tank

$1675.00 With 250-Gal. Tank

Stainless Steel Throughout—Tops in Quality and Low Cost Operation—Sure Cooling

A **Built to Finest Quality Standards Throughout**—all sizes at exceptionally low money-saving prices. Choose the size that meets your special needs.

18-8 Stainless Steel used throughout entire construction—inside, outside, in-between. Inner and outer shells, evaporator plate, supporting cradle, bracing, all internal refrigerant lines and bracings are made of this rustproof, corrosion-proof metal to give long, dependable service. Meets cooling and sanitation requirements, and exceeds present 3 A standards.

Outlet Valve is Dairy and Creamery Type Plug. Durable metal-to-metal contact eliminates wear—insures against loss. You'll never be bothered again by conventional "O" ring problems.

5-Year Warranty on condensing unit motor compressors. All other parts have a 1-year warranty. For complete details, see below.

Factory Installed Refrigeration Controls. Include: Dryer and strainer, heat exchanger, solenoid valve sight glass, expansion valve thermostat, electrical connection block. Wall-mount control panel (see picture above).

Factory-Calibrated Tanks. All include handy, easy-to-read charts in pound readings—gallons or fractions are optional.

Compressors (Included) Are Sized for every-other-day pickup. They can be installed by your local refrigeration man.

All Combinations Will Maintain a Blend Temperature of 50° and will shut-off within the first hour after completion of milking at a temperature of 38°. Direct expansion cooling (not chilled water). Write Dept. 89, Buying Office, Chicago, Ill. 60607, for additional information and sizes. Shipped by Freight or Truck from Factory near Chicago. Pay charges from there. No Money Down, up to 7 years to pay. Check Farm Improvement Terms on Page 101.

Tank Size Gal.	Ship. Wt. Lbs.	Lgth. x Width in In.	Pour Ht. In.	Combination Units		
				Catalog Number	Compressor Size	Cash Price
190	840	63x45	32	89 FB 20621F	1 HP	$1495.00
250	1000	80x45	32	89 FB 20622F	1½ HP	1675.00
315	1080	90x45	34	89 FB 20623F	1½ HP	1795.00
420	1350	96x53	35½	89 FB 20624F	2 HP	2175.00

Low as $179.00

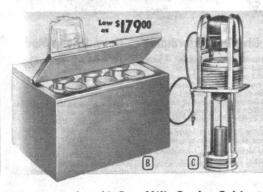

B C

Cool Milk Quickly—Economically

Quality Design—5 Year Warranty

5-Year Milk Cooler Warranty—Wards will replace or repair FREE any part of the hermetically sealed refrigeration unit that becomes inoperative due to faulty workmanship or material. 1-Year Warranty on all other parts.

Low Operating Cost. Cools milk quickly—saves electricity. Finest insulation of heat-resisting Fiberglas keeps cold in, heat out. Sold complete with agitator.

Outstanding Features. Thermostatic Refrigerant Control. Automatic—set at Factory to maintain correct water temperature. Manual Control also. Large drain pipe.

Scientific Design. Cools milk at the top first in the Cream Zone, where 90% of bacterial growth occurs.

Low at $398.00

D

6 to 10-Can Milk Cooler Cabinets

B **Replace Your Worn Out Cabinet** with one of Wards high quality Top Opening Milk Cooler Cabinets. 6, 8 or 10-can capacity. 2-in. heavy density Fiberglas insulation on all sides and bottom. 20-ga. galvanized steel inside lining, 22-ga. galvanized steel outside lining. 14-gauge scuff plate protects front of cabinet against can damage. 1-HP refrigeration unit listed separately below. Shipped from Factory near Medina, Ohio. You pay Freight charges from there.

Catalog No.	Size	Width	Height	Length	Ship. wt.	Cash Price
89 FB 20616 F	6 Can	41 in.	31 in.	60 in.	325 lbs.	$179.00
89 FB 20617 F	8 Can	41 in.	31 in.	78 in.	375 lbs.	198.00
89 FB 20618 F	10 Can	41 in.	31 in.	96 in.	425 lbs.	219.00

C **Drop-in Cooling Unit with Agitator.** Convert any cement tank or cabinet—insulated and of proper size—into milk cooler. 1-HP unit for dependable extra cooling capacity. 10-in. diameter fan cools finned-type condenser. Hermetically sealed compressor. Overload switch. One motor economically operates both fan and agitator. Use with 110-120 volt, 60-cycle AC system only. Cord and plug included. Shipped from Stock. No Money Down on Easy Terms.
89 FB 20579 R—1-HP Unit. Ship. wt. 148 lbs. . . . . Cash $289.50

6 to 12-Can Front Opening Coolers

D **Drop Milk Temperature from 90° to 47° in Less than 60 Minutes!** Easy-loading front opening ends needless exertion and back strain—just an 11-in. lift required. Efficient cooling system sprays 32° water over cans, assuring faster, cream line cooling. Hermetically sealed copper refrigerating coils controlled by copper tube and automatic ice bank thermostat. Heavy-duty, impeller-type GE pump in cabinet is controlled by time switch. Heavily galvanized interior has 3-in. Fiberglas insulation sealed in. Steel exterior in Green hammertone finish, chromed hardware. Doors completely water-tight—can be removed to save 2½-in. width when installing cooler. Slide-type spray troughs remove for cleaning. Cabinet drain threaded for standard ¾-in. garden hose. Motor operates on 110-120 V. (except 12-can size, 220 V.) 60 cycle, AC. "Ship. Note" below.

Catalog Number	Daily Capacity	Motor Size	Length Inches	Width Inches	Height Inches	Shipping Weight	Cash Price
89 FB 20640 F	6 cans	⅓ HP	55⅜	35½	43⅜	522 lbs.	$398.00
89 FB 20641 F	8 cans	½ HP	69½	35½	43⅜	600 lbs.	439.00
89 FB 20642 F	12 cans	¾ HP	100½	35½	43⅜	842 lbs.	595.00

Ship. Note: Coolers above shipped from Factory in St. Louis, Mo. You pay freight charges from there.

CBAKSDF WARDS 149

GET ALL THE CREAM

With De Laval's Super-Skimming Bowl

- Skims thoroughly for extra cream production, keep profits from flowing into skim milk. Cream going to livestock is cream you could be selling for extra dollars.
- Separates heavy cream with high fat content without danger of clogging. Gives smooth even textured cream with butterfat globules unbroken in best condition for churning.
- Simple finger-tip operated screw adjustment controls desired cream thickness.
- Super-Skimming Bowl is completely sanitary, easily cleaned to maintain hygienic conditions of milk and cream production.
- Modern Bowl Design permits long runs without reduced skimming efficiency.
- Discs are stainless steel in all-electric models, heavily tinned steel in hand model.
- Anti-splash, self-draining supply can is absolutely seamless for effortless cleaning.

Buy the Convenient Way—Wards No-Money Down Credit Terms make it so easy to obtain modern up-to-date equipment. See Page 101 for complete Credit Plan details.

Big Capacity
FOR THE LARGE HERD OWNER
$385.00
600-lb. Cap.

- Three convenient sizes—to handle 600 lbs., 800 lbs. or 1320 lbs. per hour.
- All parts contacting milk are heavy, highly polished rust-proof stainless steel.
- Special, thick, double-strength flanges allow discs to keep elasticity and shape for years of perfect skimming.
- Permanently lubricated bearings—never need oiling.

Efficient Production
AT A LOW PRICE
$80.00

NO MONEY DOWN

See Terms Page 101

De Laval All Electric Table Model Separators

250-lb. Cap. **$135.00** NO MONEY DOWN

- Economical skimming for the small herd owner.
- Bowl runs without vibration . . . seems to float.
- Discs are formed from rust-proof stainless steel.
- Self-aligning motor needs no coupling, clutch, belt.

[A] Low cost but high in quality and efficiency. No cream goes into the skim milk to be fed to pigs, chickens or young stock. Compact, streamlined, smooth-running unit—can be placed almost anywhere to operate.

Super-Skimming Bowl dynamically balanced to run true, no internal weights to get out of balance and necessitate frequent repair. Cushioned by rubber-mounted spindle bearings—no vibration, practically silent operation.

Flanged Stainless Steel Discs are precision made—the distribution holes, skimming surfaces and spacers are made exactingly to assure you of clean skimming. Supply can, bowl bottom, bowl hood and covers of finest Swedish carbon steel, heavily tinned for rust resistance. Ball bearings factory lubricated. Steel frame with attractive buff enamel finish—easy to keep clean. For 110–120 volt, 60-cycle AC or DC current. Mailed from Stock.

250-Lb. Per Hour Capacity. Skims 40 quarts in 20 minutes.
89 FB 20015 MB—Wt. 38 lbs. No Money Down. Cash **$135.00**
400-Lb. Per Hour Capacity. Skims 65 quarts in 20 minutes.
89 FB 20016 MO—Wt. 45 lbs. No Money Down. Cash **$165.00**

All-Electric Floor Models Give Top Performance

[B] **Precision-built to dependably handle huge quantities of milk.** Regulating spout is chrome-plated bronze. Supply can, covers, float assembly, super-skimming bowl and discs are highest grade stainless steel. 2 sealed ball bearings are factory lubricated. Dependable 1/6-HP motor transmits power to bowl spindle by pliable belt. For 110–120 volt, 60-cycle AC. Attractive 2-tone buff and black enamel finish. Shipped by Freight, Truck or Express from Factory in Chicago, Ill. or Poughkeepsie, N.Y. Pay charges from nearest.

600-lb. Capacity per Hour. Separates 70 gal. per hour. 42¼ in. from floor to supply can, 24¾ in. from floor to bottom of spout.
89 FB 20018 F—Ship. wt. 187 lbs. No Money Down...Cash **$385.00**

800-lb. Capacity per Hour. Separates 105 gal. per hour. 43¼ in. from floor to supply can, 24¾ in. from floor to bottom of spout.
89 FB 20017 F—Ship. wt. 222 lbs. No Money Down...Cash **$450.00**

1320-lb. Capacity per Hour. Separates 155 gal. per hour. 45½ in. from floor to supply can, 25 in. from floor to bottom of spout.
89 FB 20019 F—Ship. wt. 237 lbs. No Money Down...Cash **$505.00**

Hand Driven Model

- For the 2 to 5-cow herd owner

[C] **250-Lbs. Capacity Per Hour.** skims 40 quarts in 20 min. Produces same even texture with butterfat globules unbroken as other DeLaval separators. Super-Skimming Bowl, covers, supply can and discs are finest Swedish carbon steel, heavily tinned to resist rust for long life. Brass bowl nut. Automatic lubrication—enclosed crankcase reservoir forces oil to all moving parts as machine is turned. Steel frame, gleaming black enamel finish. Hand operation only. Ship. wt. 50 lbs. No Money Down. *Mailable.*
89 FB 20014 MO...Cash **$80.00**

Dilution Type Separator $8.95 10-Gal. Cap.

[D] For separating small amounts of milk quickly. Quicker, more sanitary than old-fashioned setting and skimming. Simply add equal part of water or ice to milk. Deep cone allows milk to be drawn off before cream reaches bottom. Conductor tube speeds process. 2 glass gauges show cream-line. Hvy. charcoal tin-plate, lock-seamed and soldered; reversible cover. 60-mesh brass wire straining screen. Green enamel finish. Average height about 40 in. 18-gallon size Not Mailable. Just Charge It. See Page 101.
89 FB 20136 MO—10 gal. Ship. wt. 12 lbs...**$8.95**
89 FB 20137 MO—14 gal. Wt. 13 lbs. **11.25**
89 FB 20135 R—18 gal. Wt. 21 lbs... **15.95**

Rebuilt Separator Bowls Low as $16.95

[E] Low prices on Wards completely reconditioned separator bowls. Retinned, rebalanced, tested for "like-new" performance. Be sure to check Wards Model Number before placing your order.

Catalog Number	Capacity Pounds	Model Number	Shipping weight	Cash Price
88 FB 31432	400	S4M	7 lbs.	$18.95
88 FB 31326	600	S6M	11 lbs.	21.95
88 FB 31389	800	S8M	12 lbs.	23.95
88 FB 31338	225	33	4 lbs.	16.95
88 FB 31261	500	37, 47, 77	9 lbs.	23.95

Separator Bowl Rings 69c Pkg. of 3

[F] Economical Bowl Rings for Ward Brand Separators.
88 FB 31450—Shipping weight 4 oz. Be sure to state name and model number of separator when ordering........Package of 3 69c

150 WARDS CKS

339

Choose Wards Graders, Save Valuable Time, Money

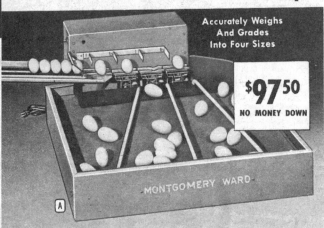

Accurately Weighs And Grades Into Four Sizes

$97⁵⁰
NO MONEY DOWN

Simplify Egg Marketing with Modern Handling Aids

Just "Charge It"
NO MONEY DOWN
See Page 101

Grades 1800 Eggs Per Hour

- Pays For Itself in Premium Prices for Properly Graded Eggs
- Electrically Operated—Easy, Automatic Operation
- Practical for Small, Average or Commercial Size Flocks
- Fast and Easy—Saves You Hours of Chore Time Each Week
- Enjoy Its Benefits Right Now—Buy It on Easy Terms

(A) Compare Wards features and new low price with others; prove to yourself that this Grader offers greatest value. Note particularly that Wards grader automatically separates eggs into *four* grades with precision accuracy. Eggs stop on each scale for stationary, accurate weighing. No experience necessary—one person can operate it easily. Scale quickly adjusts to close tolerances between grades.

1/60-HP motor assembly in steel housing moves eggs into grading position. No oiling necessary. Egg tray is steel with plywood bottom, padded to prevent breakage. Adjustable rubber tray dividers keep eggs in proper section. Off-On switch. UL Listed cord and plug for 110–120-volt AC. Instructions included. Size overall: 26 by 27 by 4½ in. high. Use with egg washers on opposite page for complete automatic washing and grading operation. Ship. wt. 40 lbs. *Mailable.*

89 FB 21031 YO—No Money Down, See Terms, Page 101 . . . . Cash. **$97.50**

Economy Egg Graders

(B) **Large Capacity Egg Grader.** For hatcheries, egg markets. Handles 60 to 90 dozen per hour. Automatically grades eggs of all weights. No electricity required. Quickly adjustable to egg sizes. Sturdy aluminum with sponge rubber egg tray, prevents egg breakage.
89 FB 21032—Ship. wt. 8 lbs **$22.95**

(C) **"Jiffy Way" Egg Grader.** Grade eggs weighing 1½ to 2½ oz. each (or 18 to 30 oz. per dozen). Dial registers 4 egg sizes—small, med., large, extra large.
89 FB 21033—Ship. wt. 1 lb. 2 oz . . **$1.79**

(D) **Acme Egg Grader.** Precision made. Simple operating mechanism. Accurately calibrated scale grades all size eggs. Sturdy aluminum for long service.
89 FB 21029—Ship. wt. 1 lb. 6 oz . . **$4.49**

(E) **Electric Egg Candler.** "Jiffy Way." Hold egg to opening in end, light ray shows blood spots, if egg is fertile. Use 15-watt bulb (not included). Soft cushioned egg cup. UL Listed cord and plug. For 110–120-volt AC or DC.
89 FB 21034—Ship. wt. 1 lb. 2 oz . . **$2.09**

Convenient Egg Baskets

(G) **Wire Egg Basket.** Heavy-gauge welded steel wires. Lacquer coated, so it won't mark eggs. Wire foot arrangement keeps basket off floor—allows free circulation of air. Helps to cool eggs—keeps them fresh longer. Holds about 12 dozen. Fine for handling vegetables too. Size: 14-in. diameter at top, 10 in. deep. *Mail.*
89 FB 21049—Ship. wt. 2 lbs. 12 oz. **$1.09**

89 FB 21050—Like above, but has plastic coated wires to reduce danger of egg breakage. Ship. wt. 3 lbs **$1.98**

(H) **Square Egg Basket.** Easier to carry. Plastic-coated so won't mark eggs. Wire foot arrangement as in (G) keeps basket off floor—allows free circulation of air. Holds about 10 dozen eggs. Size 11-in. sq. at top, 9 in. deep. *Mailable.*
89 FB 21067 M—Ship. wt. 3 lbs **$2.09**

(J) **Dirty Egg Basket.** Fastens to side of (H) above. Sort eggs as you collect from nest—place clean eggs in large basket, dirty eggs in small basket. Size: 3¼x4½x8 in. long. Lacquer coated wire, won't mar eggs. Holds 1 dozen.
89 FB 21051—Ship. wt. 8 oz **69c**

Buy All Your Poultry Needs on Credit—Remember, No Money Down at Wards— Just Say "Charge It". See Complete Details of Terms on Page 101.

Poultry Shipping Coops

(K) Safe, humane way to ship all poultry. Withstands rough handling. Double thick top. Oversize oak dowels in corners and center of sides and ends. Oak rails. ⅜-in. solid bottom. Door locks. Meets all express regulations. Use also for ducks, rabbits. 23¼ by 35 by 11⅝ in., holds 16 to 20 birds, or 60 lbs. Shipped knocked down for lower transportation charges.
89 FB 21047 MO—Ship. wt. 20 lbs. *Mail.*
Each . . . . **$3.79**, 5 for **$17.95**

Turkey and Geese Coop. Same as above, but 17¼ in. high with extra diagonal bracing for larger, heavier birds. Shipping weight 25 lbs. *Mailable.*
89 FB 21048 MO—Ea. **$4.59**, 4 for **$17.35**

(L) **Fowl Catcher.** Easy to handle. Stiff steel rod with hook—holds firmly to bird's leg—can't slip. 40 in. long. *Mail.*
89 FB 21046 M—Ship. wt. 8 oz **39c**

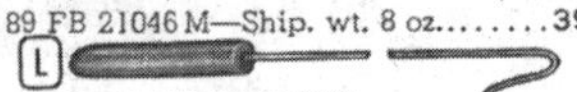

170 WARDS CKS

Attractively Packaged Eggs Will Increase Your Sales

Reduce Egg Breakage With Sturdy Containers

Buy In Lots of 1,000 And Save More

(M) **Collapsible Wood Egg Crate.** Reduce breakage on crates. Return them flat. Conserves storage space. For parcel post or express, meet U.S. Postal Regulations. Ventilation keeps eggs cool. Flats and fillers included. *Mailable.*
89 FB 21038 M—6 doz. 13x13x9 in. Ship. wt. 4 lbs **$1.49**
89 FB 21039 M—12 doz. 13x13x13 in. Ship. wt. 6 lbs 1.59

(N) (P) **Flats, Fillers.** Fit all standard crates, cases.
(N) 89 FB 21041L— 20 Fillers. Ship. wt. 5 lbs **65c**
100 Fillers. Ship. wt. 25 lbs **$2.95**
(P) 89 FB 21040L— 25 Flats. Ship. wt. 2 lbs **40c**
300 Flats. Ship. wt. 22 lbs **$4.25**

(R) **2 By 6-Row One-Piece Egg Carton.** Sturdily molded pulpboard with built-in fillers to separate and cushion eggs. Requires no extra time to set-up, shipped nested. Special tabs fasten cover down tightly. Buy in quantity and save.
89 FB 21058 MO—Holds 1 doz. *State Quantity wanted.*
250 Cartons. Ship. wt. 28 lbs. *Mailable* **$7.95**
500 Cartons. Ship. wt. 55 lbs. *Mailable* 15.75
1000 Cartons. Ship. wt. 110 lbs. *Not Mailable* 29.50

(T) **2 By 6-Row "Hawk" Carton.** Economy-priced heavy cardboard helps reduce breakage. Sets up quickly by hand. Excellent for stores and roadside stands. Shipped flat, saves on space.
89 FB 21059 MB—Holds 1 dozen. *State Quantity.*
250 Cartons. Ship. wt. 32 lbs. *Mailable* **$5.79**
500 Cartons. Ship. wt. 64 lbs. *Not Mailable* 11.25
1000 Cartons. Ship. wt. 128 lbs. *Not Mailable* 21.50

(U) **3 By 4-Row One-Piece Egg Carton.** Molded pulpboard with built-in fillers to separate and cushion eggs. Requires no time consuming set-up, shipped nested to save on space. Single (not two as shown) tab fastens cover down tightly. Durably made, stands rough handling.
89 FB 21057 MO—Holds 1 doz. *State Quantity wanted.*
250 Cartons. Ship. wt. 22 lbs. *Mailable* **$4.89**
500 Cartons. Ship. wt. 43 lbs. *Mailable* 9.49
1000 Cartons. Ship. wt. 85 lbs. *Not Mailable* 17.25

See Pages 160 through 163 for day-old chicks, ducklings, etc., the outstanding varieties, from the finest hatcheries.

SAVE TIME, INCREASE YOUR EGG PROFITS

A WARDS ELECTRIC WASHER HELPS PAY FOR ITSELF IN GREATER PROFITS FROM CLEAN EGGS

- A Trouble-Free, Efficient Egg Washer at a Low Price That Any Egg Producer Will Consider an Economy
- Complete With Egg Basket, Scrub Tub, Agitator Table, Package of Detergent Cleaner—Nothing Else to Buy
- Washes 10 to 15 Dozen Eggs in 3 to 5 Minutes

$15.89
Regular Model

$3.45
10-Lb. Box

Clean eggs look more attractive, bring better prices on market. Wards Automatic Washers are fast, easy to operate, do a job that protects the quality of the egg and eliminate most time-consuming chore. Use special Egg Washing Detergent for best results; order (B) below.

(A) **Automatically does tiresome egg washing chore.** The time and labor saved are worth the low price alone. The thorough cleaning and sanitizing, will increase your profits on the market. Gentle action permits washing both hard and soft-shelled eggs without breakage. Just set egg basket in tub and place on agitator table—swirling water bathes each egg in detergent. Basket design permits dirt and sediment to settle out at bottom. When removed, eggs are ready for market. Single fill of water handles up to four full baskets of eggs. Quiet operation.

More than 20 Years Daily Farm Use indicated by tests over 1,000 hours under continuous operation with full load. Compact, lightweight aluminum and steel construction. 11⅞-in. agitator table. Gear-type electric motor requires no belts, pulleys and no greasing or oiling. Has long-lasting, all-nylon bearings. UL Listed heavy rubber electric cord and plug. Heavy galvanized steel tub—8½ in. high, 14½-inch top diameter. Operates on 110–120-volt, 60-cycle AC. *Mailable.*

Regular Model. Complete with agitator table, sanitizing tub (not heated), egg basket and box of Detergent-Sanitizer. Operating instructions.
89 FB 21060 M—Include on Your Credit Order. Ship. wt. 13 lbs..**$15.89**

Self-Heating Model. Same as model above except sanitizing tub has built-in 1500-watt heating unit with pre-set thermostat control. Automatically heats and maintains water temperature from 110° to 120°F . . . ideal egg working temperature. Just fill tank, turn on.
89 FB 21064 M—Ship. wt. 16 lbs. No Money Down, on Wards Easy Payment terms (See Page 101 for details)................or Cash **$29.95**

Egg Basket. Specifically designed for above washers. Made of heavy-gauge wires plastic-coated to prevent breakage. Ship. wt. 2 lbs. 8 oz.
89 FB 21062—Ht. 8 in., 14-in. top. Diameter, 9-in. bottom diam... **$1.89**

(B) **Egg Detergent Sanitizer.** Cleans. Ship. wts. 10 lb. 6 oz.; 26 lbs.
89 FB 21063 M—10-lb. box**$3.45** 89 FB 21063 MB—25-lb. box..**$7.95**

(C) **Sander With Paper.** Easy to hold. Paper attaches to wooden base.
89 FB 21036—Removes difficult stains. Size 2x6 in. Wt. 4 oz.....**45c**

(D) **Sandpaper Sheets For Above.** Quickly removes unsightly marks.
89 FB 21037—Shipping weight 1 oz........................**6 for 89c**

Portable Electric Smoker—Easy To Use

$17.95

With 1 lb. Hickory Chips. For that real, honest smoke house flavor that just can't be beaten.

- Hickory smoke to deliciously flavor Meat, Fish, Fowl up to 20 lbs.
- Economical . . . easy to operate, clean, and store when not used.
- A favorite with housewives.

(E) Make an everyday treat of savory, mouth watering hickory smoked hams, roasts, spareribs, fish, fowl and game. Add to your reputation as a Specialty Cook with easily prepared delicacies. Smoke a turkey or ham up to 20 lbs., or two or three different cuts of meat or fowl at one time. Easy to operate, needs no attention.

A favorite with housewives and sportsmen; removes wild taste from game. Simply put chips in container and plug into 110–120 Volt, 60-cycle AC outlet. 170-watt chromolox heating element. Operate in garage, barn, shed or outdoors. Flavors small cuts of meat in 2 to 4 hours. Sturdy 26-gauge steel cabinet. 12 by 12 by 23 in. high. 3 removable chrome racks. Complete with instructions and smoking recipes. UL Listed cord and plug.
89 FB 21120 M—Smoker with 1 lb. of Hickory Chips. Wt. 17 lbs. **$17.95**
89 FB 21121—Extra 2-lb. Bag of Hickory Chips to use with Smoker. Ship. wt. 2 lbs...............**89c**

Oscillating Action Gently Rolls Eggs for More Thorough Cleaning

(F) Cleans 12 dozen eggs in 3 to 4 minutes. To-and-Fro thrust in moving solution makes eggs come out cleaner. Washer has 10-gallon stainless steel tub and heavy-duty mechanism that will last for years. Cast aluminum rack takes most standard baskets. Accurate, adjustable thermostat for close temperature control.
Convenient on-off switch and signal light. Handy drain and floor casters. 110-volt 1550-watt element. 25½ in. high, 17-in. diameter. Underwriters' Laboratory Listed cord and plug.
89 FB 21026 MQ—Ship. wt. 35 lbs. No Money Down . Cash **$86.50**
89 FB 21027 MO—As above but with 220-volt 3000-watt element. Ship. wt. 35 lbs. No Money Down.................Cash **$98.50**

Portable Air Cushion Egg Washer
Works Gently—Cleans Thoroughly

$189.00
1500 Watt

- Combination of air and water gently floats eggs so that there is practically no expensive egg breakage.
- Large capacity . . . washes 2400 to 3000 eggs per hour . . . approximately 10 to 15 dozen eggs in 2 minutes.
- No need to change water with every washing . . . same water can be used for up to seven baskets. Economical to operate.

(G) Deluxe electric egg washer with automatic thermostat keeps water at wash temperature. Just fill tank, turn on element (electric indicator eye shows when water is at right temperature). Cleaning action is produced by combining air and water. Eggs are gently agitated . . . agitation action is adjustable for quantity of eggs to be washed and condition of shells. Even soft shelled eggs can be safely cleaned. Takes standard egg basket . . . entire egg basket is placed inside washer. Each egg is thoroughly cleaned, even the eggs in center of basket. Timer rings bell when washing cycle is completed. Complete operating instructions included.

Heavy-duty construction . . . non-corrosive materials used throughout. Convenient casters makes washer portable. Water drains out easily . . . heavy, bronze fitted pump with stainless steel shaft and ball bearings. Equipped with General Electric motor; 110-volt, 1500-watt element. (Also available is a 220-volt, 3000-watt element model . . . *if wanted, state on order and add $15.00 to price*). Underwriters' Laboratory Listed. Size: 29 in. high, 16½ in. in diameter. Shipped from Factory near South Bend, Indiana. Pay Freight from there.
89 FB 21054 F—No Money Dn. Ship. wt. 66 lbs. ..Cash **$189.00**

CKS WARDS 171

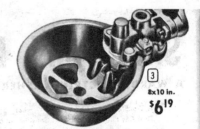

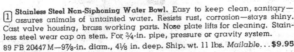

PREVENT CONTAMINATION!
Use Wards Non-Siphoning Water Bowls

- Prevent Back-Flow—Inlet Built Well Above Water Level.
- Conform to U. S. Public Health Recommendations.
- All Wards Water Bowls Fit Wood or Steel Stanchions.

① $9.95

① Stainless Steel Non-Siphoning Water Bowl. Easy to keep clean, sanitary—assures animals of untainted water. Resists rust, corrosion—stays shiny. Cast valve housing, brass working parts. Nose plate lifts for cleaning. Stainless steel wear cap on stem. For ¾-in. pipe, pressure or gravity system.
89 FB 20447 M—9⅞-in. diam., 4⅛ in. deep. Ship. wt. 11 lbs. Mailable...$9.95

② Galvanized Steel Non-Siphoning Water Bowl. Heavy construction—built to last. Trouble-free brass valve—any or all parts easily replaced without removing bowl. Built-in water flow control. Paddle moves back, not down, giving full depth of bowl to drink from, swings up for cleaning. Feed won't clog bowl. Universal inlet saves expensive pipe fittings—may be rotated so water can be piped in from below, either side, or any angle above the horizontal including straight down. Fits ¾-in. pipe. For pressure or gravity system.
89 FB 20446 M—Large Bowl 9¼x4¼ in. Ship. wt. 9 lbs. 8 oz. Mailable...$7.19

② $7.19

③ 8x10 in. $6.19

Conventional Oval Iron Bowl

③ Gray Heavy Cast Iron—gives long service. Rustproof non-corrosive valve. For high pressure or low pressure gravity feed system. Compensating valve for proper flow. Nose plate lifts for fast, easy cleaning. Connections for ¾-in. pipe at top and bottom. Bowl is 4½ inches deep. Not non-siphoning. Fits both wood and steel stanchions. Ship. wts. 14, 16 lbs.
89 FB 20450 M—8x10-in. Bowl. Mailable..$6.19
89 FB 20451M—9x11½-in. Bowl. Mailable. 6.59

Just Say "CHARGE IT"—No Money Down
See Page 101 for Complete Credit Information

Move Litter, Transport Feed, Materials—Install a Ward Carrier

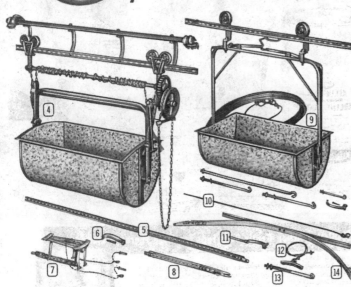

④ 10-Bushel Heavy-Duty Chain Hoist Carrier. Lowers 3 ft. on back-geared hoist. Back gearing gives extra leverage. Tub raised and lowered by chains wrapped around hoisting shaft. Positive clutch control and brake. Tub locks at both ends, dumps manually by lever. Tub 45x27x21 in. deep; 18-ga. steel with angle steel reinforcing. Soldered seams. Runs on 2 double wheel roller trolleys. For I-Beam track only (order below). See "Ship. Note" left.
89 FB 20478 F—Wt. 210 lbs....$106.50

7-Bushel Chain Hoist Carrier. Similar to above, but single geared hoist, automatic dumping. Tub 42x24x15 in. deep. 2-single-wheel roller bearing trolleys; use with any type track (order below). See "Ship. Note" left.
89 FB 20479 F—Wt. 145 lbs....$79.50

⑤ Steel I-Beam Track. 2x⅜ in. Sold in 12-ft. lengths only. With connectors. Can be bent cold. Ship. wt. per ft. 1 lb. 8 oz. Not Mailable.
89 FB 20489 F.............Per ft. 39c

⑥ I-Beam Track Hanger. 9-in. pressed steel. Screw to joists every 4 ft. for 7-bu. carrier, every 2 ft. for 10-bu. carrier. Lag screws included.
89 FB 20487 K—Ship. wt. 1 lb....59c

⑦ Two-Way Switch. Run track to all parts of barn. For I-beam track. Base attaches to joists, shifts transfer track to connecting track. Operated by chain-pull. Not Mailable.
89 FB 20485 F—Wt. 25 lbs....$13.95

⑧ Splice Connection. Join I-beam track with Rod track.
89 FB 20492 K—Ship. wt. 11 lbs.$2.59

⑨ 7-Bushel Litter Carrier Outfit. Automatically trips and dumps from either end. Trip locks at both ends of tub. Copper bearing, 20-ga. galv. steel tub is riveted and reinforced by steel angles. Size 42x24x15 in. deep. Runs on 5-in. roller bearing wheels. Malleable castings. With 100 ft. 13⁄32-in. diam. steel rod track and stay loop, 2 tension bolts, automatic trip, anchor rod and track hanger. "Ship. Note" left. Ship. wt. 160 lbs.
89 FB 20476 F—Not Mailable..$69.50

7-Bushel Carrier Only, with Trip. Use on either rod or I-beam track.
89 FB 20477 F—Wt. 85 lbs....$59.50

⑩ Steel Rod Track. With looped end.
89 FB 20490 K—13⁄32-in. diam. Mailable. Wt. per ft. 7 oz. . Per ft. 11c
89 FB 20491K—15⁄32-in. diameter. Mail. Ship. wt. per ft. 10 oz.....Per ft. 13c

⑪ Rod Track Hanger. Use at door or next to splice connection. Be sure to state size of rod track. Mailable.
89 FB 20488 K—Ship. wt. 2 lbs..$1.00

⑫ Flexible Steel Curve for Any Rod Track when run at angle to outside post. Makes 45° angle. Fastens to door frame with cable. Mailable.
89 FB 20484 K—Ship. wt. 3 lbs..$2.75

⑬ 24-in. Tension Bolt. ⅞-in. diam., 18-in. thread. With washer, nut.
89 FB 20493 K—Ship. wt. 3 lbs..$1.49

⑭ Post Curve for Rod Track. Use on outside post to run carrier from one track to another. Connect rod from each track to curve. Not Mailable.
89 FB 20486 F—Ship. wt. 20 lbs.$4.79

Extra Buckets to Fit Carriers Above $35.50 7-Bu. Size

Fiber Glass Reinforced Plastic Buckets. Lightweight for ease of operation—dent-proof, can't rust, resist urine acids. See "Shipping Note" below. Not Mailable.
89 FB20482 F—7-Bu. Size. Wt. 21 lbs.$35.50
89FB20483 F—10-Bu. Wt. 28 lbs.... 48.50

Galvanized Steel Replacement Buckets. Same as shipped with complete outfits above. End fittings included. See "Ship. Note" below. Ship. wts. 45, 55 lbs.
89 FB 20480 F—7-Bu. Size......$35.50
89 FB 20481F—10-Bu. Size...... 53.95

Important Shipping Note: Items on this page with Catalog Numbers ending in "K" or "F" shipped from Factory near Oshkosh, Wis. You pay transportation charges from there. Items ending in "K" are Mailable, those ending in "F" or "R" shipped by Freight, Truck or Express. See Wards Convenient Credit Terms on Page 101.

Keep Your Barn Clean—Use Wards Brooms, Barn Scraper

Brooms low as $1.65

Barn Scraper $3.19

⑮ Barn Scraper. Reversible heavy steel curved blade cleans wide path. Length overall 5-ft. Wood handle included. Mailable.
89 FB 20660 MO—15x7 in. Wt. 5 lbs. 8 oz.$3.19
89 FB 20661MO—24x7 in. Wt. 6 lbs. 4 oz. 3.79

⑯ TO ⑱ Heavy-Duty Brooms. Use in barns, gutters, garages, drives. Wear slowly.

(16) Straight Broom. 12-in. metal head holds bass fibers securely. 42-in. handle. Mailable.
89 FB 21585 M—Ship. wt. 3 lbs........$1.65

(17) Push Broom with High Impact Plastic Fibers—outwear natural fibers many times. Not affected by oil, gasoline, ammonia, certain acids, heat, cold; won't curl, rot or mildew. Fibers 3 in. deep from hardwood block. With 60 in. handle. Ship. wts. 3 lbs., 3 lbs. 8 oz. Mail.
89 FB 21583 M—18 in. wide............$2.79
89 FB 21584 M—24 in. wide............ 3.29

(18) Push Broom with Tough Bass Fibers. Heavy hardwood block fully packed, 6½ in. deep. No handle. Ship. wts. 2 lbs. 6 oz., 3 lbs. Mail.
89 FB 21586—14 in. wide............$1.65
89 FB 21581—16 in. wide............. 1.89

Galvanized Steel Feed Cart...Big 16 Bushel Capacity

No Money Down $76.50

⑲ Square front and rear for non-tip filling, easy unloading. 24 in. wide, 72 in. long, 24 in. deep. Heavy 18-gauge galvanized steel. 1-in. reinforcing angles at top. Dual plate steel wheels, roller bearing hubs. 10x2.75 pneumatic type puncture-proof tires. Front caster has ball-bearing swivel for easy maneuverability, 5-in. rubber tread wheel. The convenient, practical way to handle feed. Shipped partially set up. Not Mailable.
89 FB 20687 R—Ship. wt. 120 lbs..........Cash $76.50

Handy Metal Bin Trap—Easy to Install

⑳ Mounts in floor opening 8½ by 8½ in., covers 11 by 11 in. Wide flange. Leakproof. Install with 4 screws or bolts from either side of bin door. Trap door opens, closes with easy pull on rope. Tops in handling ease—ends messy spilling. Painted, ready to install. Mailable.
89 FB 20690 M—Ship. wt. 14 lbs.................$8.95

Hand Hay Hook—Low Priced $1.29

㉑ Made on genuine tool steel with selected hardwood handle. Nicely balanced. Reverse carriage bolt in handle for left hand use. Length overall 11 inches.
89 FB 20573—Ship. wt. 12 oz. Mailable..........$1.29

$8.95

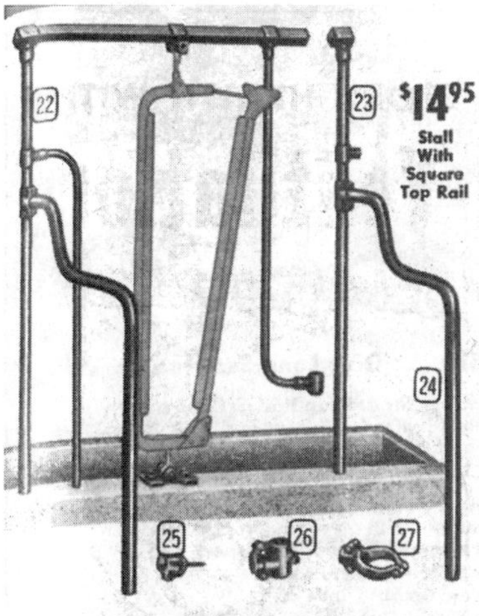
22
23
$14.95
Stall With Square Top Rail
24
25
26
27

Dairy Barn Stalls

SQUARE OR ROUND TOP RAIL

(22) **Stall with Square Top Rail.** 12 ga. 1½-in. square top rail. Welded 12-ga. tubular steel posts 1⅝-in. outside diam. Makes a stall 3½ to 4 ft. wide by 5 ft. 5½ in. high. Complete unit includes top rail section, curved partition, 1 post, 1 upper and 1 lower cow stop of 1 1/16-in. steel tubing, all clamps, fittings. Top and bottom stanchion holders provide 8-in. adjustment. With templates for setting posts. Install in concrete only. Stanchion not included (see listings at right). "Shipping Note" below. *Not Mailable.*
89 FB 20431F—Ship. wt. 50 lbs.. **$14.95**

Stall with Round Top Rail. All the features of stall above, except 1⅝-in. diam. round top rail, 1 cow stop, non-adjusting stanchion holders. Stanchion not included (see listings at right). "Shipping Note" left. *Not Mailable.*
89 FB 20432 F—Ship. wt. 40 lbs. **$10.95**

(23) **End Section.** Curved partition stall, post and clamps to complete last stall at end. *Mailable.*
89 FB 20434 K—Ship. wt. 15 lbs... **$6.95**

(24) **Curved Stall Partition.** 1⅝-in. outside diam. steel tubing. Use with wood or steel posts. No flanges. *Mail.*
89 FB 20433 K—Ship. wt. 12 lbs... **$3.39**

(25) **Post Flange.** Attach to wood post or flooring. With lag screws. *Mailable.*
89 FB 20435 K—Ship. wt. 2 lbs. .Ea. **79c**

(26) **Partition Post Clamp.** To mount curved stall partition to 1⅝-in. steel posts.
89 FB 20436 K—Ship. wt. 2 lbs.... Each **98c**

(27) **T-Column Clamp.** To mount 1⅝-inch partition or top rail tubing to 4-inch column. Ship. wt. 2 lbs. 8 oz.
89 FB 20437 K................Each **$1.19**

IMPORTANT SHIPPING NOTE: All items on this page with letters "F" or "K" following the Catalog Number are shipped from Factory near Oshkosh, Wis. You pay transportation charges from there. Items keyed "F", "R" are shipped by Freight, Truck or Express; those keyed "K" are *Mailable.*

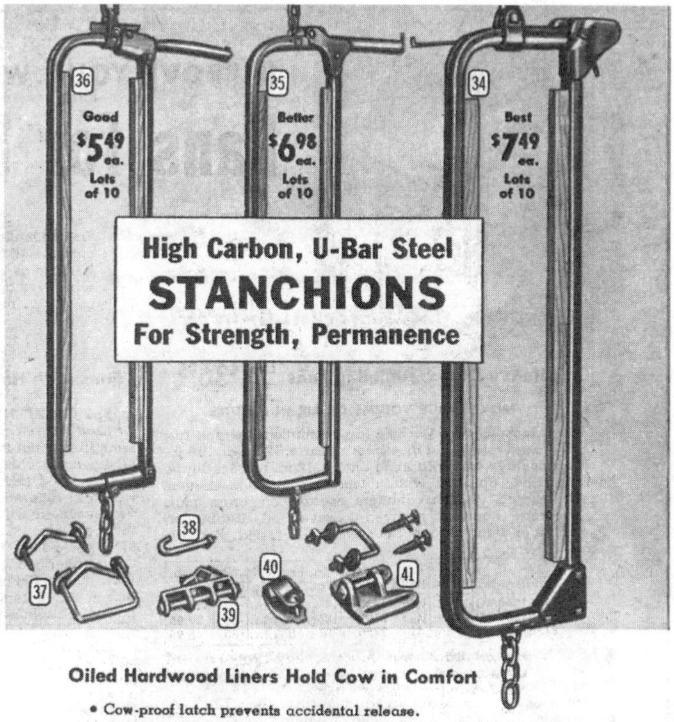
36
Good
$5.49 ea.
Lots of 10
35
Better
$6.98 ea.
Lots of 10
34
Best
$7.49 ea.
Lots of 10
High Carbon, U-Bar Steel
STANCHIONS
For Strength, Permanence
37
38
39
40
41

Oiled Hardwood Liners Hold Cow in Comfort

- **Cow-proof latch prevents accidental release.**
- **Electrically welded links anchor top and bottom.**
- **One-hand operation for quick, easy handling.**

Save—buy in Lots of 10 or more. Hardwood liners riveted into channel. *Single stanchion Mailable*, 2 or more Shipped by Freight, Truck or Express.

(34) **Best Quality.** Extra-heavy 1¼ by 1¼ by 3/16-in. uprights. Malleable iron latch opens with pressure on side. Lead bar maintains perfect alignment. Post fork prevents turning. Inside ht. about 44 in., opens to 19 in. Adjusts top and bottom 6 to 8 inches. Length overall 55 in.
89 FB 20428 MO—Ship. wt. ea. 23 lbs. Each **$8.29**; 10 or more, Each **$7.49**

(35) **Better Quality.** Heavier construction, malleable iron fittings. 1¼ by 17/32 by 5/32-in. uprights. Bottom hinge forged from U-Bar operates on ⅜-in. bolt. Latching device spring loaded to assure positive action. Inside height 42 in., opens to 18 in., adjusts for 6 to 7-in. neck. 55 in. long overall.
89 FB 20427 MO—Ship. wt. ea. 20 lbs. Each **$7.19**; 10 or More, Each **$6.98**

(36) **Good Quality.** Single hinged uprights 1 5/16 by ⅞ by 3/16 in. Inside height measures 43 in., opens to 17¾ in. Adjusts top and bottom for 5½ to 7-in. neck. 55 in. long overall.
89 FB 20426 MO—Ship. wt. ea. 19 lbs. Each **$5.89**; 10 or More, Each **$5.49**

(37) **Anchors.** For fastening bottom of single chain-hung stanchions to curb. Ship. wts. 8 oz., 12 oz.
89 FB 20439—With Clevis, 4-in. U-bolt for concrete curb...............**49c**
89 FB 20438—With forked clevis, washers, screws to fasten in wood.....**39c**

(38) **6-in. Hook Bolt.** To hang stanchion from wood beam. Nut, washer.
89 FB 20440—Ship. wt. 4 oz......**25c**

(39) **Top Alignment.** For sq. top rail.
89 FB 20441—Ship. wt. 2 lbs. **$1.29**

(40) **Steel Stanchion Clamp.** For 1⅝-in. round top rail. Complete with bolt for fastening securely.
89 FB 20442—Ship. wt. 6 oz.....**45c**

(41) **Stanchion Alignment Device.** For top adjustment on wood frame stalls or bottom on steel stalls. 5 adjustments over a total of 9 in.
89 FB 20444—With U-bolts for concrete curb. Ship. wt. 3 lbs....**$1.29**
89 FB 20443—With lag screws for wood curb. Ship. wt. 3 lbs...**$1.10**

Barn Desk Record Keeper Hangs on Wall

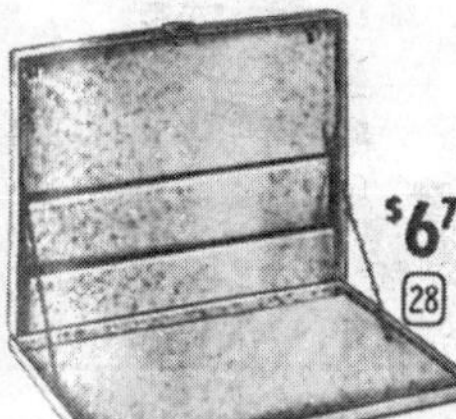
$6.75
28

(28) **Keep all your records in one safe place**—available when needed. Divided into 6 compartments to keep papers neatly arranged. One 14 by 19½-in. compartment holds breeding and milk production records; other small compartments for tags, receipts, etc. Large, smooth 20 by 15-in. writing surface. Long-lasting, heavy 26-ga. galvanized steel. Zinc-plated hinges, safety sure latch. 4 mounting brackets.
89 FB 20692 M—Ship. wt. 7 lbs. *Mailable*........**$6.75**

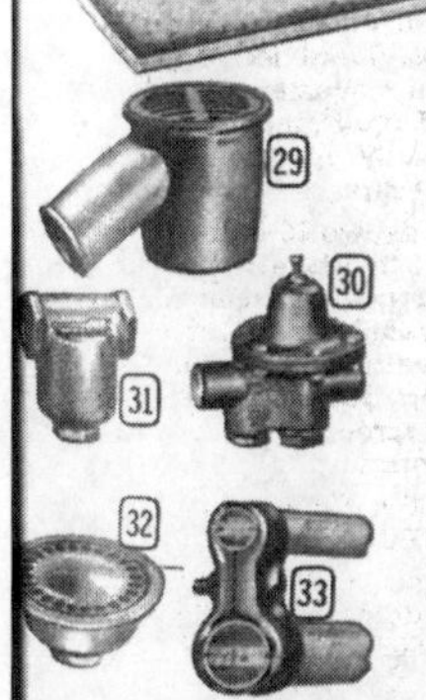
29
30
31
32
33

(29) **Gutter Drain.** 1-pc. type. Cast-iron bowl; heavy strainer seal prevents back-up. Plate opens to insert sewer rod. For 4-in. soil pipe or sewer tile. Ship. from Chicago, St. Paul or Kansas City. Order, pay charges from nearest House. *Mail.*
89 FB 20459 MBT—9x9¾ in. deep. Ship. wt. 31 lbs.....**$13.95**

(30) **Pressure Reducing and Regulating Valve.** Bronze body, stops hammer, maintains even flow. Adj. Use with pressures from 10 to 60. Factory set at 45 psi. Fits ¾-in. pipe.
89 FB 20456—5¼x7x4½ in. wide. Ship. wt. 5 lbs. 8 oz. **$14.95**

(31) **Brass Water Line Strainer.** Bronze body. Ship. like (29).
89 FB 20455 T—For ¾-in. pipe. Ship. wt. 3 lbs. 8 oz. **$8.95**

(32) **Floor Drain and Trap.** Cast iron. Bell on underside forms water seal. Top 8⅜-in. diam., drain 3½-in. diam., 4 in. deep.
89 FB 20460—For 4-in. tile or soil pipe. Ship. wt. 10 lbs. **$3.29**

(33) **Pipeline Clamp.** Use to clamp water or air line to top rail of stalls or pens. Fastens ¾-in. or 1-in. pipe to 1½-in. or 1⅝-in. square or round tubing. 10-gauge steel.
89 FB 20445—Gray enamel finish. Ship. wt. each 8 oz....**69c**

Square Track Parts...

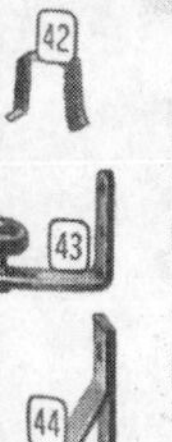
42
43
44
45

MAKE UP YOUR OWN SETS

(42) **End Caps.** For closing ends of square track.
84 FB 8729—Ship. wt. 8 oz. Pkg. 2 **29c**

(43) **Stay Rollers.** For doors up to 2¾ in. thick. Full 2-inch wheel. Rustproof finish.
84 FB 8744—Ship. wt. 1 lb. 4 oz...**55c**

(44) (45) **Track Brackets.** Fit 84 FB 8720 below. Use 2½ ft. apart. With lag screws. Ship. wts. 3 lbs. 12 oz. and 1 lb. *Mailable.*
(44) 84FB8727—For double track. **$1.15**
(45) 84FB8721—For single track. Ea. **42c**

Square Track Only. Like (46). 8, 10-ft. sizes *Not Mailable.* Ship. wts. 9, 12, 15 lbs. *State length, wanted.*
84 FB 8720 MO—6 ft. long........**$1.99**
84 FB 8720 R—8 ft. long.............**2.72**
84 FB 8720 R—10 ft. long.........**3.45**

4-Wheel Hangers. Same as in (46). Easy to install. *Mailable.*
84 FB 8719—Wt. 6 lbs. 8 oz. Pr. **$4.39**

Barn and Garage Door Roller-Bearing Hardware Sets...Smooth, Easy Operation

(46) **Box Track Hardware Sets for Sliding Doors.** 4 nylon bearing wheels enclosed in square track sets. Flexible hangers adjustable without removing doors. 16-ga. steel. 1¾x2¼-in. track needs only 6½-in. clearance above doors. For doors up to 2¼ in. thick, weighing up to 450 lbs. All parts, instr. included. Galvanized.

SINGLE-DOOR SETS. View (A). New or replacement installations.
84FB8723 YO—FOR 6-FT. DOOR. 12-ft. track. Wt. 34 lbs. *Mail*.....**$9.79**
84FB8722 R—FOR 8-FT. DOOR. 16-ft. track. Wt. 40 lbs. *Not Mail*.. **11.35**
84FB8724 R—FOR 10-FT. DOOR. 20-ft. track. Wt. 47 lbs. *Not Mail.* **13.39**

DOUBLE-DOOR SET. See (B). For two 8-ft. doors that pass each other in 16-ft. opening. Galvanized. *Not Mailable.*
84 FB 8728 R—Ship. wt. 107 lbs.........................**$30.69**

(47) **Flat Track Sets.** See view (C). Single doors to 1¾ in. thick, weighing to 250 lbs. 3½-in. roller bearing wheels. Need 5¾-in. clearance above door. All parts included. Black finish.
84FB8704 YO—For 6-Ft. Door. 12-ft. track. Ship. wt. 17 lbs. *Mail.* **$5.59**
84FB8702 R—For 8-Ft. Door. 16-ft. track. Wt. 21 lbs. *Not Mail*.... **6.69**
84FB8703 R—For 10-Ft. Door. 20-ft. track. Wt. 25 lbs. *Not Mail*... **7.54**
84 FB 8700—FLAT TRACK HANGERS ONLY. Wt. 5 lbs. 12 oz. Pair **3.05**

Flat Steel Track Only. 1¼x3/16 in. thick. Includes brackets and screws. Interlocking ends. *State length desired.*
84 FB 8701 MO—6-ft. length. Ship. wt. 6 lbs. *Mailable*......**$1.44**
84 FB 8701 R—8-ft. length. Ship. wt. 8 lbs. *Not Mailable*..... **1.89**
84 FB 8701 R—10-ft. length. Ship. wt. 10 lbs. *Not Mailable*... **2.39**

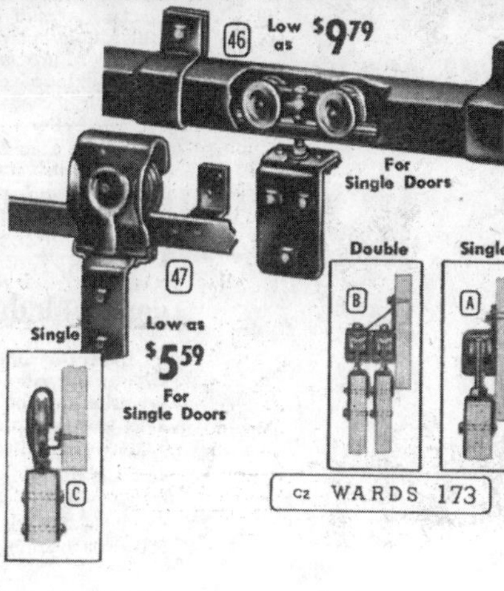
46
Low as $9.79
For Single Doors
Double
Single
B
A
47
Single
Low as $5.59
For Single Doors
C

CZ WARDS 173

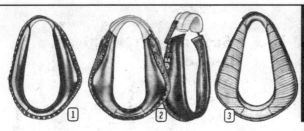
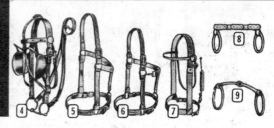

Get Extra Pulling Power with Easy Draft Collars

Long Life Performance—Added Comfort—Ward Savings

Top Quality Flexo-Face Collars Low as $15⁹⁵

[1] [2] **Top Pulling Power. No Break-in Period.** Get peak efficiency with these rugged, leather collars. Adjust for perfect fit. No pad needed. Finest, long-lasting tanned leather, oil and grease treated. Soft curled hair under lace; hand blocked, rye-straw filled. Thong laced; waxed stitching reinforced. Mailed, you pay postage from Factory near Atlanta, Ga. Just "Charge It"—See Page 101.

(1) **Flexo-Face Regular Collar.** Non-adjustable. Black leather face, back and rim. 17-in. draft. *State Size:* 18 through 25 in.

89 FB 22062K—Full Face. Ship. wts. 7 to 12 lbs...............$15.95
89 FB 22063K—Half Sweeney. Ship. wts. 7 to 12 lbs......... 15.95
89 FB 22064K—Mule Shape. Ship. wts. 7 to 12 lbs............ 15.95

(2) **Flexo-Face Adjustable Collar.** Fits for 3 sizes. Buckle, billet fasteners on each side. Black leather. 17-in. draft. Adjusts to 1 size smaller or larger. *State Middle Size:* 20 through 24 in.

89 FB 22065K—Full Face. Ship. wts. 8 to 12 lbs.............$17.95
89 FB 22066K—Half Sweeney. Ship. wts. 8 to 12 lbs......... 17.95

Chrome Retanned Split Leather Face Collar (not shown). Russet split leather back and rim. Hand laced. Rye-straw filled. Draft 17 in. Deep hame beds. *Please remember when ordering.* State Size: 17 through 23-in. neck. Same shipping point as Flexo-Face (2) above.

89 FB 22067K—Full Face. Ship. wts. 6 to 10 lbs...............$8.95
89 FB 22068K—Half Sweeney. Ship. wts. 6 to 10 lbs.......... 8.95

Economical Tick Face Collar Only $5⁹⁵

[3] **Striped Ticking** with russet split leather back and rim. Wear leathers at hame-chafes and throat. 17-in. draft. *When ordering State Size:* 17 through 24-in. neck. See "Shipping Notice" below.
89 FB 22061MT—Ship. wts. 6 to 7 lbs.........................$5.95

It's easy to say "Charge It"—See Page 101 for full details.

Economy-Priced Work Bridle, Halters, Bits . . . Give Long Service

[4] **Best Quality Team Bridle.** Fine rugged bridle. Top-grade Russet harness leather. Split crown, round winker braces. 1⅝-in. crown, ⅞-in. cheeks, brow band. ¾-in. throat, ⅝-in. face. Adjustable crown and cheeks. Polished rosette. Cup style blinds. ⅞-in. adjustable flat reins. With bit. No gag swivels. See "Shipping Notice" below.
89 FB 22084T—Ship. wt. 4 lbs. 8 oz....$6.75

[5] **Finest Riveted Lap Horse Halter.** Best Russet leather. 5-ring style. Crown .adjusts.
89 FB 22041—1¼-in. straps. Wt. 2½ lbs.$4.69

Utility Horse Halter (not pictured). Good quality grayish tan belting leather. 1¼-in. straps. 5-ring style. Adjustable chin strap.
89 FB 22037—Ship. wt. 2 lbs.........$2.49

[6] **Economy Riveted Lap Halter.** Good quality Russet leather. 1¼-in. straps. Adj. crown. Snap at throat. 5-ring style.
89 FB 22038—Ship. wt. 2 lbs.........$3.89

[7] **Cotton Webbing Horse Halter.** Low priced —strong. Will give good service. Adjustable crown. Lightweight tie rope.
89 FB 22040—Horse Size. 1⅝-in. webbing. Shipping weight 1 lb. 4 oz...........$1.95
89 FB 22039—Colt Size. Sturdy 1-in. webbing. Shipping weight 1 lb...........$1.79

[8] **Hard Mouth Bit.** 6½-in. steel link style.
89 FB 22124—Ship. wt. 8 oz.......$1.35

[9] **Malleable Iron Bit.** 6-in. jointed mouth.
89 FB 22122—Steel rings. Shipping weight 12 oz..................................65c

---